T0323163

DIFFERENT TIMES

DIFFERENT TIMES
A HISTORY OF BRITISH COMEDY
DAVID STUBBS

faber

First published in 2023
by Faber & Faber Limited
The Bindery, 51 Hatton Garden
London EC1N 8HN

First published in the USA in 2023

Typeset by Typo•glyphix, Burton-on-Trent, DE14 3HE
Printed and bound by CPI Group (UK) Ltd, Croydon, CR0 4YY

The right of David Stubbs to be identified as author of this work
has been asserted in accordance with Section 77 of the Copyright,
Designs and Patents Act 1988

A CIP record for this book
is available from the British Library

ISBN 978–0–571–35346–0

MIX
Paper | Supporting
responsible forestry
FSC® C171272

Printed and bound in the UK on FSC® certified paper in line with our continuing
commitment to ethical business practices, sustainability and the environment.
For further information see faber.co.uk/environmental–policy

10 9 8 7 6 5 4 3 2 1

To Dara and Alisha

CONTENTS

PREAMBLE

BORIS ALEXANDER

In 2011, in the sitcom *Outnumbered*, the Brockmans have taken in a German exchange student, Ottfried. The Brockmans' eldest son, Jake, asks Ottfried what English TV he likes.

> OTTFRIED: I like the comedian, he plays a character, a very funny character, the fat politician and he has funny blond hair – he sometimes cycles, I see him on the bike on the television.
> JAKE: Do you mean Boris Johnson?
> OTTFRIED: Yes, Boris Johnson – it's so funny, you like him also?
> JAKE: Ottfried, he's the Mayor of London.
> OTTFRIED: Yes, he plays the Mayor of London, a very stupid politician, very stupid, funny. We, we in Germany love him.

Michael Portillo once told Johnson he would have to make a decision between politics and comedy. It is a tragedy that he didn't take up comedy. With hints of Billy Bunter, Bertie Wooster, Jimmy Edwards, 'Boris' might have amounted to a passable, sub-Jack Whitehall confection. 'Boris' is his ursine, tousled, faux-bumbling self, whose goofs and gaffes somehow serve only to add to the affection in which he is held by the British public, despite the mortal danger of his incompetence.

For some, he was a living anachronism, a plummy old Etonian rolling around the public domain in search of a clue as to what he might do or where he might belong. For others, his very ineptitude as a politician was a bracing change from the dreary, scripted, pinstriped, managerial efficiency of New Labour. As a comedian, Boris, 'Bozza', 'Bojo', understood the value of self-deprecation.

He also stood against seriousness. He understood how seriously anti-serious a significant majority of the British people were, how much they would forgo or forgive in the cheery, bullish name of anti-seriousness.

'Boris', even 'Boris Johnson', is not all that he is. His full name is Alexander Boris de Pfeffel Johnson. Boris is his outer, bluff carapace, a fatsuit. That is 'Boris'. But driving him, like Davros inside the Dalek, is Alexander, his inner, demonic, ruthlessly ambitious, spiritually emaciated, compulsively amoral, truer self. Alexander is a perpetually famished, morally destructive creature driven by a lust not even primarily for power but for sex and for money. Alexander is an authoritarian, not because he desires to put in the effort of running a country but because his natural, ancient sense of entitlement is deeply ingrained. He has a ferociously short way with anyone who impedes his ascent.

I was at Oxford at the same time as Boris Johnson, two years above him. Coming from a state-school, lower-middle-class background, I was never more conscious of the class divide than when in closest proximity to those 'highest' in its order. They who went to Christ Church or Balliol (as Johnson did), rather than modest Hertford. They who joined the Bullingdon Club, or the even more debauched Piers Gaveston Society, or wafted briskly past you in Broad Street, their braying vowels trailing in the breeze like their college scarves. Those who descended from Eton or Harrow, took their gentlemen's thirds and then, on graduating, took up the posts in the City awaiting them like an inheritance. The likes of them and the likes of me would never consort.

We went our separate low and high ways, Alexander, Boris and I. He turned his hand to journalism, baulking at humdrum detail which, like the blame, could be left to others. Despite his affable air, he was not clubbable – Alexander would never let Boris linger anywhere for long; he was always on the move, moving on. Boris was a badly dressed shambles, he smelt, his desk was a disgrace, his attention to deadlines scant. However, he had the knack of working up an instant whip of serviceable prose.

Sent to Brussels as part of the *Telegraph*'s bureau, Boris affected to speak terrible French, but Alexander was as fluent as Richelieu in the language. And he saw an opportunity, a money-making opportunity. He realised that most of his fellow journalists billeted in Brussels were pro-EU. Alexander saw an opening for extravagant, Eurosceptic, tub-thumping copy: the straight banana stuff. 'People who complain that there's no right-wing satire in this country should forget about what goes out on Radio 4 at 6.30 p.m. and remember that Johnson's reports from Brussels for the *Daily Telegraph* in the 1990s were satires by any definition of the term,' wrote Jonathan Coe. 'And they set the tone and perspective for the British debate on Europe over the next two decades.' None of this was born out of any convictions. 'Convictions? I had one for dangerous driving but that was from years ago,' Boris once quipped, with Marlovian insouciance. Bozza.

Boris Johnson first appears on *Have I Got News for You* in April 1998. He looks like a young relic, left high and dry by John Major's honest efforts at meritocracy and the landslide of Tony Blair's victory, which buried the Conservatives. Boris is a Conservative. Let's have fun with Boris. And let's cast a dark beam on Alexander.

Ian Hislop, on the opposing team, acts as prosecutor, as ever, with Paul Merton acting as a sort of defence counsel whose counter-argument for his client consists of shrugging his shoulders and saying, 'I dunno, you got yourself into this mess.' Hislop relates the case of a taped telephone conversation between Alexander and Darius Guppy, a friend and fraudster. Boris shifts uncomfortably. He first claims not to remember the incident, a flat-out whopper of the sort the comedy-loving British public sometimes warms to. He then describes Guppy as a 'great chap', though also, he admits, a 'distinctive fraudster' and a 'major goof'. Hislop reminds him of their discussing beating up a journalist. 'That did come up,' says Boris, with admirably impeccable comic timing. In the laugh-ometer, that vital crucible in which the British test public figures, Boris has won himself a few more plus points. He recalls him and Guppy discussing mutual military heroes, including Rommel; he's floundering in contradiction when Merton quips, 'Hence Major Goof who you mentioned just now.'

Ah, the quip, the respite for Boris. Jonathan Coe, writing about this episode for the *London Review of Books*, pinpoints this as the moment when the show let Boris Johnson off the hook. In fairness, however, *HIGNFY* did prolong his discomfiture for a good few awkward moments. And there's more to come, with chair Angus Deayton adding a word or two from the bench. Boris protests he has nothing to be ashamed of. 'What are you not ashamed of?' Deayton asks him. In an instant, Boris and Alexander go into a huddle and come up with the following formulation:

'Whatever there is not to be ashamed of.'

The line goes down a storm. Boris goes on the counter-offensive, suggesting he's been 'led into an elephant trap' and using a further excuse that the incident was 'ten years ago', as if morality has a statute of limitations.

A piqued Alexander wrote a piece claiming all the so-called ad-lib wit of *HIGNFY* was, in fact, scripted. Boris would later concede that this was another whopper, but it did not queer his pitch with the show. Hislop and Merton decided they liked Boris – not as a politician but as fodder for *HIGNFY*, a useful specimen of an extinct, risible strain of Conservatism, as unlikely to make a return in the twenty-first century as the straw boater. He is invited back. Paul Merton makes a running joke about Iain Duncan Smith, then leader of the Conservative Party, actually being a set of twins, Iain and Duncan Smith. What is this thing about Iain and Duncan Smith? Boris asks. Merton explains the joke.

'Ah, I see, it's a conceit,' says Boris, as if humour were a curio to him. Boris is consciously capable of being very funny, knows about timing, knows the impact of a good line and exploiting his persona.

His face is set in a permanent half-smile, an occasional, complacent smirk. But no one ever sees him laugh out loud from deep inside. That's because Alexander, while fully understanding the use of humour, has no sense of humour at all.

In the same episode, Boris undergoes a *Mastermind*-type quiz from which he emerges with zero points. However, in this and his other appearances, through narrow eyes, scanning the room, inner machinery whirring, assessing the situation, Alexander knows he's winning.

Following this appearance, he was high-fived in the streets by students, hailed by white-van men and let off for failing to buy a ticket by the train inspector because 'You're the Bozza off the telly.'

All this, however, represented a failure to take Alexander seriously. When Angus Deayton (unlike Boris Johnson) was dismissed from public life for unforgivable sexual peccadilloes, Boris was among those subsequently invited to guest-chair the show. Merton and Hislop put to him rumours that he might become leader of the Conservative Party. 'Aidb,' replies Johnson, one of those slippery, oily, vowel-and-consonant shapes that make up many of his utterances. 'I think that's as likely as . . .' – but he doesn't finish the thought. He sings, with a knowing lack of conviction, the praises of the Iain Duncan Smith-led Tories as 'a very effective opposition that's been grotesquely let down by the media'. Guffaws ensue.

'They're laughing, Boris, they're laughing!' says Merton.

'They're clapping!' retorts Boris.

Like a political Build-a-Bear, Brand Boris is constructed on the hoof across the media. He goes on *Parkinson*, reducing fellow guest, the actor and sometime leftist firebrand Ricky Tomlinson, to fits of giggles. He's on *Newsnight* on an item titled 'When Paxo Met Boris'. Having succeeded Ken Livingstone as mayor of London in 2008, he even made a surreal appearance on *EastEnders*. Barbara Windsor as Peggy is fuming, having scoured the streets of Walford in search of Mayor Johnson, rumoured to be out and about, with a view to giving him a scolding, only for him to materialise in the Queen Vic, at which point she's reduced to a puddle of fawning. 'Such an honour to have you here, Mr Mayor,' she gushes.

Boris stands there, his customary half-smile creasing into a leer, as if he's wistfully remembering Windsor in *Carry On Camping*. 'Call me Boris,' he Borises.

Johnson also makes a series of sporting appearances. In 2006, he turns out for a celebrity England team to mark the fortieth anniversary of England's 1966 World Cup victory. His first action is to charge like a white rhino at the first German player he sees and spear-tackle him, rugby style. Bumbling Boris has got rugby confused with football, chuckles the *Telegraph* affectionately. But this wasn't Boris. This was Alexander, bared for once, exposed in all his aggressive, ruinous, pathologically inconsiderate ambition. Plus, it offered not-so-subliminal confirmation of his Europhobic credentials.

Boris Johnson's reign as mayor was strewn with attention-seeking, ill-thought-through extravagances. Spaff. Water cannon, a garden bridge, the Emirates Air Line. In 2013, when a Labour member at the London Assembly pressed him on cuts to the fire brigade, he blurted, 'Oh, get stuffed.' Alexander, the voice in his stomach. Yet Boris was able to walk away from each mess unscathed. Boris, after all, will be Boris, and more important than his serial failures was that Brand Boris be Boris, as importantly as Falstaff be Falstaff in Merrie England. During the London riots of 2011 he showed he could tickle the parts of the electorate others could not reach by picking up a broom and affecting to lead the tidy-up process. The broom became his stock prop as he did the rounds, provoking cheers as he grabbed it.

Eight years later, having decided to side with Brexit, though he'd also hedged public bets on Remain, Boris Johnson was in the running for the leadership of the Conservative Party. Martin Kettle naively wrote in the *Guardian* in May 2019, 'It is inherently unlikely that most grassroots Tories will pick a candidate for a laugh . . . they will surely ask if he or she has the dignity, the skills and the presentability of a national leader.'

A few weeks later, Channel 4 News interviewed a grassroots Tory who explained why he'd be voting for Johnson: 'Because he's a colourful character in a grey world.' Pick a candidate for a laugh? Oh, but they would. Oh, but they did.

Despite a series of parliamentary humiliations and woeful public appearances, Boris Johnson was elected prime minister on the promise that he would 'Get Brexit Done'. This would be his strategy; like Billy Bunter and his ever-imminent postal order, the perpetual promise of Jam Tomorrow. Later, this would mean world-beating test-and-trace schemes that came to grief, or a 'moonshot', a mass daily testing scheme for which there was as yet no technological basis, but which kept alive his electoral popularity; yesterday was another country, full of dead, forgotten wenches. Tomorrow, always the vague, empty fields of tomorrow, where truth, consequences and prosaic details had yet to materialise. He was elected with an eighty-seat majority not by default but by a public who positively wanted to Get Brexit Done and positively wanted Boris, Bozza, Bojo, strewing cheer at the helm of state, despite warnings from former colleagues like Max Hastings that he was unfit to be prime minister.

Boris Johnson, always wishing to be the bearer of good news, was entirely the wrong man to lead the country in a pandemic. The lockdown he imposed was too little, too late. He even blundered into catching the virus himself. His government, hamstrung by ideology and incompetence, failed tragically to implement quickly or effectively enough the sort of measures put in place in other parts of the world; but a Brexiter insistence on British exceptionalism, on not taking lessons from Johnny Foreigner, meant that no lessons were learned. Lazy and incurious about the complexities involved in running a country, Boris Johnson was for a while operated by his own externalised Alexander, Dominic Cummings. Government decisions, such as backing the climate-denying misogynist homophobe Tony Abbott as trade envoy, seemed to be made out of cachinnating malice. For one thing, Boris and Alexander/Cummings soon realised that they could avoid the punishment meted out to politicians from other parts of the political spectrum; that old codes of honour weren't binding or consequential but the equivalent of an honesty box.

Bumbling and cruel, idiotic and inept, the Johnson government barrelled on. Here we were. A very stupid politician, very stupid, but funny. We in Britain loved him. Enough to sustain him in the polls, anyway: that bewildering 40 per cent of us who were reminded of Osgood Fielding III in Billy Wilder's *Some Like It Hot*, the smiling millionaire in the speedboat accompanied by Jack Lemmon in drag, oblivious to his every attempt to persuade him he'd make a lousy wife, finally pulling off his wig and revealing he was a man. 'Nobody's perfect,' grins the millionaire.

Boris Johnson is an indictment of many things: among them, the British over-emphasis on humour. Can't-you-take-a-joke, cheer-up-it'll-never-happen, oi-oi, lighten-up, top-bantz, oggy-oggy-oggy, go-on-my-son, oi-love-give-us-a-smile, you-don't-have-to-be-mad-to-work-here, kiss-up, punch-down, 'ave it, one-up-the-bum, Boaty McBoatface, boorish, whimsical, chortling, this-is-an-ex-parrot, famous-as-bully-beef British sense of humour, sending things up but keeping us down, feet on the ground, puncturing the inflated, puffed-up balloons that might elevate us. Humour, our craven in-ability to resist humour, is what created Boris Johnson. Humour may have got us through dark days, but it might yet lead us into darker ones. Boris Johnson, he'll be the death of us, he's been the death of thousands already. His incompetence has raised the body count. Because we like a laugh. And still they chortle, still call him Boris. Because you have to laugh. Satire was supposed to laugh Boris into oblivion, but it ended up creating him: a honey monster. Satire is indicted. Comedy is indicted.

INTRODUCTION
HOW POLITICAL CORRECTNESS SAVED BRITISH COMEDY

Born as I was in the early 1960s, I've been exposed since an early age to British comedy stretching back over 130 years, on film and TV and in comics, theatre, literature. As a child, I caught Tommy Cooper, Les Dawson, Morecambe and Wise in their prime and developed an appreciation of Charlie Chaplin and Laurel and Hardy. Their black-and-whiteness didn't faze me as we didn't get colour TV until the mid-1970s. I'm also just about young enough to get my head around twenty-first-century comedy, recommended by my sixteen-year-old daughter. I get to know her TV world in a way that her generation doesn't get to get my own formative one. It'd require an active effort on their part to seek out Ken Dodd, the monologues of Joyce Grenfell or Tony Hancock. As for Laurel and Hardy and Charlie Chaplin, assumed in the twentieth century to be guaranteed immortality, they are seldom glimpsed on TV nowadays; the last time Stan and Ollie appeared on mainstream TV, the 2018 biopic apart, was a showing of *The Music Box* in 2004. This book seeks to celebrate and reanimate the Great British Comedy tradition that shed light on, lightened, lit up so many lives throughout the twentieth century and beyond, as well as to examine its failings.

I was also just coming of age as alternative comedy first began to develop, with its mission to explode hoary, unexamined assumptions, revolt against the rank, hopeless, drearily repressive complacency that had set in during the seventies and, eventually, to cleave history in two. This was as well, since with magnificent but too few exceptions, British comedy in the twentieth century was not so much about the human condition as the white, male condition. Women, when included, were generally reduced to male-scripted roles, either decorative or belligerent stereotypes, without nuance or plausible interior lives. No celebration of the comedy of this era can get round this, nor should it. It took a long time for me to gain awareness of my own privilege – white, male, cisgender, Oxbridge. Some people never did. Even in quite recent times, there were those who refused to see this as an issue of under-representation. That eminent man of letters Christopher Hitchens wrote an essay in 2007 for *Vanity Fair* titled 'Why Women Aren't Funny'. Among his arguments was that men are innately funnier because they need to be to attract women, who do not require a sense of humour to be attractive to men.

'Alternative comedy' was a dismal label (if punk had been called 'alternative rock' we might still all be wearing flares to this day), a millstone around those who practised and were associated with it. No alternative comedian, however alternative, would describe themselves as 'alternative comedian' on their calling card. As for the later terminology of political correctness . . .

And yet, amid the roll call of heroes celebrated in this volume, political correctness, which in reality means common decency and consideration for the feelings of all rather than liberal tyranny, may well be the biggest hero of them all. Political correctness didn't stifle or gag comedy, or impose on it a straitjacket of left-leaning conformity. Political correctness liberated comedy, forced it to resort to its creative imagination, helped create a new self-consciousness about what it meant to create comedy, to be more inclusive and open to new forms, new avenues of social exploration, rather than falling back on lazy, reactionary types and tropes. In 2020, John Cleese, who ossified into a bit of a reactionary himself later in his career, appeared on the *Today* programme. 'The first question I would say is: can you tell me a woke joke?' he asked. But that's missing the point. That's to regard political correctness as mere virtue signalling in lieu of comedy, like John Thomson's character in *The Fast Show*, Bernard Righton. ('An Englishman, an Irishman and a Pakistani walk into a bar. What a perfect example of racial integration.')

Political correctness was in many ways about absence – the absence of material which, intentionally or otherwise, was exclusionary or insulting to the LGBT+ community, then habitually reduced to the term 'gays', ethnic minorities, women, the disabled, who held such kick-down mockery in contempt and refused to resort to it. All of which left younger comedians with a clean slate on which to inscribe fresh ideas, new approaches, invite the lived experiences and talents of people who were previously marginalised, routinely, institutionally, if not always consciously, in less correct times.

As for the 'political' bit, well, certainly there was a shift from pre- to post-1979. There was the odd socialist such as Clive Dunn, Corporal Jones in *Dad's Army*, for example, but generally, from Morecambe and Wise to Ken Dodd, comedians inclined towards being Conservative Party supporters. In the era of alternative comedy, it was a given that the new vanguard of comedians would be left-leaning. Bob Monkhouse, himself a Conservative, once remarked that in his day, politics was considered taboo, whereas sexual innuendo was more than fair game. From the eighties onwards, it was the other way round: sex was taboo, with a disapproving 'ism' attached to it, and politics more openly discussed. In fairness, the number of out-and-out political comedians has always been exaggerated. Those few who were had to contend with the accusation that politics and comedy were a poor mix, as on a daytime TV show in which Jim Bowen, in discussion with Mark Steel, was astonished to learn that Steel was a comedian, since so far as he was concerned, he didn't have a funny bone in his body. Unfair, since one of Steel's best jokes is both political and among my most cherished. He describes his perfect day as comprising 'a workers' uprising in the morning followed by a quiet drink with friends in the evening'.

That said, the 'politics' of British comedy, before and after its 1979 renaissance, wasn't so much party political as subtly ingrained, inclined towards a sense of national superiority. This, paradoxically, is down to the English in particular (as opposed to the other home nations) being miserably monolingual, the English language being the international one, as well as the language of the last global super-power. One of the joys of English comedy is its love of the English language, its idioms, its soaring elegance, its playful turns of phrase, its thudding bathos, its profanity, its puncturing and piss-taking. However, concomitant with this is a sense that foreigners, being less able than us to pick up much more than the basics of the English language, missing its nuances, innuendo, insinuations, are dim and humourless by comparison with ourselves.

From *Fawlty Towers'* Manuel to *Mind Your Language*, from a long parade of sternly unfunny Europeans and *'Allo 'Allo* Frenchies, to ingratiating Pakistanis, this assumption went remarkably unquestioned for a long time. It didn't occur to generations of English comedians that being able to speak passably in a second language was a mark of superior linguistic skills, a greater degree of sophistication. No; we weren't having that. Foreigners' muddled English was evidence of their muddled minds. Only we, the English especially, were privy to the arcane secrets of the highest comedy of which human beings are capable. Or, as the great Al Murray, as the Pub Landlord, put it, the problem with the French is that 'they've got a town called Brest – and none of them think it's funny'.

It can feel at times like the British take refuge in the assumption that as in 1940, we stand alone, sole bearers of humour, evidence of our stoicism or pluck in the face of whatever life bombards us with. And while comedy, like music, is a significant UK export, other countries are not oblivious to laughter, and have their own comic forms that we don't quite get, and not just because we're mono-glots. Take Jacques Tati, for example. While he was influenced by the British Chaplin, he created a language of comedy based on long shots, visual puns, inadvertent symmetries, elaborate sight gags involving traffic, windowpanes, dining-room doors, all of which amounted to a gentle critique of our folly and pomposity in the machine age we had created but did not quite control.

British comedy has been successfully exported. Chaplin was the first great example, a sublime, sentimental and brilliantly acrobatic clown working in the international language of silence. Ditto Mr Bean, a calamity-prone but resourceful, rubber-faced character whose appeal stretches to every continent, not so much everyman as every un-man. *Monty Python* appealed across Europe and in America because its surrealism transcended language barriers, was not hamstrung by its English origins.

There were remakes, too. *Steptoe and Son* was remade as *Sanford and Son* in the United States, remade with an African American cast. In Germany, *Till Death Us Do Part* was remade as *Ein Herz und eine Seele* (*One Heart and One Soul*), its central character, Alfred Tetzlaff, if anything less loveable than Alf Garnett, a device to satirise the sort of angry white far-right men who still disfigured post-war Germany and retained a more sinister civic influence.

However, a lot of Britain's most beloved comedy did not enjoy significant transatlantic or European success: Tommy Cooper, for example, or Tony Hancock, despite his best efforts, or Morecambe and Wise. This could feel like solace. The foreigners didn't catch on.

Back to that conservatism, that sense that English comedy in particular speaks about our character, our predicament. You can to an extent argue that our comedy says something about the nature of Englishness, but only to an extent, as any 'national characteristic' is provisional, in a constant state of flux and development. Indeed, the idea that there is a certain, fixed and graceful state of Englishness, a self-flattering image defined by wartime, is exclusionary, particularly prevalent among a much older generation, some of whom mistake having actually fought in World War II with watching films about it as children. That's not to assert that British comedy doesn't say a great deal about British life. The very fact that we produce so much of it is not necessarily proof that we are less inhibited, less staid, more inclined to give authority a kick up the backside. All of that, yes, but all that energy devoted towards comedy and its consumption – the imperative that you have to laugh – is displaced energy, energy that perhaps other nations devoted towards converting themselves from monarchies to republics, for example.

Certainly, class has been a traditional preoccupation in British comedy; take the 1960s sketch involving John Cleese and the progressively shorter Ronnies Barker and Corbett standing in a row, signifying the descending order of the classes. For the purposes of the sketch, these three class specimens are situated improbably close to one another; across a range of sitcoms we saw the upper and lower classes consort to amusing effect in wartime situations: in *It Ain't Half Hot Mum* and *Dad's Army*, for example.

Gradually, however, in the 1980s and 1990s the upper-class figures of yore began to melt away from mainstream comedy. Come the late nineties, as comedy began to reflect the more detailed reality of life, and more complex characters were conceived, so the old stock types of a former era, including the blazered, upper-class type, fell out of favour. There was a slight return in the form of Jack Whitehall, but the aristocracy wasn't the familiar staple of yore and 'class' consequently faded from the comedy agenda. Could this be because the 'classless society' mooted by John Major had finally arrived? Hardly. Class privilege was as entrenched as ever – it's just that its beneficiaries were remote from everyday society. The reminder that they'd never gone away came with the election of David Cameron, with George Osborne as chancellor, and, before and after them, the comi-tragedy that was Boris Johnson.

British comedy has traditionally been riven with attitudes towards race, gender, disability which today would be considered hidebound, and should have been back then. Sometimes it's just single moments, but they jar like a bone in an otherwise tasty fish supper. In the 1954 film *Doctor in the House*, for instance, when Donald Sinden's amorous young doctor finds that he may have over-committed to a nurse by presenting her with a flower and, carried away during a clinch, proposes marriage to her. The situation is resolved when Kenneth More's doctor suggests he present similar flowers to every other nurse in the hospital, resulting in a reveal which sees the would-be fiancée walk in on her colleagues all wearing their flowers – including, last to turn round, a Black nurse. 'Me too,' she smiles.

You're never far from a fishbone like this if you trawl through the history of British comedy, given how heavily grounded it was in unreconstructed assumptions, and worse.

The depiction of non-white people, or simply their invisibility, is a recurring theme in this book. I am white, but my first wife was Sikh, and naturally I spent a great deal of time with her family and their everyday lives and culture, which afforded me some insight and empathy. Included in this text are racial slurs, once considered acceptable within the context of family entertainment. I suspect that even when they were spoken by buffoonish, unsympathetic characters, there was much merriment at their utterance – among writers, actors, audiences. No such merriment here. A cold pang stabs through my fingers every time I type them, but it's necessary to highlight them. I also look at blackface, the racist cultural practice first commonplace among white performers in the nineteenth-century United States but which maintained an insidious presence – experienced a revival, even – in British comedy well into the twenty-first century.

It'd be easy, so blighted is British comedy of the past with offensive caricatures, simply to recommend to young people today and future generations to give all British comedy prior to 1979 a complete swerve and start with, ooh, say *The Young Ones*.

That, however, would be a terrible proposal, like binning Shakespeare's work in its entirety because of the dubious attitudes he demonstrates towards Jewish people in *The Merchant of Venice* or women in *The Taming of the Shrew*. I am not in the least bit interested in cancellation, far from it. By all means proceed with caution when exploring the history of British comedy, but proceed nonetheless. There is, after all, the prospect of much of it becoming an endangered species. I'll try to explain how and why – why such comedy was what it was and wasn't what it wasn't, what it said about its era, how it was produced by British history, what it said about us, or, simply, the gratuitous delight it shed on us.

TV culture is very much right-here-right-now in this day and age. This, certainly, has had the beneficial effect of sparing its victims the sort of casually racist, sexist, ableist comedy that was served up routinely in my own childhood and beyond, and the pain it enabled and engendered. Today's programme-makers, producers, commissioners take these issues extremely seriously, and rightly so.

Still, kids, through no fault of their own, are growing up in a screen culture in which nothing is more than a few years old, if they even watch TV at all. Nostalgia feels like it's dying out a little more with each passing year. The black and white giants who dominated my childhood are fading into collective, middle-aged memory, from *Kind Hearts and Coronets* to the Goons, *Dad's Army* to Morecambe and Wise, and many, many points in between and beyond. This was comedy made in conditions that will never prevail again, shaped and coloured by events long past and yet still managing to say something to us, tickle us, today: about the limits of life, exasperation, boredom, absurdity, pomposity, and the ingenious ways and means comedy finds of getting around and through all that, providing a ha'penny's worth of consolation at least, making life feel just about worth living. So much comedy; not so much a source of 'pride' – they did it, you just watched – but certainly joy.

Sadly, I fail to mention everybody in this volume. Jim Davidson, for example, though since this a book about comedy, that would be a category error. Some of those who are excluded make me laugh very hard indeed: Johnny Vegas, for example. He's just bloody funny, and watching him riff dolefully and relentlessly about an internet site called Beauty's Castle, I'm so busy gasping for air I haven't the energy to try to set him in a wider context. He's the sort of comedian who makes me wonder if sometimes it's not so much a case of Britain producing comedy as comedy producing Britain, gratuitously colouring in, lending quality to our lives, rather than just arising from social circumstances. Certainly, the comedians not mentioned in this volume are in very distinguished, as well as undistinguished, company.

What of Terry-Thomas, later known for spraying sibilant contempt on his inferiors as an 'absolute shower' but who has the lesser-known distinction of appearing in the first ever comedy series on British television, *How Do You View?*, debuting in 1949? Or *The Strange World of Gurney Slade*, the surreal meta-sitcom devised by Anthony Newley, in which he addressed the camera directly as he walked through the fourth wall, bemoaning his life as a character in a TV show, at one point undergoing formal prosecution for not being funny enough?

Where's Vivian Stanshall? Ivor Cutler? Jerry Sadowitz – a comedian of inspired, revolting and burning obscenity, as well as one of the finest magicians on the planet? A shocking comedian but one driven by an obliquely moral fervour.

Sitcoms: Sean Lock's *15 Storeys High*? *Phone Shop*? Or Robert Popper's superbly farcical *Friday Night Dinner*? Meanwhile, as for my glossing over of the fine, fine *One Foot in the Grave*, the last ever chapter in the history of the exasperated suburban sitcom male before his death, the reader may well be excused for saying, 'I can scarcely credit it.'

Finally, the great musical parodist Bill Bailey, and the brilliant Kevin Eldon, with whom I briefly worked in the mid-1990s, contributing scripts to a radio series starring Alan Davies that laboured valiantly under the unfortunate moniker of *Alan's Big 1FM*. Working closely with them, alongside Graham Fellows, aka John Shuttleworth, wasn't the great career leg-up into comedy that I might have hoped for; instead, it convinced me that, unlike them, I didn't have the comedy bones, the heart, the determination, the serious/anti-serious dedication required to make it in that world. That to be funny down the pub is a world below creating comedy, building a career in comedy at the highest broadcast level. All those featured in this book, even some of the lesser luminaries in lesser comedies, had the stuff required. They and many more I've failed to mention at all. And so I dedicate this book to those who pick it up, go straight to the index, look for their name and fail to find it.

In the *Fawlty Towers* episode 'Gourmet Night', Basil, frantically retyping the menu following the discovery that his chef is dead drunk, wonders if maybe the whole experience is a dream. After slamming his head three times on the desk he concludes that it is not. 'We're stuck with it.' Being stuck with it, stuck with each other. Maybe that's what binds British comedy past and present – that sense that we are a bunch of people stuck with each other, whether we can stick each other or not, marooned on our wet island, undone by our pretensions of striking out and going it alone; we belong inescapably to one another. We are stuck with each other, not just as people but as a species, bound by difference, eventually love. From Stan and Ollie's fine mess through Hancock and *The Young Ones* to *Ghosts*. Stuck with each other, we can experience disappointment, resignation, tolerance, change, even if we don't really change, acceptance, sometimes joy and maybe even a strange, mute love.

There are other histories; this is just one.

BETWEEN THE WARS, 1917–1939
CHARLIE CHAPLIN AND STAN LAUREL

During the 1930s in particular, pre-TV and with radio still in its infancy, the stage and silver screen were where British comedy flourished, kicking on from the music hall era, heralding increasingly sceptical attitudes towards class and authority with all the energy of a kick in the pants. There was a great wave of Northern comedians who prefigured generations of rude, raspingly acerbic Lancastrians and Yorkshiremen of future decades. Will Hay, for example, and his carefully crafted bumbling persona in films like *Oh! Mr Porter* (1937). Rob Wilton, whose unhurried manner as a fire chief sees him ask a caller reporting a raging blaze if he could 'keep it going till we get there'. Frank Randle, whose irascible persona made Mark E. Smith of the Fall seem like Derek Nimmo by comparison: firing loaded guns, locking co-stars in their dressing rooms. George Formby, bumbling but always cheerily triumphant, who strummed on his somewhat phallically symbolic ukulele with a ferocity only matched by the temperament of his fearsome wife Beryl.

Or there was the Southern stand-up Max Miller. With his conspiratorial glances to the wings, as if to check the all-powerful Lord Chamberlain, responsible for censorship in the theatres, wasn't lurking in them, he would produce both a white and a blue book of jokes for audiences to choose from. Invariably they chose the blue, and he would produce a stream of highly suggestive, never profane gags which slipped, ducked and dived from the grasp of local 'watch committees', whose job was to look out for material which might offend public morals.

The two most globally successful comedians, however, were both expats, one Northern, one Southern, who made their fortunes across the Atlantic, inscribing themselves in the international firmament.

Both Stan Laurel (born Arthur Stanley Jefferson in Ulverston in 1890) and Charlie Chaplin (born in Walworth, London, in 1889) had made their starts in their juvenile years, honing the skills with which they would make their names – Stan got into an actual pickle with his father during an act at the Panopticon Theatre in Glasgow when he borrowed his suit and hat, cutting up the former and beating the latter, to the old man's fury. Chaplin's family and friends eked out livings in the music hall, but while Chaplin learned a range of pantomime and acrobatic skills, he found the often hostile audiences harrowing, finding solace in screen comedy. Still, the dying music hall was the making of them in the emerging mechanical century and age of reproduction. Once they were in America, neither man looked back, Laurel only rarely referencing his British origins on screen, Chaplin never.

When they first arrived in America with Fred Karno's comedy troupe, Chaplin and Laurel had waddled about New York, the best of pals. Once, they were caught short, desperate to pee. They dived into a bar; the barman told them they could use his facilities only if they bought beer. Both were struck by the irony of having to take on board more of the stuff that had put them in their present pass in order to be relieved from it. Chaplin doesn't mention this story in *My Autobiography*, written in 1964. It's a volume that resounds with the clanging of dropped names, but not once does he mention Laurel, his one-time drinking buddy. In *My Autobiography*, though he is honest enough to acknowledge a secret inferiority complex, Chaplin comes across as earnest, self-important, too grand for peeing anecdotes.

Chaplin was considered to be more than a 'mere' comedian – he was an artist. Jean Cocteau hailed him as the modern clown, with whose help the Tower of Babel could have been completed. Jean Renoir praised *Monsieur Verdoux* (1947) as going some way to elevating film as an art form; Jean-Luc Godard remarked that 'Today people say "Chaplin" as they say "Da Vinci".' He was embraced by the European art movements of the early twentieth century. Tristan

Tzara once claimed that Chaplin had joined Dada, in full anarchic blaze in Zurich concurrently with Chaplin's early film career. In *The Chaplin Machine*, Owen Hatherley observes that to the Russian avant-garde he was a 'mechanised exemplar of the new forms and new spaces enabled by the new American technologies, and one who promised a liberation that was decidedly machinic in form'.

I first saw his work in the 1970s BBC series *Golden Silents*. I was beguiled by the insolent, disruptive velocity of the comedy. Not just his, but that of Buster Keaton, Harry Langdon, Harold Lloyd. Chaplin, however, by 1964 did not see himself as retrospectively to be bracketed with such clowns. Lloyd gets a perfunctory mention in his book; Keaton and Langdon none at all. Chaplin saw himself rather as the confidant of great artistic minds and eminent politicians: H. G. Wells, Paderewski, Schoenberg, Eisenstein, Churchill, Roosevelt, all of whom he converses with on equal terms.

More recently, however, comedians and writers on comedy have muttered, 'Yes, but – is he actually funny?'

Certainly, in the alternative 1980s, Chaplin was increasingly unfashionable, compared, adversely, with Stan Laurel, whose short back and sides and shock of hair on top was quite the radical style in the post-punk years. Laurel and Hardy enjoyed a hip renaissance in the 1980s. In the *NME*, fans like Monty Smith and Danny Baker ensured that any Stan and Ollie short in the late-evening listings was highlighted in their TV previews column. Their slapstick chimed in with *The Young Ones*, and later *Bottom*: as if the pursuit of comedy gratuitously and above all was an anarcho-political act.

It was suspected that reverence towards Chaplin was bestowed by those themselves lacking in humour, who regarded comedy as a base medium from which truly the best should elevate themselves; the sort of critics who were relieved that with the film *Being There*, Peter Sellers had finally graduated to a serious, and therefore worthwhile, role. Although Rowan Atkinson is sometimes described as a latter-day Chaplin on account of his Mr Bean character, Atkinson himself was lukewarm about the Tramp. Indeed, in *Blackadder Goes Forth*, Chaplin is the butt of Blackadder's caustic contempt. He finds his films 'about as funny as getting an arrow through the neck and then discovering there's a gas bill tied to it' – a line Atkinson delivered with relish.

The most vivid section of Chaplin's autobiography is his account of his childhood. Chaplin recounts in painful detail a young life which saw him battered from pillar to post – with a drunken, absent father, and a luckless mother whose music hall career was curtailed when she lost her singing voice. She and her brood were forced to live in a single room in South London, surviving on 'parochial charity, soup tickets and meal parcels'. Chaplin recalls his mother's attempt to keep her children not just fed and clothed but respectable, correcting their grammar and diction. Her condition worsened; she had to forsake a living in needlework; and Chaplin found himself in the Lambeth workhouse.

Research later corroborated Chaplin's account. Real as it is, however, were it a fiction it would smack of the sentimentalism of which both Dickens and Chaplin would be accused by detractors: the woman of virtue laid low by Fate, as callous as a moustached villain in a melodrama foreclosing the mortgage of a helpless widow. Chaplin was a fan of Dickens – one of his earliest successes in his youth was his portrayal of a character from *The Old Curiosity Shop*. And although he is considered the 'first man' of twentieth-century comic creation, he was also a bona fide Dickensian creature.

Stan Laurel's background was more privileged. Brought up in Ulverston, then Bishop Auckland and North Shields, Laurel was sent to boarding school rather than the workhouse. As with Chaplin, he came from a showbusiness background, though his father was rather more successful; Arthur Jefferson was not just an entertainer but an entrepreneur. In 1910, Laurel Sr joined forces with Fred Karno, a tireless showman who would provide the vital bridging point between nineteenth-century music hall and early-twentieth-century two-reel comedy, short, silent features that ran to twenty minutes.

Chaplin had joined Karno's troupe two years earlier. The pair travelled to America with Karno's Company of Clowns, with Laurel as Chaplin's understudy. They took lodgings together and were thick as thieves, though some suspect there was thievery involved in Chaplin's adaptation of a tramp-like character Stan had developed at their lodgings, based on the vaudeville comedian Dan Leno.

By 1914, Chaplin had left Karno to forge his own film career; as Chaplin rose to fame, however, Laurel descended back below the waterline of obscurity. He found himself briefly back in England, resuming a fitful music hall career. He looked on from afar at the rise of his one-time drinking partner but held on to the conviction that if Chaplin could make it, he could too, and persisted in a variety of roles on the lower rungs of the silent movie industry. In 1917, back in America, he met his old friend Chaplin, who received him rather coolly, seeing him as a reminder of his modest past and perhaps the true provenance of the Tramp character. For a while, Laurel was part-nered on screen with Mae Dahlberg, briefly his romantic partner, but that ended acrimoniously. It wasn't until the mid-1920s that he would find the partner he needed.

Stan Laurel shared his name with his character. Charlie Chaplin's Tramp, however, did not. The character was, by his own account, born in the haste with which all film comedy was conceived in those days. He was on set with Mack Sennett, who was short of gags for a picture and told Chaplin to go grab some 'comedy make-up' that might prompt the necessary missing chuckles. Chaplin claimed no premeditation was involved; once he adopted the scruffy garb of baggy pants, tight waistcoat, big shoes, small hat, the ensemble topped off with a cane, the character flowed into the clothes: 'a tramp, a gentleman, a poet, a dreamer, a lonely fellow, always hopeful of romance and adventure'.

Thus was Chaplin inscribed in the cultural firmament, as recog-nisable as Mickey Mouse, and later Hitler, a recently arrived, fully formed, freshly minted creature born of a fast-cranked, flickering machine age, a self-performing marionette without family or back-story. His ancestry is of the music hall tradition; he is an immigrant, created in the old country from a series of exaggerated comic types, scruffs with airs and graces. But in his movements, his quick, improvised thinking, his grace and pratfalls, he was an original whose impact on mass audiences was immediate.

Modern audiences might wonder at the Tramp's appeal. In his debut, *Kid Auto Races at Venice* (1914), he is basically a pest. It is a film about a film: attempts by a cameraman to film a 'baby cart' race in Los Angeles. His efforts are thwarted by Chaplin's Tramp continually interrupting, strutting about in front of the camera, ruining the race, caught between not knowing where to put himself and enjoying the mischief of disruption. Today, there would be little sympathy for such an attention-seeker, who would be ejected by stewards to universal applause. However, a silent movie periodical greeted *Kid Auto Races* as 'the funniest film ever made'. The mere presence of the Tramp announcing 'here I am' was enough.

Weeks later came *A Film Johnnie*, in which the Tramp falls in love with a girl on screen, making a nuisance of himself at the cinema as he does so, then trying to break into Keystone Studios to find her, triggering further mayhem involving a firehose. Again, in our era of stalkers and court injunctions, it is harder to cheer on the Tramp, but maybe the key title of this film is: 'We don't want any bums around here.' This was the character that audiences, the huddled American masses who identified all too well with the shunned, friendless, pushed-about 'bum', were crying out for. Yay, bum!

Bums, vagabonds, immigrants, floorwalkers – these were the types Chaplin would play. When he first arrived in America, he was struck by the coldness of New York, a place where business was conducted at skyscraper-high level, moving on up, leaving the rest behind. He found little of the European sense of community and conviviality. He recalled saloon bars with no seats, merely brass rails for customers to rest a foot on, and clean but characterless restaurants. Chaplin would evoke their charmless interiors and the 'eat it, get out' attitude of their waiters, ready to become bouncers at a moment's notice, in his films.

The Tramp faces an endless stock supply of irascible cops, heavies, crooks, cruelly indifferent passers-by, competitors for scraps, disapproving, matronly women. There was the occasional kind stranger, however, and Edna Purviance as his recurring love interest. She appears opposite him in *The Tramp* (1915), in which he chances upon a family farm, which he helps defend from thieves, before being taken in to do odd jobs and falling in love with the farmer's daughter (Purviance). On this occasion, he is disappointed: he discovers, in a moment of well-turned pathos, that she already has a boyfriend. He sighs and sets back off along the dusty road, but revives his spirits with a kick back in the air, as if dispensing lightly with the setback. In subsequent films starring Purviance, however, they did head into the sunset together.

There are jarring moments in early Chaplin films. There's a running joke in which he repeatedly jabs a pitchfork up the backside of his fellow dim but undeserving farmhand, for example. Similarly, in *The Bank* (1915), the Tramp seems unaccountably cruel to his fellow janitor, delivering him kicks up the backside and assaults with a mop that might better have been reserved for his 'superiors' upstairs. Considering the McCarthyite allegations later levelled at Chaplin, the Tramp seems incapable of socialism even to a fellow worker. Chaplin was paradoxical. Yes, he identified with the underdog, but he was excited, as he crossed America, by its go-ahead architecture, 'throbbing with the dynamism of the future'. For all his Dickensian hard luck and sympathy for the little guy, the Tramp was a character of rare mechanical speed, and his successes were individual rather than for the benefit of a wider community.

Even today, the velocity of those early shorts alone is formidable; Chaplin prefigures the great cartoon characters of the twentieth century, his inventiveness and athleticism unmatched, anticipating the likes of Tex Avery. Then there are the visual gags; in *The Immigrant* (1917), he can be seen dangling over the side of a boat, his entire body heaving, as if in the throes of seasickness. Only when he hauls himself back do we realise that he is actually hooking a fish.

Still, watching the meticulous, fast-cut choreography of Chaplin, the ducking, the tumbling, the swivelling planks, brings to mind the story Chaplin told of the ballet dancer Nijinsky, who looked in on the shoot of *The Cure* (1917). As the crew and onlookers chuckled away, Nijinsky sat 'looking sadder and sadder', albeit with great attentiveness and appreciation. At the end of the day, face weighed down with solemnity, he congratulated Chaplin and asked if he could return for the next two days. Chaplin reluctantly agreed, but told his cameraman not to bother putting film in the machine as he was put completely off by the unsmiling Russian. At the end of the three days, Nijinsky congratulated Chaplin, describing him as 'balletique . . . like a dancer'. Watching Chaplin today, one can sympathise with Nijinsky; one admires the choreography, without necessarily smiling.

Although Stan Laurel was more business-minded than his character, he was never able to strike that great a deal. No such problems with Chaplin, who always retained enough raw nerve to realise that a fellow prepared to offer him $150 a week would probably be willing to pay $175. Whereas Stan and Ollie did all their best work tethered to the Hal Roach Studios, Chaplin moved from Keystone to Essanay, on to Mutual and then First National, where he was allowed creative autonomy to make films at his own pace and with as many takes as he felt necessary. In 1919, he formed United Artists alongside D. W. Griffiths, Douglas Fairbanks and Mary Pickford. At his peak, he was earning $13,000 a week, and in his Tramp guise he achieved a universal recognisability that even today feels beyond deconstruction; the irrationale of celebrity, once in motion, takes on a momentum of its own.

Except celebrity doesn't quite sum up the Chaplin/Tramp phenomenon; for all his fame, it is not the tanned, bowler-hatless, wealthy young Chaplin who was branded on the collective consciousness. The Tramp was a human animation, much imitated, generating much merchandise, but who of necessity remained a vagabond, an exile, an outsider on whom the camera must fade the moment he enjoys a happy ending, only to be reset as a down-and-out for his next feature. He's the little guy at whom you can marvel in his defiance of authority, of burlier opponents, yet he is nevertheless unenviable, pitiable. You're badly off? This guy is worse. His abject poverty was as comforting to mass audiences as his victories.

Chaplin is sentimental – lachrymose rather than socially prescriptive, emotionally indulgent rather than intellectually nourishing. However, he created masterpieces of sentimentality. During a scene in *The New Janitor* (1914) in which he is imploring to be reinstated in his job, he had seen that a fellow actor, Dorothy Davenport, was weeping real tears. Chaplin considered what he was doing mere pantomime, but he must have carried over more of the tear-jerking adversity of his early life than he realised. He resolved to exploit this, and exploit it he did in those masterpieces of sentimentality, *The Kid* (1921) and *City Lights* (1931). For all the ingenious comedy routines of *City Lights*, its most affecting scenes are its concluding ones. Our hero has been released from prison and is shambling pitifully down the street. This is more than pathos. The Tramp was never a 'Tramp' in the true sense but a spry music hall creation with a defiant waddle and as firm a grip on his sense of dignity and adventure as on his cane and bowler hat.

Here, dragging himself hopelessly along the street, caneless, hat battered and torn, he is an actual tramp – a marionette with all his strings cut, broken, spent, mocked by street kids, before the most tender and moving of conclusions as he chances upon the heroine of the picture, whom he saved from blindness. But briefly we see a de-romanticised glimpse of the Tramp, enduring the personal ruin that would befall so many during the 1930s' Great Depression.

The chasteness of the Tramp's on-screen romances contrasted with Chaplin's off-screen love life, which was considered controversial in his own time and has not aged well. Chaplin had a penchant for girls around the twenty-year-old mark, sometimes younger. He met and married Mildred Harris in 1918, when she was either sixteen or seventeen. They separated after the death of their only child in 1919. He first met his second wife, Lita Grey, when she was twelve, and they had an affair when she was fifteen. They married in 1924, when Chaplin was thirty-five, and divorced in 1927, by which time she was nineteen and a bored Chaplin was seeking solace with other women. Oona O'Neill was eighteen when Chaplin met her; he was aged fifty-three, but their marriage did last until the end of his life. The only occasion his on-screen character reflects his off-screen proclivities is *Limelight* (1952), in which Chaplin's washed-up comedian, Calvero, becomes attracted to a twenty-one-year-old Claire Bloom (Chaplin was at this point sixty-two). Gallantly, he steers her towards another young man, played, hmm, by his son, Sydney.

All this affected the perception of Chaplin; following accusations of 'perverted sexual desires' by Grey during her divorce proceedings in 1927, women's groups tried to organise boycotts of his films. However, by the time of *City Lights*, the challenge facing on-screen Chaplin was the arrival of talkies. It became increasingly clear that the Tramp's days were numbered. What would happen when he talked? 'This was unthinkable,' he wrote, 'for the first words he ever uttered would transform him into another person. Besides, the matrix out of which he was born was as mute as the rags he wore.'

By the late 1920s, Chaplin was in a quandary. For Stan Laurel, however, fame was at long last arriving. Unlike Chaplin, he could not cut it alone.

The on-screen relationship he struck up with Oliver Hardy, born in Harlem, Georgia, in 1892, was one of interdependency. And, although they rose to prominence as silent screen partners, they were constantly chattering mutely, waiting to give vent to their voices. The orotund Hardy, with his fastidious, courtly phrases punctuated by primal cries of exasperation at the constant mishap visited on him by Stan: 'Why don't you do something to help me?' Stan, meanwhile, would reply with his flat-footed, diffident English diction and innocently tactless, dumb interjections. Dialogue would not be a hurdle to overcome for these thus-far silent comedians. Dialogue would be key to Laurel and Hardy.

Before they teamed up, Laurel had appeared in fifty films, Hardy more than 250. They first appeared together in 1921, but only with 1928's *Leave 'Em Laughing* do we begin to get an inkling of their future partnership. Sharing a bed out of economic necessity and a deep friendship to which fate has abandoned them, we see Stan whimpering like a five-year-old at a bout of toothache, and the wonderfully familiar body language of Ollie's exasperation at his role as keeper of this man-child, tempered with genuine solicitude.

They made several more shorts, developing and exploring what at the time must have seemed a potentially tricky relationship between two men against the world, rather than the conventional sole protagonist (Lloyd, Chaplin, Langdon, Keaton). Like the Tramp, Laurel and Hardy had constant run-ins with beat cops. However, as they embarked on the classic eight or nine years of talkies by which they are defined, their comedy, mostly conceived by Stan Laurel, would be of a very different, often contrasting order to Chaplin's.

In a typical Chaplin two-reeler, for example, the Tramp would start off right down on his luck, but rise to a happy ending, or at least vindication. Not Laurel and Hardy, in their shorts. In these, we see the worlds they inhabit, whether as prosperously middle-class or sleeping on a park bench, fall apart piece by piece, with Oliver, sitting on his backside amid the ruins, staring at us from down the decades with infinite, searing dismay as Stan fumbles self-consciously with his fingertips, scratching his head, as if wondering if he might have had some vague role in his friend's downfall, and either bursting into tears or trying to extract something from the wreckage, such as the still-functioning horn at the end of *Towed in a Hole* (1932).

Laurel and Hardy are neither romantic nor sentimental. To assuage the sensibilities of the time, we are assured of the boys' heterosexuality thanks to storylines that see them in amorous pursuit of young women; later, the women would be battle-axe wives, antagonists in the miserable marriages in which the boys found themselves entrapped. Somewhat reductive female roles, for sure, but Laurel and Hardy were involved in a bizarrely durable bromance, one rarely manifested in affection or verbal acknowledgement, but one with which the marriages in which they find themselves entangled are ultimately irreconcilable. The nearest they ever got to expressing these sentiments was in a deleted scene from *Laughing Gravy* (1931), in which Stan receives a telegram announcing that he is due to receive a huge inheritance from an uncle – so long as he severs ties with Ollie. Stan won't let him see the telegram until Ollie rips it from him – only for Ollie to express a moment of chastened tenderness for his old pal. Lovely as the scene is, they were right to drop it. Explicit, potentially cloying moments like this were more Chaplin's forte. The joy and love between Stan and Ollie is best implied rather than declared. Then there are the moments when they temporarily fall into sync, whether pitted against Charlie Hall in *Tit for Tat*, or united musically, as in *The Music Box*, in which they snap into a makeshift waltz to a player piano tune, or *Way Out West*. It's moments like these that affirm their bond: how unthinkable one would be without the other.

The film *Stan and Ollie* (2018), starring Steve Coogan and John Reilly, offers an authentic glimpse into the real-life relationship of the two actors. In truth, Laurel was Paul Simon to Stan's Art Garfunkel: responsible for ideas as well as performance. He was (relatively) more aggressive and confrontational in business dealings, whereas Ollie, minus his imperious glue-on moustache, was soft 'Babe' to one and all.

There are other contrasts between Chaplin and Laurel: Stan's smile, for example, one of cheerful, gormless, blank-faced, infantile innocence, arcing across his face like the acid house smiley symbol. The

Tramp's beam is much less broad: a mere baring of the teeth, generally when he is making eyes at his leading lady. My mother found Chaplin films hard to watch simply because his small, obsequious smile gave her the creeps.

Chaplin insisted on absolute creative control of his output, including composing the soundtracks – to *City Lights*, for instance. His music is lacquered, amply signalling the surges of sentiment in his films. The relationship between Laurel and Hardy and the incidental music in their shorts is more intriguing. The main theme, 'Dance of the Cuckoos', was written by Marvin Hatley. It takes a polytonal approach; the melody represents the prancing, puffed-up Ollie, accompanied and undermined by the recurring 'cuckoo' harmony that represents Stan, before the clarinets unite – for Ollie, ultimately, for all his pretensions, is just as dumb as Stan.

It's not this, however, or Ballard MacDonald and Harry Carroll's 'The Trail of the Lonesome Pine' (from *Way Out West*), a posthumous hit in 1976, that is crucial to Laurel and Hardy. It's the incidental music written for them by Leroy Shield, tunes such as 'If It Were True', 'Smile When the Raindrops Fall' (featured at the beginning of *Busy Bodies* as they trundle along to work in an open-top car), 'Bells', 'Dash and Dot', 'Colonel Gaieties' (used in *County Hospital* as Stan eats his hard-boiled eggs) or 'Rocking Chair', whose rising, bluesy motif comes into play when Stan is going through his customary range of sentiments to camera, from sorrow to blank denial, having inadvertently visited calamity on Ollie.

The recurring use of these tunes was an act of cheapness on Hal Roach's part; 'Beautiful Lady', for instance, was initially written to signal the on-screen appearance of Thelma Todd, a co-star in early Laurel and Hardy features such as *Another Fine Mess* (1930) before her untimely death. However, it was reused many times after that. These incidental tunes, light and effervescent band music, have a dual effect. They are, firstly, cheering reminders that we are watching Laurel and Hardy. However, they also function similarly to the recurring tunes in Larry David's *Curb Your Enthusiasm*. They are a reminder that these characters are doomed, for our entertainment, to blunder into the same pitfalls, come the same croppers as they always have, always will. They also mask the hiss and crackle of old film stock, although much of this survives in the Laurel and Hardy shorts – as off-putting to twenty-first-century children, in my sad experience, as the films' black-and-whiteness. Yet for me, even the ambience of the crackle has a deep charm, like a fireplace, a reminder that the embers of this comedy still glow decades on.

Another contrast: although Chaplin reused certain actors, they are generally foils; only the central character is of real interest. Laurel and Hardy certainly dominate their films, but they did allow for a regular ensemble to make their own individual impressions, which somehow adds a familial feel to their comedies, for all the misery they inflict and have inflicted upon them by Stan and Ollie – the Birmingham-born Charlie Hall, for example, the pint-sized, angry foe of *Them Thar Hills* and *Tit for Tat*; Mae Busch as the henpecking spouse and terroriser of Ollie; Billy Gilbert, who played a range of characters, including the apoplectic recipient of the piano in *The Music Box*; Walter Long, who played violent heavies, including the sea captain in *The Live Ghost*, who makes good on his threat to twist Stan's and Ollie's heads 180 degrees; and James Finlayson, he of the broom-like moustaches and double and triple takes, whose 'Doh!' pre-dates Homer Simpson by several decades.

Chaplin's shorts move at a busy pelt – a contrast again with the ponderous pace of Laurel and Hardy, who proceed almost ritual-istically through their slapstick routines. When watching back the 1930s shorts years later, Stan Laurel was shocked at how slowly they proceeded. However, those lengthy pauses after Ollie has been pitched face first into a body of water from a ladder dislodged by Stan were inserted so that audiences could recover from their fits of laughter. Today, they move us in a different way. Ollie's colossally exasperated stares to camera, cast down from deep in the last century into our own, pleading sympathy for his perpetual torment; Stan glancing up with shy, boyish contrition, fiddling with his fingers – these are the most lingering, mutely soulful moments of Laurel and Hardy, comedy twelve-bar blues.

Moreover, Chaplin's Tramp may start at the bottom, but with his enterprising speed of mind and movement he's generally able to advance himself. Laurel and Hardy shorts move more slowly because Stan and Ollie themselves are slower, bringing up the rear of the human herd, victims not just of the Depression but of innocent helplessness in the face of adversity. Despite their interdependence, they are impeded by the contrast between them, at odds with one another: Oliver Hardy is from the Deep South, the land of courtly, grandiose graces, whereas all this is foreign to Stan, a man trying to make it in America but very much made in Britain.

Their transition into talkies saw them lose the hand-cranked pace of their silent pictures. In *Men O' War* (1929), they're sailors on shore leave, hooking up with two young ladies at a soda bar in the park. Short of cash, Ollie persuades Stan to refuse a drink when he offers him one, as they can afford only three sodas. Stan nods but then repeatedly accepts Ollie's offer, forcing Ollie to take him aside. 'Can't you *grasp* the situation?' he asks him – whereupon Stan stares at us with the most whitewashed, blankest of blank expressions, face drained of sense or any hint that he possesses the apparatus to make sense. His ignorance is almost divine, as if he abides by the deeper logic of a preternatural clown. This is Laurel logic, and he applies it at the soda bar. Stan and Ollie are supposed to split their drink, but Stan drinks it all. Ollie, aghast, asks him why, to which Stan replies pitifully, 'My half was on the bottom.'

By this time (1929) Stan Laurel was almost forty and, for all his infantile tics, he also looks rather elderly, and beleaguered, not unlike Godfrey in *Dad's Army*. He looks worn down by decades of failure to grasp either end of the stick, his voice withered, his face often wreathed in a weak, nervous smile, his body language dithery, as if he knows from many years' dumb experience that he's about to get it from Ollie, despite his best intentions. Pity poor Stan, quite incapable of dealing with the essential responsibilities of the adulthood he's aged, if not grown, into, the lowest human being of all, browbeaten by the second lowest, the both of them, as Oliver would announce to an old lady in *One Good Turn* (1931), 'victims of the Depression'.

So it is in *Perfect Day* (1929), a short about a picnic at which the boys, their wives and a grouchy uncle never arrive: they are stalled outside their house by a series of setbacks, including a malfunctioning car. What is Stan to do when Ollie yells at him to 'throw out the clutch'? Naturally, he unscrews the clutch pedal and throws it out of the car. Generally, Ollie bears the worst brunt of the slapstick: stepping on the roller skate that pitches him down the stairs (*Brats*); falling through a glass window after Stan thoughtlessly removes his foot from the ladder Ollie is halfway up (*Our Wife*). It's funnier that way; he has further to fall, and his hollers of horror, like bison upended, are the hilarious stuff of pure anguish. The punishments he visits on Stan, however, are things of beauty in themselves, the more so because we know how impervious is Stan's skull. In *Perfect Day*, Ollie assaults him with the loosened clutch, bringing a wonderful 'clang' as it bounces off his head. Elsewhere, there's a certain elan in *Busy Bodies* about the way he picks up a saw, tests its elasticity by folding it back with a musical spoing, then snaps it atop Stan's cranium.

With each new film, the boys appear to have undergone a complete memory wipe of their previous calamities – those same characters appear in completely new universes, whether as tramps, labourers or respectable middle-class men, though regardless of their circumstances, their appearance hardly differs. Whatever they are, however strenuously they are trying to get somewhere, they are destined to tumble all the way to the bottom, like the piano in *The Music Box*.

So, in *Our Wife* (1931), Ollie is a well-heeled bachelor who is to be married to his sweetheart Dulcie, a soulmate of matching circumference. Stan is best man. At Ollie's apartment, he makes a series of errors, beginning with the smashing of a needlessly large pile of plates he's brought into the dining room. Ollie reproaches him irritably – 'I don't know how anyone could be so clumsy' – before himself colliding nose first with a wall as he attempts to re-enter his bedroom.

Stan continues to fail to repay the confidence Ollie mysteriously places in him, ruining the cake with fly spray, which Ollie then mistakes for throat spray and nearly burns his tongue off. With James Finlayson as Dulcie's father disapproving of the marriage, the pair are forced to elope. It's when they reach the house of the local Justice of the Peace that Stan's lack of grasp of the basic situations of existence reaches levels that would be considered Beckettian if they weren't also funny. The exchange, as the truculent wife of the Justice answers the door to Stan, is worth quoting extensively:

JP's WIFE: What do you want?
STAN: What do we want?
OLLIE: We want to get married!
LAUREL: Oh, yeah. We want to get married.
OLLIE: Not we. Us!
STAN: Not we. Us.
JP's WIFE: Well, how about it?
STAN (to OLLIE): How about it?
OLLIE: How about what?
STAN (to JP's WIFE): How about what?
JP's WIFE: What are you talking about?
STAN (to OLLIE): What are you talking about?
OLLIE: Tell her we want to get married!
STAN: We want to get married.
OLLIE (as STAN returns to the car, nursing a bloody nose after
    one question too many): Well, how about it?
STAN: How about what?
OLLIE: What did she say?
STAN: Who?

The whole thing feels like some twentieth-century philosophical exercise, an interrogation of the fundamental nature of all things and the limits of language. Except it's Stan being Stan, a man who, as one of the opening titles has it, has 'no thoughts of any kind'.

Actually, Stan is capable of coherent thought and will occasionally come up with an aphorism of sorts – 'You can lead a horse to water but a pencil must be lead' – or even a clever idea, as in *Towed in a Hole*, in which the boys have set up a nice little business selling fish. He suggests that they buy a boat so they can catch the fish themselves. Unfortunately, when Ollie asks him to explain the scheme again, we realise Stan is incapable of properly reassembling an idea once it has left his mouth. 'Well, if you caught a fish, then whoever you sold it to wouldn't have to pay for it. And the profits would go to the fish . . . if . . . er . . .'

No thoughts, with Stan, means no thought for other people, too. His ignorance may be divine, but he is no saint. In *County Hospital* (1932), he brings a convalescing Ollie hard-boiled eggs and nuts – his own favourite snack, you suspect – rather than the chocolates Ollie would have preferred, because 'You didn't pay me for the last ones I brought you.' Yes, he puts himself at Ollie's beck and call, without question, out of lowliness. And in his moments of whimpering distress it's Ollie he turns to, like a child with nightmares crawling into bed with their parents. But like a child, he's also capable of utter indifference to his fellow man, that man being Ollie.

In *The Music Box* (1932), we also see how unfiltered his social behaviour is, when he kicks a young nanny up the behind after she guffaws at his and Ollie's predicament with the piano; 'right in the middle of my daily duties', as she complains to a policeman. No conventions or social delicacies bind him. Stan is by no means completely passive, and holds in reserve a tempestuous rage. In *One Good Turn* (1931), when Ollie mistakenly accuses Stan of robbing the old lady who provided them with a meal, only to realise his 'faux pas',

Stan's ears flap with fury and he exacts a physical revenge on Ollie he wouldn't normally undertake.

Stan also possesses supernatural qualities, or 'white magic'; it's as if he is able to suspend the laws of nature, being wholly ignorant of them. He demonstrates in *Way Out West* (1937) an unassuming ability to convert his thumb into a cigarette lighter, and when Ollie forces Stan to eat his hat after he made a rash promise to do so, he is able to convince himself that it is as tasty as roast beef. Of course, the normal laws resume when a curious Ollie tries to eat the hat and finds it tastes exactly like a hat.

In 1940's *A Chump at Oxford*, the boys find themselves sent to the great English university, where, following a bump on the head, it transpires that Stan is actually Lord Paddington, the greatest scholar and sportsman in Oxford's history, who suffered a similar bump on the head years earlier and wandered from the university.

Lord Paddington resumes his Oxford career, even taking a call from Einstein to give him some tips regarding his theory of relativity, as well as smashing various track and field athletics records. However, a further bump on the head sees him to revert to being Stan. It's a lovely, theoretical explanation of the enigma of his origins and sublime lack of sense: a man of huge, latent capabilities who simply suffers a loose screw that causes total wipeout. It would have been a great point on which Laurel and Hardy could conclude.

What followed *A Chump at Oxford* was not good – their wartime adventures and, later on, the unwatchable *Atoll K* (1951), with Stan looking dreadfully unwell. Already in the late 1930s they looked conspicuously out of their element as their films suffered the dubious benefit of enhanced Hollywood values – bigger, brassier soundtracks, slicker cinematography. In their own shorts, cocooned in those recurring soundtrack tunes, among a small ensemble of familiar actors, in that decayed footage, with that bed of crackle, they're in the grainy, monochrome, impressionistic suspension in which they belong. Even the way the light falls on Stan's ultra-pallid face perfectly conveys how utterly drained he is of capability, of understanding: it is an angelic glow of gormlessness.

By 1940, Chaplin and Laurel and Hardy were equals in terms of public recognition and international fame. For all their dissimilarities, they did have one great thing in common, absolutely central to their identities: their attachment to their bowler hats. Ollie even wears his in the shower. ('I didn't want to get my hair wet,' he explains bashfully, in a moment that shows that deep down, he is not that far removed from Stan.) Chaplin, Hardy, Laurel all hold fast to their hats in the midst of their predicaments and vicissitudes, as if to their dignity, their esquire status.

But whereas Chaplin's Tramp draws our admiration as one plucky guy coming up trumps against the world, there is something more moving and exemplary about Stan and Ollie's friendship – an enduring example of the brotherhood of man, unbreakable despite all, and for which they were loved by millions in return. There's a constancy about their pairing for which Chaplin has no equivalent – he passes from Edna Purviance to the Kid to Paulette Goddard, but essentially he's a loner.

Chaplin sometimes found mass adulation difficult. He was a celebrity before such things were understood, internationally famous before he even realised it. But once famous, and despite his sympathy for the downtrodden, one of whom he had once been himself, he took permanent refuge among the great and good. There's the story of his emotional return to his old school at Hanwell; moved, he promised to come back and make them a gift of a motion-picture projector. Out of shyness, however, and a horror of the crowds he might expect, he failed to keep the appointment, lunching with, of all people, the Conservative MP, anti-Semite, anti-Catholic and, for a while, Nazi sympathiser Lady Astor instead.

He also eventually disappointed those Russian avant-gardists who saw him as a 'mechanised exemplar', the supreme proponent of the new 'machine art' of the twentieth century. *Modern Times* (1936) begins with a wonderful Eisensteinian moment, a visual metaphor of a black sheep amid a white flock pouring forth; Chaplin's Tramp is that sheep, a human being working on an assembly line, frantically keeping pace with the conveyor belt as he screws pair of nuts after pair of nuts. A chat with his pal Gandhi had disabused Chaplin of his enthusiasm for the machine age. *Modern Times* is an indictment of the cruelty of industrialisation and the drive for profit. The boss figure, surveilling and broadcasting diktats remotely via a screen, is like a precursor to Big Brother, while the indignities suffered by workers like the Tramp prefigure the present-day conditions endured by employees of today's corporations such as Amazon. *Modern Times*, sadly, retains its relevance.

However, the film emphasises that the Tramp is no political revolutionary. This is highlighted in a scene in which a red flag falls from the back of a truck, and as he chases the vehicle, brandishing the flag trying to attract the attention of the driver, he finds himself heading a mass demonstration. Freud once said that in his films, Chaplin was perpetually re-enacting the privations of his childhood, and here is an example; the factory is a more modernistic workhouse. Following a nervous breakdown in which he runs riot, the Tramp finds escape in the world of cabaret entertainment, as a singing waiter ironically discovering his 'voice' (singing a nonsense song made up of French- and Italian-sounding gibberish) and heading out on the road, as he so often does in his films, hand in hand with his saviour, played by real-life wife Paulette Goddard. This is how he finds salvation: not by insurrection, or seizing the means of production, or joining any brotherhood of man, but by individual escape.

By 1940 and *The Great Dictator*, Chaplin had, however reluctantly, embraced talking pictures. He insisted that the barber was not the Tramp, but there is some overlap; in a show of his dominance as the first great icon of the twentieth century, Chaplin is able, without conceit, to describe Hitler in his autobiography as no other human could: as a 'bad impersonation of me'. The final scene, in which the moustached barber delivers a speech, anti-Nazi to its very last syllable, could be seen as the moment in which Chaplin himself and his Tramp, his long series of adventures at an end, merge in a moment of didactic triumph, the first man of the twentieth century merging with his creator in absolute opposition to its worst:

> Don't give yourselves to these unnatural men – machine men with machine minds and machine hearts! You are not machines! You are not cattle! You are men! You have the love of humanity in your hearts! You don't hate! Only the unloved hate – the unloved and the unnatural! Soldiers! Don't fight for slavery! Fight for liberty!

It was with such vigour that Chaplin had campaigned for a second front to assist America's allies the Soviets; for these sins he was branded a 'communist' in the McCarthy era – an absurd accusation completely out of kilter with his capitalist inclinations as a businessman. He left America, only returning to collect an honorary award at the 1972 Oscars. He received a twelve-minute standing ovation.

Chaplin was a virtuoso, a hugely capable polymath who added to comedy a physical, acrobatic dimension for the film age, for one, whose work is rich with pathos and whose appeal to the burgeoning international masses of the twentieth century is beyond calculation. His rise from abject poverty to Hollywood superstardom was a colossal effort of individual will and ingenuity, an ascension reflected in the heroic struggles of the Tramp against all obstacles. He achieved a status, a prestige no other comedian will ever match, transcending comedy, reaching into other realms, such as art and politics. He was . . . Chaplin.

Stan Laurel was, however, funnier. Perhaps that is to do with his, and for that matter Oliver Hardy's, humility and lack of pretension, their artfully clumsy grace, their fundamental sweetness. We find them easier to love, easier to empathise with, as they stare into the camera at us with the intimacy of eternal contemporaries, in exasperation and confusion at their inability to advance more than a step in the world without taking a backward, crashing tumble. We relate, comedically, better to their failures than to Chaplin's and the Tramp's 'successes'. As Charles Schulz, creator of the *Peanuts* cartoon series, once said, 'Winning is nice but it isn't funny.'

Both Laurel and Chaplin, however, even if they are in danger of disappearing from our screens and, therefore, the consciousness of generations to come, were undoubtedly responsible for taking the music hall stuff of nineteenth-century English comedy and using it to lay the foundations for the screen comedy of the twentieth.

FROM EALING TO EAST CHEAM
COMEDY 1945-61

The UK emerged from World War II ready to play, but also grappling with such issues as austerity, the loss of empire and reduced global status, and a newfound scepticism towards figures of authority, born out of bitter wartime experience. All this would be reflected in the best of British comedy.

There was a rise in radio situation comedy, including the homely *Meet the Huggetts* (1953–61), in which Jack Warner reprised his role as patriarch Joe, based on a series of films featuring the family made in the late forties and fifties. There was also *Take It from Here* (1948–60), the creation of the brilliant Frank Muir and Denis Norden, featuring Jimmy Edwards and June Whitfield, whose dysfunctional family, the Glums, mocked the tendency towards 'nice' families on UK radio, such as the Huggetts. And there was *Educating Archie* (1950–60), which featured, as grandparents would have a hard time explaining to their grandchildren, a ventriloquist act. On the radio. It was here, however, that Britain's first great sitcom actor, Tony Hancock, made his debut.

On the film front was Norman Wisdom, whose movies were still being broadcast regularly in the 1970s. As evidenced in *Ask a Policeman* (1939), he was literally unable to follow his father's footsteps; his lack of inches prevents him from joining the constabulary like his dad, though Norman being Norman, that doesn't stop him from having a go. 'Norman' was gauche but deceptively acrobatic, well-meaning but incompetent, the bane of irascible employers such as Mr Grimsdale, a less effete precursor of Frank Spencer (he turned down the role of Spencer in *Some Mothers Do 'Ave 'Em*, finding it unfunny), more pitiful and sentimental than George Formby; his appeal was laced with mawkish musical interludes, such as the song 'Don't Laugh at Me ('Cause I'm a Fool)'. Wisdom inspired more fondness than admiration but enjoyed widespread domestic and international success in unlikely, repressive corners of the globe such as Iran under the shah and Albania. The reason is that his films, his persona, were considered innocuous, free of any adult, subversive content or subtext despite being made in the decadent West.

However, the greatest comedy film legacy of the post-war era was born out of Ealing Studios.

THE EALING COMEDIES

Chaplin and Laurel were expats, drawing on their English experience to launch themselves in America, with a style of comedy that was international, universal in appeal. But neither spoke much about their native country.

The comedy output of Ealing Studios, however, spoke very much to England, to Britain. Theirs was in many ways a patriotic mission to depict British experiences and British character affectionately, with all its virtues, as well as its numerous foibles. If other British film comedy of this era was given to the carefree play of out-and-out daftness, from the caperings of Will Hay, Frank Randall and the Crazy Gang to the haplessly loveable Norman Wisdom and George Formby, there was a certain composure about Ealing comedies, an underlying seriousness of purpose, albeit one expressed through arch irony rather than ham-fisted didacticism. They did not really do earthy, regional authenticity very well, still less the accents. They did not do slapstick as such. They were disdainful of picture-post-card bawdiness. They treasured language, crisp, breezy and well spoken. In many ways, they are closer in spirit and feel to the films of Powell and Pressburger (*A Matter of Life and Death, The Life and Death of Colonel Blimp*) than they are to other British film comedy of the time.

Ealing films sought to depict the times as the British pieced themselves back together following the war and were shadowed by sombre
reality – of post-war austerity, the impending nuclear age, relationships between workers and management – as well as the joy at last of
play and plenty once more. There is a sense that they were seeking to
piece back together a sense of national identity and character which,
if it had not been shattered by wartime and a new, reforming Labour
government, was in its final years. Ealing's Britain is not today's
Britain. And yet, their films are among the stately homes of British
comedy, still standing, masterpieces of (generally) black and white,
with shades of grey cloud and silver linings galore.

I was born in Edgware General Hospital, and, for a few weeks,
raised in West London, before my dad's work meant that we moved up
to West Yorkshire, to a village near Leeds. I pined for London, images
of which recurred teasingly on TV, especially in old British films, in
chipper, silvery footage of central London and the well-connected
outlying suburbs. As for Leeds in the 1970s, I found it a miserable,
surly, toxic, haggard, ugly place. I hated the perpetual undercurrent
of male violence, whether it be the football team or that inflicted by
the odd sadistic schoolteacher or bullying schoolkids. There seemed
to be a sour, male, Yorkshire pride in gruff, anti-'puff' conformity,
in the language of scuffling, of knacking and braying and thinking
of nothing beyond the miserable, heads-down, hands-in-pocket here
and now, in which Doc Martened breaktimes were spent standing
in a circle, spitting into a communal patch of mucus and making
claims of sexual conquests that were dubious coming from a group of
thirteen-year-old boys. I kept my virginity a secret shame.

I took my pleasures where I could, in football, sweets, TV and
bikes, like any seventies kid, but there were times when Yorkshire
felt like a prison sentence. I was an exile. And so the most profound
solace I took was in any sort of depiction of London life, especially
the black and white variety; bright capers from the 1950s were a
particular preference. My dad occasionally spoke of the 'Ealing

comedies', which spoke to my depths: Ealing in West London, scene of the childhood I was robbed of.

Whenever such films were on, I lapped them up like bank holidays, while feeling pangs of that most profound sense of nostalgia: the nostalgia for things you have never experienced. I personally basked in their London-ness in particular, their gleaming, tootling, bracing, prelapsarian energy, the freedom of characters to be openly well-spoken without getting head-butted, as well as the lawksamercy accents of characters who, as privileged as those who lived by the seaside, got to live in London every day of their lives, Big Ben only a bus ride away. Furthermore, I was conscious enough of history to realise that these were characters still brimful of exuberance at having beaten the Germans in a straight, fair fight – no pile-ons in the corridors or dark, snide, cowardly bullying tactics, but in exchanges carried out in the blue skies above the Garden of England by Kenneth More as Douglas Bader.

Later, I understood that far from depicting some metropolitan idyll, these films were set in a London that was still being rebuilt. *Hue and Cry* (1947), for example, a caper about schoolkids inspired to rise up against a gang led by a cast-against-type Jack Warner, took place amid rubble. I also developed a scepticism about the films' cherished, quintessential Englishness, a very white Englishness, and worried that the source of the nostalgia for them, when repeated of a Sunday afternoon, was a pining for a post-war but pre-*Windrush* era. Yes, Paul Robeson had starred in *The Proud Valley* (1940), but how truly was Ealing a reflection of the actual make-up of the country? Who and what might it be excluding?

For British cinema audiences in the 1940s and 1950s, however, these films offered not nostalgia but the here and now. And for them, the appeal of Ealing comedy was a reaction against the sort of earnest fare the Ealing Studios themselves had produced in wartime.

The head of Ealing Studios, Michael Balcon, was a man who regarded Britishness as a core Ealing value. He disdained the British

expats who had fled to Hollywood. Wartime cinema had had its bit
to do – boost morale and portray to British audiences models of
their best possible selves in adversity. Hence *Convoy* (1940) and *Went
the Day Well?* (1942), gripping films exemplifying the selflessness
required in times of national emergency. Or there was *The Proud
Valley*. Its underlying message concerns the hardships of life in a Welsh
mining community, as well as its solidarity, with Robeson making
the ultimate sacrifice for the sake of his trapped comrades. Much of
the studio's wartime output was sinew-stiffening, and the austerity
continued for some years following VE Day. It became habitual, this
gross decency. Upper lips were set permanently to stiff. There was a
disposition to worthiness, to bleakness, such as a drama about the
lives of Bethnal Green folk, Robert Hamer's *It Always Rains on a
Sunday* (1947), whose subjects complained that the film had made
their lives look worse than they actually were.

Ealing comedies weren't just a respite from post-war hardship
but from the gruel of propaganda about the stoical, courageous,
decent British character on which cinemagoers had subsisted.
Ealing comedies were a charabanc holiday from the pull-together
high-mindedness with which audiences were feeling browbeaten by
the late 1940s, a 'freedom from rationing and petty restrictions', as
Ealing stalwart T. E. B. Clarke put it. They were about the joy of
lapsing into the illicit, the foreign, criminality even, and the thrill of
maybe, just maybe getting away with it, like the Outer Hebridean
community in 1949's *Whisky Galore*, seizing on a cargo of their
favourite spirit that had run aground in heavy fog.

Passport to Pimlico, released in 1949 but set in 1947 and directed
by Henry Cornelius, was another example. It tells the story of a
detonated bomb leading to the discovery of a charter drawn up
by Edward IV, which reveals that Pimlico is technically still a part
of Burgundy, and therefore exempt from restrictions imposed on
the UK, such as licensing hours and rationing. The locals take up
independence with gusto, with the latter-day Duke of Burgundy

even visiting the territory. Complications ensue, however, including water shortages and black marketeers, leading to headaches for grocer and prime minister Arthur Pemberton (Stanley Holloway) and his governing council.

Passport to Pimlico has echoes of Henry V, who wages war against France based on an ancient legal claim to the throne. Only here it is somehow deemed very British for the citizens of Pimlico to declare themselves independent of Britain. Betty Warren as Conny Pemberton puts it succinctly: 'It's just because we are English that we're sticking up for our rights to be Burgundians!'

The film is set in the heatwave that prevailed in London in 1947. The stifling heat makes for a lovely oppression, exuded like steam from the screen. In a heatwave England is temporarily not quite England, a midsummer night's dream; moreover, it brings to a head simmering romance. Frank Huggins (John Slater) longs for Pemberton's daughter (Barbara Murray), who herself has fallen for the Duke of Burgundy. Even the mode of living feels continental: communal food and wine. A very English desire to be un-English underscores the film.

A caped Margaret Rutherford, playing Professor Hatton-Jones, the academic who verifies the authenticity of the charter, raises a few laughs, playing Margaret Rutherford to the hilt (much as the 'character actor' Miles Malleson could always be relied on to play a single character, the rotund, genial, chinless, bumblingly oblivious fellow forever humming and hawing and drumming his lapels with his fingers, Miles Malleson). And yet, bracing as it is, *Passport to Pimlico* isn't a gag fest. It's a cheery joyride, an adventure in irony, of being careful about what you wish for. Much of its energy derives from the symphonic exuberance of not an English composer but a Frenchman, Georges Auric, one of Les Six, assembled as would-be acolytes by Erik Satie after World War I. An associate of such doyens of the avant-garde as Jean Cocteau, he was also a member of various leftist groups, if not an outright communist, whose first film score

had been for René Clair's 1931 film *À nous la liberté*. He wrote the
scores not only for *Passport to Pimlico* but also *The Lavender Hill Mob*
(1951). In both cases, his orchestrations are rich, vivacious, blossoming, outpouring; the sense, temporary perhaps but overwhelming,
is of liberation. He soundtracks not the action but the underlying
current of the movies, their spirit, their appeal.

The Lavender Hill Mob starred Alec Guinness as Henry Holland, a
bank clerk who plots to steal the gold bullion he oversees and smuggle
it abroad. He finally sees his chance when he meets fellow lodger and
foundry owner Alfred Pendlebury (Stanley Holloway), and together
they hatch a scheme involving Eiffel Tower souvenirs.

Although they work with career criminals played by Sid James and
Alfie Bass, we can never shrug off the feeling that somehow Holland
and Pendlebury are not cut from the same common criminal cloth as
this pair of ne'er-do-wells – that they are people like us, respectable
and decent, understandably tempted by a strictly one-off caper like
the bullion job. There may not be honour among thieves, but there is
certainly a very British sense of class. And no one gets hurt, that's the
beauty of it. Although justice is ultimately obliged to be done, you'd
have to be very dedicated to the rule of law indeed to root for John
Gregson's police officer. We see Guinness coming to the end of a year
living the high life in South America on the £25,000 he has managed
to retrieve from the botched robbery; it's faintly Graham Greene-ish,
our man in Rio de Janeiro. British we may be, in Britain we may
belong and British remain in demeanour wherever we may wander,
but as with the wistful, romantic Francophilia of *Passport to Pimlico*,
paradise lies in foreign climes. In ration-hit post-war Britain, travel
abroad was as remote a dream for the vast majority as travel to the
moon. British we were, not least because we were generally confined
to these isles, our place, our station.

Alec Guinness was adept at playing, as he did later with George
Smiley in *Tinker, Tailor, Soldier, Spy* (1979), an Englishman whose
diffident blandness belies a secret knowledge shared only with very

close confidants and us, the audience. His default expression is a
discreet half-smile. Only a dim glow in his eyes betrays the cunning
intent, the illicit desires he harbours within. He embodies the very
proper and respectful way we of these isles go about our criminal
business, as if that very respectability in some ways exonerates us.

Guinness starred again in *The Man in the White Suit* (1951), as
Sidney Stratton, a chemist working at a textile mill who is convinced he
is on the point of inventing an everlasting, dirt-resistant fibre that will
preclude the need for both washing and buying new clothes. Stratton
is an idealist – the white suit he devises is also representative of his
unspotted, otherworldly soul. However, he is oblivious to what both
workers and management realise quickly enough – that his invention
will be the ruin of the mill, and all mills, to the disadvantage of both
capital and labour. Only Daphne (Joan Greenwood), daughter of
Cecil Parker's millionaire mill owner, is sympathetic to the idea of the
new cloth, delivering a rhapsodic speech in those distinctive straw-
berry tones of hers about the liberation housewives will enjoy from
drudgery. Certainly, to us, the audience, it's a fleetingly tempting
thought, an imaginary, prospective break from the oppressive norm.
However, order must be restored, the 'equilibrium' between workers
and management and their common interests preserved, the post-
war consensus, for all its onerous, dutiful drabness, maintained, the
hare-brained ideals of a Stratton kept in check.

Again, a few amusing explosions apart, *The Man in the White
Suit* is less a 'comedy' than a satire, a sombre one, on the definite
and real threat posed by science for science's sake in the dawning
nuclear age – there is a disquieting radioactive glow about Guinness's
suit. Better the hell you know. There are shades of the dark and the
satanic about the mill setting, against which Guinness in his suit
exudes such threatening purity, and certainly in the saturnine, Mr
Burns-type countenance of the oldest and nastiest of the mill owners
seeking to suppress Stratton's work. The cinematography affords a
grim treat, a nostalgia for the monochrome, skewed geometry of

yesteryear's backstreets and indoor stairwells.

The drama of *The Man in the White Suit* was further enhanced by the services of a prestigious composer, but as with Auric, it was one who went against the grain of Ealing's supposed all-English spirit. Benjamin Frankel was a gifted, idiosyncratic composer of Polish Jewish parentage who, at the time this film was released, was still a member of the Communist Party of Great Britain.

The Ladykillers (1955) is considered by many to be the apotheosis of Ealing comedy, its finest, ripest flowering of a morbid wit and very British criminality, but it would also turn out to be its swansong. As with *Whisky Galore* and *Passport to Pimlico*, Michael Balcon had hoped to enlist Alastair Sim for the lead role of Professor Marcus, but once again he was disappointed. Alec Guinness, however, more than compensated with a set of false teeth and a performance that was very much a pastiche of Sim, while drawing deep from the dark wells of his own versatility.

The Ladykillers benefits from the richness of Technicolor, from the lopsided, cubistic charm of the isolated house occupied by widow Mrs Wilberforce and her avian charges to the sulphurous surroundings of King's Cross railway station, the engines snorting steam with all the menacing significance of the locomotives in Zola's *La Bête humaine*. Her house, denoted by the dreamy jingle of a music box, is a last outpost of Victorian gentility on the cliff edge, below which lies the roiling, stormy reality of the industrial age.

There are strong similarities between *The Ladykillers* and *The Lavender Hill Mob*. Both star Alec Guinness as an unlikely criminal mastermind; both involve elaborate and successful robberies which come unstuck due to the tiniest of hitches, rather than the long arm of the law. In this case, Professor Marcus, a man whose meticulous, erudite and oleaginous manner belies a hidden, maniacal streak, has plotted a security van robbery near King's Cross. He has assembled a group of criminals who take lodgings with Mrs Wilberforce, affecting to be a string quintet. The ingenuity of the scheme is to have Mrs

Wilberforce take delivery of the trunk of swag on Marcus's behalf, which she innocently does; she even enlists the assistance of two police officers to carry it into the house for her.

Comparisons break down, however, in the composition of *The Ladykillers'* gang. With the exception of Cecil Parker, cast against type as a well-spoken fellow who somehow stumbled into a life of crime, these are scary guys. Herbert Lom plays Louis, a continental gangster; One-Round is an ex-boxer, merciless with his fists, while Peter Sellers plays an unscrupulous spiv. These are creatures of a far more sinister stripe than Sid James's and Alfie Bass's reassuringly common or garden ruffians in *The Lavender Hill Mob*, creatures of an impending Technicolor age of Teddy Boys, looser morals, ruthless pursuit of wealth, sleaze, decay; the genteel fabric of Old England hangs by a single thread.

The Lavender Hill mob, however, did not have to reckon with Mrs Wilberforce, played to dainty but determined perfection by Katie Johnson. We get a hint that there is more to her than meets the eye when she activates her kitchen pipes with a rubber mallet, showing more strength than might be expected. She has learned to cope with her loneliness, which is offset by frequent trips to the police station to report, for example, a suspected UFO incident. Dotty and delicate she may be, but she is nevertheless not to be denied.

In his study of Ealing Studios, Charles Barr fancifully suggests that *The Ladykillers* might be a metaphor for the incoming Labour government of 1945, come in to take over the 'house', adopting a respectable air while embarking on a radical scheme of wealth redistribution, who are laid low by their internecine squabbling and debilitating respect for the ancient establishment in all its abiding serenity, represented by Mrs Wilberforce. However, the gang's intention is to redistribute the loot solely among themselves, not society. Moreover, Balcon described himself and his Ealing colleagues as the sort of people 'who voted Labour for the first time' after the war. Still, there's enough about the theory to account for the tiniest sense of exasperation one experiences at the china-delicate Mrs Wilberforce's survival: the old linger, the new cannot be born. Ironic also that the snorting, belching forces of the steam age which seem to threaten Mrs Wilberforce's house from below would in just a few years themselves be supplanted by the diesel engine.

Despite the triumph of *The Ladykillers*, Ealing wound down thereafter. The Britain, chirpy and doughty, albeit devil-may-care and even devilish, depicted in Ealing was changing. Peter Sellers's Teddy Boy suit in *The Ladykillers* was a hint of what was on the horizon: pop-cultural, demographic, ethnic transformations that would render the world depicted by Ealing anachronistic. Rock and roll. Modern conveniences. And TV. Balcon sold Ealing Studios to the BBC for £350,000 in 1955. It all felt shabby to long-standing Ealing employees. Furthermore, there were rumours of Ealing-type skulduggery: that the son of Balcon's second-in-command Reginald Baker was a Tory MP but also an embezzler, compelling his father to take all his money out of Ealing Studios to pay off his debts. One can imagine Baker being played by Cecil Parker, his son by a young Peter Sellers.

It would be remiss to leave Ealing without recalling its finest comedy, a masterpiece of wit and jet-black irony. *Kind Hearts and Coronets* (1949) was directed by Robert Hamer. Its theme is in keeping with the Ealing tradition, but in other respects it falls outside the studio's output. It is a period drama with little bearing on the immediate social condition of post-war Britain, set as it is in Edwardian England, though its theme of class distinction is universal. It endures, however, not least because of its timeless, finely ground wit, but also because in so many respects, despite the affected propriety and straitlacedness, it is exquisitely cynical, impeccably queer, bristling with Wildean paradox and expedient deceptions.

The title is from a Tennyson poem about the importance of decency rather than rank or social status, a sentiment misapplied by Valerie Hobson's Edith D'Ascoyne to Louis D'Ascoyne (Dennis Price), taken in by what he himself describes as 'my impersonation of a fellow of sterling character', For all his charm, grace and eloquence, Louis's heart has been reduced to a homicidal cinder by the injustice done to his mother by the haughty D'Ascoyne family. This made him all the more appealing to audiences yearning for a change of moral pace from the heroic likes of Jack Hawkins.

The film begins in Louis's prison cell. He is due to meet the hangman in the morning and is spending his last hours composing his memoirs. We learn that he is half Italian; his father was an opera singer, with whom his mother fell in love and then married, leading her to become estranged from the D'Ascoyne family. All of Louis's Englishness is on the surface, his cultivation, his manners, while his Italian side informs his passions, both romantic and for a revenge which, as he observes, the Italians say that people of taste prefer to eat cold.

Following his mother's death, Louis resolves to take revenge on the D'Ascoyne family, all played by Alec Guinness, and seize the dukedom. One by one, and with unflappable efficiency, he dispatches them, including the arrogant young Ascoyne D'Ascoyne, the imbecilic Reverend Lord Henry D'Ascoyne (by poisoning his port while posing as the visiting Bishop of Matabeland), the suffragette Lady Agatha D'Ascoyne ('I shot an arrow in the air; she fell to earth in Berkeley Square') and the affable amateur photographer Henry D'Ascoyne (by contriving a fatal explosion in the dark room to which he is wont to retreat for the alcoholic refreshment forbidden him by wife Edith).

This series of tragedies does not appear to trouble the police, who, as so often in Ealing comedies, appear oblivious to criminal goings-on. Except that, at a ceremony marking his attaining his title, he is visited by an inspector from Scotland Yard. He is charged with murder.

For all his cool, Louis's romantic appetites undo him. Despite regarding her as a 'prig', Louis has courted Henry D'Ascoyne's widow. When with her he maintains his impersonation of a fellow of sterling character. However, his baser yearning is for his childhood friend Sibella (Joan Greenwood). They meet, discreetly. With her he is unmasked in his manner, regarding her with a mixture of casual lust, physical adoration, vengeful spite for having rejected him and easy contempt: he sees her as a bit on the side but, with her sub-urban ways, beneath his station – for despite his contempt for the D'Ascoynes' high-handedness, Louis, like his late mother, is quite the snob himself.

Kind Hearts and Coronets wilfully lacks the gusto of other Ealing comedies. It is not heavily soundtracked, for one thing, save the odd operatic flourish or motif. Its special effects are poor. This scarcely matters. As Hamer intended, this is a film in which the English language plays a starring role, its speciality of understatement featuring strongly. The use of Louis as narrator throughout means that the cinematography doesn't have to do much heavy lifting. *Kind Hearts and Coronets* is perfectly funny, with barely a single ill-judged or extra-neous moment. Its narrative and dialogue are like an unending series of delicious, exquisite savouries, which can be relished time and again: 'It is so difficult to make a neat job of killing people with whom one is not on friendly terms'; or the Reverend D'Ascoyne conducting a trip of his church with Louis's 'bishop': 'And I always say that my west window has all the exuberance of early Chaucer without, happily, any of the concomitant crudities of his period.'

Joan Greenwood as Sibella epitomises the acid, cold sensuality of *Kind Hearts and Coronets* bustling beneath its prim and formal surface. She played 'modern women' capably in Ealing comedies – *The Man in the White Suit* and *Whisky Galore* – but in such roles was only allowed to play up to the conventions imposed on young leading women as written by Ealing. However, it's in period pieces, corseted and extravagantly behatted, that her sultry, camp charm is put to best effect, her every utterance a roseate moue of calculated, voluptuous restraint. Although she later starred alongside Dawn French and Jennifer Saunders in their sitcom *Girls on Top*, she is not ahead of her time, waiting for the permissive era to happen so that she can really let rip. Prim and pouting, she is of her era, a strikingly coy representation of buttoned-up, simmering sexuality. She stars in Anthony Asquith's film version of *The Importance of Being Earnest* as Gwendolen, daughter of Edith Evans's redoubtable Lady Bracknell. Greenwood is the perfect Gwendolen, quite just-so, especially when insisting on a formal marriage proposal from Michael Redgrave's Mr Worthing, while conveying in advance that she intends to accept. As Sibella, meanwhile, she is comically ravishing in the way she swills and elongates every word, including 'Louis', extracting every last droplet from its vowels, and adding some of her own.

In terms of its Wildean spirit, as well as its period setting, *Kind Hearts and Coronets* is quite the throwback to Victorian and Edwardian mores. At the time of its release, Spike Milligan was assembling the troupe from which he would make up the Goons, meeting at Grafton's, a London pub, every Sunday night. A new modernity was in the offing. And yet, for today's audiences, *Kind Hearts* is probably easier to relate to, has held up better than the earliest *Goon Show* offerings, revolutionary as they were. *Kind Hearts* has retained its discreet subversiveness, its ruthless sexuality ('You're a lucky man, Lionel. Take my word for it,' Louis tells the groom on the occasion of his and Sibella's wedding day), as well as an utterly deadpan air of high camp that is more down to Joan Greenwood's extravagant headwear than Alec Guinness's cross-dressing. Sex lurks in every Ealing comedy to a greater or lesser degree, unmentioned, unperformed, smouldering discreetly beneath corsets, girdles and layers of thick, grey clothing, but undoubtedly there.

Robert Hamer left Ealing after Balcon vetoed a project set in the West Indies and featuring a stronger sexual undercurrent than that which courses beneath the faultlessly proper Edwardian surfaces of *Kind Hearts and Coronets*. In 1960, however, he was reunited with Dennis Price in *School for Scoundrels*, based on the 'gamesmanship' books by Stephen Potter. Starring Alastair Sim and Ian Carmichael, the film is one of the final flowerings of a pre-erotic fifties British comic sensibility, bristling with romantic longing, preceding what Philip Larkin hailed as the birth of sexual intercourse in 1963. April Smith (Janette Scott) is an English rose, not an object of erotic desire, which is what makes Delauney's (Terry-Thomas) attentions towards her so caddish. His every 'hello' and 'I say' was smothered with lecherousness, his every 'hard cheese' dripping with snickering, brazen insincerity.

Terry-Thomas brought some of the eyebrow-twitching mischief of his films to real life. In *Bounder!*, his biography of the actor, Graham McCann recounts that when in the South of France once, Terry-Thomas found himself chatting to Pablo Picasso. 'I say,' he said to the artist, 'has anyone ever asked you, "Can I have a word in your eye?"' Picasso was unamused.

BEYOND EALING

Concurrent with and subsequent to Ealing, there were films that felt like they might have emanated from the studio. *Genevieve* (1953) had originally been pitched to Michael Balcon by director Henry Cornelius, but with his schedule full, he passed on it and advised Cornelius to take it to Rank Productions. In the finished film, John Gregson and Kenneth More, as two veteran car owners, both enter the London-to-Brighton car rally, where their friendship turns to rivalry, to the exasperation of their girlfriends Dinah Sheridan and Kay Kendall. Distinguished by its cheerful Larry Adler harmonica soundtrack, *Genevieve* is a capsule of a Britain that still lingers in its rural byways and country pubs and excessive preoccupation with motor vehicles. It is very British and, therefore, all the more surprising that it was scripted by an American screenwriter, William Rose.

Frank Launder and Sidney Gilliat inaugurated the *St Trinian's* series with *The Belles of St Trinian's* (1954). This was based on cartoonist Ronald Searle's wonderful, scratchy caricatures of the anarchic but resourceful schoolgirls of an educational establishment whose

appallingly lackadaisical standards were shared by senior staff as well
as the pupils. Ealing could never have sanctioned such a comedy; it
would have regarded as too permissive the depiction of the older 'girls'
as stockinged seductresses. Yet there's a strange innocence about the
sexual implications of having a character like George Cole's spiv Flash
Harry sneaking about the grounds of a girls' private school. Such implications would scarcely have occurred to 1950s audiences. *St Trinian's*
may be 'sexual' in a way Ealing wasn't, but it's an unreconstructed,
quaintly pre-feminist sense of sexuality, and as such has dated worse
than the heaving restraint of *Kind Hearts and Coronets*.

The girls themselves provide a backdrop of raucous energy. They
are a monstrous regiment, a fractious blur of hockey sticks, burst
pillows in dorm fights and fearful screeching. Comedy honours
are shared between Joyce Grenfell as an undercover police officer
posing as a games mistress and Alastair Sim. He upstages himself as
a dodgy bookie playing his twin sister, Miss Fritton. In drag, Sim
does not make the mistake of projecting an exaggerated femininity,
a falsetto warble or mincing gait. He alters the register of his voice
only slightly and plays the character rather than the gender, a character of thoroughly respectable unscrupulousness.

Funnier, however, is Launder and Gilliat's earlier *The Happiest
Days of Your Life* (1950), a brilliantly constructed farce originally
devised by John Dighton (co-writer of *Kind Hearts and Coronets*),
who co-scripted alongside Launder. Here, Rutherford, Sim and
Grenfell co-star, all at the peak of their game and working with
prime material. A civil service blunder has meant that an all-girls
school, St Swithin's, is accidentally billeted at Nutbourne College, a
boys' school. Sim plays Wetherby Pond, headmaster of Nutbourne,
who must reluctantly co-operate with Muriel Whitchurch, head of
St Swithin's, especially as she has it in her gift to prevent him attaining an appointment to a better school, on which he has his sights set.

With the civil service proving sluggish and indifferent to the predicament it has triggered, the two schools must coexist as best they

can, but are put to the test when two tours of the school coincide, one by the girls' parents, the other by a group of governors from the school of which Pond hopes to be headmaster. The ultimate descent into chaos contains within it the wistful foreboding of the coming decline of schools like Nutbourne and the rise of a post-war secondary, mixed-sex state-school system and, Lord forfend, bearded schoolteachers. *The Happiest Days of Your Life* is about a Britain, a black and white Britain, coming to an end.

As with *Kind Hearts*, *Happiest Days* revels in language: pupils 'bursting for a hot bath and peckish for their high tea'; 'topping grounds for the Guides and Brownies to muster in'; 'I say, you girls are bang on seventeen'; and, from Rutherford's Whitchurch, 'I have a brother who grows groundnuts in Tanganyika.'

Rutherford Rutherfords to the hilt in *The Happiest Days of Your Life*, with her armoury of characteristics and facial gestures: the tongue planted thoughtfully in the cheek, the peremptory silent snort, the wry downward glance, the way she trumpets her lines, the glint of battle in her eye as she sweeps her gown over her shoulder; her lack of deference to the male of the species and imperviousness to their charms, her irritability at the weaknesses of her own gender. She is prepared to waver on matters of principle, however, when prudence dictates; blackmail and deceit, for example, must be deployed if the natural order of things is in jeopardy, though this causes a frisson of fretfulness when she leads the girls' parents on a tour of the school. 'You seem to be in the most delightful spot,' one of the parents comments.

Alastair Sim, like Rutherford, brings a great deal of himself to his roles, but even within that limited range, his is an immense, welcomely familiar presence. He is Scottish but vowed early on that he would not play the 'professional Scotsman'. He is hangdog, doleful, lugubrious, regarding the world through wide, watery eyes, both sad and dryly amused at the folly of his fellow man. He can be a chuckling fount of wisdom, but also highly strung, easily moved to indignation and horror, feigned or otherwise, pained beyond endurance, eyes rolling back into his head. And he is economical with his morals. When Richard Wattis's schoolmaster points out that Pond's proposal to censor the boys' mail presents an ethical dilemma, Pond brusquely replies that it is 'not one which I propose to look into too deeply'.

Miss Gossage, played by Joyce Grenfell, is a more callow version of the police sergeant Grenfell plays in *The Belles of St Trinian's*. Like her, she is a games mistress, ironically lacking in physical grace. She's a victim of nervous, over-enthusiastic and unrequited infatuation: 'Call me sausage,' she blurts to Richard Wattis's schoolmaster, leaning forward, a tremulous, gawky mass of shyness and desire. With her loping gait and diffident body language, Grenfell in her every movement created a sort of ballet of gaucheness, pressing through life in the only way she knew how. One imagines that her declaration of the school netball cry, 'Effort, St Swithin's, effort,' is her own mantra.

Although her aristocratic background and twittery, cut-glass tones made Joyce Grenfell appear to some the quintessence of English womanhood, both her parents were American: a socialite mother from Virginia and a millionaire architect father. She could easily have lapsed into wealthy anonymity. One of her great virtues, however, was her curiosity about her fellow human beings, which she expressed through her capacity for imitation, never malicious, always acute. Her facial features were a great asset. Though at rest hers was a radiant and kindly expression, suffused by her strong Christian beliefs and essential, humane decency, her nose, eyes, mouth and teeth were all a little too big, vital tools in her caricatures.

With *The Happiest Days of Your Life* she embarked on her golden cinematic decade: she has a cameo, for example, in *Genevieve*, in which she plays the proprietor of a bed-and-breakfast whose fat-lot-of-use facilities she presents in the best possible light. 'There's no hot water?' cries out Dinah Sheridan's Wendy on arriving at the establishment late at night. 'Yes, hot water is provided between half past two and six,' replies Grenfell, with a blandly ingratiating, pearly smile.

Of these three actors, Margaret Rutherford made the most significant incursion into the 1960s, in the Miss Marple series of films, in which she played Miss Marple as Margaret Rutherford. The film's distinctively jaunty theme vibrated with anticipation at the incipient energies of the new decade, but Rutherford, well into her seventies, wound down. Following 1960's *School for Scoundrels*, Sim all but bowed out of cinema, unimpressed by the turn the scripts were taking. He returned to the stage.

In a decade in which British comedy was dominated by the *Carry On* series, in all its exuberance and concomitant crudity, Grenfell's screen work dwindled also in the 1960s; she, too, seemed out of temper with the swinging times. Come 1972, however, BBC controller David Attenborough decided to bring her back from the cold. She was given her own show, in which, with minimal props, she delivered a series of songs and monologues, which in their warmth, wisdom, originality, underlying sadness and, above all, uproarious wit are only more impressive with each passing decade. She did upper-middle-class ladies, but also homelier types, her Northern accent spot on, uncondescending and unexaggerated. Songs like 'Stately as a Galleon', about gentleladies forced to dance with each other at a tea dance for want of menfolk, would have wowed them in the old nineteenth-century music halls, while her depiction of 'Lumpy Latimer', about a lady back from Kenya attending a school reunion, thrives on the technology of the close-up. At one point, Lumpy Latimer gets carried away with one of her exclamations and it comes out all schoolgirly raucous, in a manner that uncannily prefigures Queenie's aggressive rasp in *Blackadder II*. These characters were based on observation: the infant schoolteacher's admonition 'George – don't do that,' teetering right on the end of her tether with her charges, rings true with all those who have care of small boys who will insist on doing that. Others, such as the English literature don, she created, she said, while brushing her teeth; she made an adjustment of her upper lip, began to speak and wondered aloud what a person who spoke thus would say. From that speculation, she created the character of a highly intellectual woman whose amiability lies in her assumption that everyone she talks to is as well read as she is. Britain hosted no funnier or greater talent than Joyce Grenfell.

It could be that I'm nostalgic, living as I do in overpriced London, exhaust fumes from the South Circular Road blackening my finger-nails on a daily basis. I often yearn for the halcyon, bucolic days of my childhood, for the proud, civic majesty of Leeds. I share a similar hankering for the Britain Ealing represents. The credits alone, those major and minor players. Alastair Sim, Margaret Rutherford, Joyce Grenfell, Terry-Thomas, yes, but also Miles Malleson, Cecil Parker, Raymond Huntley, Irene Handl – and James Robertson Justice, who, as evidenced in Sir Lancelot Spratt in *Doctor in the House*, played a series of burly, bearded, blustery, irascible characters from the early fifties onwards, all of whom seemed to be about sixty-eight years old, before dying, in 1975, aged sixty-eight.

When Ealing Studios was sold on, Michael Balcon erected a plaque that read, 'Here during a quarter of a century many films were made projecting Britain and the British character.' It's hard not to entertain the feeling that something was lost with the passing of the era they represented – a pull-together spirit, inherited from the war, perhaps, which Conservatives in particular have attempted to invoke in lieu of public spending. But these films do not represent the mean-spirited insularity and nostalgia for a war not personally suffered that is characteristic of the Brexiteer. These films were viva-cious, a joyful release from the misery and austerity of war, embraced all of the British Isles, dreamt international dreams and involved European and American talent, queer as well as hetero (*Kind Hearts and Coronets*, for example, with its gay director and leading actor), with women afforded distinctive comic roles that were not always the norm in the coming decades. The people who made these films,

Balcon himself declared, were essentially 'liberal-minded'. Michael Frayn characterised the Ealing comedies as belonging to culture of 'gentle herbivores' whose spirit was also evident in the Festival of Britain of 1951, but who were increasingly under attack from the countervailing culture of 'carnivores', represented by the shrill, churlish tones of the *Daily Express*, the restoration of the Tories under Churchill and the continuing dominance of bastards like *The Man in the White Suit*'s Sir John Kierlaw. All things pass, but some endure. These films will.

HANCOCK: THE LAD HIMSELF

With the advent of radio, followed by TV, in the post-war years, there was a sense of mainstream comedy shrinking to its new dimensions. In lieu of Ealing, with its expansive, large-screen capers and lavish soundtracks, comedy became more domestic, constrained in scale.

From the 1950s right through to the late 1980s, two writing partnerships – Ray Galton and Alan Simpson, and Dick Clement and Ian La Frenais – explored, in various ways with a series of highly memorable characters, the comedy of confinement. The prison walls could be literal but often they were metaphorical – thwarted ambition, the dead weight of obligation and family ties, the inability to revisit yesteryear. These were male writers and the confinement was seen as a predicament of maleness. But from these wells of rueful self-pity were drawn some of the greatest characters of British situation comedy, with the emphasis on 'situation'. The lineage began with 'the lad himself', Tony Hancock.

Face to Face, which ran between 1959 and 1962, featured only one face – that of the interviewee. Of John Freeman, the politely forensic inquisitor, we saw only the back of his head. This added a godlike air of authority to his questioning; Freeman spurned the spotlight, which was to be shone, civilly but remorselessly, on the guest alone, sunk in a chair amid the intimidatingly highbrow trappings of the show – the Greek masks, the Feliks Topolski portraits, the Berlioz theme.

Normally mistrusting interviews, Tony Hancock, the first great British star of radio and TV situation comedy, was enticed to appear on *Face to Face* on 7 February 1960. It's been argued by some, including his brother Roger, that in so doing, he lost everything.

Freeman bats him a gentle starter: why are you a comic? Hancock modestly states that looking as he does, it was the only thing he could do. Of the world, he says that it is both funny and sad, 'the two basic ingredients of good comedy'. He admits that the Hancock character is largely based on himself; he disavows religion, which he has replaced with a tentative ethical curiosity. All reasonable and thoughtful enough.

Hancock's facial expressions throughout, however, reveal a man ill at ease. His plasticine jowls, the play of his lips, his darting eyes are the virtuoso instruments of his comedy, but here their furtive movements, twitches, wavering, tics betray a wary mass of anxiety under both Freeman's scrutiny and self-scrutiny of his own performance. Freeman notes Hancock's body language and asks if something is troubling him.

It isn't that he wants out of the studio. Rather, it's as if he has fallen prey to the pretentiousness of his own character, affected by the osmosis of being on a show which also featured titans such as Carl Gustav Jung. According to his brother Roger, it triggered a wave of agonising: a still deeper, morbid voyage into the inner life, which would cut him off from his colleagues and loved ones in a futile search for his core essence which would lead to his oblivion. 'You try and clear away the rubbish and get down to what is really your own personality – you find yourself discarding, not gathering,' Hancock says on the show. But in the end, he discarded everything.

For all that, he remains a bringer of joy, a divine light shining through every one of his orotund vowels, the wild surmise of his eyes, that great, wobbly, fatuous canvas of a face of his. Why did he worry?

Born in Birmingham in 1929, raised in Bournemouth, educated in Reading, Hancock's accent is more pan-English than regional, with plummy touches signifying a desire for self-improvement, and a bit of Cockney earth rubbed in when his character, star of the radio show *Hancock's Half Hour*, settled at 23 Railway Cuttings, East Cheam. He might not seem especially ill spoken by modern standards, but his tones were intended to contrast with the impeccable tones in which the 'Ladies and gentlemen, we present . . .' introduction to his show was delivered – the faultless, default tones of the BBC establishment, from which Hancock's flat-footed vowels were considered an amusing deviancy. Hancock was a creation born out of himself, with florid additions: hence his name in full, Anthony Aloysius St John Hancock.

Hancock's Half Hour was co-scripted by Ray Galton and Alan Simpson, who met during a post-war spell in a sanatorium and developed an instant rapport. There's a musical understanding in their scriptwriting, like a tight rhythm section; you feel it in the swoop and cadence of their best lines. In the early days, they didn't write especially well for women – fine stalwarts like Hattie Jacques and June Whitfield were poorly served by the pair. However, they understood men, everymen, aspirational men, thwarted men, confused and blind as to why they weren't able to reach a higher station in life. Like Hancock.

Hancock was there at the dawn of British situation comedy, but the earliest radio shows are more like sketch shows, with the star cast in a variety of roles, from comedian to would-be boxer to soldier on national service to Monte Carlo rally driver. Right until the end, Hancock deviated from sitcom inasmuch as he was never in the same situation. Some weeks he was well to do, others down on his luck.

Hancock was a natural product of 1950s England, that drab period in which, despite the recent war, Britain's imperial glory was a distant memorial glimmer, a nation of boiled eggs, cut-out coupons, Spam fritters and hand-me-down furniture. The all-mod-cons consumerist future teasingly promised on advertising hoardings hasn't permeated the net curtains of East Cheam. In Situationist terms, this gleaming, spangly Society of the Spectacle contrasted with the abiding mundanity of the vast majority of British life. For the dreamer, the would-be Man of Action like Hancock, the way to progress is thwarted by a host of human obstacles; his every encounter, whether with a hotel receptionist or a dinner lady, swiftly becomes a battlefield of petty antagonism, culminating in an exasperated exhalation of 'Oh, this is ridiculous!' And yet this world is his natural element; with his jowls, 'pains and pullovers', he is part of it, nothing special himself, hence the difficulty he has in escaping from it.

In the radio series, one of the most successful shows, amid the far-fetchedness of other plots, including Hancock playing cricket for England, only to find that his friend/nemesis Sid James is chair of the MCC, is the episode 'Sunday Afternoon at Home' (1958), a capsule for future generations of what British life was like in the fifties on the Day of Rest.

> 'Stone me, what a life.' (Deep sighs, miserable draughts of stale air, almost sinking into the void of radio silence). 'Are you sure it's only two o'clock? Doesn't the time drag? Every Sunday it's the same, nowhere to go, nothing to do. Just sit here waiting for the next lot of grub to come up.'

This was the naturalism to which Hancock would eventually come down: the drab, petty, circumscribed, suburban imprisonment against which he fidgeted and chafed so irritably, wearing his Homburg and big overcoat like he was carrying the weight of a wilfully dull world.

The early TV editions of *Hancock*, with their flimsy sets, were no-expense-incurred affairs. At times, Hancock felt like the only three-dimensional, flesh-and-blood character amid an ensemble doing stock turns, such as Kenneth Williams and June Whitfield in 'The Alpine Holiday' (1957), which turns on a strained, farcical misunderstanding involving hotel room numbers. In another, Hancock is an inept barrister who ends up prosecuting the man he is supposed to be defending. Meanwhile, with retakes at a premium, mistakes are left in, adding the wartsy charm of a Morecambe and Wise sketch.

As the TV series progressed, players such as Bill Kerr, Graham Stark and Hattie Jacques fell away. All this could be seen as evidence of Hancock's growing reluctance to share the spotlight. Yet Hancock was always laudatory about his fellow actors and critical of himself.

Hancock adapted superbly to TV, however. His face was a veritable circus ring, a jowly lexicon of comedy. One particular scene takes full advantage of his acrobatic countenance, as he tries to remember a name that's on the tip of his tongue; his face dances, lights up, recedes in puzzlement, springs to life, as his mind scampers about like a butterfly catcher in search of the elusive word.

Eventually, the series was reduced to essentially Hancock and Sid James. James was antithetical to Hancock: a face craggily etched like a wrinkly map of the ways of the world, as opposed to the pudgy innocence of Hancock; a man of worldly, villainous cunning with no qualms about exploiting Hancock's naivety. In 'The Red Planet' (1955), Sid manages to convince Hancock he has discovered a new body in the heavens simply by painting a red blob on the lens of his telescope, which he enlarges every day. In later series, such capers were eschewed in favour of more realistic situations arising from James's irritation at Hancock's ceaseless restiveness.

Finally, however, Hancock decided even Sid would have to go. He suspected a perception was growing that they were a double act. Hancock disagreed. Sid James was a fine actor, experienced in both film and TV, whose performances could be mistaken for simply turning up on set and being Sid. However, that intrinsic-ness, that anti-acting on James's part, was a result of his extreme professional-ism, and, while he was hardly a virtuoso in the Kenneth Williams mould, his was an inimitable presence.

Still, he wasn't of the same order as Hancock. While he handled the matter shabbily, Hancock had made a correct decision in terms of his own development. James, like Williams and Hattie Jacques, immediately established himself as a long-term regular in the *Carry On* series. Alone, in his final TV series with Galton and Simpson, Hancock would embark on TV work of another level.

That 1961 series saw Hancock also eschew the trappings of the Homburg and East Cheam, migrating to similarly cheerless surroundings in Earl's Court. The opening episode sees both writers and performer rise to the challenge of solitude; it is set entirely in Hancock's bedsit, spinning gold thread from the dross of boredom.

From nervously applying aftershave to his cut-up face, to idly puffing smoke rings into an expanse of time, to attempting to peruse a stack of weighty tomes, including Bertrand Russell, in the hope that merely having them piled about the place might transmit moral improvement, this is a man befogged in a deep, grey cloud of ennui, some generated by the era, some self-generated; he's trapped not just by a lack of opportunity but by his own inability, even disinclination to haul himself out of his circumstances. He's in his comfort zone, bellyaching, adding further to the grey clouds with his gaseous, despairing monologues. The brief prospect of a possible party invitation brightens his spirits and he excitedly clambers into jeans and a black shirt; but a follow-up call immediately snuffs out this prospect, leaving Hancock alone, once more, with the cold company of his books.

'The Radio Ham' (1961) sees Hancock prefigure the internet, with his vast rig of equipment enabling him to make global connections ('friends from all over the world – not in this country but all over the world'). But when the adventure he craves arrives in the form of a mayday call, his essential incompetence – he is a man who, for all his verbiage, 'knows nothing about anything', as Galton and Simpson put it – finds him out.

As with Laurel and Hardy, Hancock's character found himself in very different situations in each of his outings, as if living out alternative, successive historical timelines, while at all times remaining consistent to himself. In 'The Bowmans' (1961), for example, a parody of *The Archers*, the long-running radio soap opera still broadcast to this day, Hancock is the leading member of a cast who is about to be violently written out by producers fed up with his ad-libbing.

Finally, 'The Blood Donor' (1961), in which Hancock masterfully conceals the fact that he is mostly reading from cue cards, following a car accident which left him concussed days before production. All Hancock's virtues/vices come into play – pomposity, self-delusion, cowardice, snobbishness, ill-informed bluster, his prickly relationship with authority figures, an un-sentimentalised loneliness which prompts him to venture into the world, make human connections and come a complete cropper. The scene in which he learns that he's required to give a pint of blood and the precisely honed rhythm of his outcry – 'That's very nearly an armful!' – is the pinnacle of Hancock legend.

He declares his pride in his blood ('One hundred per cent British. Undiluted for twelve generations'), giving away Hancock's underlying belief that merely to be born British is to be of a certain 'calibre', a cut above ex-colonial types like Bill Kerr, with no strenuous effort required on his part to maintain this distinction. Hence his constant disappointment that life does not make good on his entitlement. Hancock is a symptom of the British post-war hangover, all too aware that the romantic days of swaggering imperial adventure are the stuff of yellowing volumes of *Boys' Own*. But the 1960s are coming, and Hancock is an increasingly isolated figure, his colleagues in the process of moving on in a way he cannot.

The Rebel (1961), Hancock's first foray into cinema, is often maligned by Hancock purists. But it's a fine introduction to Hancock the character, released from his customary monochrome austerity into a richly coloured cinematic adventure. Hancock, office clerk by day, justly struggling artist by night, escapes to Paris (reflecting the real-life Hancock's Francophilia) and finds his appalling daubs heralded as the work of an avant-garde genius, inaugurator of the 'shapist' school of art. His success prompts roommate Paul Ashby, an actual artistic genius, to quit and move to London, leaving behind his works. When the art critic Sir Charles Brewer (George Sanders) visits his studio, he immediately sees Hancock's infantile works for the rubbish that they are but is full of praise for Ashby's work, which he assumes to be Hancock's also. The latter reluctantly goes along with the misunderstanding and becomes Europe's most celebrated artist.

The Rebel was reasonably successful; alas, it did not match Hancock's ambitions, particularly of conquering America, and he made the ill-fated decision to part company with Galton and Simpson. Hancock's comedy shines with relevance even in our own times, yet it was as if he had no place, no resonance in the sixties, a drastically different decade from its predecessor; he could not survive alongside the Beatles, cope with the new swing of things, being too conspicuously a fixture of the previous decade. He regressed, making TV appearances whose very lack of lustre was compounded by the sadness of his decline. He made a second film, *The Punch and Judy Man* (1963), in black and white; it's hard to watch in retrospect. He descended into alcoholism and, alone in Australia in 1968, took his own life with pills and vodka. He was what he was: a victim of a certain English, envious, frustrated, aspirational spirit in a country of limited social mobility, which he played on so well as a comedian. But his very appeal was that he lacked the glitz, the glib pizzazz, the Sellers stardust to have become the international celebrity he yearned to be. He was anti-showbiz; he represented the lumpy gravy of reality. That was the basis of his appeal. J. B. Priestley, however, encapsulated his tragedy in the comment that Hancock was 'a comedian with a touch of genius, and no enemy but himself'.

THE GOONS: SPIKE MILLIGAN –
DELICATE FLOWER OF MODERNITY

If Hancock and his subsequent lineage were about confinement, then the comedy authored by Spike Milligan was absolutely unbound, breaking the chains of drab cliché and laboured puns, as well as the limits of reality itself, which weighed like kitchen sinks on the comedies created by Galton and Simpson.

Not for nothing was Spike Milligan voted the Funniest Man of the Last 1,000 Years in a 1999 poll. He is comedy's own Picasso, the man who conceived modernity in post-war British comedy. It was Milligan who enabled comedy, its words, its ideas, to fly off at limitless tangents beyond the dreary railroads down which it had previously been routed. He was the human spanner who, with *The Goon Show*, broadcast between 1951 and 1960, hurled himself into the works, at the expense of his health, his sanity, his happiness. The Goons were a quantum feat of imagination. Without Milligan, no Python, no Rik Mayall, no Chris Morris, no Eddie Izzard, all of whom received permission for their own unbound adventures from *The Goon Show* and Milligan's subsequent TV series, *Q*.

One only has to revisit the archives, the preserved radio sessions, the YouTube clips to bear witness to the . . . . okay, here I must slow down, guide the narrative into a lay-by, switch off the engine and level with you. I really don't find Spike Milligan very funny. And when I say not funny, I mean deadeningly unfunny. About as funny as a man going cross-eyed. Great comedians have not only got away with but thrived upon delivering duff material, showering us with corn; Tommy Cooper springs to mind. But we love Cooper, or his onstage persona at least. Spike Milligan is harder to love, and not because his truculence was never far from the surface of his public being. His default expression is one of twitching self-satisfaction at his own mirth, often corpsing (especially in *Q*) at the direst material. I sometimes feel that if just one reader is persuaded, after reading this book, not to bother watching *Q*, this entire enterprise will have been worthwhile.

Milligan is praised for his wordplay, but too often this amounted to no more than abysmal puns: 'Contraceptives should be used on every conceivable occasion.' Here's another, a *Goon Show* 'classic': 'Are you a spy?' 'I'm not a spy, I'm a shepherd!' 'Ah! Shepherd's pie!' At this, the Goons ensemble explode like grenades with laughter, as if the laff-line of the century has just been delivered, as opposed to a punchline a Christmas cracker would be too embarrassed to dispense. Then, in *Down Among the Z Men* (1952), Milligan divines that the word 'guerrilla' sounds a lot like 'gorilla'. So delighted are he and Harry Secombe at this discovery that they flail gibbon-like for many seconds. Now, you could argue that these were the 1950s and this verbal coincidence was freshly minted, but he was still cracking the joke in correspondence to George Martin in 1984.

That young men in particular tuned into *The Goon Show* and found it cathartically hilarious makes you wonder how funereally atrocious radio comedy was prior to the arrival of Milligan and co. Perhaps it was the funny voices. These, however, have proven desperately perishable for reasons which, in fairness, can't all be ascribed to Milligan. As with Peter Cook's E. L. Wisty, the expediently distinctive voices adopted by Sellers, Milligan and Secombe for maximum radio impact were widely adopted by a mass of dullards who felt it was enough to imitate these voices to be funny.

Milligan traded in surrealism but also in stereotypes, especially in *Q*. Military men were peppery, brusque; the police preceded their enquiries with ''Ello, 'ello, 'ello'; a psychiatrist would speak in zer funny German accent; barmaids were busty and there to be ogled at and molested; and as for Asians . . .

Milligan came a cropper more than once when dealing with race. Maybe he wasn't a racist. He detested the National Front and recalled with horror his awful mother, during his early upbringing in India, forbidding him to play with 'little Black boys'. Let's just say he had a morbid obsession with racial matters and devoted much thought to the subject. He received flak for opposing the building of a mosque in Regent's Park in 1977, but responded to critics with a letter to *Private Eye* gaslighting them as the real racists, insisting that his objections were purely 'aesthetic', before musing without basis that the justice system was inhibited in its treatment of 'coloured' people because to convict a Black person of a crime was considered by some 'racist'.

Comedy of a certain vintage is rife with racial stereotyping, but with Milligan it felt obsessive, although it was hard to see what helpful point he was trying to make. It's no excuse to say that since he himself was born in India, he had a pass to go 'brownface', as he so frequently did, any more than it would be acceptable for a white man born in the United States to claim it was okay for him to wear blackface because he was from the same nation as African Americans. This obsession culminated in *Curry and Chips*, a 1969 sitcom written by Johnny Speight and starring Milligan, gleefully blacked up, in which he played Kevin O'Grady, an Irishman of Pakistani heritage. The supposed inherent comic value of Asians was made much of throughout the series, which was pulled after six appalling episodes. Speight made the mistake he did in *Till Death Us Do Part* of imagining that audiences were laughing at the satire on racism rather than enjoying the guilty pleasure of the racism itself. Unapologetically, Milligan had another pop with 1975's *The Melting Pot*, which he co-wrote with Neil Shand. Milligan again browned up as illegal immigrant Mr Van Gogh. Again, it featured 'racialists' such as Colonel Grope, whose invective certain sections of the audience greeted with relish rather than revulsion. This spectacularly unwise commission was again pulled, this time after a single episode – this in an era when *Love Thy Neighbour*, *Mind Your Language* and *It Ain't Half Hot Mum* all received a pass. Unrepentant, Milligan recycled elements of *The Melting Pot* into his novel *The Looney* (1987), in which the n-word features abundantly.

Milligan did use Black actors, in fairness. But the effect could be hideous. Take a 1970 TV sketch, in which he opens his front door to a Black postman. 'Blackmail!' he puns, as he takes the letter from him. And then he offers him a tip. 'Daz!' (the detergent whose boast was that it 'washes whiter').

The problem is with Milligan himself. Despite his love of children and care for the environment, a lack of love for humanity is at the hollow core of his work, which merely acts out the free-associative contents of his own head. He is an arch-solipsist. He considered himself always to be the most supremely relevant being on the planet and never accepted that alternative comedy had supplanted his hack-neyed worldview – hence his rudeness to Rik Mayall when the latter sent him a letter of praise. He may have deconstructed comedy but was himself unreconstructed.

That said . . .

One of Milligan's distinctive qualities was gravity. He was deeply affected by World War II, but also by the world itself, the very fact of human life. He was beaten by his mother, his father was a remote figure, but his brother survived the same trauma much more robustly. Milligan had one skin too few. As for the war, his memoirs of his service are his most affecting work; they begin as a romp, but darken as Milligan comes up against the horror of war, its absurdities, its bereave-ments, its shock impact, none of which Milligan deflects or makes light of. With strange exceptions, including Bernard Manning, who as a young soldier was responsible for guarding Rudolf Hess and Albert Speer at Spandau jail, no British comedian experienced the reality of war as deeply as Milligan. Certainly, none made as much of it as he did. For Milligan, it was formative in his comedy, not just in terms of his unsuitability for active service but the impact it had on any faith he might have had in God, human nature and the order of things.

He found little solace in the rations of comedy doled out to him and the forces. He described ENSA, the forces' entertainment organisation, as Every Night Something Awful. He also despised the protocols of variety, which insisted that comedy be broken up by mawkish, punitive bouts of middle-of-the-road crooning. *The Goon Show* would be comedy, a tsunami of comedy and nothing but the comedy. Buckets of custard, not rationed spoonfuls.

And while audiences lapped up the pre-*Goons* comedy staple fare, with shows like Arthur Askey's *Band Waggon* (1938–40) commanding audiences of up to thirty million, much of their success might have been due to the poverty of options. Listening to the antics of Askey, Leslie Hatton and the endless procession of comedy charladies, from Mrs Mopp to Suzette Tarri, is as unendurable as cold Spam to modern audiences, but back then you got what you were given: puns about the RAF being a 'flighty lot', and Arthur English's spiv reflecting on his employee, 'She's the latest thing in secretaries – well, they don't get any later than her, she doesn't get in till twelve.'

It's not too far-fetched to say that the Goons formed a significant part of the post-war avant-garde, in which the ruins of war were a metaphor for the explosion of old artistic forms and assumptions. This manifested itself in the Theatre of the Absurd, which carried through ideas developed by the existentialists and the Dadaists, who had had a similar reaction to the events of World War I. In music, it found expression in electronic music and *musique concrète*, as developed by Karlheinz Stockhausen and Pierre Schaeffer, using or repurposing new technologies to create music that in its sources, expansive abstraction and departures from the pen-and-ink constrictions of conventional notions visualised new realms for contemporary music.

Milligan wasn't a fan of electronic music, which he equated with the muzak he regarded as a blight on the modern world. However, he was fully conscious of the way he could use the studio and radio to realise his impossibly surreal ideas, taking liberties with space and time. Milligan was very keen on availing himself of the BBC Radiophonic Workshop, commissioning them, for example, to create the noise of Major Bloodnok's stomach and its consequent flatulence, as well as the effects in 'The Scarlet Capsule' (1959), a parody of *Quatermass and the Pit*.

Milligan knew how to exploit the invisibility of radio in his gags: In 'Rommel's Treasure' (1955), he has the field marshal order that a box be buried ten feet above the ground. 'But people will see it!' someone objects. 'That's a chance we'll have to take.' And so the box is duly buried ten feet above ground. What's beautiful about this exchange also is 'That's a chance we'll have to take,' the sort of heroic, plucky sentiment all too familiar to watchers of war movies. Major Bloodnok, voiced by Peter Sellers, 'late of the 3rd Disgusting Fusiliers', he of the bilious stomach and also an avid womaniser, was a monstrous model of military fatuity. The mockery he made of military authority was vital at a time when the upper echelons of Britain were anxiously seeking to preserve the hierarchical norms and respect for seniors and betters of the pre-war era.

As for the rest of the Goons – Bluebottle, Neddie Seagoon – the first impact of the ridiculously enervated, insipid voices of these un-men was extraordinary; radio comedy, with its limited stock of class and regional types, had never before conceived of such creatures. Eccles is the closest to Milligan himself, a creature incapable of adulthood but strangely clear-eyed, indomitably innocent. Asked 'What are you doing down there?' Eccles replies, 'Everybody got to be somewhere.' Or, when asked what time it is, he replies, 'I've got it written down here on a piece of paper.' On the piece of paper is written eight o'clock. But what if it's not eight o'clock? 'Then I don't show it to them.' But how does he know when it is eight o'clock? 'I've got it written down on a piece of paper.'

Much of Milligan's output is dated, crass. And yet amid it all there are exchanges, moments that could only have come from the mind of one man. On losing his dog and putting an advert in the newspaper that reads, 'Here, boy.' Or 'I have the body of an eighteen-year-old. I keep it in the fridge.' Or routines like 'The Dustbin Dance', which in its inspiration leaps unbidden and pointlessly from the void. 'When you're feeling lonely and you can't find romance,' warbles Milligan, 'jump into a dustbin and do the dustbin dance.' Upon which he and his fellow Goons jump about with furious, slamming futility in metal bins.

Milligan's uniqueness, his raging nonsense, sprang from his implacable sensitivity. He was probably doomed never to be truly, happily at ease. In 1967, he wrote the poem 'The New Rose':

The new rose
trembles with early beauty
The babe sees the beckoning carmine
the tiny hand
clutches the cruel stem
The babe screams
The rose is silent –
Life is already telling lies.

Milligan's Q could be pretty wretched, but there are moments that feel like they could have been drawn from contemporary art: the skeleton and mannequin you can just glimpse sitting in the waiting room in a psychiatry sketch, for example. The collapsing plywood shambles of the series, its Brechtian refusal to abide by sketch-show norms, were a direct inspiration for *Monty Python's Flying Circus*, and on Terry Jones in particular. When trying to conceive of the show, and the shape it would assume, he saw Spike Milligan's *Q5*. 'Fuck, Milligan's done it!' he exclaimed. He was impressed at how Milligan's sketches eschewed conventional beginnings and conclusions, drifted in and out of one another.

For all his terrible flaws, for all that sections of his work are unwatchable, sections of his literature unreadable, the sensibility of modern comedy owes its origin to Spike Milligan. Innumerable subsequent comic geniuses had their minds unlocked by the free associations and gleeful subversions of his own work. The future began with him.

SATIRE, SEX AND HOW'S YOUR FATHER
THE 1960S

I was born in 1962, and once I developed a dawning sense of the world and its contents, I found myself exposed to the fitful, monochrome worlds of pop music and TV. As a child, I liked any pop music so long as it was up-tempo, fast-moving. I liked any comedy so long as it had a laugh track. My earliest heroes were Harry Worth, the opening credits to whose show saw him stand at the corner of a glass-fronted department store and make a floating star man of himself by lifting his left arm and leg, which were duly reflected in the glass. Another was Freddie 'Parrot Face' Davies, whose gimmick was, I should explain, that he had a face like a parrot. The appeal of these men and others to my seven-year-old self was simply that they were not men, with all the unsmiling discipline and authority that entailed.

The sixties appeared to create a generation gap, with established stars like Ken Dodd and Morecambe and Wise seeming to represent a middle-of-the-road old guard of light entertainment that was about to be supplanted by the wave of the revolutionary new. There's footage of the Beatles meeting Eric and Ernie, and insolent showbiz arriviste John Lennon teasing Eric: 'It's not like it was in your day.' Ironically, however, Morecambe and Wise were not the only entertainers of their generation who would outlast not only the Beatles but also such Beatles-esque phenomena as the Satire Boom of the early sixties. Nonetheless, it was this boom that brought the curtain down on the 1950s, a decade, an era that was in danger of outstaying its welcome.

THE NOT VERY ANGRY YOUNG MEN:
THE SATIRE BOOM

Even those who feel familiar with late-1950s Britain through period
TV and film recreations would be fazed were they to be airlifted back
to that era. Sure, there was rock and roll, but that did not feel like
a permanent transformation but a passing fad, already faded by the
end of the decade, by which time a trad-jazz revival was mooted as
the next thing. Rock and roll had slowly faded into the grey, thin air,
stifled by the determined dullness of a monochromatic Britain, living
in permanent shades of grey.

What would strike them? Not immediately the quiet bigotry, the
bitter stoicism, the bewildered feeling that Britain had been demoted,
rather than exalted, following the war. The monocultural blandness of
everyday life would be the first shocker. The Spam fritters, the golden
syrup, the dismal lack of options, be it in clothing, TV and radio,
or places to eat and drink, especially when immigrant culture – and
the flavours of variety it might provide – was firmly, even violently
marginalised. For most people, a restaurant treat meant the Lyons
tea rooms or the municipal dining halls left over from wartime. Most
likely, a meal would be taken at home, diners sawing morosely away
at a chop, washed down with nothing stronger than a mug of tea.

The Swiss photographer Robert Frank documented the London
and Wales of the 1950s. His grainy images vividly capture a settled
air of pervasive toxicity, particularly prior to the Clean Air Act of
1956. What with the fug of peasoupers and the plumes of smoke
exuded by ubiquitous and unrestricted cigarette users, Britain must
have felt like a country where the sun hadn't broken through since
1935.

In the late 1940s, the welfare state had been constructed, but
Britons did not permanently adopt a socialist mindset, resented
the austerity of continued rationing and by 1951 decided to vote
Winston Churchill back in. The Tories would remain in power for

thirteen years, presiding first over the humiliation of the Suez crisis, in which America effectively reminded the UK just who was running the world now, and eventually over a consumer boom in the late 1950s, in which a host of labour-saving technologies at last added modern respite to British lives.

At the cinema, the pictures presented a chipper view of Britain to itself, in the crisp tones of Pathé news bulletins. These consisted of clipped news items, often clipped of context; a goal in a sports report would be illustrated by second-long footage of a ball hitting the back of a net, accompanied by a mighty cheer. A lack of context also characterised their current affairs reportage, mini-documentaries focusing on fractious events on the international scene, particularly the former colonies. However, bulletins would generally conclude, in a 'thank heavens' spirit, with items on the royal family, a model family representing a haven of stability, prosperity and continuity. For as much as Britain benefited from, and took as a given, the welfare state, there was a similarly strong impulse in people to hark back to Britain's halcyon, pre-war conditions in which the aristocracy played a starring role.

Such was the hierarchical deference of the times, despite their increasing shininess and exuberance. There was a gaping absence of scepticism in the public discourse. The word 'satire' was barely known: it was a reference to the ancient Greeks, perhaps, or maybe the Weimar Republic.

Britain's apparent return to prosperity had been presided over not by men who projected youthful, go-ahead vigour but by leaders prone to incapacity – first Churchill, then Anthony Eden, before ill health saw him give way to Harold Macmillan. Despite being dubbed 'Supermac' by an obliging press, Macmillan exuded patrician decrepitude. And, while his efforts as PM might mark him out as an honourably constructive, one-nation Tory, to a restless generation on the verge of the meritocratic youthquake that would rock the 1960s he embodied a party that had been in power far too long.

However, these men were protected from juvenile jibes by the personage of the Lord Chamberlain, a member of the Royal Household, who until 1968 exercised the power to censor material for presentation in the theatre which mocked or undermined those in public life. Anything written for the stage had first to be submitted to the Lord Chamberlain and his blue pencil. And so it was considered unthinkable, for example, to impersonate the prime minister, any more than a fifth-former might openly mimic the headmaster during a school assembly.

A concatenation of factors, however, prompted a new generation to go about getting around these ancient taboos and protocols. The imminence of the sixties and their myriad promises of modernity was one (sexual intercourse, the Beatles, moon landings, a Labour government, perhaps). Exasperation on the part of bright young men forced to endure two years of national service ('a complete waste of time', complained the *Private Eye* journalist Paul Foot) may also have impressed upon some the obsolescence of the *ancien régime*.

However, with the exception of one studious young man from humble Yorkshire origins, the perpetrators of the impending Satire Boom were drawn from a similar stratum of privilege as those they sought to lampoon. They were almost entirely men, and not particularly angry young men, still less particularly angry about the continuing marginalisation of women across the board in British society. Bored, highly facetious, yes; angry, no. They were as capable of being hidebound and reactionary as they were iconoclastic and radical. But at a strikingly young age they found themselves with a Britain that was providentially falling at their feet.

One such clique formed in Shrewsbury School in Shropshire. Four of the *Private Eye* team met there in their teens: Paul Foot, Willie Rushton, cartoonist, humorist and eventually high-profile household name, Christopher Booker and Richard Ingrams.

John Peterson, headmaster of Shrewsbury School, later described these four boys as 'pillars of happy citizenship' compared with the generation of pupils who succeeded them. Able, staid even; hardly troublemakers. They took over the school magazine, *The Salopian*, turning it into a journal of precocious adolescent humour, poking fun at school institutions such as speech day. But by and large they were indulged.

These men decided to preserve their working camaraderie, born in adolescence. They also took on other personnel, including John Wells, the inspiration for 'Gnitty', the parody of the sword-bearing figure on the *Daily Express* masthead. The invention of Letraset was helpful in the creation of *Private Eye*. Ingrams was initially set on naming the magazine *The Bladder*, a title more reflective of his jesting, piss-taking for piss-taking sake's spirit, but Rushton objected, since a relative of his was suffering terribly from a bladder infection. It was as well. *Private Eye* much better conveys the magazine's most vital purpose, as an ahead-of-the-curve investigative journal, as opposed to a vehicle for its uneven humour.

One reason the *Eye* has survived is the obdurate, intensely frivolous perversity of Richard Ingrams, whose idiosyncratic character has hugely determined that of *Private Eye*. A bear-like man, yet one who in his younger days exuded a handsome charm to which he appeared oblivious, Ingrams hated confrontation and yet loved to make trouble, to see how far and for how long you could poke your stick in the hornets' nest. He was not a nonconformist. He did not burn with rage at the iniquities of the establishment. He was socially conservative. He took a dim view of homosexuals or 'homosexualism'; early *Private Eyes* are rife with references to 'pooves'. He was a fellow who, as he repeatedly said, hated boredom, the most detestable of the human conditions. As editor he was lax when it came to fact-checking, going on a vague instinct he described as the 'ring of truth'. When writs were issued, a part of him probably reacted with glee that the right nerves in the body politic were being touched.

Ingrams's initially shambolic, laissez-faire editorship, coupled with a general sense that the Satire Boom was winding down, saw the *Eye*'s sales dwindle from 90,000 to 25,000 in 1964. They might have succumbed to despondency had it not been for the magical intervention of their unlikely proprietor, Lord Gnome himself, Peter Cook.

Born in 1937, Cook later described himself as 'raised by goats'. This surreal remark was typical of the way he looked at life, the way he deflected from introspection or self-examination. What he meant was that he had been raised by nannies – nannies, goats, nanny goats. His was a materially well-to-do but emotionally straitened upbringing. His grandfather had committed suicide, a tragedy his grandmother successfully kept secret throughout her life. His father worked in the Colonial Office, in Nigeria. He was a geographically remote figure to young Peter, who throughout his youth experienced a series of 'goats', ersatz parental figures.

He also experienced the misery of being packed off to boarding schools, first St Bede's and then Radley; the loneliness, the bullying. Like others, Cook used humour as a defence mechanism, but what was unique to him was the exquisitely honed nature of his wit. He didn't merely play the amiable class buffoon. There was about his humour – sarcastic, verbal, gimlet-eyed, unflinching – a quality that mirrored that of bullying, that was, in its own way, equally devastating, non-violently sadistic. In his teens he wrote what he considered the finest sketch of his life, the 'One-Legged Tarzan' sketch, in which a 'unidexter' actor applies for the role of King of the Jungle, with Cook as a casting agent who, rather than dismiss the hopeful (later played by Dudley Moore, hopping optimistically around his office), goes to great lengths to preserve the feelings of the thespian applicant ('Your right leg I have nothing against. The problem is, neither do you'). Actually, this displays a corollary to Cook's character, a certain considerateness.

Having managed to emerge unscathed from the privations and passages of a 1950s upper-class education, Cook went up to Cambridge and made his name as one of the university's foremost wits, evidenced in such unlikely places as his college's food complaints book, in which he composed lengthy essays, developing his calculatedly long-winded, unrelenting, unwavering comic voice.

He gravitated towards the Cambridge Footlights, where he encountered, among others, the earnestly left-wing John Bird and David Frost, who was seen in Oxbridge circles as a 'hack', one of the lowest sorts of creatures – lacking obvious talent but industrious, ingratiatingly on the make. Cook felt rather sorry for him.

Cook saw the hierarchical set-up of the 1950s as rotten – maintained by a spirit of pomposity and artifice. This would be the next phase of his work. While the left writhed with indignation at the re-election of Harold Macmillan, the wrinkly, drawling embodiment of 1950s complacency, Cook poured his efforts into honing the unthinkable: an impersonation of the premier, all the more devastating for its pitiless detail.

And yet, Cook was not a radical. He was as scornful of Labour as he was of the Tories. He looked on at the world with an amused, penetrative glare of contempt, rather than fervent idealism. Moreover, he showed no great inclination to revolt against his own upbringing, despite its miseries. Even as his comic career was flowering, he was studying for the Foreign Office, happy to follow in his father's footsteps, genuinely deflated when he failed the exams. He spoke wistfully of how he could have cheerfully lived the life of a governor of Bermuda, wearing a plumed hat, looking down on the everyday absurdities of colonialism and its bureaucracy. He wished to mock the world, not change it.

Cook's achievements as a writer, comedian and performer were staggeringly prodigious for one aged twenty-two. When *Beyond the Fringe*, a synthesis of the Cambridge Footlights and the Oxford Revue, was conceived in 1960, Cook already had an agent, having written a West End revue for Kenneth Williams. Indeed, using his agent, Cook negotiated a higher fee than his *Fringe* co-stars, though once the agent took his commission, Cook ended up with less money. Those co-stars were Jonathan Miller, a medical student; Dudley Moore, a diminutive comedian and highly gifted jazz pianist;

and Alan Bennett, a bright young grammar schoolboy from Leeds with a diffident, clerical air that belied a withering eye for the English establishment, particularly the clergy.

The immediate success of *Beyond the Fringe* suggested a troupe pushing at an open door, like the Beatles, supplying something people had been crying out for without knowing it. Cook wrote most of the material. He most effectively lampooned the senility of post-Suez Britain, confident in its speech patterns and the notion of British supremacy that they signified, but losing its grip on the modern world. This disconnect was best encapsulated in a sketch in which a crusty Cook character is anxiously asked what could be done in the event of a four-minute warning following a nuclear strike. 'I would remind those doubters that some people in this great country of ours can run a mile in four minutes.'

Or there was the Great Train Robbery sketch, featuring an Arthur Streeb-Greebling-type police chief explaining in self-assured but wholly unconvincing tones that the robbery was being dealt with effectively by the British investigating authorities. 'When you speak about the Great Train Robbery this in fact involved no loss of train,' he told his inquisitor Dudley Moore. 'We haven't lost a train since 1943.' He then went on to opine that 'We believe this to be the work of thieves.'

Cook's knowledge and mastery of the tones and cadences of the class into which he was born were vital. He understood fluently the layered mass of subtle assumptions which kept aloft the politicians, administrators, military officers and civil-service men who still believed they were running the world. As for the new world, the handsome and socially magnetic Cook found himself its darling. The success of the *Fringe* was transatlantic: it was a hit in New York, and a performance was attended by President Kennedy and his wife Jackie.

Cook was at the height of his powers. And yet one sketch from the *Fringe* at this time seems prescient in retrospect. He's in character as the distinguished, befuddled octogenarian Sir Arthur Streeb-Greebling, explaining how he has dedicated his long life to teaching ravens to fly under water, at the behest of his fearsome mother. Is it difficult? he is asked. 'I think the word "difficult" is an awfully good one here,' he replies with cultured understatement. It soon emerges that he has never once, in forty years, succeeded in teaching a raven to fly under water. Fly, fly, you devils, he urges them, only to watch in repeated dismay as the birds 'spiral very slowly down to a watery grave'. Sir Arthur can only conclude that his has been an entirely 'wasted life'.

There's a lot going on here: his faultless realisation of a crusty relic of the upper classes, learned through a lifetime of close listening, and the sense that, for all their persistence and confidence, whatever strange mission aristocracy has undertaken is as doomed as a drowned raven. Maybe this is Peter Cook already at the stage of Marcel Duchamp's *Sad Young Man on a Train* – the work of an artist who had already reached his own zenith of modernity and would effectively cease producing art from 1923 until his death in 1968. Maybe Cook has arrived, too soon, too young, at the realisation of the futility of things. He himself was sharply satirical when it came to the subject of satire itself; he spoke of all the political cabarets of Berlin in the thirties 'which did so much to prevent the rise of Adolf Hitler'. His investment in *Private Eye* was born out of an understanding more of the potency of its serious, investigative journalism rather than its joke pages. That, at least, was something.

A corollary to Streeb-Greebling is the rather less well to do E. L. Wisty, who began life as a *Fringe* character, based, supposedly, on one Mr Boylett, table butler at Radley College. In his distinctive vowels, Wisty reflects that he could have been a judge, but 'didn't have the Latin'. Cook didn't so much deliver as inflict Wisty monologues on tadpoles, bees and human innards, unsmiling, in a merciless, monotonous drone, on and on and on in an endless stream of invention, unfurling like an intestine, buttonholing his victims with the absolute confidence that he was doing anything other than wasting their time entirely.

By law, only Cook should have been allowed to do the Wisty voice. Unfortunately, from very shortly after Wisty's creation, masses of far less able copyists took up the 'voice', usually to denote mirth in lieu of anything actually funny. The 'Wisty voice' is a cover, also, for English self-consciousness, the sort dropped into when wanting to make an awkward, perhaps pretentious or confessional point; a vocal act of displacement, created by the master of displacement.

Still, this was the 1960s, with a Tory government on its last legs. If there was one ruffle in the elegant feathers of Cook's effortless rise, it was the TV success of David Frost. Something about his doggedness, his will to impress, his upward slickness, made him perfect for the medium. *That Was the Week That Was* began in 1962 and featured a range of talents, from singer Millicent Martin, who would render in jazzy verse a précis of the week's events, to producer Ned Sherrin, Kenneth Cope, Roy Kinnear, Willie Rushton, Lance Percival and a revived Frankie Howerd. Writers included stalwarts such as Frank Muir, John Betjeman and Keith Waterhouse, as well as Graham Chapman, John Cleese, John Bird and Bill Oddie. *TW3* was absolutely of its day, tilting at a tottering, barely upright government. Deliberately shambolic, with actors reading from scripts, stagehands and cameras visible in a Brechtian display of consciousness of the artifice of its medium, abrasive, this was not satire diluted for TV. Whether they were discussing police brutality or the apartheid system in South Africa, no punches were pulled, no concessions made.

TW3 lasted only two series, the BBC pulling it on the pretext that with 1964 being an election year, the Corporation was obliged to remain impartial, though many thought this was an excuse for nervous governors to pull it altogether. However, it was also felt by 1964 that the work of the Satire Boom – to remove the rotten Tories and replace them with the white heat of a Labour administration – was done. Given that most of its exponents were left of centre, taking Labour, a party whose rise to power most of them had longed for, to task would be far less fun than taking a rapier to the saggy flesh of the despised Tories.

Cook certainly relished flaying Tories, though he later admitted to voting for them out of 'selfishness'. In *Private Eye*, he was responsible for a photomontage of Tory cabinet minister 'Rab' Butler bearing the slogan 'FLABBY FACED OLD COWARD'. Meanwhile, he had founded the Establishment, a members' nightclub designed to circumvent the attention of the Lord Chamberlain. The Establishment was hardly a countercultural haunt; Willie Rushton complained that much of the audience came from the same top drawer as the victims of their jibes. Even Harold Macmillan looked in. 'It is a good thing to be laughed over – it is better than being ignored,' he said, damn him. Cook spotted him one night and, realising that a poke in the eye rather than a dig in the ribs was what the situation required, laid directly into him during an onstage monologue. 'There's nothing I like better than to wander over to a theatre and sit there listening to a group of sappy, urgent, vibrant young satirists with a stupid great grin over my face.' However, the Establishment, too, though it played host to the likes of Lenny Bruce, went into decline, not least once it began to attract the attention of local gangsters.

If satire was done, where did this leave *Private Eye*? It might have sunk like *TW3* had Peter Cook not returned one day in June 1964 when the magazine was at its financial lowest, like a fairy godmother, injecting £2,000 of his own cash into the *Eye* and, more importantly, showering the office with jokes ('We'd almost forgotten about jokes, we were so depressed,' recalled Peter Usborne, co-founder of the magazine). The first of these was a cover featuring the *Raft of the Medusa*, with one of the survivors saying, 'This is the last time I go on a John Bloom holiday,' a reference to a dubious entrepreneur of the early 1960s, one of whose specialities was cut-price vacations to Bulgaria. The magazine was re-energised with the addition of flexi-discs, featuring contributions from Cook himself. One of these I acquired as a reissue twenty years later. I made the mistake of playing it in front of my parents, assuming they might appreciate some of the now-quaint public schoolboy jibes of yesteryear, much as they might do Flanders and Swann. Cook piped up. 'People ask me how I can be a working-class trade unionist and vote Conservative. The answer is, because I'm a stupid cunt.'

In the mid-1960s, Cook towered like some latter-day Psmith in his effortless elegance and casual brilliance; as Alan Bennett might have said, in a very real sense he was the tallest comic of his generation. The *Fringe* members peeled away, but Cook and Dudley Moore formed a duo that took television by storm with the same ease as Cook had the West End and New York. *Not Only . . . But Also* coursed almost libidinally through the mid-sixties, on the same monochrome, modernist wave as the Beatles (John Lennon even appeared in the show, as a doorman at the most exclusive public lavatory in London).

As the sixties began to swing, for a spectacular few, at least, and the Tories were no longer available as the butt of the joke, satire was giving way to sex. Amid all this, Cook wrote maybe the greatest ever sketch about the awkwardness of passing on the Facts of Life from father to son. Cook is an ageing, upper-class patrician, Moore his schoolboy son, whom he summons to his study to explain to him, from a vast emotional distance, 'the method whereby you came to be brought about'.

'Some of the boys say very filthy things about it, sir,' remarks Moore, earnestly, before Cook explains, 'It was necessary for your mother to sit on a chair that I had recently vacated . . . Something beautiful happened and sure enough, four years later, you were born. You mustn't think less of your mother – she had to do it, she did it.'

Sex is regarded distantly and deludedly by Pete and Dud as two scarved and cloth-capped geezers. There's a Cook trope involving him being lusted after and pestered by Hollywood actresses, some approaching old age even by the mid-1960s, including Betty Grable and Greta Garbo, who, driven mad by desperation in the mind of Cook's character, has come to his house. 'Stark naked . . . hanging on to the windowsills . . . white knuckles . . . "Pyeter! Pyeter . . ." You know how these bloody Swedes go on.'

Sex again, thwarted again, in *Bedazzled* (1967), in which Cook and Moore burst, *Sgt Pepper*-like, onto the big screen; a comedy which, like Cook himself, exuded as much style as it did laughs, though that was as much down to the swinging soundtrack supplied by Moore, wretched butt of the film, as the finesse of Cook's script. Moore plays Stanley Moon, the name by which the gaffe-prone John Gielgud referred to him in a letter praising *Beyond the Fringe*, a cook in a Wimpy restaurant in London who is infatuated with waitress Margaret Spencer (Eleanor Bron). Cook plays Satan, assuming the form of one George Spiggott, who, in exchange for his soul, offers Moon seven wishes in order to win Margaret's heart.

Finally, rebuffed by Moon, Spiggott's concluding rant sees him promise to visit all the ruinous miseries of modernity on earth. 'I'll fill it full of concrete runways, motorways, aircraft, television and automobiles, advertising, plastic flowers and frozen food, supersonic bangs. I'll make it so noisy and disgusting that even you'll be ashamed of yourself.' *Bedazzled* is the essence of 1967; it exudes halcyon, Carnaby Street chic. Cook's bleak vision of what is to come does foreshadow the functional mediocrity of life in the seventies, from instant mashed potato to rising pollution. Once the promise and magic of the sixties had petered out, Peter Cook would rather peter out too. It's as if his visionary genius was anticipating a decline to come.

The first taste of failure Cook would experience was with his chat show, *Where Do I Sit?*, in 1971. For someone as apparently effortless as Cook, a chat show should have been a cinch. However, it did not go well. He was no Frost, and was exposed as unversed in the discreet arts required to maintain the deskbound blandness of a smooth-running talk show. *Where Do I Sit?* was panned. In the retrospective phase of his career, Cook was fond of telling the story of having Kirk Douglas on as a guest and, meaning to ask him,

'How are you?' instead blurted, 'Who are you?' Cook was at his best answering questions, taking them like a ball and dribbling off down surreal mazes.

Self-confidence was key to Cook's humour. Dudley Moore was a paragon of self-deprecation. Cook never went in for that. While not arrogant and disliking arrogance in others, he never belittled himself in his comedy. He was always coolly Olympian. But with his self-confidence affected by the failure of *Where Do I Sit?*, Cook's drinking increased. Boozing affected his relationship with Moore and dissipated the application required to maintain him at the highest levels of showbusiness.

He continued working over his remaining years, but his projects had a fitful frivolity about them. A Holmes and Watson film with Dudley Moore; the surly host of a post-punk TV series, *Revolver*; a speaking role on a concept triple album by former 10cc artists Godley and Creme; playing Richard III in *The Black Adder*, the first and least successful of the series. He was supplanted by former juniors: John Cleese and the Monty Python crew; Bill Oddie, even.

However, Cook never forgot how to be funny. He would still pop up with his Macmillan imitation ('Millions unemployed. Millions more out of work'). He was always a fine chat-show guest, correcting Michael Parkinson, for example, when he asked the boxer John Conteh if he obeyed the rule about not having sex before a fight ('It's no sex during a fight'). The *Derek and Clive* series, albums based on recordings made by him and Dudley Moore which were initially put about by word of mouth for the private amusement of those in the know, were, initially at least, masterclasses in the verbal martial art of foul-mouthedness. Take this exchange: '. . . And he comes back, "You fucking cunt" . . . I said, "You fucking cunt" . . . I said, "You cunt . . . you fucking cunt" . . . and the cunt come back with, "You fucking cunt – I said, "You calling me a cunt you fucking cunt?"' As a rhythmical exercise in minimalist delivery and parody of empty male belligerence, it's fucking unmatched.

As the eighties and nineties progressed, Cook's own life, a chaotic, drunken, jolly affair, became his most potent form of comedy. In 1986, a long-time foe of the *Eye*, the irascible, thin-skinned and litigious *Daily Mirror* proprietor Robert Maxwell, was attempting to produce a rival publication to the magazine, entitled *Not Private Eye*. Cook hatched a plan to purloin the dummy first edition. First, he sent over a crate of whisky to the production team putting the magazine together. Then he put in a follow-up call to the team to confirm receipt of the whisky, and that the team were utterly smashed. He and a gang from the *Eye*, including Ian Hislop, then took a cab down to the *Mirror* buildings. There, Cook charmed and breezed his way past security. He and the *Eye* crew then headed for Maxwell's suite, where the pages of the dummy were conveniently strewn. Cook settled himself in the absent Maxwell's chair and put a call through to him, inviting him to guess where he was. An enraged Maxwell at once called his security, ordering them to eject the trespassers immediately, but when they arrived, Cook smothered them with charm and alcohol, and they, too, joined the party. The *Eye* then showed the dummy of *Not Private Eye* to W. H. Smith, persuading them that an image in it depicting Richard Ingrams as Hitler was libellous. *Not Private Eye* was duly sunk, as was Maxwell in 1991, the most high-profile victim of the 'Curse of Gnome', the misfortune that awaited all *Eye* litigants.

There were rampages around town. Stephen Fry recalled being with Cook late one evening when he was denied access to Stringfellows on account of the nightclub's strict dress code. 'Give up my lucky trainers? Are you mad?' retorted Cook to the doorman. On a more melancholic note, he would, late at night, among the other calls to friends he was wont to make, phone up a late-night chat show on LBC in the guise of Sven, a sad Norwegian fisherman, another projection of his own fundamental depression and loneliness, which his code as a comedian and repressed member of the British upper classes prohibited him from being candid about. Here was a man who did not merely detest boredom; he feared it, sought to submerge it in booze. It doesn't feel right to pity Cook. His legacy is enormous, his talent never dimmed. He was not just a comedian but one of the authors of the 1960s, in his handsomeness, charm, the glamorous and well-booted cut of his jib, his style, his sexual frisson. He was the first of a new sort of creature – handsome in both body and wit, self-assured, non-deferential, acutely alive to the abiding, archaic absurdities of his country and unafraid to point them out. All modern comedy, not just satire, owes him a debt for the possibilities of being he opened up. His legacy can be found in the work of, for example, the late Sean Lock, who, like Cook, was taken far too soon, aged fifty-eight. During his final days in a hospice, when asked what it was like, Lock answered, 'It's all right actually, and the sex is amazing.' Cook would have approved.

Still, there was always a crucial lack of strenuousness about the man. Things happened as a matter of natural course, or not at all. And so his 'decline' was a merry one; he was, if not free from sadness, a walking antidote to sadness. He left the world a better place than when he entered it, not because he changed the world but because he existed in it.

Although Cook and Moore cut an obvious contrast to each other, Alan Bennett was still more antithetical to Cook. It wasn't just Bennett's humble origins – he was raised in Leeds as a butcher's boy, who went on to do exceptionally well at grammar school. Unlike Cook, who tended to avert his eyes from his own backstory, Bennett meditated penetratingly and publicly on his background and upbringing, from the cobblestone perspective rather than peering down like Cook. Although his was not a traumatic upbringing, the solace he took in books spoke of a boy who did not see his future in butchery. And yet, throughout his life, Bennett seemed to have one foot in the past, retaining homes in both Yorkshire and London, prone to such wistful, detailed reminiscence about his childhood (memories of Otley, Filey, Nidderdale) and adolescence as to leave him a hostage to parodists. But this wasn't Proust's madeleine cakes replaced with Hovis. Bennett saw in his family a microcosm of the English character: its diffidence, the strange bathos of its humdrum cadences, its mass of small taboos, its craven sense of class distinction, its vulnerability to embarrassment; also, a longing to leave one's surroundings, the place in which one has been set down, but a feeling of being overcome by anxiety when the chance to do so occurs. And, like the Catholic sense of original sin, the British sense of original shame. 'Every family has a secret,' remarked Bennett in the documentary *Dinner at Noon* (1988). 'And the secret is that it's not like other families.'

After his *Fringe* days, Bennett departed quickly from satire as such. 'I've a dreadful feeling I may have thought I was doing some good,' he said. Which is not to say he did not make some brilliant contributions; he could hardly have held his own in the quartet if he hadn't been capable of such routines as 'The Aftermyth of War', in which, stiff-legged à la Douglas Bader, he delivered a monologue that glided elegantly through every trope and cliché common to the black and white, airbrushed, almost nostalgic version of the conflict presented in films like *Reach for the Sky*. He would go on to cast a broader beam, surveying the English condition, sometimes with affection, sometimes with loathing, but knowing it was a condition that he shared. He satirised his North London neighbours, the 'Knocker Threws', in a 1966 TV special *On the Margin*, and, though he was not a product of it, the public school system in 1968's *Forty Years On*. Increasingly, however, he dwelt on his Northern origins for inspiration. *Dinner at Noon* alluded to the Northern habit of not taking lunch and then supper, but dinner during the day and then a more modest repast, tea, in the evening, often no more than a snack. When Bennett became well to do enough to take his parents out for meals, they would find the prospect daunting, whether trying to navigate the wine list or wondering, as Bennett's mother once did, whether they might have a simple poached egg on toast. These small observations of the inhibited nervousness of the British class system are the sort the loftier Cook would be unlikely to notice or personally feel.

When he was much younger, Bennett would be mortified by his parents' little gaffes, all born out of a fear of undue airs and graces, of 'putting it on'. It wasn't long, however, before he came to harvest them for material. Moreover, the unease that Bennett himself might be 'putting it on' with his Oxbridge chums prompted him to alight on what he describes as his 'own voice', one he has maintained throughout the decades: unabashedly Northern, creased and crinkled with his formative experiences.

There is a duality about Bennett highlighted in *The Lady in the Van* (2015), starring Maggie Smith as Mary Shepherd, the elderly, eccentric woman on whom Bennett took pity and whom he allowed to stay in her filthy van in his driveway, a kindness she exploited without gratitude till her dying day. There are two 'Bennetts' played by Alex Jennings: his actual self – fretful, trying to do the right thing, entangled in the daily doings, excremental or otherwise, of Miss Shepherd – and his 'writer self', who is fully conscious of what good material all this mayhem makes for. The very sense of guilt that prompts Bennett to introduce this device is similar to the advanced sense of liberal guilt that makes him take in Miss Shepherd in the first place – as if, being of humble stock, he is unentitled to the comforts and privileges of 'getting on' and must pay a penance.

Bennett delights in people who, as was said of the characters of Charles Dickens, 'are themselves', uninhibited, in no way stricken by his own particular consciousness and the attendant discomfiture it sometimes brought, whether it was Peter Cook or Miss Shepherd, a woman of absolutely fixed opinions and wholly unburdened by any regard for the feelings of others. Or there was his friend Russell Harty, whose cheek, self-interest and flamboyance were so against his own nature but which he could not help but admire. He told the story of Harty driving him around town in an expensive Jaguar and occasionally tooting at an old lady at a bus stop and waving cheerily to her:

She would instinctively wave back and, as we drove on, one would see her gazing after us, wondering who among her scant acquaintance had a cream-coloured Jaguar. 'Brought a bit of interest into her life,' he would say, and that was as far as he got towards a philosophy; that most people are prisoners in their lives and want releasing, even if it's only for a wave at the bus-stop.

Women, often old women, and often queens, figure heavily and empathetically in Bennett's writings. There are lovely encounters, amid the more high-minded reflections on churches, art and politics in the diaries, such as this one from 1989, in which he temporarily thinks he has stumbled on a kindred spirit. He is accosted by a woman who tells him her sob story of being put in a hotel by the council with her three kids. 'They said they'd send me my books, but they haven't.' After giving her his spare change, Bennett sympathises, but then realises 'she is not talking about her treasured copies of Anthony Burgess but her social security books'. What do books mean? the author ruefully reflects.

As for queens, there is little need to watch the Netflix history *The Crown*, since Elizabeth II is so much more brilliantly imagined in the scene in Bennett's *A Question of Attribution* (1988, filmed 1991), in which she is played by Prunella Scales, who, finding herself 'kicking one's heels' one afternoon, stops by to chat to the traitorous Sir Anthony Blunt (James Fox), surveyor of the queen's pictures. Bennett, a monarchist by temperament, invests Elizabeth with an imperiously dry wit, one cultivated, perhaps, to amuse herself in her gilded cage of undemonstrative dutifulness. For Bennett, the queen was, in her own way, stuck in her place in the class scheme of things, much like his own mother.

Forty Years On, *Prick Up Your Ears*, *The History Boys*, monologues like *A Cream Cracker Under the Settee*: Bennett has created the most impressive body of work of the *Fringe* boys. In the TV play *A Day Out* (1972), set in the summer of 1911 and featuring a cycling club on a day trip, the leader of the club warns his *compadres* as he traipses ahead of them across cowpatted rural terrain to watch out: 'This field's in a disgusting state.' But Bennett's humour is overshadowed by larger, cloudier themes; in this play, we learn that most of the club members perished in the Great War a few years later. Again, Bennett's intimacy with the ways, attitudes, odd phrases and small aspirations of the sort of folk who would have joined this cycling club combines well with his ability to pan back and look at the wider sweep of history. These weren't mere matchstick men.

Bennett has been much parodied. When Mrs Thatcher stood down, he recalled being asked for his thoughts by the *Guardian*. He offered some words, which, he noticed, were prefaced in the final copy by the phrase 'ooh 'eck', words he hadn't offered the journalist, and all subsequent aitches were dropped in his comments. But beneath the caricature there has always been about him a seriousness, a steeliness, a resolve on which he has always delivered. In his eulogy to Russell Harty, who died of hepatitis in 1988, there were jokes, but the most searing passage was a rebuke to the tabloids that hounded the entertainer even as he lay dying. 'One saw at that time in the tireless and unremitting efforts of the team at St James's [hospital] the best of which we are capable, and in the equally tireless, though rather better rewarded efforts of the journalists, the worst.' Bennett may be victim to a mass of small guilty feelings, but he has always known who the real guilty are, and the scale of their guilt.

The history of British satire is a male-dominated one, as if the radical impulse required to be actively feminist was considered inimical to the true satirist, antennae quivering with mirth at the attendant seriousness of feminism. For years, for example, *Private Eye* ran a series entitled 'The Naked Cow', in which readers were invited to submit such 'loony feminist nonsense' as placenta stew. For the *Eye*, such earnestness was as worthy of derision as Tory corruption.

From the outset, there was an unexamined assumption that satire, like darts, rugby or driving fast cars, was a young man's game.

Women's involvement in the genre was too often to embody male fantasies under the pretext of 'liberation' as the new decade dawned. Little was made, or attempted to be made, of women's own possible self-determination – what was funny about that? – and their lack of any scriptwriting role assured that remained the case.

'The girls are clever and personable but they are not encouraged to be funny,' observed the critic Kenneth Tynan on a first viewing of *Beyond the Fringe*. It was an acute observation. Jonathan Miller, recalling those halcyon years, referred to them as 'mini-skirted', and regarded the era as being as much about the discovery of sex, a male discovery of female objects, as it was about defying the authority of the Lord Chamberlain. Peter Cook had at one point fantasised about a running joke in the *Fringe* that would involve a naked Julie Christie walking occasionally across the stage, saying nothing.

However, the few women who did manage to find a berth in the Satire Boom proved themselves lifelong creative forces to be reckoned with. Millicent Martin's role in *That Was the Week That Was*, if not merely decorative, was restricted to providing a certain jazz glamour to proceedings. She was later given her own series, *Mainly Millicent* (1964–6), which featured a somewhat prescient spoof in which she played opposite Roger Moore in a James Bond sketch, with Moore playing 007. In 1970, she starred in *From a Bird's Eye View*, an ambitious, if ultimately unsuccessful, British–American series in which she played an air stewardess alongside Peter Jones. The opening episode was written by T. E. B. Clarke, an old Ealing stalwart who scripted *The Lavender Hill Mob*. He could take kudos for one scene, in which Martin is the object of some unwelcome lecherous attention from a male passenger. The prim older woman sitting next to the passenger bridles in disgust and demands to change seat. It's not the passenger she wants to get away from, however, but Martin. 'No nice young lady would allow a man to talk to her like that.' Her comic talents received belated recognition when she was cast as Gertrude, Daphne's mother, in *Frasier*.

There were other exceptions. There was Caryl Brahms, the ballet and theatre critic who along with Ned Sherrin co-wrote the elegantly topical lyrics to *That Was the Week That Was*'s title song. She had previously co-written with S. J. Simon a series of comic thrillers, including *A Bullet in the Ballet*. And there was Eleanor Bron.

Speaking to *Varsity*, the Cambridge University newspaper, in 2014, Bron told the story of going on a date. When he asked her what qualities she liked in a man, she reversed the common trope and said that she liked a man whom she could make laugh. As for what he wished for in a woman, he said, 'A voice that is "soft, gentle and low"' – the qualities King Lear declared to be 'excellent in a woman'. And so, for the rest of the date, she spoke in an ever softer, gentler, lower voice. She made him laugh.

Bron has been a deceptively soft, gentle, low presence in British comedy ever since 1959, when she joined the Cambridge Footlights revue entitled *The Last Laugh*, co-starring with Peter Cook. She was the first ever woman to do so – previously, women had been played by men in drag. (Sadly, if she broke down Cambridge's barriers for women, they were later re-erected. In 2014, Bron complained that the current Footlights tour consisted only of men.)

Even when playing a ditzy debutante, Lady Pamela Stitty, in shows like *Not So Much a Programme, More a Way of Life* (1964–5), she insisted she was never 'token'. Though she is impeccably beautiful, impeccably well spoken, there is about Bron a certain intensity, a dark, penetrating gaze which undoes the complacency of the beheld and lends itself well to the scrutinising element of satire, self-scrutinising or otherwise. However, her fundamental seriousness – excellent, if not essential, in a comedian – led her to hanker after roles with more gravitas.

She gave more to her more famous film roles than they gave back to her, except in terms of exposure. She lent some class to the Beatles' *Help!* (1965), a thoroughly daft film whose narrative structure was determined by the locations the Fab Four fancied holidaying in, as the high priestess Ahme. Meanwhile, in *Bedazzled*, as Margaret Spencer, she brought substance to her Cook-created role as an object of desire. She observed that perhaps the reason she had not made the wholly successful transition from comedy to 'high' drama was that it was considered far more delightful for serious actors like Judi Dench to perform comic roles than it was for comic actors like herself to trek in the opposite direction – an uphill struggle from 'low' to 'high'. It was certainly a disappointment to her when she received a call from Ken Tynan and, expecting to be called to the National Theatre, learned that he wanted her to appear in the sex-related revue *Oh! Calcutta!*

Bron was able to enjoy some degree of success as a serious actor, but thankfully she always kept her hand in comedy over the decades, even if there is a feeling that she was under-regarded by a wider audience. The likes of John Bird and John Wells, however, understood her abilities, with Wells regarding her as being as capable in her inventiveness as Peter Cook. Some of her early revue work is strikingly clever and well turned even by current standards, including a sketch in which she played a nervous young postgraduate being seen home after her first date with an equally nervous young man played by John Fortune. Their dialogue is an exquisitely naturalistic study in sexual shyness and longing.

Although emblematic of the 1960s, she shone intermittently in the 1970s. She did a marvellous turn at *The Secret Policeman's Ball* (1979), playing a chatty, guilt-ridden but incorrigible middle-class woman in conversation with God: 'I am guilty of the sin of anger towards my sister . . . this is my younger sister Janice, the one who lives outside Watford – but thou knowest which sister I mean . . .' In 1979, she even made a brief appearance alongside John Cleese in a Douglas Adams-scripted episode of *Doctor Who*, swaddled in a mauve scarf-cum-turban, as a pair of art appreciators in a gallery taking in the TARDIS, temporarily parked there, which they assume to be an exhibit. She remarks how the TARDIS's line and colour are 'curiously counterpointed by the redundant vestiges of its function'.

In the 1990s, she was one of the many guests to appear in *Absolutely Fabulous*: she played Patsy's mother (a figment of Patsy's distorted recollection) as a monstrous aesthete, a gorgon-cum-earth mother surrounded by dancers, poets and bereted women playing guitar in a European garret.

Bron once said that during the Satire Boom she was less interested in politics than things like class and the relationship between the sexes. 'I find it comic. But then, I find most of the civil service comic,' says her under-secretary character in a *Yes Minister* episode from 1982 regarding the woeful shortage of female under-secretaries. And yet her political views have always been explicitly left of centre – she rejoined the Labour Party in 2015 solely to vote for Jeremy Corbyn – and far more deeply felt and unwavering than those of some of her more overtly political but flippantly noncommittal colleagues.

STEPTOE AND SON AND, AT LAST, THE WORKING CLASSES

Hancock had been unable to find a place for himself in the swinging, sexy, satirical sixties; he felt like a grey, almost ghostly anachronism of a dead past. He mistakenly felt that he needed a change of script-writers. But while Hancock withered, his ex-writers Galton and Simpson flourished. *Steptoe and Son* originated as *The Offer*, one of six Comedy Playhouse pilots they made for the BBC in 1962. It emerged fully formed. Here was a comedy very much of the sixties, an era of political enlightenment, the era of Labour, in which the working classes, their hopes, aspirations, dreams and disappoint-ments, would at last be given a proper, sympathetic hearing. And yet this was also a decade in which the material promises and sexual fantasies of a new year were tantalisingly remote for many. Moreover, the old bitterly refused to let go, refused to die, clung desperately to the shirt tails of the young, failed to let them take flight, kept them in their 'place'. Times were a-changing but also staying very much the same. All of this was embodied in the father–son relationship central to *Steptoe and Son* – a comedy of contrasts, of bonded conflicting opposites, which could be deeply touching, almost tragic at times in a way Hancock never was.

Harold Steptoe, played by Harry H. Corbett, did have aspects in common with Hancock: a desire for self-improvement, a feeling that he was cut out for better things and a manner of speaking that floated into the pretentious high registers of the cultivated, before tumbling back down to the natural, earthy tones of a London rag-and-bone man.

The taboo of accent as a signifier of class status or worth has been fought against in our own time with some success. In the 1960s, however, the necessity of well-spokenness as a condition for 'getting on' held firm sway. England manager Alf Ramsey, Beatles producer George Martin and Radiophonic Workshop pioneer Delia Derbyshire were among those who felt obliged to lose their regional accents if they hoped to enjoy career success and be taken seriously. (Derbyshire, incidentally, is most famous for her electronic arrangement of the *Doctor Who* theme, written by Ron Grainer, also responsible for the *Steptoe and Son* theme.) Listening to them today, Ramsey's and Derbyshire's accents in particular sound oddly deliberate and contrived. Harold Steptoe's wonderfully idiosyncratic accent is a comic exaggeration of this tendency, attempting to take flight like a clumsy fowl, in stark contrast to the unapologetic bog-coarseness of his old man.

Born in 1925, Corbett had been just old enough to serve in World War II. According to his daughter, he had killed two Japanese in New Guinea while on service, a reluctant depth of experience of which he rarely spoke. Like Harold, he lost his mother early, when he was aged eighteen months, while his father died in 1943. He began working life in Joan Littlewood's Theatre Workshop, an eager participant in all the backstage *Sturm und Drang* that came with the Stanislavski method. He was described as an 'actor's actor', a British Brando, perhaps. That he should have ended up playing in a sitcom set in a rag-and-bone yard is thought by some to mirror the thwarted ambitions of Harold Steptoe – but no one put a gun to his head to force him to return, series after series. Moreover, when it came to comedy, Brando was no Corbett.

Corbett's first meeting with Galton and Simpson followed their seeing him in a production of *Macbeth* at the Old Vic. After five days of rehearsal as Harold, Corbett was puzzled to see seats arranged in the TV studio. They're for the audience, Galton and Simpson explained. 'Audience?' he replied; and then, with the solemnity that would become a trademark of the character, he said, 'I shall have to rethink my entire performance.'

While there was some overlap between Harry H. Corbett and Harold Steptoe, this was not the case with Wilfrid Brambell, who played the wizened, seedy, manipulative father, Albert. Brambell was a dapper fellow, Irish by birth, his career surviving a conditional discharge in 1962 for 'persistently importuning' at a Shepherd's Bush public lavatory. Only thirteen years older than Corbett, he played men older than he was – Paul McCartney's grandfather in *A Hard Day's Night* (1964), for example – but without much make-up. Audiences could plausibly accept, as in the episode 'Homes Fit for Heroes' (1963), that, aged fifty, he could play a character who were being put in an old people's home.

Whereas Hancock's failures were down to his own incompetence, Harold is frustrated by the very man who should have been a mentor to him – his own father, who is terrified of being left alone and with no scruples about playing the guilt card. Driven by fear that Harold's aspirations to make something of himself will lead him to fly the nest, Albert undermines and belittles Harold at every turn, showering him in constant, caustic discouragement.

Galton and Simpson were keen to have a serious actor play the role of Harold. Although Hancock's career ended in tragedy, there is always about his character a fundamental lack of seriousness, even when he embodies the ennui of post-war Britain. Nor is he sentimental. Tears do not belong in the comic world of Hancock, and you're glad of that. Nor did romance. Hancock has his amorous moments, but generally he makes little real effort to attract women. Hancock the actor laid down an edict that his character should be regarded as female-repellent.

Harold's disappointments, however, excite real tears. When Hercules the horse dies, or when Harold fails in his futile effort to pull his cartful of possessions out of the yard in 'The Offer' (1962), a 'stone me, what a life' won't do – Corbett draws deeply on his thespian training. The violin soundtrack weeps for him, in a manner similar to the soundtrack to the closing scenes of *Schindler's List*. His yearning for a girlfriend, to 'pull a bird', is sexist yet deeply moving. Unlike Hancock, he is, his bent nose apart, a handsome young man, willing to put the sartorial effort in for the romantic cause. But all the perfumes of Araby can't conceal the inescapable stench of his rag-and-bone prison and his father, the jailer.

Harold Steptoe is thirty-seven in 1962, the same age as Corbett. However, over the next fourteen years, he would age only a further two years. He would be beset by the same thwarted desires, the same frustration at being denied his right to enjoy the best years of his life, the same feeling of being humiliatingly left behind as the sixties swung and the seventies soared. And yet millions of viewers identified with Harold – perhaps because of the singular absurdity of his domestic situation. Who isn't familiar with the feeling that whatever is embarrassing about our upbringing is unique to us, making it all the more humiliating? That is Harold's lot – he carries a burden peculiar to him.

Concurrently with the Beatles, *Steptoe and Son* was an overnight sensation, as much a harbinger of the new decade as the Fab Four. The only difference was, whereas they were getting action, Harold was longing for it.

Aficionados of *Steptoe and Son*, as with Hancock, have long suspected that had Galton and Simpson subtracted all the gags, it would be taken more seriously, with Harry H. Corbett, in this harrowing, contemporary drama about the ties that bind, lauded at last as the finest actor of the British stage. None of that, thankfully. For all its finesse, audiences revelled in the coarseness of old man Steptoe, which constantly offended Harold's nostrils, and Harold's own linguistic coarseness when berating him. *Steptoe and Son*'s dialogue boasted a pungent topsoil of invective that fell just short of swearing: 'bleedin'', 'sod', 'cobblers', 'knackered', 'bog', 'pillock', 'toerag', 'grotty'. Later on, the occasional testicular reference was allowed – Albert's Christmas puddings were 'black as a gorilla's goolies' – while the first *Steptoe and Son* movie (1972) features a very satisfying 'wankers'. There is also the Scrabble board in 'Men of Letters' (1972), which freeze-frame technology reveals to contain the words 'bum', 'spunk', 'cock', 'tit', 'privit', 'bristols', 'vibrators', 'rape' and 'crumpet' – a 'display of calculated filth', laid down by the old man to Harold's disgust.

Then there's the set – the outdoor khazi, the interior bric-a-brac, the optics filled with dregs from the rounds, the detritus of a hundred years or so, the skeleton, a constant reminder of death. Only Harold's bureau provides sanctuary. In the gentrified world of the twenty-first century, the Steptoes might be considered to be living in real-estate paradise: a large, detached, West London address whimsically furnished with a riot of antiques; scratch out 'Steptoe', think Mumford & Sons. In 1962, however, the emphasis was on the modern, the plastic, the plywood panel to conceal unsightly Victorian fireplaces. 24 Oil Drum Lane was regarded with shuddering, hideous pleasure by a society increasingly steeped in mod cons.

Take 'The Bath' (1963), in which Albert is abluting in a tin tub in the sitting room, barely minutes before Harold's latest 'bird' is due to arrive. Albert, accompanying his bath with pickles, drops some of them in his bathwater. He reaches into the water and retrieves one from his rectal orifice, presumably, given his expression, and puts the remainder back in the jar.

Albert undermines his son's romantic aspirations, but in 'The Stepmother' the boot is on the other foot. Albert brings home a lady friend, only to find Harold sullenly resentful at his prospective mother replacement. 'My mum could cook a steak and kidney pudding,' he jeers, turning his nose up at her own burnt offering to his sensibilities.

Here, Harold's voice takes one of its many turns: he assumes the tones of a small boy, still doting on his late mother, whose inability to commence an adult life has left him developmentally arrested. He is impeded by immaturity, as well as class, from making his way in the world. There is no voice quite like Harold's, one that reflects the range of his turmoil, fluttering about like a caged bird, the uniqueness of his circumstances reflected in the distinctiveness of its tones. His frequent variations on the word 'dirty', as in 'you dirty old man', slither from 'duutty' to 'dzzzirty' or even 'zirty', as if in proclaiming the word, he is indulging in one of the few little pleasures available to him, like savouring a liquorice allsort.

Galton and Simpson strove for a degree of naturalism with *Steptoe and Son*, but by twenty-first-century standards, it falls short. They were not interested in depicting the reality of life on a London 'totter'; they were interested in character and situation. There are frequent implications that Oil Drum Lane and its environs have become predominantly occupied by ethnic minorities in recent years. Albert is particularly and unfortunately prone to pointing this out. However, these minorities make only fleeting, non-speaking appearances in *Steptoe*: a bus conductor; a landlady in St Stephen's Gardens in West London, then part of a run-down bedsitland where Harold takes temporary, pathetic lodgings, today a road in which properties exchange hands for £3 million. It's a shame Galton and Simpson did not create Black characters, allow them to speak, rather than be othered, alluded to, *in absentia*, as 'wogs' by the racist old man with whom some of *Steptoe*'s audience would have had a more than sneaking sympathy. In mitigation, unlike Hancock, there are hardly any recurring characters in *Steptoe and Son*. It is essentially about Harold and Albert alone, marooned from wider society.

Politics features frequently in *Steptoe and Son*. In 1964, Harold Wilson asked the BBC to put the show on at a later hour, after the polling stations had closed, so that Labour voters would not be tempted to stay home and watch *Steptoe* rather than vote. The BBC refused; Labour won, just. Although affronted by Wilson's request, which they regarded as insulting to working-class people, Galton and Simpson were committed socialists, albeit not without an ear for the long-winded tendencies of left-wing idealists. Harold is Labour, as was Corbett himself, his father Conservative, doubtless a dynamic that was played out up and down the country in sixties Britain. 'You're a traitor to the working class,' Harold tells his father. 'I'm not working class!' protests Albert. 'That's right,' reflects Harold. 'You're a ponce.'

In 'My Old Man's a Tory' (1965), Harold hosts a meeting of the Labour Party, in the hope of being put up as a candidate for the local council. Harold votes Labour not so much out of solidarity but because theirs is the intellectually superior political position. Moreover, he fantasises about political soirées, hobnobbing with cabinet ministers, 'choice wines, superb food'. However, Harold's bid is unsuccessful. Anticipating the era of Mandelson and Blair, of guacamole rather than mushy peas Labour, the local rep explains to Harold that the demographic of the area is swinging towards the middle class. 'The cloth cap image has worked against us in such areas.' And so, yet another kick in the teeth for Harold, the sort he takes on a per-episode basis. Albert has refused to leave the living room throughout the meeting, but for all his awfulness as a father there are moments when blood is thicker – and this is one of them. 'I know which way your seat would swing if I put my boot up it!' he snarls at the rep.

For all Harold's failures, *Steptoe and Son* was, in line with a good deal of the monochrome drama of its era, successful in putting working people centre stage, rather than as mere comic underlings in long brown coats who delivered cheek but never showed any ambition to rise above their underling status. Although its second phase coincided with Edward Heath's Conservative administration, it was broadcast in an era in which Harold Wilson and Labour were establishing themselves as a force to be reckoned with, one in which the rights and demands of working people to be heard and understood were gathering strength, their frustrations and predicaments given a fair hearing.

As writer Robert Ross has observed, one of Galton and Simpson's great innovations with *Steptoe and Son* was to allow working-class characters to 'instigate the humour' rather than be the occasional butt of it. This would eventually be taken for granted, and, by later, more nuanced standards, *Steptoe* might seem broad. However, it's instructive to look back, for example, at 1940s and 1950s Pathé news documentaries, about railwaymen and the like, to see what reluctance there was to allow the working classes their own voice. In these documentaries, over silent footage of the workmen, a narrative is supplied by the plummy Pathé narrator, assuming the less refined accent of the lower orders and giving a version of their thoughts as they go about their business, rather than resorting to the dangerous precedent of allowing them to speak for themselves and goodness knows what dirt to come tumbling from their mouths.

After *Steptoe*, a deluge of working-class comedy – beginning with *The Likely Lads* (1964–6), scripted by Dick Clement and Ian La Frenais. They sympathised with the Galton and Simpson ethos – 'All the best sitcoms are about people who are trapped in certain situations,' remarked Clement. Like Galton and Simpson, they met young, in a pub in Notting Hill, while Clement was struggling to make a living writing radio sketches, and remained lifelong working partners, having struck up an immediate synergy which is evident when you interview them. Profoundly influenced by Galton and Simpson, they wished to reflect the shifting social order of the 1960s – not least the gap between aspiration and reality.

The Likely Lads was first broadcast in 1964. Set in the Northeast, it stars Rodney Bewes as Bob Ferris and James Bolam as Terry Collier, factory workers and best friends since the Scouts. As with *Steptoe*, it tapped unexpectedly into the decisively shifting, transformative mood of the early sixties.

The Likely Lads' credits sequence betrays a devil-may-care laddishness which wouldn't sit well today – the boys cycling down a towpath, Terry arrogantly discarding a cigarette into a canal. Though they are best friends, they are antithetical characters who take a malicious pleasure in each other's misfortunes. Terry is the cannier, worldlier of the two, with a youthful swagger that belies his dubiously sourced, conservative views ('It's a well-known fact . . .'). Bob is more naive, more inept, fatuous and flabby-faced but more aspirational. In 'Rocker' (1966), Bob puts a down payment on a motorbike, seeking to get a toehold in 1960s mobility. However, the bike he purchases is no Vespa but a nondescript affair, his helmet a pitifully unmod-ish 1930s throwback. Bob's road skills are abysmal – he crashes the motorbike twice in a week and is outdistanced in a race by Terry on his bicycle. And yet you always sense that Bob will get on in the world, not Terry, if only because he wants it more.

The first series of *The Likely Lads* ends with Bob persuaded by two older hands that he could make a life for himself in the army. He joins up, only to be rejected because of his flat feet. Terry, meanwhile, has decided to sign up himself, to keep Bob company. He is accepted and, to his horror, ends up being shipped off, while Bob remains at home. The sundering of their partnership felt like the breakdown of the early, Who-like, mod-ish moment of British self-confidence. The sixties would transmogrify in their absence.

QUEER COMEDY AND *CARRY ON*

Albeit discreetly, British comedy was not entirely preoccupied with the heterosexual longings of *Steptoe* and *The Likely Lads*. Julian and Sandy, two strikingly flamboyant characters, featured in *Round the Horne*, first broadcast in 1965. I would say 'gay', except at the radio series' end in 1968, they were revealed to be married men. *Round the Horne* starred Kenneth Horne and featured a cast of characters, including sometime 'gaiety girl' Beatrice, Daphne Whitethigh (a parody of TV cook Fanny Cradock) and Rambling Syd Rumpo, a warbler of seemingly suggestive, actually nonsensical rustic ditties. However, it was Julian and Sandy, played by Hugh Paddick and Kenneth Williams, both gay, who were the real stars, running florid rings around the seemingly oblivious Horne. Ostensibly out-of-work actors, they cropped up in sketches as lawyers, booksellers, but always themselves, interweaving a richly delicious seam of double entendres, audacious insinuations about gay activity and outright use of Polari, a code used by gay men at a time when homosexual relations were illegal in the UK. These included 'bona' (good, with the added bonus of a homophonic relationship to the word 'boner') and 'vada' (look, or see). When Horne approaches the pair, as lawyers, to ask if they will take on his case, Julian replies, 'Well, it depends on what it is. We've got a criminal practice that takes up most of our time.'

Julian and Sandy's dialogue bristles with suggestion, even when it wasn't clear to those listening on the wireless exactly what was being suggested. At one point, Horne chides them for their choice of words. 'The audience may have seen a secondary meaning.' 'Secondary meaning?' jeers Sandy. 'They don't even see the first meaning.'

Also left to the imagination was the physical appearance of Julian and Sandy, their outré bodily and sartorial language, as implied in the swoop and swerve of the delivery of their lines. *Round the Horne* exploited the limited dimensionality of the radio, but transferred less well to the small screen. That said, many of the gales of laughter at the recordings of *Round the Horne* were at Williams's facial comedy at the microphone, which might occasionally have bewildered listeners at home. According to Williams, however, by 1968, writer Barry Took felt it was taking a 'filthy' turn: 'We might as well write a series called *Get Your Cock Out*.'

Was the show a boon for Britain's gay community, who, at the time of Julian and Sandy, were struggling to attain legality, let alone for their voices to be heard? There was certainly a jubilation and vivacity about the pair that could not be denied, which left Horne as the 'straight' man sounding very straight indeed. They represented also, as writer Paul Baker suggested, a refreshing change from the customary depiction of gay men in serious cinema or high drama as afflicted or doomed by their sexuality, like Dirk Bogarde in *Victim* (1961).

Granted, Julian and Sandy's dialogue was written by heterosexual men, principally Barry Took and Marty Feldman. At least Paddick and Williams themselves were gay, however, and could bring that authenticity to the parts; better that than, say, Dick Emery (or sundry Python members) doing their received, mincing, 'Hello, honky-tonk, how are you?' voice. The use of Polari added a sense of authenticity, though their 'outing' of the code was perhaps less helpful.

Despite his struggles to reconcile himself with his own sexuality, Kenneth Williams exudes an absolute ease in *Round the Horne*. He would attain wider fame, however, much to his own chagrin, in the *Carry On* series, which would dominate British film comedy in the 1960s. Williams castigated the films for their 'vulgarity', but what was most insidious about them, at their worst, was their underlying ethos.

Carry On was a different, tamer animal in its first few years, when Norman Hudis was on writing duties, before he was lured to the American TV market. The *Carry On* title had a dual meaning: on the one hand, a carry-on, as in a bit of a bawdy romp, a weekend charabanc adventure; but carry on also in the sense of the Keep Calm and Carry On injunction on those war posters which were to be put up in the event of a German invasion.

The earliest films, including *Carry On Sergeant*, *Carry On Cruising*, *Carry On Cabbie* and *Carry On Spying*, generally involved a bunch of improbable incompetents, featuring Charles Hawtrey, Kenneth Connor and Barbara Windsor, recruited in some capacity or other, suffering multiple mishaps but with admirable determination getting there in the end. These capers are mild by the later, spicier standards of *Carry On*. There are even moments of tear-jerking sentimentality and decency, as in *Carry On Teacher* (1959).

Kenneth Williams appears in these early films, young, rounder-faced, smirking and twitching with suppressed insolence in the face of his immediate superior, often played by an irascible, sergeant major-ish Sid James (the captain in *Carry On Cruising*) with Williams dishing out cheek rather than being affronted by it.

There are aspects of early *Carry On* that are consistent with the 'golden age' movies of the sixties and seventies: the opening themes, generally composed by Eric Rogers, whose scores had a British trad-jazz, gorblimey, racy feel to them, setting up the promise of what was to follow; bawdiness, but nothing too near the knuckle; and not a hint of rock and roll and the degeneracy and bad kind of permissiveness it threatened. However, it was in 1964, with the Technicolor splendour of *Carry On Cleo*, that *Carry On* was truly reborn. Hereafter, the films, scripted by Talbot Rothwell, lurched merrily from one wordplay gag to the next. *Carry On Cleo* has some belters: Caesar's 'Infamy, infamy, they've all got it in for me' – but there were others, which supposed that even viewers of low romps like this would have some Latin. There's Sid James as Mark Antony emitting a '*Puer, puer, oh puer*' when he first catches sight of Cleopatra or, almost thrown away, the bark of '*Sinister, dexter, sinister, dexter!*' (Left, right, left, right) as the centurions march.

Rothwell had been an avid fan of Max Miller, and as writer of the *Carry On* films, he saw the opportunity to bring to the British comedy film screen a riskier sense of the risqué, a bawdiness which had taken on a new, electric energy post-Beatles, but which had its tradition not just in Miller but also in the marginal paraphernalia of seaside postcards. But this wasn't some European-style pornographic 'liberation' – he stopped well short of that. This was a very British bawdiness, bound by an abiding conservatism, patriotism, even.

That patriotism is embodied here by the fighting pluck of Jim Dale's Horsa, fending off Romans five at a time to try to win time for Boudicca's armies to rally. Kenneth Connor plays Hengist, a snivelling, anxious bungler. There's a scene which could almost have belonged in *Monty Python's Life of Brian*, when, making haste across country to alert reinforcements on his square-wheeled bike, Connor gratefully accepts a lift from the wagon taking away the British captives, including Dale's Horsa, en route for Rome. Connor doesn't realise what's going on even as he's manacled. Charles Hawtrey plays Caesar's father-in-law, the first in a succession of *Carry On* roles in which he is as knock-kneed and effete as he is heterosexually lecherous: a mockery of male desire.

However, it's the casting of Sid James and Kenneth Williams that represents a radical break from early *Carry On*. Overnight, Williams, his facial features now more angular, is promoted from junior to senior, a jumped-up authority figure to be goaded and shocked to his core by the vulgarity surrounding him. Hereafter, he would bring to the *Carry On* series a gamut of expressions, ranging from smugly urbane to swift descents into Cockney snideness, with many a whoop and a gasp and a rolling of the 'r's in between, a human long whistle.

Sid James, meanwhile, retained his alpha male status, but now lecherous geniality is added to his persona. We'll hear more of his 'hwa hwa hwa!' chuckle, more raucous cheek and the occasional loud raspberry, with Williams as often as not his stuffy adversary. In *Don't Lose Your Head* (1967), James plays the Scarlet Pimpernel-type figure the Black Fingernail, a paragon of British pluck determined to rescue the French aristocracy with a laugh and an effortless swagger, the peasantry having risen up against them out of wanton bloodlust. Williams, meanwhile, plays Citizen Camembert, who, in his puffed-up Frenchness, unmanly pomposity and bureaucratic insistence on emancipation for the masses, is just the sort of joyless upstart *Carry On* is pitted against.

Carry On continued throughout the sixties to parody established genres, such as the Western (*Carry On Cowboy*), with Rothwell's unapologetically puerile penchant for comic nomenclature coming to the fore (the Rumpo Kid, Jim Dale's Marshall P. Knutt, etc.); Hammer horror (*Carry On Screaming*); and the Foreign Legion movie (*Follow That Camel*). Sid James appears in neither *Screaming* nor *Follow That Camel*: the leads are taken by *Steptoe and Son*'s Harry H. Corbett and Phil Silvers of *Sergeant Bilko* fame respectively. Neither actor is stretched beyond playing the characters for which they were already famous. *Carry On Screaming*, set in the Edwardian era, is especially fine, with Corbett as the painstaking Detective Sergeant Sidney Bung, who is seduced by Fenella Fielding's Valeria, sister of the cadaverous villain of the piece, Dr Watt (Kenneth Williams), whose monster has been abducting young women. Fielding puts in one of the best female performances in *Carry On* history, funny, impossibly uber-sexy. The puns are pricelessly creaky ('Fangs ain't what they used to be,' delivered with apparent relish by Williams). Peter Butterworth, a friend of Rothwell's from his days in a POW camp, was an excellent, lugubrious addition to the ensemble, often playing sidekicks, like a wheezy, eager but dim-witted old bulldog.

With *Carry On Doctor* (1967), the series returned to the present day. Despite its often right-wing political subtext, *Carry On* shared the British public's deep-seated fondness and gratitude for the NHS, socialist in origin but proudly British nevertheless. However, it has its other uses as a setting – as a respite from marital life, for one. Sid James is only contriving to retain his hospital bed with a mysterious illness to avoid home life with his nagging wife (Dandy Nichols). Francis Bigger, the 'mind over matter' guru, is played by Frankie Howerd, again very much in his deliciously pained and pursing persona, all squeals, arched backs and rasping, exasperated asides.

Having married sidekick Joan Sims, who turns out to consider his teachings 'rubbish' and resolves that he get a proper job, Bigger pulls off the same trick as Sid, affecting a nasty injury which will necessitate a lengthy stay in hospital. There is much suggestion of sex in *Carry On*, but not much love, while marriage is generally a disaster, the enemy of roving male lechery.

Hospitals also involve young nurses, beds, states of undress, as well as deep, heaving lust lurking beneath the prim, uniformed surface. It was Hattie Jacques's fate in *Carry On Doctor*, and again when she reprised the same character in *Carry On Camping*, for a bassoon motif to strike up every time she strode down a corridor. Here, as in *Camping*, she can't resist eventually bursting with infatuation all over a horrified Kenneth Williams.

Carry On Camping is among the best loved of the series. Jim Dale apart, every one of the classic ensemble appears – James, Williams, Hawtrey, Sims, Bernard Bresslaw, Windsor, Jacques and Terry Scott, playing a Hancock type enduring the purgatory of wife Betty Marsden and her whinnying guffaw. The campsite as comedy site is perfect. On the one hand, while ostensibly representing the healthy wholesomeness of the outdoors, it also poses the possibility of nudity, which attracts James and Bresslaw, as well as escape from the tyranny of the domestic household, represented by Joan Sims's mother (Amelia Bayntun). 'Camping' is also apt since many of the most uproarious moments of this most heterosexual of films belong to Hawtrey and Williams, including Williams leading his young female charges, stripped to bras and pants, in an aerobics session.

Sid James's 'hwa hwa hwa!' resounds throughout *Camping*. By now, his role was well established – an on-screen conduit for the audience's amusement at the frolics, pratfalls and jumped-up, sex-denying characters around him, an embodiment of the saucy, fun-loving, laddish British spirit that carries on through the films, an aversion to taking things too seriously. In *Carry On Henry* (1971), it almost amounts to historical propaganda. He plays up to the fond image of the king as he existed for centuries in folk memory, the embodiment of Merrie England, whose unique solutions to the vexations of matrimony, the true tyranny in *Carry On*-land, and love of a bit of blonde crumpet (Bettina, played by Barbara Windsor) are sympathetic vices, throwing his tyrannical tendencies into the shade.

As for Kenneth Williams, he applies to Rothwell's scripts a relish they don't always merit, swilling them as if they were fine wines before spitting them out, swooping up and down the gamut of his comic range, often in mid-sentence. That he was most known for these roles, that he returned to them faithfully time and again, might lead you to think he treasured *Carry On*. His diaries, however, tell a different story. He is disparaging from the outset; they were beneath the dignity of a thespian who had pretensions to intellectualism.

It's telling that the rise of *Carry On* parallels the rise of the *Sun* newspaper (founded in 1964, the same year as *Carry On Cleo* was released), which went tabloid in 1969, the same year as *Carry On Camping*. Both *Carry On* and the *Sun* represent the 'permissive-reactionary' tendency of Brits in the sixties, seventies and beyond, an age of increasing irreverence, decreasing religious observation, but not necessarily egalitarian enlightenment.

Take *Carry On Camping*. *Carry On* is all for sexual liberation when it means Barbara Windsor being liberated of her bra, but when it collides with the world of rock music and the progressive attitudes it represents, the attitude is one of horror and hostility. When Farmer Giles allows a rock concert by a travelling group of hippies, the Flowerbuds, to take place in a neighbouring field, the regulars rush to the gate and look on with revulsion. A plan must be hatched, and it falls to chuckling Sid, reprising some of the spirit of the Black Fingernail, who disguises himself as a festival-goer and, with the assistance of the lecherous coach driver, cuts off their electricity supply. There's a wistful moment as the girls from the finishing school join the Flowerbuds' departing convoy, however, as if accepting that rock and roll has claimed the youth and that *Carry On*'s days are numbered. (The series eventually fizzled out with the ignominious *Carry On Emmannuelle* in 1978 – Kenneth Williams starred, complaining to the last.)

TILL DEATH US DO PART –
LAUGHING AT, OR WITH, BIGOTRY?

Johnny Speight's *Till Death Us Do Part*, which debuted in 1965, was, on the face of it, much more on the side of the angels – a riposte to the bigotry that still abided in the swinging sixties. It is set in the household of Warren Mitchell's Alf Garnett, a racist raging against the scorn of daughter Una Stubbs, son-in-law and 'Scouse git' Tony Booth and Dandy Nichols as his wife. It ought to have been clear that Alf is a buffoon, a relic of outmoded, plain wrong attitudes. His defence of 'Mary Whitearse', who had condemned the show not for its racism but for its coarseness, backfires, as it is meant to. However, the explosions of studio laughter whenever he rants about 'bladdy coons', their limbo dancing and 'jungle juice' are horribly telling. Such language was generally not featured on the BBC, not for the sake of racial equality but for politeness and tone. And so, when Alf uses this language, the audiences are reacting not with derisory scorn at his bigotry, but with catharsis.

Alf Garnett was a huge character, played to the voluminous hilt by Warren Mitchell. He takes all the best laugh lines, negating the impact of him being, supposedly, the butt of the overall joke. As a defiant relic he could sometimes be a figure of pathos. The fine movie based on the series, harking back over decades, highlights this. At the end, he and his terraced neighbours are being rehoused in high-rise flats, not quite the ideal they are presented as in this film. Alf is dead against them, and gains a sympathy from us that he's perhaps not meant to. Conversely, there's a joyous scene in which he and his son-in-law temporarily make their peace to go and watch England win the 1966 World Cup final at Wembley. Cut to the early hours and the pair stumbling drunkenly back home, with Dandy Nichols waiting in curlers and hairnet at the door, demanding to know where they've been. 'They played extra time, didn't they?'

Mitchell complained in interviews that he was often approached by strangers giving him a 'Good on you, Alf!', retorting that they had missed the point of Alf entirely. They had, but he and Speight shared some responsibility for this. They had invested too well in Alf as a character, so much so that it felt like he was speaking the language of the suppressed. It did not help that, with the exception of such extras as the Black fan Alf accidentally kisses at the final whistle at Wembley and a cameo appearance by Kenny Lynch in a 1967 special, Black characters barely featured in the show.

MONTY PYTHON – ONE GIANT LEAP

A wholly different response to the onset of modern life that drove Alf Garnett time and again to the pub in despair was taken by a group of young Oxbridge men only in their late twenties, but already seasoned in writing and performing comedy.

Python's giant foot landed on earth just three months after Neil Armstrong set foot on the moon. It was the era of satellite transmission, in which events such as the May 1968 student demonstrations, Tommie Smith's Black Power salute at the 1968 Olympics in Mexico City and the assassinations of Martin Luther King and Robert Kennedy impinged onto the British media environment, made their reverberations felt. It was a time of fire, violence and chaos, but also of fresh possibilities, the overthrow of the old black and white order of things. The Pythons were not revolutionaries, and beneath their zaniness they hankered for reason – but their determination to explode old forms and toss the fragments in the air made them auspiciously right for revolutionary times.

Along with Michael Palin, Terry Jones had been writing and performing for TV since the early 1960s, when the pair came down from

Oxford. The same went for John Cleese and Graham Chapman, who went up to Cambridge a year before Eric Idle. They'd overlapped on the kids' show *Do Not Adjust Your Set* (1967–9) and *At Last the 1948 Show* (1967), working alongside David Jason, the Ronnies Corbett and Barker, Marty Feldman, Tim Brooke-Taylor and Bill Oddie. Monty Python didn't quite explode from the blue. It was as if the Sex Pistols had comprised former members of Cockney Rebel, Roxy Music and Mott the Hoople.

All, however, were frustrated by the limitations of TV comedy, of seeing their material completely rewritten, or having to work at the behest of producers with hidebound ideas about format. As a collective of writer/performers, they would be able to create an overall product that was at least to their own liking.

The first *Python* series appeared in 1969, in colour from the outset. This was vital. The visual quality of these broadcasts, not just the colour but also the definition, makes them feel connected to the televisual language of our own times, as opposed to shows broadcast just a year or so earlier in relatively grainy, blurry monochrome. The Britain of 1969 that they depict is one in which rock music has barely happened; in fairness, that is how the late sixties would have felt, an era in which Britain swung far less than has subsequently been supposed. Outdoor scenes are set against a backdrop of humdrum, silent, suburban London streets. *Python* dealt in stock period signifiers, albeit in surreal settings. Workmen wore caps and light brown overcoats; civil servants and city gents wore bowler hats; teachers wore black gowns; creative types wore cravats; young women, as the sketches progressed, wore next to nothing.

For, despite their radical thrust, their desire to explode clichés and tired formats, the Python team were of their time in some respects. They didn't really do women, and didn't really apologise for the fact much in later life, either. ('How many men were there in the Spice Girls?' Eric Idle protested, feebly.) Idle himself wrote many sketches which conveniently involved young, nubile women draping themselves around him or throwing themselves at him to no obvious comedic end – one in which he is in bed, crooning Blake's 'Jerusalem' and strumming on a guitar, for instance, or playing the marriage guidance counsellor who seduces busty Carol Cleveland in front of her husband Michael Palin. (That said, Idle was responsible for the immortal, unimpeachable 'wink-wink, nudge-nudge' sketch, in which he tries to initiate a bawdy conversation with Terry Jones's stranger. That sketch does have a punchline: 'What's it like?')

Although Cleveland was very much accepted by the team as the 'seventh Python' (songwriter Neil Innes graciously stood down from the competition for this honour), the boys themselves played multiple roles as women, the 'pepperpots', those squawking, monstrous parodies of middle-aged English womanhood. Funny as they invariably were, if only for the simple comic appeal of men dressed as women (once more, the 'un-manning' of men), this did represent a failure to break away from the old, exclusionary Footlights custom of eschewing women in favour of male actors in drag. It enabled them to present a caricature of femaleness while bypassing female agency or curiosity about the real condition of womanhood, to wonder, what's it like?

Cleveland was initially hired by the Python team to play 'the pretty girl', but they did not reckon with her multidimensionality and comic talent. Her heroines were Lucille Ball and Marilyn Monroe, and she had worked with Roy Hudd, the Two Ronnies and Spike Milligan, among others. She herself coined the phrase 'glamour stooge' in relation to the unsatisfying roles she was asked to play, and, in fairness, these did not immediately improve when she joined *Python*, something for which Michael Palin, at least, was awfully apologetic. The Pythons were impressed with Cleveland and insisted she stay on for longer than the mere four episodes for which she had been initially slated. She would go on to appear in all four series, as well as the films. However, when they excitedly told her that they had at last come up with a character worthy of her talents, she was a little crestfallen to learn that the character went by the name of 'Vanilla Whore'.

There was a marginal improvement in the deployment of Cleveland, including some drag-in-reverse scenes, such as playing a moustached soldier in the jungle, complete with pith helmet, khaki shorts, eyelashes and lipstick. She also took over the role played by Graham Chapman in the Spanish Inquisition scene, following his death, of the old woman tortured by cushions. Unlike Connie Booth, who appeared in only a handful of *Python* episodes, Cleveland has never turned down *Python*, loyally taking part in revival after revival, even into her seventies. However, in interviews she has referred more than once to *Python* as a 'ball and chain', and perhaps wishes she had been bolder in forging a post-*Python* identity or speaking up more at the ideas stage. She was at once included and excluded: a dubious idea of the sacred chemistry and symmetry of the Python Six proved resistant to strong female involvement. Come the nineties, and such exclusion would be unthinkable – a *Fast Show*, for example, without Arabella Weir and Caroline Aherne?

Homosexuality was another problematic area. Graham Chapman was gay, and for innocents like Palin, he represented a first introduction to gay culture. But Chapman considered himself 'butch' gay and disdained the more hello-honky-tonk, mincing queer; he took against David Bowie, once he found out who he was, whom he considered not just too 'poofterish' but also phony. Which is perhaps why he seems not to have vetoed his fellow Pythons' depictions of camp-voiced hairdressers and the like. Palin, meanwhile, enjoyed a little too much the novelty of gaydom. One sketch involves him playing a man whose wallet has been stolen and who alerts a police officer (Cleese). Not much he can do about it, Cleese informs him. After a well-timed pause, Palin asks, 'Want to come back to my place?' Cleese agrees. Whatever the structural merits of this sketch, it relies on the idea that a policeman, a traditional authority figure, who turns out to be gay is inherently comical – surreal, even. Sorry, Brian Paddick. And there's

Palin's lumberjack, for that matter, who delivers one of *Python*'s most famous songs, culminating in the booming revelation that far from being 'rugged', as his best girl Connie Booth had hoped, he enjoys dressing up in women's clothing and wishes he was a girlie.

Far from delivering material like this in a snickering, half-guilty spirit of political incorrectness, it is quite possible that the Pythons considered it to be go-ahead and taboo-breaking, touching on matters that the comedy establishment of the day considered unmentionable. There's a cartoon sequence by Terry Gilliam, featuring a young Edwardian couple in a formal pose for the camera. The male of the couple, with one tug, removes the woman's clothes, revealing her in her more truthful state of bare-breasted nudity. The head of a policeman then hoves into view, upon which he instantly puts back her clothes. 'Just checking,' harrumphs the constable, before disappearing; whereupon the man swipes away the woman's clothes once more. It's as if the undressing of the woman and the revelation of her tits represents a blow in the struggle for sexual liberation; that it is the woman who is 'liberated' from her clothing, and not the man, says much about how male-determined, how cis-heteronormative, ideas of sexual freedom were in the 1960s and 1970s.

Back then, *Python* never felt like the hit-and-miss experience it can feel like to a more sceptical viewer over half a century on, but an initiation, a rite of passage into a higher realm of comedic consciousness, juvenile and anarchic yet seriously adult. The surrealism of the format was vital – refusing to entertain, to ingratiate, pander or beam broadly with showbiz sincerity. For young, white grammar-school boys like myself it was a moment of cultural puberty, akin to when you were invited by a select circle of classmates to leave behind pop and delve into the more sophisticated LPs of Led Zeppelin or Genesis. This was certainly the case at the all-boys school I attended: it was an initiation. The equivalent for schoolgirls of the same age remained elusive. I recall suspecting that girls simply did not 'get it', failing to grasp that they were actually being given relatively little to get.

The first episode of the first series, broadcast on 5 October 1969, begins with a ragged Michael Palin wading through sea water to collapse on the beach, before uttering, 'It's . . .' It's what? Cleese's stern voiceover of the title, despite the crisp clarity of his tones, doesn't relieve the opacity. Who's Monty Python? Why is the circus airborne? Don't ask. Everything is designed to disorientate. Over a montage by Terry Gilliam involving municipal-looking buildings, cherubs, naked ladies, a robed French cardinal, more naked ladies and finally a giant, squelching foot, the Band of the Grenadier Guards strikes up with 'Liberty Bell', the American military march. Gilliam came up with this; he felt that the brisk, let's-get-down-to-business spirit of the tune was at once appropriate to introduce a new TV series and completely at odds with its contents.

Our senses duly slapped about, wet fish-like, Graham Chapman sits down in a TV presenter's chair, as if he's come to bring order to proceedings. But he's barely uttered a formal 'good evening' before he places his rear end in his chair, only for it to make a squealing noise. This is marked off on a chalkboard. Now Cleese as Wolfgang Amadeus Mozart, introducing recreations of famous 'wonderful' deaths, beginning with that of Palin as Genghis Khan, falling stone dead and receiving a score of 28.1 points from the judges. Over to Michael Palin as an Eddie Waring-style presenter who shows us the tally of scores thus far, with Khan only sixth, behind, among others, Lincoln, Joan of Arc and St Stephen. This'll be a recurring motif of *Python* – eminent figures of history iconoclastically reduced to competing in popular events, from quiz shows to wrestling bouts.

Finally, a sketch: Terry Jones as a tutor introducing himself to an adult class learning Italian. It fairly quickly becomes clear that his class is filled with enthusiastic Italians, who have apparently taken the class out of an eagerness to please their teacher with their grasp of Italian. There's no explanation, no revelation; just the quiet bemusement of Jones's teacher as to why on earth these people have chosen to take lessons in a language they know full well. Then a Gilliam montage, in which a human head is cracked open, egg-like, on the head of a fellow advertising Whizzo Butter.

The Whizzo Butter advert crosses over into real life, with the Python team playing a gaggle of menacing housewives as Palin presides over a plate of the butter and a dead crab – who can tell the difference? And now for something completely different – 'It's the Arts', a parody of the sort of improving, late-night shows which abounded in the more paternalistic late sixties. It's a Cleese–Chapman classic, with Cleese as the interviewer, initially obsequious to his guest, Chapman's film-maker Sir Edward Ross. 'Edward's all right? Splendid. Sorry to have brought it up. Thank you very much indeed,' etc. Edward becomes 'Ted', to which Ross testily agrees, but then baulks at 'Eddie baby'.

The episode culminates in a parody of wartime, Bletchley-style intrigue, in which the funniest joke ever written, deadly to those who read it, is taken up and developed by British scientists, working in 'joke-proof' conditions, to be inflicted on the Germans. Again, the parody of breathless TV docu-drama is acute, while the point is emphasised again that this series will not be about working to big bass-drum, pants-dropping punchlines but is more of a con-tinuum, to which the audience must learn to adapt and in which it must swim.

The Pythons' intimidating lack of desire to ingratiate manifested itself in their attitude to laughter. It was imperative that they never raise a smile in their performances. Peter Cook could make Dudley Moore corpse, Spike Milligan could laugh at his own material, while Tommy Cooper roared at his own terrible jokes. Alf Garnett's family could laugh scornfully at his ranting and raving. Not *Python*. Yes, the audience apart, there was 'laughter', as in the 'Funniest Joke Ever Written', or characters like the Cheap-Laughs, but this was laughter at a remove. The Pythons frequently took a sledgehammer to the fourth wall but never by laughing at their own material.

It's not that they were po-faced. Gales of laughter doubtless pre-vailed in between takes and in their after-hours drinking sessions.

It's just that they were meticulous, driven not by tediously bonkers zaniness but by a fierce logic, in the missionary way they upturned clichés, tropes of complacency, stale formats. It was about the method, never the 'madness'.

For all their radical attitude to comedy form, they weren't especially radical by temperament. Terry Jones was the group's left-winger; in a tearful tribute to Jones after his death, Palin spoke fondly of the political rows they had had, Palin belonging to the softer left. They certainly weren't the comedic corollary to the Angry Brigade. The likes of Mao and Marx were subject to the same, iconoclastic irreverence as Alan Whicker.

Although he was clear-eyed about the deceptive sense of authority perpetuated by his own class to maintain their power, John Cleese was no lefty. His Reg in *Life of Brian* (1979) was a deeply felt creation, in the tradition of Peter Sellers's trade unionist Fred Kite. Cleese would consider Labour too extreme, opting to join the Social Democratic Party in the 1980s. Underneath all the silliness, the surrealism, the Pythons' call was an implicit one for sensibleness and sanity.

The dynamic between the Pythons involved a measure of tension, though only Cleese was estranged for any time from the group, skipping series four because he felt *Python* was repeating itself. He would never have cared to direct, for example. Jones, on the other hand, felt a strong inclination to shape *Python*, and consequently exercised a strong but discreet influence within the group. He and Cleese got on the least well; Palin, by contrast, Jones's writing partner, was liked by all. Gilliam was the most anarchic in spirit, the outsider – it tickled Cleese no end throughout the *Python* years that Gilliam was American.

Eric Idle wrote solo. As well as writing, he had a more entrepreneurial role as a Python and the strongest connection with America and Hollywood, which would prove vital as the Pythons made the transition from TV into filmmaking. I interviewed Idle when he was doing press for the 1988 Gilliam-directed *Adventures of Baron Munchausen*. Idle was conscious of the 'juvenile', in the best sense of the word, nature of comedy – it was essentially a 'young man's game', implying that it was a game he could no longer play to any great effect.

Chapman, meanwhile, was, in terms of his personal character, the toughest to work with. It was primarily his severe alcoholism that irritated Cleese, and also his indolence. Cleese remarked that when asked just what Connie Booth actually contributed to their writing partnership, he would reply, with asperity, 'A lot more than Graham Chapman ever did.'

And yet, the contributions he did make were telling. There's the story of Chapman puffing away on his pipe as Cleese read out to him a sketch about returning a faulty toaster. Yes, yes, said Chapman, but it should be a parrot . . .

Python lasted until 1974. It's not all gold. Cleese himself has remarked that there are two or three items in each show that make him wonder how the group ever managed to find them remotely amusing. Without being over-topical, it spoke to its own time and place: the media landscape, the British landscape of Alan Whicker and Spam, city gents and door-to-door salesmen, which are no longer everyday features of UK life. But that which does endure accounts for acres and acres of British comedy's evergreen forests. There was inspired inversion: Eric Idle as the college-educated young man who's defied his irascible Northern father, a redoubtable literary scion, to join the mining industry ('You know what he's like after a few novels,' interjects Terry Jones's mother, trying to make peace between the warring father and son); Michael Palin as Bicycle Repair Man, a hero in a society of non-mechanically minded Supermen ('See how he uses the spanner to tighten the nut').

There's so much more. Discussion of the mysteriously forgotten German composer Johann Gambolputty de von Ausfern-schplenden-schlitter-crasscrenbon-fried-digger-dingle-dangle-dongle-dungle-

burstein-von-knacker-thrasher-apple-banger-horowitz-ticolensic-
-grander-knotty-spelltinkle-grandlich-grumblemeyer-spelterwasser-
kurstlich-himbleeisen-bahnwagen-gutenabend-bitte-ein-nürnburger-
bratwustle-gerspurten-mitzweimache-luber-hundsfut-gumberaber-
shönendanker-kalbsfleisch-mittler-aucher von Hautkopft of Ulm,
whose name Cleese's presenter dutifully insists on pronouncing in full,
so much so that a surviving relative dies as a question about him is put
to him. 'Your majesty is like a dose of clap,' in which Oscar Wilde,
James Whistler and George Bernard Shaw sadistically goad each other
into explaining their apparently insulting witticisms to Edward, Prince
of Wales ('You bastard, I never . . . '). Mrs Premiss and Mrs Conclusion
staring with only mild curiosity at a penguin atop a TV set. 'I just
spent four hours burying the cat . . . it wouldn't keep still.' The RAF
sketch, in which no one can make head or tail of each other's banter in
the officers' mess ('Charlie Chopper's dropping a handful . . . sausage
squad up the blue end . . . cabbage crates coming over the Briney'). Eric
Idle's door-to-door practical jokes salesman with an array of unnerving
devices, including CS gas canisters and real snakes – 'guaranteed to
break the ice at parties'.

Sketches involving Cleese are clustered at the top of the tree.
Sometimes these involved him practising the sort of choleric, impotent
ranting he would perfect with Basil Fawlty: a sergeant major trying
to impress on a sceptical class the importance of defending yourself
against attack from a piece of fruit. Or an architect outlining his plans
to a group of property developers, explaining how block residents
will be systematically slaughtered on entering the building. When the
developers object, he bridles at this slap in the face to the creative planning spirit: 'You sit there on your loathsome, spotty behinds, squeezing
your blackheads . . .'

Cleese enjoys a silly voice, be it Gumby, mad housewife or disgruntled
parrot owner, but he's most effective deploying the naturalistic tones
of the professional class into which he almost entered (he was training
for the law, before comedy, with its marginally superior wages, enticed

him). Take the Ministry for Silly Walks, for example. This sketch only works as well as it does because of the plausibility he exudes as a high-ranking civil servant; like the bowler-hatted men that recur in the art of René Magritte, the ultra-normal is married with the surreal. It's not just the accent but the unbendingly complacent self-assurance he projects. Interviewing a humble member of the public applying for funding to develop his own walk, he remarks, 'Not very silly, is it?' with confidence-sapping disparagement. He goes on to explain the realities of budgetary pragmatism in the practised tones civil servants have perfected over the decades to maintain the sensible equilibrium of our way of life, brooking no objection to the fundamental absurdities, far worse than any silly walk, that it preserves. Or there's the sketch in which he plays a chartered accountant approached to make a donation of £1 to a charity. He mentally audits the proposition before asking for forgiveness if he is being obtuse, observing that he comes out a pound down on the deal.

Monty Python's Flying Circus percolated only slowly into the national consciousness. Initially it was esoteric, wilfully so, making no effort to ingratiate itself with the norms of TV and mainstream audiences. Early on, certainly, it did not enjoy the universal appeal of the great sitcoms of the era, grandparents, even parents, frankly, were oblivious to it, my own, certainly. Its avant-garde absurdism and allusions to great thinkers and philosophers might have appealed to a continental sensibility the series was eventually popular across Europe.

The eventual national treasure status of *Python* can, however, be put down to the advanced form of Britishness it represents: for absurdism, read silliness (silly voices, silly walks); for formalist reworking of comedy, read wackiness; for iconoclasm, read cocking a snook at our betters. It's not quite so far from *Carry On* as you might imagine, certainly in its bawdiness, even if it affected to be somehow 'progressive' in that respect. Much of the work still stands, but some of it has been reduced through repetition, like E. L. Wisty.

Some of the *Python* spirit can, sadly, be found in the David Brents of this world, the sitters in bathtubs full of baked beans for charity, the wearers of coloured rimmed glasses, tiresome sorts whose lives are over-determined by comedy. The Pythons themselves became house-hold names, but in old age have in some cases become reactionary figures, bleating about wokeness and cancellation. It's worth fighting backwards through all this, getting back to the original work, in all its colour and clarity, and seeing what remains brilliant in it.

SUNSHINE, DESSERTS, DARK DAYS AND GRIM RESPITE

THE 1970S

The 1970s is considered a moribund decade politically, the Wilsonian promise of White Heat in the mid-sixties having faded to a lukewarm grey. Whether people were mourning the loss of sixties idealism or of empire, there was a general air of decline. The ruefulness this engendered might well account for the sheer quantity, as well as quality, of light entertainment during these years. From *Agony* (1979–81), starring Maureen Lipman, not desperately funny but creditably progressive in its depiction of its gay characters, to the rather earthier *Yus, My Dear* (1976), starring Arthur Mullard, well over a hundred sitcoms were broadcast across the decade, most of them on BBC1 and ITV. These were augmented by dozens more light entertainers, the vast majority white and of a certain age, veterans who had served long apprenticeships now at last coming into their own in the age of colour TV. But as the decade drew to a close, they would find their dominance called into question by a younger generation radicalised in their own way by the spirit of punk.

DAD'S ARMY (AND BREXIT)

Most of the seventies sitcoms have faded from memory, while even the best of them tend not to be rebroadcast on mainstream TV, marred as they are by kipper ties, flares and garish kitchen decor. There is also the matter of those fishbones of racism, sexism, homophobia. *Dad's Army* (1968–77), however, by virtue of being a period drama, is a flares-free zone, while its essential innocence preserves it from the serious accusations levelled at other seventies comedy. Part of this is through avoidance. Apart from the 'fuzzy-wuzzies' of Corporal Jones's febrile Sudan reminiscences, no person of colour appears in

Dad's Army, and while the *Dad's Army* film (1971) contains the odd moment of mild homophobia, such aberrations in the series are rare. It was a time capsule in the sixties and seventies for viewers who retained vivid memories of 1940, sweetened with excerpts of songs of the period between scenes, including 'Keep Young and Beautiful' and 'Run, Rabbit, Run'. *Dad's Army* stands today as a vivid relic of Britain as it once was, a perpetual, self-deprecating but comforting reminder of aspects of the British character, ranging from pomposity and ineptitude to comradeship and courage, to a deflating sense of humour and a mistrust of would-be despots.

And so, as arrière-garde as *Monty Python* and Spike Milligan were avant-garde, *Dad's Army* has nonetheless been a constant on the TV-scape, like an old fort abutting a small-town shopping precinct. It's a unique British constant – it has been rerun practically without pause since its inception, a show for all time and out of time. It comforted the nation through the strains of the early seventies, such as the three-day week, and has continued to console us with the power of a perfectly brewed mug of tea.

Dad's Army survives also because it doesn't strain to be the greatest, the funniest, the most boundary-testing, genre-busting comedy of all time. As Bill Pertwee, who played Captain Mainwaring's gruff nemesis, ARP Warden Hodges, put it to me in 1990, '*Dad's Army* was chuckling comedy. Humour has become more aggressive today because life has become more aggressive. It's down to fear, in a way. In our day we knew we were quite good, quite amusing. We weren't saying, "Laugh at us."'

When the series was first aired on 31 July 1968, however, it was quite out of keeping with the incendiary spirit of the times. Fire raged everywhere, from cities up in flames in the wake of Martin Luther King's assassination to the rocket burners of Apollo 8, to Jimi Hendrix's guitar set alight to the Czechoslovakian students who burned themselves alive in protest at the Russian invasion of their country. After all the overtures for peace and love in 1967, 1968 was a year of growing, angry militancy, including the May demonstrations in Paris, London, New York and West Germany. The sixties were at once experiencing a violent death and instigating a violent birth of who knows what. It was impossible for anyone with a television set not to be buffeted by these inflammatory events.

What place had a series like *Dad's Army* in such a world? Certainly, among less revolutionary Brits, nostalgia for Britain's finest hour was rife in a steady diet of war films – staples like *The Dambusters* and *Reach for the Sky* – while comics like *Victor* and *Warlord* featured the adventures of beefy Brits strafing 'Jerries' and 'Japs' with bullets and gusto. A small boy at the time, I spent many an hour with a pencil and sheet of A4 paper, writing up stories of triumphant sorties by the Royal Air Force, while blackening the other side of the sheet with images of Messerschmitts going down in flames.

Dad's Army ran counter to all of this. For all the presentation of arms and Corporal Jones's thrusting bayonet, it was a fundamentally gentle series. No one dies, throughout. The very little violence that is meted out is by, of all people, the diffident Sergeant Wilson, who more than once proves surprisingly adept with his fists. The combative Captain Mainwaring does not strike a single blow, though he does suffer a black eye following an altercation with his unseen wife, Elizabeth. It was a wartime series and yet in the very best sense it was cosy, reassuring and, despite its aged characters, ageless, a reminder of something of what we British are – motley yet indomitable, a nation of victorious losers.

The very first episode takes place in the year 1968, with all members of the platoon still alive (including, poignantly, James Beck's Walker). Though Corporal Jones, for one, would have been in his late nineties at this point, they were all vigorous and active citizens still, at a function in honour of the 'I'm Backing Britain' campaign. This was where Britain was at, economically and politically, in 1968, with the pound having been recently devalued, and this setback felt symbolic of the country's standing. The campaign began with a group of Surbiton secretaries who volunteered to work an extra thirty minutes a day unpaid to help boost productivity, and briefly caught the imagination of the Captain Mainwarings of this world, before foundering, not least due to the opposition of trade unions, who saw the initiative as an attempt to exploit workers while leaving management inefficiency unexamined.

Wilson affectionately introduces guest of honour Alderman George Mainwaring, who begins by reminiscing on the days of the Home Guard, founded in 1940. 'Then, we all backed Britain. It was the darkest hour in our history . . .' The action then cuts to a 1940 newsreel, then to Mainwaring's bank manager's office, leading some to speculate that the entire series, running from 1968 to 1977, is one long flashback. Over nine years, the series covered the period from 1940 to 1942, before the threat of Nazi invasion receded.

Co-creator Jimmy Perry, himself a young member of the Home Guard, conceived the idea of what was originally termed *The Fighting Tigers* while walking in St James's Park in London. Perry realised, on visiting a library and finding no books on the subject, that the very existence of the Home Guard had been practically forgotten. With the assistance of producer David Croft, he set himself the potentially delicate task of recreating this aspect of the wartime effort in the medium of comedy.

There were qualms at the BBC that the series might be seen to be mocking the war effort. It was its genius that, for all the laughs it extracted at the expense of its often inept, inadequate characters, it never did any such thing. The title *Fighting Tigers* was replaced with the more engaging *Dad's Army* at the suggestion of BBC Head of Comedy Michael Mills. It was ironic, really, since none of the series' main characters, with the secret exception of Sergeant Wilson, were actually fathers. There were early missteps. An initial opening credit sequence featuring harrowing early wartime footage of fleeing refugees was replaced by a graphic of the Nazi advance across Europe; even then, the earliest episodes featured audience laughter as the British triangles hastily withdrew across the Channel. That was swiftly removed, but it's still disconcertingly preserved on DVD reissues.

All this was fine tuning, however. In 1968, when social historians might think the country's mind would have been preoccupied with more contemporary swinging matters, its TV viewers warmed immediately to this platoon of game but elderly duffers standing to attention with broomsticks in readiness for an invasion which, with happy comic relief, we knew would never happen.

The opening episode sees Mainwaring's ear pressed to the radio as Anthony Eden announces the formation of the Local Defence Volunteers as fears grow of a Nazi invasion. Mainwaring seizes the initiative and the church hall, and before anyone else gets the chance, bags himself the position of captain of the Walmington-on-Sea platoon. His assistant at the bank, Wilson, is appointed his sergeant.

One by one, the characters troop in to sign up and introduce themselves to us. First in, Frazer, played by John Laurie. He had played many a Scot before and would continue to do so afterwards, and it was as if his very demeanour had taken on the weather-beaten, jagged contours of a West Scottish isle. For all that brusque, no-blather, physical air of authenticity, however, and the glee he takes in others, Mainwaring especially, being 'exposed to the world', he's an old fraud himself: he claims to have been a chief petty officer in World War I, but in a later episode is rumbled, exposed as having worked in catering.

Laurie had appeared in the 1944 screen version of *Henry V*, playing the Scotsman Jamy, and as such is a connection with a cultural ancestor to *Dad's Army*, with Shakespeare's play depicting a sometimes comical, fractious band of men united against stiff odds in a military battle, from callow youths to wide boys to elderly duffers to proud members of the other home nations dedicated nonetheless to the British cause.

In shuffles Godfrey next. Mainwaring issues a stark warning of the treatment he will mete out to this stooping paragon of Edwardian diffidence when Godfrey asks for a 'receipt, or something'. 'This is a fighting unit – not a dry cleaner's!' snaps Mainwaring, who never makes any concession to Godfrey's age or infirmity. So far as Mainwaring is concerned, Godfrey should be held to the same standard as an Andy McNab.

Next up is Joe Walker, local 'wholesale supplier', who, owing to his vital role, not least to Mainwaring himself, of getting his hands on scarce goods such as whisky and knicker elastic, has been afforded the status of reserved occupation. More youthful, good-looking and resourceful than his fellow privates in the platoon, you sense in the early episodes that Walker might dominate *Dad's Army*, with his sixties-friendly chirp and cheek and charm, putting the codgers in the shade. However, as the series progressed, Walker, though always integral, fades back into line as the alcoholism that claimed actor James Beck's life in 1973 took its slow toll. It was his hangovers, rather than the infirmity of his co-players, which often held up filming.

And now Jones, a rickety seventy years old, played by the more youthful and agile make-up specialist Clive Dunn, frequently called upon for physical, slapstick roles necessitating hanging upside down from belfries and enduring various predicaments involving the hindquarters. He was inspired by a former sergeant of Perry's who would tell his charges as he brandished a bayonet that the enemy 'did not like it up 'em', as if this were a sign of their weak moral fibre, rather than an understandable aversion to having several inches of sharp metal inserted hard between the buttocks. Jones's virtue, but also his undoing, is his constant willingness to volunteer. In the series one episode 'Sergeant Wilson's Secret', when a stand-in is required for Mrs Pike in a mooted wedding rehearsal, a volunteer, about Mrs Pike's height, is required. 'I'd like to volunteer to be about her height, sir,' says Jones.

Ian Lavender appears as Pike the junior clerk, seventeen going on twelve; his voice and delivery are not quite yet fixed, but his relationship with his cosseting but sharp-tongued mother Mavis (and very dear friend of Pike's 'Uncle' Arthur Wilson) is already established.

Mrs Pike and Mainwaring are at constant loggerheads over her concerns for her son's weak chest, necessitating the wearing of a scarf and prompting Mainwaring's sputtering indignation at such disregard for the ascetic demands of a fighting unit.

Catchphrases were abundant among the platoon. 'Do you think I might be excused?' 'We're doomed!' 'I'm all wet, Mr Mainwaring!' 'Permission to speak, sir.' A staple of comedy, the catchphrases in *Dad's Army* are a sign of reassurance: that sitcom characters, for all that they go through, never ultimately change their spots. Also, they are another illustration that in comedy, predictability, the expected, is as vital a factor as the unexpected.

Finally, there is the central and most important relationship in the series – intimate, distant, passive, aggressive, jealous, truculent, exasperated, caring – between Sergeant Wilson and Captain Mainwaring. Much has been made of the vital masterstroke of making Wilson the sergeant and Mainwaring as the captain. John Le Mesurier had traditionally been cast in senior roles, achieving brusque authority through his well-spokenness alone – for instance, as the office manager in Tony Hancock's *The Rebel* (1961). Arthur Lowe, meanwhile, had previously played modest roles as a responsible middleman, be it the fellow dispatched by *Titbits* magazine to secure Lous D'Ascoyne's memoirs at the end of *Kind Hearts and Coronets* or the officious Leonard Swindley in *Coronation Street*. In a lesser comedy, it would be Captain Wilson commanding the platoon with suave, indolently assumed authority, with Sergeant Mainwaring, his tubby, red-faced, coarser little inferior, adding an extra rasp when barking out his orders to the platoon. 'You heard what the captain said!'

Making Mainwaring the captain and Wilson the sergeant upturned the class conventions that persisted into the 1960s, while also highlighting them. Perry and Croft did provide Wilson with a backstory – he was born in Gloucestershire in 1887, his uncle a member of the House of Lords; he was educated at a public school and tended to by a nanny; a lack of concentration seems to have hampered the career paths set out for him. He did, however, receive a commission as a captain in World War I. What appears to have bent his spirit, however, is a marriage to 'one of Charles Cochran's Young Ladies'. They had a daughter, but his wife soon left him. The daughter, having joined the WRNS, turns up briefly on leave to visit Wilson in 'Getting the Bird' (1972).

After this, Wilson drifts resignedly into low-level banking, eventually catching the eye of a widow, Mavis Pike, in Weston-super-Mare. When he makes the move to Walmington-on-Sea, working under George Mainwaring at the bank, she follows him.

Wilson's customary upper-class drawl is a constant source of infuriation to Mainwaring. Despite many efforts, he never drills out of him his casual manner in falling the men in: 'I say, would you mind awfully forming a line?' Admiring Jones, despite his doddery manner, for at least having the light of battle in his eyes, Mainwaring remarks, 'It'd be nice to see the light of battle in your eyes, Wilson.' But he never will. Yes, Wilson is as brave as any man in the platoon; in 'Absent Friends' (1970), he even single-handedly dispatches a pair of IRA suspects holed up in the church hall with fisticuffs learned while at public school. But this is not enough to assuage Mainwaring's deep-seated dissatisfaction with Wilson, ultimately based on class resentment.

Mainwaring relishes the war because, despite only having seen action in 1919, to 'clean up the mess', he is a fighting man, having had to fight for whatever status he has achieved. His is the pugnacity of the aspirational lower middle class. In the episode 'A. Wilson (Manager)?' (1970), he erupts. Wilson has been appointed manager of the Eastgate branch and also received a commission with the Eastgate platoon. Wilson is blameless in all this – which, however, makes it worse for Mainwaring, who detests the effortlessness, the privilege with which rank is conferred on him. 'You've never had to fight for anything in your life – brought up by a nanny – father something in the City – you just had to sit back and let it all come to you.'

Wilson and Mainwaring survey each other sceptically through-out the series, each taking a keen and at times mockingly malicious interest in each other's occasional quirks or stylistic try-outs. Mainwaring is goaded when Wilson takes to wearing a monocle in 'If the Cap Fits . . .' (1972): 'It makes you look like an advertise-ment for Sharp's toffee.' They have at each other in 'Keep Young and Beautiful' (1972), when, alarmed at the prospect of being displaced in the platoon by younger men, Mainwaring solicits Wilson's opinion on a wig he has bought, bringing forth only a torrent of helpless guffaws from the sergeant. 'Watch out, Wilson, you'll snap your girdle!' snaps Mainwaring, in reference to the 'gentleman's abdominal support' Wilson is wearing. And yet these men are bound by duty, and a duty of mutual care, never more so than in 'Something Nasty in the Vault' (1969), when both men find themselves in the basement of the bank, unable to move as they are clutching an unexploded bomb in their laps.

Mainwaring could easily have been rendered with one fewer dimension by a more poorly cast actor; there was talk of giving the role to Jon Pertwee, who, although versatile, might have lacked the roundedness, the finesse to play Mainwaring. Arthur Lowe was born to the role. Much of the depth he brings is summarised by Graham McCann in his volume *Dad's Army: The Story of a Very British Comedy*. Lowe as Mainwaring, notes McCann, 'listened to each character as they spoke'. Lowe is the funniest and greatest actor in *Dad's Army*, but it's rarely him that delivers the jokes. Rather, he sets up lines for others, huffs and puffs himself up in order to be pricked, or draws out the comedy value of the platoon's fatuous suggestions as he listens to them in full, rubbing his chin, removing his glasses, staring in a pained, watery manner into the middle distance – no more so than when Frazer embarks on one of his expansive, bleakly cavernous yarns of his seafaring days, when Mainwaring asks if anyone has a diving suit. Minutes pass as the Scotsman wends slowly towards the end of the tale of his poor pal Wally, stricken by the bends, before we cut to Mainwaring, whose expression bears the full weight of the saga's diversionary irrelevance. 'So, I take it you have a diving suit?' he responds.

As Mainwaring often informs Wilson, his life has been far from carefree; shy and ignored as a child, he strained without support to get to a decent grammar school, voluntarily subjecting himself to cold baths to clear his mind and maintain focus. This joyless, dutiful sense of application enabled him to work his way up from office boy at an Eastgate bank to the post of bank manager in Walmington-on-Sea. Somehow, he was diverted into marriage to Elizabeth, a brittle but exacting woman who never appears on screen. His voice rises a nervous octave when he is on the phone to her.

Though not quite a Blimp, Mainwaring has swallowed Pathé News's wartime propaganda whole. Addressing the platoon, he refers to Hitler 'licking his wounds' after the drubbing administered to him at Dunkirk and generally paints a sanguine picture of the conflict. As for the Nazis, we are spared full cognisance of their genocidal evil and the geopolitics of the war. 'We shan't go into all of that,' he says dismissively, when Godfrey asks why we are allied to Stalin when he is a communist. The scale of the mass death in World War II never casts its shadow over *Dad's Army*. During the period of its first broadcast, consciousness of the Holocaust was not generally that great in Britain. The *The World at War* (1973–4) episodes covering it were broadcast after 11 p.m., so as to avoid distressing the show's viewers, but this did not help raise awareness about the topic. *Dad's Army* never broaches it at all. This is a straight fight between Britain and the Nazis, with belated and slightly irksome assistance from the Americans.

Mainwaring's principal objection to the Nazis is their 'shabbiness', the unsportsmanlike manner in which they are conducting the war – sneaking around the Maginot Line, for example, rather than squaring up at the wicket. He even delivers a lecture to the men, explaining why the Nazis don't play cricket. Nevertheless, for all his delusions about the havoc his hand-picked fighting men could wreak on Hitler's invading hordes, there is never any doubt about Mainwaring's courage – his or any of the platoon's.

Mainwaring enjoys the war; it invests his loveless, humdrum life with drama and meaning. He cannot, therefore, understand why his platoon would sometimes rather sag off down to the pub than stay behind at the church hall brushing up on their sloping of arms or reading military manuals. One of Mainwaring's most frequent tropes is at the expense of everyday life in all its convenience and fun-loving triviality. 'This is war, not Sainsbury's!' 'This is war, not a cocktail party!'

All of which makes it all the more satisfying when Mainwaring does reveal his heart's true longing, in 'Mum's Army' (1970), when he becomes besotted with a Mrs Gray, played by Carmen Silvera, better known for playing Edith in *'Allo 'Allo!* Silvera brings an authentic, sympathetic fragrance to the part of the widow, recently having moved to Walmington-on-Sea with her mother from London to avoid the bombs. Romance rarely impinges seriously on *Dad's Army*. Wendy Richard occasionally features as Walker's blowsy, sharp-tongued girlfriend; Wilson's relationship with Pike's mother sees him as put upon as he is by Mainwaring; the cheerful, buxom Mrs Fox is a likeable seaside-postcard creation; while Mrs Mainwaring is left entirely to the imagination. Mainwaring and Mrs Gray's temporary and wholly respectable dalliance is as unforgettable as it is fleeting. Their final scene at the train station, as she reluctantly flees an illicit relationship, heavily parodies *Brief Encounter* to soften the emotional blow. As he watches the train pull away through the smoke, eyes blinking behind the glasses which, she said, 'cut off the warmth of a person's eyes', we feel the warmth of his grief nevertheless. *Dad's Army* did not often deal in sentimentality, but when it did, it did so unerringly.

Mainwaring is a great drunk also, on those memorable occasions when alcohol gets the better of him. He's waylaid by fellow officers in a game toasting the health of Cardinal Puff, weaving unsteadily back to his tent and distinctly repentant in the morning. Lowe also did a tremendous turn as Mainwaring's brother, Barry, a travelling salesman and inebriate, turned up at Walmington-on-Sea to demand a pocket watch from the captain. Or there's 'The War Dance' (1969), in which, having organised a morale-boosting do as if it were a military exercise, Mainwaring turns up at the event with a black eye administered by his wife and, as the evening unfolds into a disaster, decides, basically, sod it, looking on as he chooses for once to let some other bugger take care of things as he gets genially sozzled.

Mainwaring deserves to be the butt of so much of *Dad's Army's* comedy – it is him, after all, who puts the men through pointless exercises in military drill, with frequent inspections of hair length, uniform and even feet. Episodes often begin with the captain in teacherly mode, stick in hand, undermined by interruptions from the platoon's pupils. His stiffest sanctions, meanwhile – ordering Wilson to take down Pike's name, for example, or sending Walker home – hardly feel calculated to have the men trembling in their boots. The more slapstick conclusions to episodes often involve frantic capers across country in pursuit of wayward balloons or similar predicaments. To resolve these, however, requires on-the-spot improvisation, with the undisciplined Walker often coming up with the goods, rather than ramrod army training.

And yet Mainwaring's creators have a finely calculated respect for his dignity. Rather than use his being busted down to private in 'Room at the Bottom' (1969) as an excuse for jokes at his expense, we're invited to admire the way he buckles down to his reduced rank. Meanwhile, in 'If the Cap Fits . . .', he finds himself stitched up, saddled with leading his men at a ceremonial event playing the bagpipes. Croft and Perry resist setting Mainwaring up for the indignity of a disastrous, make-shift, skirling cacophony. It turns out he learned to play the instrument on honeymoon in Invergeikie. 'The nights were long and there was nothing else to do.' He leads the platoon, playing impeccably.

There is a sense of underlying sadness, if not weakness and ill-suitedness, about the *Dad's Army* platoon. These are not the barrel-chested men of action of the *Warlord* comic. Mummy's boy Pike, spiv Walker, blabbermouth Frazer, senile Jones, the barely continent Godfrey, the enigmatically passive Wilson and Mainwaring, with his rather fraught home life and upbringing, could have been lonely, unfulfilled men without the war. Only banding together in the Home Guard has lent these gamma males a sense of common purpose and collective strength. Losers they may be, but they are on the winning side and deserve to be so for the bravery and solidarity they would certainly have shown had they been overrun.

Much is made of how the writers of *Dad's Army* based the characters on those of the actors themselves. This is true, to a degree, of the older members, though not Clive Dunn, whose politics veered from a flirtation with fascism in his youth to a lifelong commitment to socialism. Certainly, John Le Mesurier was temperamentally akin to Wilson, for sure, all 'awfully's and 'dear boy's and 'delightful's. Arnold Ridley possessed a similar temperament and sense of misfortune quietly endured to Godfrey. During World War I, Ridley suffered a bayonet wound which left him with permanent damage to his right arm. Sent home early, he found himself the recipient of a white feather from a woman in the street, who assumed he was shirking conscription. He said nothing – much as he said nothing in 'Branded' (1969), when Mainwaring and the platoon assumed he had been a World War I 'conchie' out of cowardice. In fact, as his sister was obliged to explain on his behalf, Godfrey had worked as a medical orderly, and, like Ridley, took part in the Battle of the Somme, going out into no man's land, saving several lives. Some of the unhappiness of the lives of Ridley, the alcoholic Arthur Lowe and the cuckolded John Le Mesurier carries over into the roles they play.

Bill Pertwee was the complete opposite of his character, Hodges: he was the soul of conviviality on set and the man to whom it fell to warm up audiences during shooting. 'Yes, Godfrey was very Godfrey,' he told me.

> And John [Le Mesurier], well, he just played himself, didn't he? Oddly enough, in the case of John Laurie, it was a remark of his in real life that became a hallmark of Frazer's throughout the series. When *Dad's Army* was first mooted, he was very sceptical. He said to Jimmy Perry, 'It's rubbish! Och, it's just a bunch of silly auld men running about in a field, it'll never catch on.' And then when it was successful, he told Jimmy he'd always had faith in the show from the start! As for Arthur Lowe, he had a lot of Mainwaring in him. He had a curious habit, whenever we met socially for a meal, of addressing us all by our character names. He'd organise for everyone to get together, saying, 'What time shall we be on parade?' And he'd say things like, 'Oh, do wake up, Godfrey,' if Arnold Ridley looked like dozing off – and when the bill came he'd wave it away, saying, 'Oh, give it to the warden. The warden'll take care of it.' So I'd always end up paying the bill.

One suspects Arthur Lowe's real-life character lay somewhere between Mainwaring and his alter ego Barry. He did a great deal of work before, during and after *Dad's Army*: as one of the regular players in the films of Lindsay Anderson, starring in sitcoms such as *Potter* (1979–80), as a retired sweet manufacturer and an amiable priest in *Bless Me, Father* (1978–81), as well as a one-off part as an exceptionally dim Watson opposite John Cleese as Sherlock Holmes. He once said that it was as well for actors to have as little personality as possible, so that all their efforts at characterisation could be invested in their work. Lowe seems to have revelled in the smallnesses of human life; he obsessed over food and meals, and liked to be sure that there was a newsagent at hand where he could purchase Craven A cigarettes. He was a Tory, but not an especially thoughtful one – the sort of Conservative for whom the politics is an excuse to grumble and cherish unexamined petty prejudices.

He may well, as Hodges attests, have played up to the role of Mainwaring in private life in superficial aspects, but Mainwaring would have been horrified at Lowe's lax attitude to preparing his lines and his heavy drinking and smoking, the signs of a quietly nihilistic soul: taking oneself not too seriously taken to a sad extreme. The very last footage of him is a 1982 interview on *Pebble Mill at One*. He died hours later following a stroke, aged sixty-six but looking puffier and older. The flood of tributes to his acting career, however, was richly deserved; his is a legacy immaculately preserved.

The durability of *Dad's Army* is in large part due to the quality of the writing and of the characters and the warm familiarity they engender. These episodes aren't just a reminder of wartime solidarity but of all our TV times over the past fifty years. They have accrued redolences for so many of baked beans on toast and the warm, damp aroma of ironing in the living room, of shag-pile carpets and long-dead pets.

By 2017, there was a growth in the use of *Dad's Army* as a metaphor for Brexit: the idea that, with British character and improvisation, we could see off Europe against the odds, proud island race that we are, yea even unto Agincourt. A quote from TV presenter Chris Tarrant, interviewed by the *Guardian* in 2018, about why he now wanted the UK to leave the EU sums up an attitude of exceptionalism that persists among more senior types: 'I think the sooner we get out, the better. We will survive and carry on very nicely because we're British.'

Dad's Army became a battleground for both Brexiters and Remainers. On the one hand, Nigel Farage concocted the rousing soundbite, 'Who do you think you are kidding, Mr Juncker?', while European Commission deputy president Frans Timmermans once accused then-prime minister Theresa May's negotiating team of running around like '*Dad's Army* idiots'.

What might the cast have made of Brexit? One can imagine Mainwaring being mustard keen, initially at least, with Corporal

Jones hopping about enthusiastically, promising 'a touch of cold steel' to obstinate EU negotiators, Wilson rubbing his chin with a 'Do you think that's wise?', Frazer dismissing the exercise as a Sassenach folly, Walker minding only insofar as it affects his import/export business, Pike made to vote Remain by his mum, who, we learn, has shares in the Channel Tunnel, and the vicar simply wishing the whole beastly business could be done with.

The last word on this subject should go to Jimmy Perry himself, speaking to Francis Gilbert in *The Times* in 2009. Unlike many Britons of a certain age who have convinced themselves they are part of the war generation but were actually born several years after it ended, Perry experienced World War II at first hand and came to very different conclusions from some of the junior, boomer generation. 'It does worry me that many young people today aren't interested in the wider issues connected with Europe,' he said. 'For example, I think anyone who lived during the war appreciates the European Union, if only because it's much better to be trading with each other than blowing each other's heads off.'

As it happened, it was the younger generation who voted for Remain in droves, who understood all too well what generations of *Dad's Army* watchers preceding them failed to – but not its co-creator.

KEN DODD, LES DAWSON, MORECAMBE AND WISE, TOMMY COOPER

In our own somewhat fragmented and atomised media age, in which larger numbers of people don't watch TV in real time at all, with multiple outlets and fewer shared TV experiences, it is hard to convey the sense of warmth and consolation that the best TV comedy afforded to mass British audiences. *Dad's Army*, nestled safely in the known past, offered its own form of assurance as to how our character might bear up in our darkest hours when power cuts were visited on the UK, following industrial action by electricity supply workers. I vividly remember how cruel indeed it felt to have the comfort blanket, the perpetual fix, of the ever-switched-on TV removed. Then, more than any decade since, or even before, you watched the telly as a family, albeit reluctantly. The good, the bad, the rubbish, the grown-up and incomprehensible: you watched the telly because the terrible alternative was not watching the telly. And in that age of quantity as well as quality, comedy played a starring role, not just in reflecting the British character but also in feeding it in some way. Those middle-class parents who put locks on their TV cabinets or banned their children from watching TV altogether were not being progressive or responsible, as they imagined, but enacting child cruelty. The playground was a lonely place for those children.

There was a raft of familiar faces in the early seventies. But five comedians in particular whose fame was at its zenith in that era represented a Britain that was not 'with it', mostly had to do without it. They were weather-beaten, as familiar as old slippers, and their working lives and formative experiences stretched back to a previous age, to the end of World War II. These were Ken Dodd, Les Dawson, Morecambe and Wise and Tommy Cooper.

These were hardly our finest men – not our handsomest, or most go-ahead, or most heroic. They could well have lined up in the second rank of Captain Mainwaring's platoon. They were not iconoclasts or trailblazers. They were certainly not radicals; they were not, as a rule, overtly political, which was probably fortunate. They were middle-aged men who at times affected, perhaps genuinely felt, a sense of innocent confusion at the pace of social change in Britain after the war; they had the air of men left behind at the starting gun, looking at each other, at us, in confusion: 'What happened?' Their physical condition seemed to speak about the British condition – a nation very able to laugh at itself, with much to laugh about. But they were gentle creatures whose point was existential rather than bitter or reactionary. Simply to regard their countenances was to experience at once their warming familiarity and the guarantee of hilarity they represented, before even opening their mouths. They were highly distinctive but had elements in common. None enjoyed international fame; they tended to vote Conservative, despite their natural identification with the underdog, the put-upon, the down-to-earthness of the regions, the gauche. They were often careful with money, a meanness born out of insecurity about their success. And yet all were so loved that they simply had to appear from behind a stage curtain to raise a laugh.

Loved as they were, they were not necessarily easy to love in private, whether workaholic, inconsiderate of others, politically unpalatable or financially criminal. It was as if they left the best of themselves onstage. But for all that, they were, in uncertain, fraying times, a source of assurance and joy.

'Really?' said Lenny Henry, initially with some surprise but then, after a moment's consideration, a nod of approval. It was 1989, and I was interviewing him for *Melody Maker*. I told him Ken Dodd had been voted the comedian's comedian by the *Observer*. 'By Jove,' he whistled, a casually perfect Doddy impression. He then went off on a general appreciation of a certain mode of comedy in which 'it's the bloke that's funny, not the joke'.

Ken Dodd was one such 'bloke' who managed to burrow a place for himself deep in the affections of the British people on the strength of his intrinsic qualities alone: his face, his demeanour, his very being.

Although there's much for young comedians to learn from studying Dodd, few in today's darkly suited, observational stand-up milieu would emulate his onstage appearance, which bellowed, 'Here, I'll tell you what, you're going to be tickled pink by this, I guarantee you,' which is generally considered an unwise preface to the delivery of comedy. Dodd, however, was the clown prince of exceptions. Take his 1999 Royal Variety performance, for which he sported a full-length red furry coat with outsized white buttons, a Union Jack topper and a selection of his tickling sticks, all of this combined with a scarecrow riot of hair and buck teeth.

The massive hit he had with 'Tears' notwithstanding, Dodd was a comedian, the whole comedian and nothing but the comedian. He was, in other respects, a man without qualities. He lived and died in his family home in Knotty Ash, the Liverpool suburb whose name took on a certain Doddiness by association. He had two major relationships, both involving lengthy engagements, the first curtailed by the death of his fiancée Anita Boutin, the second, to Anne Jones, culminating in his marrying her on her deathbed. In 1989, he was charged with tax evasion and was considered lucky to have got off.

Dodd found early success in radio and TV, emerging around the same time as the Beatles, with whom he was interviewed as if they were all part of the same up-and-coming Liverpudlian showbiz wave. His own comedy, however, belonged to a world in which they never happened, a saucy, picture-postcard milieu. He would throw in contemporary references – his 1999 routine included cracks about New Labour stalwarts Peter Mandelson and John Prescott – but right into the twenty-first century, his frame of reference implied a long-gone, once-upon-a-time Britain of 'housewives' and the 'gas board' of which he himself was a survivor, and a comforting reminder. You could deplore him as the ultimate specimen of British anti-seriousness – a Tory, like many of his contemporaries, which might well suggest a lack of real moral empathy or reflection on the evolving state of society, a living specimen of the little man at the heart of the British soul, stunting its growth by repeating in its ear over and over, 'You have to laugh.' (You don't have to laugh.) But Doddy's relentlessness brooks no such qualms. With him, you do have to laugh.

He lost his regular TV berth, his appearances drying up somewhat after 1982 as the sensibilities of commissioning editors, unlike Doddy, began to shift with the times, but this didn't put him out. He considered his true home to be the stage, and spent the remainder of his life mostly on the road, happy playing to audiences in the low thousands, subsisting gleefully on the gales of their laughter rather than TV audience ratings.

If there's an underlying theme to his work, it's the inadequacy of manhood, which he conveys with a nod and a wink to the ruefully understanding 'missus' to whom he addresses the bulk of his comedy. From his sidekicks the Diddymen – including Stephen 'Tich' Doyle, Little Evan, Hamish McDiddy, Nigel Ponsonby-Smallpiece and Ben 'Tiny Ween' Winston – to his tickling stick, it's all about willies and the smallness thereof. He himself, and the ridiculous figure he cuts, embodies man as disappointing animal. A YouTube compilation of his work attracts a multitude of comments congratulating him on the lack of 'smut'. Well, one of his routines involves a wizened little woman, a leprechaun, who tells a passing man that she will grant him wishes, to which he gratefully responds, opting for a large house and a beautiful woman awaiting him there. The leprechaun says she will grant his wishes on the condition that he fucks her. The man reluctantly fucks her, then asks for his wishes. 'How old are you?' asks the wizened woman. 'Thirty-four', answers the man. 'And you still believe in leprechauns?'

Of course, Dodd's version isn't as I paraphrase it, but couched in much more euphemistic, granny-friendly language. A rib-tickling, buck-toothed tale of wee leprechauns, by Jove.

In Doddyland, it's a perpetually lovely day for mischief, of jam butty mines and a private language in which we are tickled, marmalised and discumnockerated into submission. Dodd's lengthy sets worked by cumulative effect, like a boxer who overwhelms his opponent with flurries of light punches rather than a knockout blow. At one point, watching one of these routines, I turned the sound down. The comic effect was largely undiminished – Dodd gesticulating to the rafters, his face set in an expression of merriment, both anticipatory and self-celebratory, and his head jerking about like that of a ventriloquist's dummy.

Bob Monkhouse said of Dodd that his 'entire presentation has been a disguise', that when he eventually left the stage he 'dies a little death and becomes once again the ordinary bloke that Kenneth

Dodd is in real life'. You might say that he was both ventriloquist and his own dummy, for whom coming off stage meant going back into the dull box of everyday life. In which case, it's small wonder that he wished to defer the moment of departure for so long. He toured to the end of his life, a reminder of a pre-'smut' Britain that never was.

By contrast with Dodd, Les Dawson was a man of the written word. When his TV career began to peter out, he consoled himself that he could now dedicate more time to his great love, writing. His routines feel composed. He was a paradox – a man of elegant and refined abilities who nonetheless bore the put-upon demeanour of a crushed grape on a cobblestone. He would soar rhetorically aloft before crashing down to earth in a bathetic splat of flattened vowels. His face was creased and caved in, a mishap in a boxing bout in his youth rearranging his features so that he could face-shift freely. Gurn and bear it.

Dawson was born in 1931 in Collyhurst, Manchester, and spent his formative years and beyond developing his comedy skills, influenced by Northern comedians such as Rob Wilton (on investing in a greyhound: 'I wouldn't say it was slow but on the first race a hare bit its leg'), while also mugging up on essayists like Charles Lamb, who fed his love of language and its higher, purple realms. His was a lengthy spell in the school of hard knocks and the University of Life, from which he emerged not exactly with distinction but with a certain resilience. Only when he appeared on *Opportunity Knocks* in his mid-thirties did he establish himself as a household name.

The Dawson persona was a miserabilist, an exquisitely vulgar man who held you in his thrall with his penetrating, hangdog stare. He often dressed as John Bull, the stout, Union flag-waistcoated personification of the United Kingdom created by the friend and contemporary of Jonathan Swift, John Arbuthnot; he represented a divot of England that was forever stoical, perhaps too stoical. He was alive to the privations endured by many in the North in the 1930s, but was politically averse to the idea of anything being done about it. In 1985, he looked back on his childhood wistfully: 'If two men fought it was with fists and fair play, and all the policemen were beefy Sons of Erin who corrected an offender with a judicial clout, not a charge sheet.' Beautifully put, but merely an elegant spin on clichés about bobbies fetching wrong 'uns a clip round the ear before the dark days of the welfare state.

Dawson expanded on this in a *Parkinson* interview at the height of his fame, in 1974, when recession was pawing at the door of British society. He felt it could be character-building, reinstil the lost sense of community of his youth – 'Tightening our belts could be the best thing for us.' A return to the thirties, before everyone was cut off indoors watching their colour televisions. The irony of a well-to-do comedian extolling the virtues of poverty and decrying the very medium, television, which was responsible for his national fame was lost on Dawson. He would further elaborate on his fears for modern Britain in one of a number of novels he wrote, *A Time Before Genesis* (1986), in which he envisaged Britain falling to a far-left government, the Socialist Union Movement Party, in which entertainment was reduced to live sex shows, while comedians, free thinkers like himself, found themselves imprisoned. It was the most eloquent and extended expression of the latent fears of the old-style comedian in a modern Britain they imagined was imminently susceptible to leftist extremism.

Fortunately, Dawson was never defined or disfigured by these thoughts. Yes, he told mother-in-law jokes, but these were understood, not least by his own mother-in-law, as so ridiculously over the top as to be more ritual than misogynistic sniping. Their surreality sprang from the reality among the working class of having to live cheek by jowl with elders even when married. Dawson's 'mother-in-law' is simply a device for invention so grossly far-fetched it could touch no nerves. 'She once went for a swim in Loch Ness, and the monster got out and picketed the lake.' Her house is 'decorated in early Dracula'. 'When she hangs her brassiere up to dry, a camel makes love to it.'

And then there were Cissy and Ada, first introduced as sketch characters on the *Sez Les* show (1969–76), a priceless pairing whose gossipy exchanges descended into silent lip movement whenever the topic of unmentionables was broached. Dawson said that this was inspired by women millworkers who were forced to communicate with one another above the din of the machinery, but it's a wonderful device for conveying the implicitness of British comedy, these lapses into silence which leave so much to the imagination. Roy Barraclough played Cissie as a lady of advanced years with a certain sense of social superiority, but in reality no better than Dawson's Ada. He, by contrast, makes little attempt to conceal his not very comfortable-looking undergarments, even extracting alcoholic miniatures from them or adjusting his brassiere. Cissy and Ada are beautifully observed specimens of piety and prurience, affecting handbag-clutching disgust but all ears when the beans are being spilled.

In 1984, Dawson took over *Blankety Blank*. He made much of his inadequacy and incongruity amid the glitz of a primetime quiz show, while holding himself a cut above its fiscally constricted naffness and the B-list celebrity guests he had to suffer. On one occasion, the British boxer Terry Marsh offered a less than adequate response, at which Dawson turned to camera and said, 'One punch too many.'

The last time I saw Les Dawson was in a piece in which he revisited his old Lancastrian haunts with a TV journalist. He stared out onto the grey west coast sea on a bracing day and remarked of the cold waters, 'The fish wear mittens.' In 1993, he died. Yet watching him again it feels like just yesterday. Although decidedly Northern and decidedly of his generation, he regarded the North–South and generational divides as 'delusional'. Add to that the divide of decades.

Dawson brought to 1970s British comedy a certain bracing rain; Eric Morecambe and Ernie Wise brought sunshine. Although they had risen to fame much earlier than Dawson, there was more of a youthful skip about the pair, a showbiz dynamism that contrasted with Dawson's perpetually sunken jowls. Morecambe was a Lancastrian, like Dawson, Wise from Leeds, but there's far less of a sense of cobblestoned Northern origin about the duo, whose ostensible ambition it was to ingratiate themselves with the great and good of showbiz. But as with Dawson on *Blankety Blank*, celebrities generally ended up coming a cheerful cropper on their shows.

In one of the best-known Morecambe and Wise sketches, they invite André Previn to conduct Grieg's piano concerto. Eric, in full tails, is the pianist; unfortunately, his progress during the opening bars to the keyboard is prancing and circuitous, so that when Previn jabs his baton in his direction, he's not settled in his seat. Rather than adjust his walk, he suggests Previn lengthen the introduction 'by a yard'. This works, but this time, on reaching the keyboard, he plays a jaunty ditty unrelated to the score, which brings a priceless stare of horror from Previn. He upbraids him, only for Morecambe to curtly inform him that he is playing all the right notes, 'but not necessarily in the right order'.

What's striking is the role of Ernie. A more conventional straight man might have offered profuse apologies for his imbecilic partner to the distinguished guest. Instead, however, he looks on approvingly as Eric belts out the ditty. He maintains his hostly respect for 'Mr Preview' but is nonplussed as to what his objections to Eric's playing might be.

Such was the closeness between the Eric and Ernie personae. They bickered; Ernie had a short way with Eric's messing about, especially during the plays what he wrote, while Eric slapped the smaller man's cheeks and lambasted his 'short, fat, hairy legs' and supposed toupee. However, they were an inseparable proposition. They were ultimately loyal to each other, as Eric demonstrated in a late sketch, in which he suspects a magazine journalist is seeking to stitch Ernie up for his terrible plays. Eric takes her aside and warns her off. 'You hurt him, you hurt me . . . You know that he can't write. I know that he can't write. He thinks he can, and that's good enough for me.'

Morecambe and Wise were entering their Saturday-night heyday as

I began to become conscious of television, in around 1970. The seventies would belong to them, but unlike later decades, which belonged to younger and more quickly broken comedy superstars, they had been awaiting the big time since World War II. They first teamed up in 1941, in their teens, a product of the variety era – the stage curtain persists on their TV shows, as much a prop as a throwback to the music hall. They made a poorly received TV series in 1954 but had a second chance with the series *Two of a Kind* during the 1960s, before moving to the BBC in 1968. It was only when they hired the writer Eddie Braben in 1969 that they reached their career zenith and made the work for which they're held in eternal public affection.

They weren't really a straight man/funny man combo – more like a funny man and a very funny man, Eric. Other great comedians might have used their eyes as part of their armoury of comic effects, but not Eric. His thick, black-rimmed glasses were his strongest visual motif, but even up close you could barely make anything out through their lenses. Unlike Ken Dodd, there was nothing innately amusing about Eric's stage appearance: regular suit, middle-aged baldness, those glasses; he could easily have passed for a secondary-school geography teacher, were he not so famous for being who he was.

Instead, with Eric, it's not so much looks as a gamut of wheezing and hawing facial expressions, especially when he's faced with a situation in which he has to consider his next response. Take the scene in which he's been presented by Ernie with an album by Des O'Connor. The boys share a series of gags at Des's expense – 'Where did you get it from?' 'Boots!' 'Did you need a prescription?' 'I got it at the poison counter!' – only for Des to stroll onstage behind them. Eric spots him before Ernie: a nervous cough, an adjustment of the specs, jowls buried shamefully in his chest; it's a delightful visual phrasing of the comedy of realisation. He immediately changes tack, praising O'Connor's charm and lovely singing voice.

By this point, the Eric and Ernie personae were long established: Ernie, with his desire to elevate the tone of the show with his plays, to maintain at least a semblance of showbiz sanity in his introductions, while Eric is the epitome of Northern worldliness, a contrast to the show's invariably grand guest stars. He is a totem of ridiculousness, there to puncture the balloons of oratory in Ernie's theatre pieces or introduce the subject of football at the most inappropriate moments. 'What news of Carlisle?' asks Peter Cushing, in a segment of cod-Shakespearean historical drama. 'They won 3–1,' says Eric. Again, Ernie lets all this pass, rather than perpetually exploding, Peter Glaze-style. He's too much in love with Eric to do that.

Morecambe and Wise shared an insecurity with the likes of Dodd and Dawson, a fear that what they had worked for all their lives could disappear overnight. With Morecambe and Wise, this insecurity manifested itself in workaholism. They never took their success for granted. In between TV series, they would be flat out touring the regions, the city halls, the Winter Gardens. However, this placed undue strain on Eric, who had a weak heart, suffering a major attack in 1968 and dying of heart failure in 1984, aged fifty-eight. Vic Reeves and Bob Mortimer, who bore a superficial resemblance to Morecambe and Wise, decided they were overdoing it at the height of their fame and took a sabbatical – but as with professional footballers, they were earning bigger bucks than their predecessors. Eric and Ernie never felt secure enough to do the same.

All of which is ironic since they commanded massive TV audiences in their heyday, albeit in an era where there were fewer channels. Such was their success, especially in the Christmas schedules, that they had at their command the whole gamut of UK showbiz, from high dramatists like Glenda Jackson to Vegas doyennes like Shirley Bassey and Tom Jones. It was a mandatory rite for all in the firmament that they should participate in one of Ernie's costume dramas and be cut down to size by Eric, their appearances generally culminating in some old-school dance routine, and they certainly look as though they were enjoying every minute.

Among their most popular shows, however, were those featuring

BBC presenters. Their parody of *South Pacific*, for example, featured newsreaders Peter Wood and Kenneth Kendall, as well as Barry Norman, Eddie Waring and Frank Bough in sailor outfits belting out 'There Is Nothing Like a Dame' and 'performing' acrobatics clearly executed by stunt doubles. Previous to that, in 1976, they had featured newsreader Angela Rippon, who performed a dance routine with Eric and Ernie which sent the nation's popular print media into palpitations. Today, the crossover between newsreaders and entertainment is commonplace – Chris Hollins on *Strictly Come Dancing*, for example – but in the seventies, a high-kicking Rippon represented an unprecedented and much-needed act of levity, a form of national catharsis.

Ben Elton once complained that whenever the BBC put together a package of the best of Morecambe and Wise, they always lazily reached for the Angela Rippon clip. Why don't they ever show those sketches of them in bed together, in their flat, bickering about nothing, making comedy out of nothing? A police car flashing by, siren at full blast, and Eric remarking, 'He'll never sell any ice cream going at that speed.'

Looking up some of their less frequently broadcast sketches can be disquieting, however. The writer Andy Medhurst used the word 'homosocial' in reference to Bob and Terry in *The Likely Lads* – men who, while not gay, clearly preferred and sought out the company of their own sex over any other, despite rubbing each other up the wrong way. Morecambe and Wise were another such pairing. However, notes Medhurst, it is necessary for homosocials, in homophobic word and deed, to stress frequently that they are not gay. With Morecambe and Wise, there is a sketch in which they visit the dressing room of actor Eric Porter. He's not immediately available, but they are welcomed in by his somewhat camp assistant, played by Michael Ward. Eric bridles uncomfortably in his presence. 'I don't know about you, but I'm off!' Backing stiffly away, he tells Ernie, 'Don't start anything you can't finish.'

When they are cooped up together, Ernie working on one of his plays, Eric mooching about idly, they seem bored: Eric opening and shutting doors, messing about with a fishing rod trying to 'catch' Ernie's toupee. In one unfortunate sketch, their tedium is relieved only when a young female neighbour calls in on some flimsy pretext and, after a bit of coy back and forth, Eric and Ernie speedily take her by the arms and repair to the bedroom. 'Fade out, roll captions, off to bed,' quips Eric. This is not the best of Morecambe and Wise.

What such sketches do reveal is that Eric and Ernie were more than a close duo; they were practically a single entity – one of the reasons why they worked so frequently with guest stars. Even as a duo they weren't self-sufficient. They craved the company of third parties to work off.

Still, for all of this, Morecambe and Wise were deservedly beloved, the sunshine to Ken Dodd's happiness, who broke through the perma-grey clouds of the 1970s with their vitamin D. They were everywhere in my childhood – on chat shows, presenting a show featuring scripts written by kids, at Graham Hill's funeral, in boys' football annuals, on *The Sweeney*, in comic books. They were all our uncles. The 1977 Christmas show was watched, according to some estimates, by up to twenty-eight million people. However, at this point the duo chose unwisely to switch to ITV, upon which they sank into irrelevance. By going to ITV they forfeited their place in the TV firmament, jettisoned a vast section of their significance in British life. They were Tory voters but they felt very much at home in the Wilson era, as binding agents of the post-war consensus in the UK. With them disappeared a very different Britain, a pre-Thatcher Britain, whose worn fabric they helped pull together. And Christmases were indeed never quite Christmases again.

There is, as we have seen, the occasional bone in the comedy fish served up by Morecambe and Wise – a British Rail-related sketch involving blackface and a Jimmy Savile reference makes for particularly unfortunate viewing. Tommy Cooper, by contrast, is virtually boneless. A comic presence in the UK since being demobbed after World War II, there is about him a flat-footed, weather-beaten hapless-ness and unfitness for serious purpose that speaks directly to the nature of British self-deprecation. As with all this group of five comedians, he did not enjoy great international success – he remained as exclusive a part of the British experience as brown sauce. One can be excused a certain feeling of national pride in that.

'What you've got there is a Stradivarius and a Rembrandt. Unfortunately . . .'

You're laughing already. No comedian had more ability to make people laugh before even cracking a joke than Tommy Cooper. There's a story of him getting off jury service out of fears that his very presence, simply sitting quietly alongside his fellow jurors, would inevitably be a distraction from the serious court business at hand.

It helps that he never attempted seriousness. Even Eric Morecambe published a novel. Cooper reserved all his seriousness for his craft. There's a story of Cooper as a child pulling off the trick of appearing to be reading a newspaper as he rode a bike at full speed. He did it by cutting two small holes in the newspaper so he could see where he was going. He wasn't reading the newspaper at all. He didn't take in current affairs; sports news and politics passed him by. He had a childlike indifference to such preoccupations. Barry Cryer recalled him being in a bar when such adult conversations were going on all around him, socially adrift. To draw attention back to himself, he would perform a magic trick, from his vast trove of tricks, which he practised constantly, obsessively, even on the toilet. As a man, Tommy Cooper was guilty of many things: infidelity, stinginess, inebriation. But on stage he was the epitome of innocence, sharing with the likes of P. G. Wodehouse a wholly successful failure to take things seriously – a very British trait, not always a desirable one, but one which he manifested to supreme advantage.

Cooper was one of a generation of gifted comedians who tried their luck in showbusiness after being demobbed, rising to prominence in an age when the old rules lay in ruins and new opportunities to make fun were up for grabs. Though he was well established by the 1960s, what survives best is Cooper's colour ITV output from the 1970s.

What are we laughing at? A Tommy Cooper with decades of stagecraft behind him; a seasoned Tommy Cooper, a well-known and well-loved Tommy Cooper, those watery eyes brimming with mirth and haplessness, and an incomprehension in part genuine. He himself could not put his finger on his innate appeal. What are you laughing at?

The face. A beat-up face, bulging chin, a downturned mouth, lips that have long lost their pucker, a bulbous red nose; a face knocked out of shape by bad living, forlorn and lugubrious, yet cracking open time and again as he breaks the golden rule of comedy: don't laugh at your own jokes. Only Basil Brush laughed harder. It's an infectious, inviting laughter, the biggest guffaws saved for the worst jokes and props: 'Horn-rimmed glasses!' he declares, donning a pair of specs with animal horns attached. Props like a pair of gloves stitched together are picked up and discarded immediately, jokes likewise: 'I've always been unlucky. I had a rocking horse – it died.'

Cooper didn't suit every element. He was once denied the opportunity to appear on *The Muppet Show*, which might have helped him break America, but it's hard to see him striking up a chemistry with Kermit, Miss Piggy and Fozzie Bear. He'd get lost in the show's format. Hard also to imagine him in a sitcom, with all the grown-up dimensionality required. Film? He performs creditably in *The Plank* (1967), written by and co-starring Eric Sykes, about two dim workmen and the misadventures they have with a length of wood. However, it feels like a poor (English)man's response to the much more sublime Jacques Tati.

Cooper did sketches to variable effect. In one, he plays a down-and-out-looking character in a scruffy bedsit, desperate for work, who auditions for a revival of a 1940s musical. He somehow gets the job, which involves some prolonged business involving him completely at sea in the dance routines in top hat and tails. Prior to this, however, he has a piece of dialogue with his own mirror reflection. 'I'm sick of you!' 'And I'm sick of you!' he replies to himself. It's an absurdist, uncomfortable scene, grist to those of Cooper's colleagues who suspected that in private, not unlike Marilyn Monroe, Tommy Cooper felt himself to be a separate entity from the 'Tommy Cooper' who appeared onstage.

Cooper never seemed at ease interacting with other adults – not other men, not even Alan Cuthbertson, his long-time straight man, not other women, who often made him nervous. He was hardly undersexed – as well as his wife Gwen, Cooper had a long-term lover, Mary Kay, as if it took two women to provide the necessary emotional care for this man-child. But generally, Cooper did not go in for the sort of gurning and phwooaaring of other seventies comedians – Les Dawson, Sid James – whenever a 'dolly bird' hove into view.

In December 1980, he was, bizarrely, booked to support the Police, in a large, overcrowded marquee in Tooting Bec. Partly fazed by the sea of potentially querulous post-punk types in the crowd and partly because he was dead drunk, he did not perform well; the irritable audience began booing and baying for him to leave the stage. Sting himself, a Cooper fan, intervened and, in full schoolteacherly mode, told the crowd that if they did not pay Mr Cooper the proper respect due to him, the Police would not be playing that evening; but, as Cooper himself admitted, he had flopped.

Cooper, however, generally thrived before an audience, be they his peers, as a guest on *This Is Your Life* to the likes of Bill Fraser, or as guest of honour at a Variety Club speech ('I went to the doctor's and he looked in my mouth and said, "A little raw," so I said, "Raagghhhr"'). Or a TV audience, as on his various appearances on *Parkinson* or Bob Monkhouse's chat shows, walking onstage with a saucepan on his head or wearing huge chicken legs. This extinguished any prospect of probing into that less happy character, the 'real' Tommy Cooper, unintellectual, fiscally mean, a long-term adulterer, whose lack of punctuality and increasingly heavy drinking would eventually all but end his TV career.

Cooper is at his joyous best against the white backdrop of a TV stage, topped off with a fez, a table of props to his right. There's no blackface accompaniment to his wearing of the fez; there's the faintest association of the snake charmer vis-à-vis his magic, but really the fez is an unexplained act of comic incongruity that became utterly congruent with Cooper, essential to his identity.

Despite his act itself being a mock shambles, Cooper himself doesn't shamble. He isn't static or lumpen. Generally in immaculate evening dress, he glides, sashays, flutters. He moves from left to right, in circles around his table, as if establishing his space. Even his mock-nervous cough is delivered with a certain panache. He shoots his cuffs, he fingers his lapels. All this fastidiousness is the perfect counterpoint to the cropper he invariably comes in his act.

For all his physical grace, the poise with which he holds an audience in the palm of his hand, conscious that a judicious silence on his part will inflate a titter to a mass belly laugh, for all his thorough foreknowledge of precisely where every prop for his magic tricks sits on that table, stumbling and mishap are ingrained into his act. No ad-libbing, no real cock-ups – everything is meticulously scripted and planned. Even sober, he slurs. His accent slithers all over the shop. Born in Wales, he was moved as a child to Exeter, so a Devonian burr is there in mix, alongside a touch of Cockney. Words are lost or compounded as he delivers his lines; scissors becomes 'swizzers', other words are misshapen, phlegm-soaked emissions, a gravelly mess, but it doesn't matter – his laughs aren't contingent on impeccable delivery. In any case, quite often, the noise, the sludge from his throat, *is* the joke – not just the 'little raw' but the noise of an X-ray machine buzzing in his mouth, his ludicrous magical incantations as he makes a spoon dance in a jar.

It's poignant that so many of Cooper's jokes are doctor jokes, given the ailments that befell him: thrombosis, bronchitis, asthma, heart attacks. Given his onstage demise in 1984, collapsing and dying of a heart attack in front of an audience of millions in mid-performance on the ITV variety show *Live at Her Majesty's*, it's retrospectively saddening to see him clutch the left side of his chest after an unexpected onstage bang, or being frightened by entering a dark cupboard. But then, part of what makes Cooper funny is his physical stricken-ness. And, indeed, the jokes.

'I went to the doctor. I said, "I've broken my arm in several places." "Well," he said, "you shouldn't go to those places."'

It's the extended jokes, however, where Cooper truly takes you for a joyride. Sometimes the punchline is the weakest bit; sometimes he scrunches up and throws away the punchline so offhandedly that key words are unintelligible. But it's the business along the way that counts. Example: a bloke goes into a bar, takes a drink, looks to the people to the left of him and shouts, 'You're a bunch of idiots!', then looks to the people to the right and says, 'And you're a bunch of fools.' Then downs his drink and leaves. Next day, he does the same thing. 'You're a bunch of idiots! And you're a bunch of fools.' Downs drink, leaves. At which point, one of the bar regulars says, 'If he comes in here and does that again, I'm going to say something.' Whereupon Cooper picks an imaginary argument with the audience, at the potential expense of the entire joke; and in so doing, with every indignant pause, picks up half a dozen extra laughs.

Finally, his magic, the epitome of an act free of slickness, of adult accomplishment. The blindfolded wooden duck picking a card, the spoon dancing in a jar quite clearly attached to a piece of string, the blue handkerchief dyed white and the white handkerchief dyed blue 'magically' transposed. P. G. Wodehouse once described his Lord Emsworth, surprised to discover an item about his person, as having the 'air of an inexpert conjuror whose trick has succeeded contrary to his expectations'. Cooper is an expert conjuror whose tricks fail exactly in accordance with his expectations. He's a master bungler. Every rule of showbusiness, of showmanship, he breaks like a vase.

Yet he knows exactly what he's doing, and so do we: wasting our time in the best possible way. His comedy is non-observational, non-analytical, non-referential, unenlightening, a trestle table of inconsequential junk, throwaway visual puns, basic blokes in pubs, doctors; it is childlike, sexless, rarely problematic. All of which not only lends his comedy an enduring universality; it makes (non)sense regardless of your age, ethnicity, background. If you're left cold by Tommy Cooper, there's something wrong with you. Go to a doctor.

FAMILY FUN – THE MEMORABLY INDIFFERENT SITCOMS OF THE 1970S

Dawson, Dodd, Cooper, Morecambe and Wise were long-nurtured, prize-winning fruits of the seventies comedy garden, but they were part of a general zenith. Those who lived in that era recall not necessarily all the comedy but a less fragmented televisual age, in which the TV was central, the choice at once scarce (three channels) yet plentiful in feel. For watching television, regardless of what was on, was what you did, the unthinkable option being to switch the TV off and go do something infinitely more boring instead. Power cuts hit hard; the TV schedules were all.

The times did not feel especially glad, however. It became pretty clear soon into the seventies that this was not the dawning of the Age of Aquarius. The news, such as it made sense to my kid self, mostly consisted of querulous, joyless, grumbling men in thick spectacles and obdurate accents, or snooty Tory types trying their hardest to look down their noses at the masses addressed by the TV camera, as they explained how 'we' were all going to have to lower our expectations. For all the grumbling, the strife and rancorous exchanges between capital and labour, there was still something in that 'we': a relative lack of polarisation, of huge distance between the main parties, taking it in turns to keep the shambles of political life into degenerating into outright chaos. The country was down in the dumps but on solid ground, in it together, one nation. 'We' were all British, after all. Or so it seemed to me, aged eleven.

TV comedy was a unifying force in the UK, binding families in the living room. A show like *Man About the House* (1973–6) appealed as much to my grandparents as it did to me; TV and its abundance of shows was still a relative novelty for my grandma, born in 1898, as it was for me, born sixty-four years later. It created fabrics of varying quality, from silk to nylon, from the sow's ear of the imperceptibly slow but sure decline and deterioration of (so it felt) a once proud, dominant, self-assured and optimistic country. It was the comedy of ruefulness, of self-deprecation, of mishap and mild confusion at modernity, of disappointment but not despair, defeat shrugged off with good humour, even at some level welcomed as a British trait in these garish yet glum post-imperial times. Ultimately, British comedy benefited from, even reflected at times, the indolent, indoor habits of a country lacking either Scandinavian strenuousness or continental cafe culture.

Some 1970s comedy was too adult for me. *Dave Allen at Large* (1971–9), for instance, wreathed in cigarette smoke, bore the redolence of intriguing albeit undrinkable beverages like whisky. Still, I watched. I knew everything about Dave Allen: his vocal intonations, his missing half-finger, his catchphrase ('May your God go with you'), everything except what he was on about. However, I unjustly hated Peter Tinniswood's *I Didn't Know You Cared* (1975–9), because its nuances were just so much dour, incomprehensible ugliness to my ears.

Generally, however, in the 1970s, TV comedy felt as if it were tailor-made for me. I didn't catch half the jokes, laced with innuendo incomprehensible to me, but those frequent bursts of audience cheer cheered me in turn. I watched everything. Reruns imply that because programmes were broadcast in colour from about 1969, they were experienced as such in UK households. Mostly, they weren't. My parents acquired a colour TV set only in 1976. Prior to that, the cathode blaze of monochrome emanating from the

TV screen provided an electric refuge from the prosaic colour of everyday seventies life, which ran to browns, oranges, dark yellows, turgid greens. This meant *The Two Ronnies* and their multi-pronged comic approach and tirelessly risqué wordplay: a news item about two men at a ball bearing factory, one of whom had lost his bearings, the other . . . Or in one of their spoof detective dramas, a scene which took place in Paris in La Rue de remarques. Or *The Dick Emery Show*, wonderfully predictable in its catchphrases, a predictability later emulated by *The Fast Show*.

I even watched Roy Clarke's *Last of the Summer Wine* (1973– 2010), an extraordinarily long-lived sitcom considering its premise – three pensioners spending their twilight years enjoying a second, mischievous boyhood, mooching around a Northern town in the aimless spirit with which they would have kicked around stones and teased irascible locals in their school holidays. It was as old as the hills from the beginning – the hills down which a goggled Compo rolled in a bathtub familiar to me, having played football for my school on those very hills, in Holmfirth. Written in seaside-postcard Clarke-ese, *Last of the Summer Wine*, with its harmonica musings, wasn't so much funny – not even remotely – as a perennial reminder of Sunday evenings, baked beans, tea shops, drystone walls. Over its unbelievably long run, it would become an informal retirement home for yesteryear's stars: Thora Hird, Russ Abbot, Bert Kwouk, June Whitfield. All our British yesterdays, a balm for a British TV-watching demographic who, like the perennial Peter Sallis, had felt past it for decades.

Jane Freeman was a long-serving member of the cast of *Last of the Summer Wine*, only Sallis matched her longevity, appearing in the series from 1973 till its conclusion in 2010. As Ivy, she had a rough side to her tongue, keeping the elderly rascals in check and quarrelling with husband Sid (John Comer), and was not above inflicting corporal punishment with a tray to customers who stepped out of line. However, at heart she was no monster, kind when needs be.

In 1972, however, Freeman had starred in *The Fishing Party*, in the *Play for Today* series. Written by Peter Terson, it told the story of three Derbyshire miners having a jolly boys' break in Whitby. On fetching up there, however, Art (Brian Glover) is struck by the resolve that he and his pals should be models of respectability, so as to defy the expectations of their wives that they will spend their break getting roaringly drunk. It's a study in what passed for service, respectability and the desire for self-betterment in early-seventies Britain, with its mean-spirited, fraying sense of propriety.

To this end, they decide to check into an unlicensed bed-and-breakfast ('sheets, serviettes'), a place where, Art says, they will 'act respectable, with respect for property and standing'. And so they roll up at a guest house run by Audrey (Freeman), a formidable paragon of mean-spiritedness, and her put-upon husband, who craves only a spot of fishing rather than the work agenda set out for him by his wife, culminating in Christmas at her mother's.

When Art and his pals turn up on her doorstep, she coldly affects a posh accent as she clocks their rods and tackle. 'The season's ewver, I'm sew sorry.' However, this hauteur only encourages the would-be guests, even as she insults them ('You might get fixed up somewhere where folks aren't so particular'). After consultation with her husband, the nominal manager, she agrees to let the group stay, 'at great personal inconvenience'.

The boys are quite taken with their dismally spartan lodgings, whose attractions are headed by 'hot and cold running water'. However, Audrey's guest-house pride is not sufficient to stop her contemplating not giving the lodgers fresh sheets, thereby making a cash saving. After all, she says in justification, rough-looking as they are, they are unlikely to notice, especially as they will most certainly roll in dead drunk.

As it happens, they do get drunk but turn up nonetheless to breakfast. There, Art is disappointed as he tries to order sausage, bacon and eggs, merely to be told by Audrey that he can only order either sausage and eggs or bacon. 'I cannot tamper with the menu.' As for the kippers they crave, they are off, she announces, triumphantly. 'They were never on.' Kafka reborn in a boarding house.

The Fishing Party might be seen to deal in stereotypes – battle-axe seaside landlady, henpecked husband – but such is the quality of Terson's writing, and Freeman's playing in particular (she was a highly accomplished *Play for Today* regular), that it speaks Alan Bennett-esque volumes about class consciousness and its tensions, a certain wilfully austere misery played out in what should in theory be a vortex of gaiety, the seaside guest house. Freeman was a long-standing TV fixture as Ivy but victim at times to the broad, cosy, un-exploratory limitations of Roy Clarke's writing. Audrey, by contrast, is a lost companion comic specimen to Basil Fawlty.

I even watched ITV comedies when I was permitted; they had a greasy allure, like fish and chips instead of cottage pie. Among them was *Nearest and Dearest* (1968–73), featuring the diminutive Hylda Baker. I laughed then at her strange intonations, coated in would-be poshness and respectability, and the way she gurned and shimmied, or occasionally accidentally showed her voluminous bloomers, her malapropisms soaring over my pudding-bowl haircut.

Nearest and Dearest, like *Sykes* (1972–9), involved a brother–sister relationship, expediently maintaining a man–woman tension without having to deal with any sexual component, or children. Sexual intercourse might have been happening since 1963, but several years on, it had yet to happen in this corner of England.

Baker played Nellie, obliged to endure her ne'er-do-well brother Eli (Jimmy Jewel) as a condition of co-ownership of the pickle factory they had been bequeathed. It's a reminder that despite the Tupperware revolution and Habitat, many families still dwelt amid the cobbles, terraces, pollution-belching factories and handed-down dark brown fixtures and fittings of the twenties, thirties, forties. Jewel is an adequate foil as sitcom wastrel Eli, with his football rosette and habit of stumbling into the parlour at inopportune moments, such as when Nellie is trying to impress two women from a select local businesswomen's club. 'Have you ever been in the club?' one asks Nellie. 'No, I'm not married,' she replies, to rocketing guffaws.

This is poignant. Baker's first marriage broke down after she suffered two ectopic pregnancies, and while she lived in splendour at the height of her fame, her childlessness was a lifelong regret. Indeed, she traded for her fame on a persona humorously excluded from the possibility of sexual attraction or intercourse. Furthermore, the amusing confusion of mind she exhibited with her malapropisms ('I'm a maiden lady – I can say that without fear of contraception') manifested itself in real life, as she suffered from dementia in later years. Still, she was a redoubtable comic force, vibrating and bristling with insinuation, indignation, innuendo, eyes narrowing and glowering, snooty and raspingly crude – the funniest of her kind outside *Coronation Street*.

Whereas *Nearest and Dearest* harked back to a pre-sixties 'normality', its sequel, *Not on Your Nellie* (1974–5), sees Baker's character (Nellie Pickersgill, distinct from Nellie Pledge) relocate to London, again to take over a business run by an ailing father – a pub in Chelsea. This plunges her right into the sitcom seventies, leaving her frequently discombobulated. She is put out by a Black policeman, asking him if he is 'any relation to Al Jolson' and commiserating with him on being a 'foreigner', but it is she who is the real foreigner in London, having arrived as if from another country (the North) and another era (of blackfaced men singing 'Mammy'). In the opening episode, she finds herself at eye level with the breasts of a seaside-postcard busty barmaid and a window cleaner whose sideburns alone bristle with confessions, and she makes the acquaintance of a gay couple, or at least scriptwriters Roy Bottomley and Tom Brennand's notion of a gay couple, called, cleverly, Gilbert and George, Gilbert being particularly ooh-duckie in his flash, white, strawberry-laden ensembles. Another regular was an Asian Tube worker, who despite some 'yes please, thank you' dialogue is not the most egregious depiction of an Asian in a 1970s sitcom. The joke is that he gets beaten up a lot. There's a mutual tolerance among these characters – they are London. Baker, meanwhile, with her clog dances and practised lines recycled from her stage days ('It's quarter past – I must get a little hand put on this watch'), is a remnant of the old school, the old England still abiding in the age of glam rock, gay lib and immigration, solace for older viewers.

SOME MOTHERS DO 'AVE 'EM, THE GOODIES – YOU HAD TO BE THERE

A stranger fish was Frank Spencer (Michael Crawford), of *Some Mothers Do 'Ave 'Em* (1973–8). Much as the Bay City Rollers ruled the airwaves and groups like Lieutenant Pigeon reached number one, so we watched programmes like *Some Mothers Do 'Ave 'Em*. Not just watch, but enjoyed immensely. Odd, but there it is.

Frank Spencer is unique, a creature of comic imagination rather than nature: uniquely incompetent, although much of his stunt comedy was born of the supreme physical competence of Michael Crawford, unique in his trademark choice of trenchcoat and beret, uniquely effete, yet never camp. He's married to Betty, played by Michele Dotrice, whose mildness makes her probably the only woman on the planet Frank could be married to. He's heterosexual, somehow, we're assured, but his constant assertion 'I'm a man' is a giveaway. He says 'da' instead of 'the'. His theme music is played on piccolos. His catchphrase is 'Oooh!' He's in the British comedy tradition of un-men, from Stan Laurel through to Kenneth Williams, the Young Ones to Mr Bean. This is a drawback in the 1970s, the days of the 'labour exchange', when, as it is throughout *Some Mothers*, the word 'men' is synonymous with 'workers'. He is constantly pitted against other men, real, gruff, impatient men, like his neighbour (Glynn Edwards) or Mr Bradshaw, manager at the employment exchange. He fails catastrophically at everything he turns his hand to – postman, plumber's mate, ticket collector, security guard, night porter, trainee journalist. In a sense, however, he triumphs against every effort on the part of other men convinced they can make a man of him, mould him, reducing them as he does to paroxysms of frustrated rage as he drips like wet putty through their fists, leaving fire, collapse and electrical mishap in his wake. He is indomitably useless.

Massively popular, and a boon for trainee impressionists, *Some Mothers Do 'Ave 'Em* stands alone, a period one-hit wonder. Which it was for Raymond Allen, who, unusually for successful sitcom writers, succeeded with little else but *Some Mothers*.

Another uniquely seventies phenomenon, rarely broadcast since, was *The Goodies*, whose lifespan (1970–80) matched the decade exactly. Comprising Bill Oddie, Graeme Garden and Tim Brooke-Taylor, they came from the same undergraduate set as Pythons Graham Chapman, John Cleese and Eric Idle, and overlapped with them in their early careers: Brooke-Taylor was co-responsible for the 'Four Yorkshiremen' sketch, featuring four well-to-do Northern elderlies outdoing each other with tall tales of their deprived childhoods. (This is often mistakenly cited as a *Monty Python* sketch but was first broadcast on *At Last the 1948 Show* in 1967.) It became a truism to say that *The Goodies* was *Monty Python* for kids. This kid loved it.

'We do anything, anywhere, anytime' was the Goodies' motto, and certainly the mazy, zany range of their imaginations makes them hard to encapsulate. Initially, they were Goodies, hired on various missions to put the world to rights. Except sometimes they were baddies, crazed mercenaries, dictators or wild experimentalists accidentally letting enormous kittens loose on the city of London. As characters they represented a triangle of sorts: Graeme Garden represented science, reason, the bespectacled boffin of the group; the patriotically waistcoated Tim Brooke-Taylor represented the hubristic ruling classes, though he was the first to panic when things went awry – no prizes for who would have voted Remain and who would have voted Leave. Bill Oddie, meanwhile, represented Everyone Else, the miscellaneous common people.

Unlike Frank Spencer, eternally identifiable in his beret and coat, the Goodies adopted countless garbs. Among those garbs was blackface, for which they showed an unfortunate fondness. There was the big-lipped Black American boxer in the 'Ecky Thump' episode, halloo-dah-ing away. Or themselves dressed as Black and White Minstrels, in an episode showing how their ancestors had been kidnapped and forced to perform thus; or a promotional film for apartheid featuring Tim Brooke-Taylor in blackface, or Bill Oddie changing his name to Rastus Watermelon. Or the time when they bought a horse and, admiring its blackness and beauty, decided to call it . . . cue the atomic drop of the n-word.

Their mistake was the same as that of subsequent blackfacers: to assume that because their liberal credentials were so evident, no one would take them for 'true' racists. However, that's a hard ask indeed for those whose skin colour is being so crudely parodied for laughs, and the Goodies are worthy of reconsideration, if not TV revival. In the limitless scope of sagas like 'The Goodies and the Beanstalk', they anticipate *The Young Ones*. Furthermore, no one, Morecambe and Wise excepted, persuaded so many contemporary figures to make guest appearances on their shows: Harry H. Corbett, Patrick Troughton, John Cleese, Joan Sims, John Le Mesurier, Michael Aspel and Raymond Baxter (in string vest and pants, hailing the new invention of string).

Funniest are the silent slapstick sequences, cranked up à la Benny Hill, but much more imaginative in their spree of sight gags. A sequence of them at a seventies gymnasium of vaulting horses and medicine balls was a reminder to me of why I had doubled up to this series as a boy.

They attempted to come to terms with Mrs Thatcher and punk rock (*Nationwide* presenter Michael Barratt dressed as a punk), but these were both forces that would bring the seventies to a premature close, turn everything inside out and upside down, including comedy itself. They were done.

Some Mothers and *The Goodies* were, to seventies audiences at least, hysterical – my mum cried torrential tears of laughter at Frank Spencer; one man had literally died laughing watching *The Goodies*. Other comedies, however, were of a different, more melancholic register, the comedy undercut by deeper hankerings, a desire to rediscover lost ways. And others again were flat-out reactionary.

BAD, UNFORGETTABLE COMEDY – *ON THE BUSES, ARE YOU BEING SERVED?*

In the opening montage of *Mutiny on the Buses* (1972), a bus is trundling down a suburban street towards Inspector 'Blakey' Blake, standing by the bus stop. Beneath him at the kerbside lies a large puddle that looks suspiciously like it has been hosed into place, as the remainder of the street shows no sign of a recent downpour. A lesser series would have seen Blakey end up with a thorough soaking, and since *On the Buses* is a distinctly lesser series, that's exactly what happens.

On the Buses was a half-cooked oven chips of a comedy, an insult to the ITV viewership who watched it in droves for years. The first series in 1969 was differently configured, however, from its better-known successors: Reg Varney played Stan the bus driver, but his mother was played not by Doris Hare but by Cicely Courtneidge, who made her name in stage comedies in the Edwardian era. There's a faint air of *Steptoe and Son* about the way she smothers him, keeping him a man-child. Varney turned fifty-three in 1969, ten years older than Stephen Lewis, who played Blakey, his senior at the depot. Stan was quite the ageing lothario, face as creased as Sid James's. Creased with laughter – like James, his job was to do a great deal of chuckling, from the opening credits onwards, so that we didn't necessarily have to; like James, he rubbed his hands with glee at the spurious parade of 'dolly birds' in the employ of Luxton and District Motor Traction Company. His accomplice was conductor Jack (Bob Grant), a toothsome, seedy, sallow specimen who nonetheless enjoyed numerous sexual favours throughout the series. Typical *On the Buses* moment: Stan and Jack, in the canteen, ask the woman behind the counter if she's 'got any dumplings'. Cue reveal, as she turns around, this trained actor, displaying her ample endowments bulging from a low-cut blouse, delivering a glassily vacant stare.

The many Black British workers employed by London's bus companies in the 1960s and 1970s were represented by an occasional extra named 'Chalky'. Plotlines were desperate. In one, the blokes at the depot are pitted against an all-female team, the Basildon Bashers, in a competitive football match. Somehow the blokes persuade a professional footballer, Arsenal's Bob McNab, to join their team as a ringer. Unfortunately, McNab suffers an injury while training. The Basildon Bashers, a monstrous regiment indeed, win the game by foul means, which Blakey, as referee, is unable to put a stop to because the pea is stuck in his whistle.

On the Buses was not a good comedy. Like much of the output of its era, it lied about what Britain actually was, and what it was becoming. And yet it is a remembered comedy: it inveigled its way into the hearts of the viewing public, many of whom watched it for want of anything else to do or out of familiarity with the characters. As with the *Carry On* series, it reinforced a piss-poor conservatism, a host of backward social attitudes which lurked beneath its supposed good-natured foolery.

On the Buses had a decent ensemble: Anna Karen as Stan's sister the sex-starved Olive, Michael Robbins as her grumpy, sexless husband, Doris Hare as a less-than-stern matriarch of the household in which she, Robbins, Karen and Varney lived a crammed existence. This, at least, was a semblance of working-class life, an alternative to the detached tweeness of the suburban sitcoms featuring the likes of Wendy Craig, Patrick Cargill and Hannah Gordon.

On the Buses is not just remembered, vividly, its ensemble were even loved. When Anna Karen died in a house fire, there was a pang of grief among those who remembered her as a familiar living-room face of the early seventies. Such was the potency of the second, even the third rank of British TV comedy at the time.

Are You Being Served?, first broadcast in 1972, was ahead of the curve in one respect: it pre-dated Pink Floyd's 'Money' (from *Dark Side of the Moon*) in its use of the cash till as a musical instrument in its theme. That apart, even in its time, it seemed as if the department store in which it was set was a quaint and fading institution, a metaphor, perhaps, for Britain in the 1970s. In its opening episode, we see Mrs Slocombe and Miss Brahms clamber down from a lift which has stuck midway between floors. This metaphor for British malfunction also made it seem as if the store is some sort of twilight world, a bit like Platform 9¾ in the *Harry Potter* series – not so much a store as a quandary. Every photo of the characters has the air of a group of people caught in a predicament, as opposed to employees.

On one level, the series is a compendium of innuendo of the sort the British warmed themselves with in the dark days of the early seventies as if at a two-bar heater. Mrs Slocombe's pussy features on a per-episode basis, conjuring up at times quite surreal images: 'a diamante collar for me pussy'; 'My pussy's just like an alarm clock.' Meanwhile, John Inman's Mr Humphries, he of the gamely trilled 'I'm free!', is a fountain of suggestion that would make Julian and Sandy raise an eyebrow in recognition. 'My horoscope said I was going to get a new position – I interpreted it quite differently'; 'a roving reporter, a stringvestite and a dustman with a very interesting tale to tell'. The tape measures wielded by the sales staff, meanwhile, feel like metaphorical props, suggestive of penile inadequacy, of failing to measure up, an indictment of the country at the time, too.

Certainly, shabby and faded as the world of *Are You Being Served?* is, there's a sense that it speaks to Britain about Britain, the kind of people we are: sexually repressed, grumpy but not militant, cheeky but not revolutionary, amused at relics like Captain Peacock but deferential to their benign authority. For all their complaints about the shabbiness of their work conditions, industrial action is the bane rather than the salvation of their lives. In a piece for *The Quietus* in 2020 arguing that the show contained the seeds of Brexit, Alexei Monroe highlights the episode in which the staff find themselves stranded in the store due to a transport strike. They make the best of it, recalling the spirit of Churchill through poor impersonations and making jokes at the expense of the Germans. For, bad as it might have been to be a Brit in the mid-seventies, at least we weren't German or, as we discovered in the 1977 film based on the series, set at the Costa Plonka resort, Spanish.

STEPTOE AND SON RIDE AGAIN, *THE LIKELY LADS* RETURN, *PORRIDGE* – COMEDY OF CONFINEMENT

By 1965, after four series, Galton and Simpson felt that they had explored every facet of the Steptoes and it was time to move on, to cinema, to Hollywood. Harry H. Corbett and Wilfrid Brambell were not short of work in the interim. Both appeared in *Carry On* films, Corbett taking the lead in *Carry On Screaming* as Detective Sidney Bung. The shadow of *Steptoe* hangs inescapably over *Screaming*, the Ron Grainer theme even being quoted in the soundtrack. Galton and Simpson's Hollywood dreams foundered, and in 1970, *Steptoe* resumed, the tragicomic note immediately struck with the death of Hercules on the rounds. 'Why didn't you bring him back home?' demands the old man. 'What, sling him round me neck and walk home? I'm not bleedin' Desperate Dan!' protests Harold.

Steptoe and Son remained event TV in 1970. The most watched BBC programme that year was *Miss World* (26.5 million viewers), followed by England versus Brazil and West Germany respectively in the World Cup, as well as the Royal Variety show and the Apollo 13 splashdown. An airing of the 1964 film *633 Squadron* was watched by 20.5 million viewers; but apart from the Morecambe and Wise Christmas show, the only comedy on the list was *Steptoe and Son*, pulling twenty million viewers per episode.

The years between 1965 and 1970 were hugely consequential. It was an era of blossoming psychedelia, idealism, violence, disillusion – a cultural shift from monochrome to vivid colour. *Steptoe and Son* was now broadcast in colour, though the majority of Britons rented, rather than owned, black and white sets. Galton and Simpson were worried that colour might adversely affect the feeling of the show. 'We thought it would make it look too pretty,' said Alan Simpson. However, colour rendered more lurid, rather than prettified, the Steptoe premises, revealed now in their full gaudy anti-splendour of rich greens and pinks and grimly faded dark browns, while the tattiness of the cardigans is rendered at stitch level.

For all the changes the late sixties had wrought, however, nothing had changed for *Steptoe and Son*. Harold was now thirty-nine rather than thirty-seven, while his father had gone up from sixty-four to sixty-six. Harold is still desperately captive, though more domineering over his frail father, constantly on the edge of clouting him one. An apotheosis is reached in 'Divided We Stand' (1972), as Harold loses his rag and delivers the following tirade in the impervious face of his old man: 'You are a dyed-in-the-wool fascist, reactionary, squalid little know-your-place, don't-rise-above-yourself, don't-get-out-of-your-hole, complacent little turd. You are morally, spiritually and physically a festering, flyblown heap of accumulated filth.'

Harold goes so far as to redesign the house in the manner of East and West Berlin, with a turnstile functioning as 'Checkpoint Charlie' and each living on separate sides of makeshift divides. Unfortunately, this means sharing the screen of the TV set they now co-own, and when Albert changes channel from Harold's beloved ballet, he solemnly reminds him of his obligations in the matter of agreed screen time. 'I have the law of contract on my side,' says Harold. 'I've got the knobs on my side,' retorts Albert.

'Divided We Stand' was followed by 'The Desperate Hours'. When Tory politicians talk about the 'dark days of the 1970s', this episode is a taste of the 'darkness' in the folk memory of older voters. Except this wasn't the Labour era but the single Conservative term over which Edward Heath presided, beset by miners' strikes and power cuts, leaving the country forced to huddle together and entertain itself by candlelight.

In 'The Desperate Hours', the Steptoes aren't victims of a power cut, but the business has had a terrible spell and they can't afford to maintain the electricity; the only sound is the howling of the wind and the rumbling of Harold's stomach. All he's had to eat that day is half a carrot – 'and I had to fight to get that out of the horse's mouth'. Matters worsen when two escaped convicts from Wormwood Scrubs, played by Leonard Rossiter and J. G. Devlin, break in. They demand food, money, a getaway car, only to realise that their victims have none of these things ('We can't make a getaway on a horse'). As it becomes clear to the fugitives that they were better off back inside the nick, it's evident also that Rossiter and Devlin are the criminal equivalent of *Steptoe and Son* – the older man holding the younger one back, going right back to the job for which they were collared, with Devlin overstuffing his pockets with gold bullion. Both Harold and Rossiter share glances of shuddering sympathy as Devlin gratefully champs down a plate of lumpy porridge and the older men complain, richly, about the ingratitude of the younger generation. The convicts leave on friendly terms with the Steptoes, a few cigarettes lighter than when they broke in. The imprisonment metaphor is clear enough, but it took actors of the calibre and presence of Devlin (initially considered for the role of Albert) and especially Rossiter to match, even outshine Corbett and Brambell. This happened only once.

There were two *Steptoe and Son* movies. The first, released in 1972, is sublime – in its crudity, in its hilarity, in the real depths of sorrow it plumbs. The excellent Carolyn Seymour is cast in the most convincing female role Galton and Simpson ever created, as Zita, the stripper for whom Harold falls. His father, who had been leering at her earlier, is appalled that his son should fall for a 'scrubber', but she is a far better drawn and more durable character than the previous 'dolly birds' who flitted briefly into Harold's life, only to be repelled by his flea-infested dad. Much of this is down to Seymour herself: born Carolyn von Benckendorf and of Russian–Irish descent, she does not play for laughs but brings a dramatic heft and seriousness of purpose to this often quite emotionally harrowing comedy. She would later bring her skills to bear in the post-apocalyptic series *Survivors* (1975), and still later in villainous roles in *Star Trek: The Next Generation*.

They marry, though the old man subverts the relationship at every turn, from ironing his son's trousers sideways on the wedding day to insisting on accompanying them on honeymoon in Spain. 'You're worse than a fly around a cow's arsehole,' Harold moans.

The film brings out all the aspects of the sadly unbreakable relationship between Harold and Albert: the old man's selfishness, as well as his vulnerability; the tininess of the toss he gives about making a good impression, beating a carpet adjacent to Harold's best shirt on the washing line, engulfing it in billowing clouds of dust; his sanitary indifference, which sees him take a bath in the sink or eat a sandwich directly after patting down horse dung. As for Harold, his emotional inexperience, his doomed romantic expectations, in contrast with his seen-it-all father, are tragic in a middle-aged man. And yet there are moments, as with the arrival of the baby, when Albert can give Harold the benefit of his experience, moments in which they work together, bonded not just by circumstances but, somewhere beneath the junk, the invective, the squalor that fills up so much of their lives, by love.

There's a moment in the film when Albert is taking a bath in the kitchen sink, naked save his hat and socks, using OMO detergent in lieu of soap. Kitchen sink comedy. It prompts again the thought that had this film been forged as kitchen sink drama, with moments like this eschewed, it might have been regarded as the frankly classic, harrowing study in cruelly thwarted aspiration that it is.

By 1974, there were signs that *Steptoe* was winding down. 'The Seven Steptoerai', their take on the kung fu craze gripping Britain, was silly, not something you could often say of *Steptoe*; theirs was generally not the funny of silly. Then there were the cross-dressing capers of 'Live Now, PAYE Later', with Albert dressing up as his late wife to collect her pension and being given the glad eye by a retired policeman. Highly amusing, but at the expense of any credence whatsoever, evidence of a sitcom broadening rather than deepening. There were, however, satisfying moments for Harold – 'Upstairs Downstairs, Upstairs Downstairs', for example, when he realises that that 'perpendicular ponce upstairs', the old man, has been feigning a back injury and stealing downstairs while he's out to nick his beer and sweets. Harold's revenge is stinging: a bed bath, and a generous application of surgical spirits to his 'little bum'. And, in the final episode, the final ever scene of *Steptoe*, we see Harold at last rid of the old man, following an elaborate ruse to send him on holiday to Europe using the proceeds of their swear box – while he and a lady friend jump into a sports car and head for Bognor. Desserts at last.

As with *Steptoe and Son*, there followed a seven-year hiatus for *The Likely Lads* after 1966. However, whereas *Steptoe* resumed where they had left off, *Whatever Happened to the Likely Lads?* (1973–4) is deeply conscious of the passing of time in Britain. The two meet by chance on a train back to Newcastle. Terry bemoans having missed out on all the exciting cultural shifts that took place in the late 1960s and early 1970s, due to having joined the army. He's not referring to the May 1968 demos, psychedelia and the rise of feminism, but '*Oh! Calcutta!*, topless waitresses and see-through knickers'. He has returned to resume his working-class station, finding jobs as and when he can. Bob, meanwhile, has gone up a class, and is now working for his fiancée Thelma's father's building firm, his life a round of badminton, dinner parties, bridge and foreign holidays, a new, Cinzano-tinted world of things to aspire to which still has a freshly painted whiff of novelty about it. For all this, Bob as pinstriped middle-class man has a harassed, guilty look about him, as if forced into a game of middle-class cosplay about which he has nervous misgivings.

That Bob should be working in construction is apposite. During the sixties, Newcastle in particular had been subject to slum clearance and ambitious city planning under the aegis of the leader of the council, T. Dan Smith. It was a time in which the old was being torn down; communities were moving on, being rehoused. For Bob, regeneration is a mixed blessing; it provides him with gainful employment, but he shares Terry's dismay at the eradication of their past haunts, their lost youth, those carefree, monochrome days; as the Mike Hugg-composed theme to the new show has it, 'What became of the people we used to be . . . It's the only thing to look forward to, the past . . .'

Terry dismisses Bob as a class traitor, but despite Bob's hectic social schedule, the two find time to hang out a great deal, fugitives together from obligation and reality, as well as news bulletins, as in 'No Hiding Place' (1973), when they spend the day avoiding the score to an England football match so as to save themselves for the highlights.

Twenty-six episodes of *Whatever Happened to the Likely Lads?* were made, twenty-seven including the Christmas edition, but all were broadcast between 1973 and 1974, making the series a time capsule: the era in which Sam Tyler fetches up in *Life on Mars*. The wistful mood of the characters is more in keeping with Britain in general, losing its chromium lustre, politically stagnant. The demise of the Beatles, who were desperately missed, having disbanded in 1970, left nothing but an increasing sense of Great Britain's busted-down significance. As for the England football team, in 1973 they were in the process of failing to qualify for the World Cup they had won in 1966, losing out to Poland of all teams. What became of the people we used to be?

As if in compensation for this glumness, fashions ran to the stylish and colourfully extravagant. In the episode titled 'Guess Who's Coming to Dinner?' (1973), in which Terry takes great pleasure in reminding class-conscious hostess Brenda of her humble, chip-shop origins, the decor is so garish by today's post-Habitat, post-IKEA standards that it is a major distraction to modern eyes – a lurid riot of exploding green-patterned wallpaper – to say nothing of the huge flares and massive collars. Only Terry, not au fait with seventies sartorial mores, looks like he could walk about without comment in our own times.

All this may offend the eye and preclude the repeat viewing enjoyed by a *Dad's Army*. Terry's roving eye for the women, meanwhile, feels like a laddish relic of the pre-*Young Ones* era. That said, in Bob's fiancée Thelma, Clement and La Frenais scripted an excellent character, brilliantly realised by Brigit Forsyth. She is certainly not to be trifled with, and not for nothing does Bob often harbour a look of pale, piggy-eyed terror when he displeases her. But she has too much about her to be a mere dragon – she's a woman whose demands of life, if a touch bourgeois-trendy at times, are not unreasonable, and she is forced to overlook a great many failings in the man she loves. She takes a dim view of Terry but is not unsympathetic to him, nor are we to her, having long understood that there is a bond between Terry and her husband which she has no hope of sundering.

As a rule, women feature only peripherally in the work of Galton and Simpson, Clement and La Frenais. Their own sense of frustration or confinement is not explored, as a rule; if not mere fleeting 'floozies', they are supposed to be grimly happy with their lot, at once subordinate and authoritarian, be they bolshie canteen workers or housewives. Forsyth exceeded these bounds. She was an excellent actor who was unlucky in the roles that came her way after *Whatever Happened*. She co-starred as the primly middle-class Harriet in the Johnnie Mortimer and Brian Cooke-scripted series *Tom, Dick and Harriet* (1982–3), starring Lionel Jeffries, which, after a promising start, petered out after two series; then as the primly middle-class Elsie in the sitcom *Sharon and Elsie* (1984–5). She deserved more, and better.

The feature film *The Likely Lads* was released in 1976, a pearl-studded movie whose best lines aficionados quote with the same affection as fans of *Kind Hearts and Coronets*. Bob's disillusion with the 'chocolate box of life' is principal among them. He is sinking into boredom with his marriage; meanwhile, the pub of his youth is about to face the wrecking ball. Terry, however, is on the up, a beneficiary of slum clearance as he stares out of the window of his new flat. He also has a Finnish girlfriend. Terry tries to comfort Bob, within reason – 'I'd give you a beer but I've only got six cans,' he tells him when Bob joins him as he fishes.

The film is a hilarious if aimless farce, involving the boys returning from an off-licence to a caravan site, only to find themselves lost amid the caravans; Terry urinating loudly outside the caravan during a game of bridge (Thelma: 'It's the first time I've known what was in his hand all evening'); and a mishap which sees the boys return, trouserless, from a misadventure in Whitley Bay, only to find Thelma and Terry's sister Audrey back at the flat and required to explain themselves. Finally, it's Bob's turn to be inadvertently shipped off abroad as he falls asleep, drunk, on a boat leaving from Newcastle docks, next stop Bahrain.

And that was that. James Bolam, who had never really got along with the genial but sometimes irritating Bewes, used the pretext of an indiscretion by Bewes during a press interview to sever links. The pair were never reunited on screen, Bolam blocking any possibility of their working together again. Thus we were denied the possible privilege of seeing how Bob and Terry navigated middle and finally old age. Bewes died in 2017. Bolam would go on to star in the period drama *When the Boat Comes In* (1976–81), which would finish the work *The Likely Lads* had started of establishing the presence of the Northeast, and its accent, on the map and in the British consciousness. In this respect, it broadened the scope of comedy in the UK, considering not just its class structure but also its regions – the horizontal, as well as the vertical.

Clement and La Frenais set to work on *Porridge*, which debuted in 1974. Set in Slade prison, it starred Ronnie Barker as Norman Stanley Fletcher, former 'King of the Teds' turned housebreaker, who, we learn from the judge's remarks from the bench in sentencing, is 'a habitual criminal' who regards arrest as an occupational hazard and presumably prison in 'the same casual manner'.

Despite the reluctance of the prison authorities to co-operate with the making of the series, *Porridge* does not indict the penal system or reflect its grimmer realities. Given twenty-first-century TV's demand for authenticity, it is unlikely that any mainstream channel would today commission a prison-based comedy, unless it were a remake of *Porridge* (which, regrettably, they did).

It's in keeping with Clement and La Frenais's ongoing theme of male confinement. Though it's not explicitly stated, one early episode, in which Fletcher is lying on his bed trying to 'relax' with an adult magazine, only to be assailed by a stream of visitors through the open cell door, is about thwarted masturbation, further emphasised when he starts rubbing his leg with his foot. And yet, despite such little agonies, he has a generally contented air, free of the caged suffering endured by a Hancock, Bob Ferris or Harold Steptoe, taking pleasure in 'little victories' against the penal system. While looking out at all times for number one, he's a fine mentor to cellmate Lenny Godber (Richard Beckinsale). Keep your head down, son. Don't let them grind you down.

With its stream of non-swearing, in which 'naff' means 'fuck', *Porridge* is a highly agreeable fiction, never brutal, harrowing or hopeless. Slade can feel more like a boarding school than a prison, with the inmates more like classmates, with Fletcher as the cheeky lad happier keeping up a stream of quips than knuckling down. The supporting cast, including 'Horrible' Ives, Harris, Christopher

Biggins's 'Lukewarm', David Jason's elderly 'Blanco', feel more like rambunctious fellow pupils than criminals.

Despite the ramrod Caledonian airs of principal officer Mr Mackay, Fletcher has the full measure of him, while his fellow warder, the stammering, liberal Mr Barrowclough, is putty in his hands. We see this when Mackay sends out Barrowclough to negotiate with Fletcher for his missing false teeth, half-inched by Fletcher after Mackay sneezed them into a large bowl of curry. 'Now, I've been instructed to go no higher than £5,' burbles Barrowclough. 'Well then, the sooner we get up there, the better,' counters Fletcher. It's 'genial' crime boss Harry Grout who really runs Slade, and Fletcher knows it.

Porridge ran for three years before Ronnie Barker decided he did not want to be saddled with the role indefinitely. However, in 1979, Fletcher was back in the nick for the *Porridge* movie, yet another example of the much-maligned film version of the sitcom rising to the cinematic occasion. There's a brilliant recurring joke in the movie concerning the Prison Officers' Club set up enthusiastically by Mr Mackay, but whose dungeon-like environs make it less than popular with the officers. It's a reminder that, as an arriving inmate jeers at his captors, 'you're just as much prisoners as we are'.

Following their reluctant involvement in a prison escape organised by Grout during a football match between the prisoners and a dis-appointing 'celebrity' eleven ('See him? Reads the weather for Anglia television'), Fletcher and Godber are compelled to break back into prison, finding their way to the cellars of the Prison Officers' Club. It had been wise of their captors, explains an inebriated Fletch to the governor, to lock them in there, as it was the only place in the prison where no officers were to be found.

Clement and La Frenais enjoyed further success with the confine-ment theme with *Auf Wiedersehen, Pet* (1983–6), making hay of British brickies in recession-hit Britain forced to take work in West Germany, a reminder of humiliating post-war decline. Their living conditions do their sexual prospects little good, as in the scene in which Brummie Barry (Timothy Spall) attempts to chat up a couple of women with the enticing line, 'Would you like to come back to our hut?'

Confinement is often a literal situation in Clement and La Frenais's work. However, it's notable that their captive characters, be it the largely cheery inmates of Slade prison or the construction workers living in prison camp-type conditions and in economic thrall to the Germans, seem to be having a better time of things than the ostensibly 'freer' characters they and Galton and Simpson created. They are at least free of onerous domestic responsibilities, able to console themselves with laddish larks or boys-together capers, while Fletcher's adventures, unlike Hancock's, generally end in some small success.

The confinement of the likes of Hancock, Steptoe and Bob and Terry is a more complicated one. What restricts them is their inability to become the 'men' they are supposed to be – a disinclination, even. It's embedded. Hancock is the 'lad himself', Bob and Terry the 'lads', Harold Steptoe the 'son'. 'What are we?' Jerry once asked George Constanza in the diner in *Seinfeld*. 'We're not men.' So it is with these men. They are not men either. In different ways, they are unable to escape their juvenile condition, whether it is Harold condemned to live out his best years with his father, Bob and Terry trying to hold fast to their boyhoods, even taking part in a weekly kickabout with a bunch of eleven-year-old kids in *The Likely Lads* film, or Hancock caught somewhere between his lost boyhood and a manhood he is not up to.

And so it must be, for the situation comedy requires that they are confined thus; with each episode, they are put back in the box like chess pieces, to start over another day.

DECLINISM – *THE FALL AND RISE OF REGINALD PERRIN, THE GOOD LIFE*

Two of the most popular sitcoms of the seventies shared a theme: escape from suburbia. They reflected a feeling that Britain was, as the country's 1977 Eurovision Song Contest entry asserted, at 'Rock Bottom', though given the levels Britain has drilled down to since, there is cause to envy this 'bottom'. Indeed, the first thing that might strike twenty-first-century viewers of *The Fall and Rise of Reginald Perrin* (1976–9) and *The Good Life* (1975–8) is how two middle managers in single-income households could afford to live in West London houses now worth well over a million pounds. Whatever else was far-fetched about these sitcoms, however, this wasn't considered to be so.

The Fall and Rise of Reginald Perrin commences with Leonard Rossiter as Perrin removing most of his clothes and swimming out to sea, not to commit suicide but to erase his identity. By coincidence, the Labour politician John Stonehouse had pulled the same trick in November 1974, only to be rumbled a month later. Although it first appeared in 1976, *Perrin* was based on a novel its creator David Nobbs had written prior to the Stonehouse affair. The coincidence gave the series an air of seventies zeitgeist, however.

Perrin works at Sunshine Desserts, the letters from whose sign are dropping away like rotten teeth: another symptom of decay and the 'declinism' of the series. Bored rigid by the routine of his everyday life, suffering from impotence and subject to bizarre fantasies, Perrin first resorts to sarcasm and self-sabotaging recklessness before deciding to erase himself. He returns, however, and founds Grot, dedicated to the honest purveyance of absolute rubbish – square hoops, sprout wine (which, contrary to his expectations, and owing to the perverse psychology of consumerism, is a success).

There is some dodgy 1970s cultural politics to navigate in *Perrin*: a mother-in-law depicted in Perrin's mind as a hippopotamus, a dalliance between his brother-in-law Jimmy and his own daughter, and his creepy admiration of his secretary's breasts. What mitigates some of this is that much as Perrin's life sees him condemned to tread the ritual circuits of a suburban commute and work routine – the same route, the same train carriage, the same eleven-minute delay – so *Perrin* is itself walking through the rituals of the conventional seventies sitcom – the suburban situation, the pretty secretary, the catchphrases ('Great!' 'Super!' 'I didn't get where I am today . . .'), the low-level scatology (Sunshine Desserts boss C. J.'s flatulent chairs), the batty relatives, the Ronnie Hazlehurst theme. Much as Perrin was anxious to remake himself, Nobbs was anxious, if not to subvert, then to remake the peak-hour sitcom. It is a meta-sitcom.

Rossiter's Perrin is by far the most fully realised character; like Paddington bear in the seventies animations, it is as if he has more dimensions than the cut-out characters around him, who play their limited parts in the ritual of the series. He is everyman and eccentric, delivering his dialogue like a virtuoso saxophonist, stammering, slipping and gliding, tack-sharp, timing perfect. Politically, he occupies a neutral zone somewhere between his son-in-law Tom, a *Guardian*-reading type who believes a 'total breakdown of civilisation' is at hand, and his brother-in-law Jimmy (Geoffrey Palmer), whose belief that the 'balloon is going up' chimed in with alleged plots by right-wing dignitaries and MI5 to unseat Harold Wilson. Their exchange, when Jimmy announces his plans to set up a secret army, is worth quoting in full, not just as a torrential demonstration of Nobbs's writing skills but as a cross-section of prevailing social attitudes sloshing about in a murk of casual prejudice, of fear, loathing, perception of decline and fall, conspiracy theory, inaccurate foreboding and what still felt up for grabs in the still-smouldering idealism and febrile militancy of the seventies. Jimmy rails against:

> wreckers of law and order. Communists, Maoists, Trotskyists,
> neo-Trotskyists, crypto-Trotskyists, union leaders, communist
> union leaders, atheists, agnostics, long-haired weirdos, short-haired

weirdos, vandals, hooligans, football supporters, namby-pamby
probation officers, rapists, Papists, Papist rapists, foreign surgeons –
headshrinkers, who ought to be locked up – Wedgwood Benn, keg
bitter, punk rock, glue-sniffers, *Play for Today*, Clive Jenkins, Roy
Jenkins, Up Jenkins, up everybody's, Chinese restaurants – why do
you think Windsor Castle is ringed with Chinese restaurants?

Perrin replies:

You realise the sort of people you're going to attract, don't you,
Jimmy? Thugs, bully-boys, psychopaths, sacked policemen,
security guards, sacked security guards, racialists, Paki-bashers,
queer-bashers, Chink-bashers, anybody-bashers, rear admirals,
queer admirals, vice admirals, fascists, neo-fascists, crypto-
fascists, loyalists, neo-loyalists, crypto-loyalists.

Jimmy: 'Do you think so? I thought support might be difficult.'

For all its wit, there's a melancholy about *Perrin*, which Ronnie
Hazlehurst's theme captures well: a Britain drifting on, and slowly
submerging into, a grey sea of seventies boredom. Housing was
affordable, jobs less scarce, society more economically equal, the
NHS unthreatened. All of this, however, was taken for granted. But
the boredom, a boredom which no amount of Sunshine Dessert
could dispel, the boredom . . .

John Esmonde and Bob Larbey's *The Good Life* was set not
far from Perrin's home. It was a reaction to a seventies stirring of
environmentalism and more sustainable lifestyles, as evidenced by
the PEOPLE party, which held that oil was a finite resource and we
could not take our consumer lifestyles as forever granted.

Tom Good (Richard Briers), like Perrin, is forty-something and
bored with his job – in his case, one involving plastic products. With
the conveniently ready agreement of his dream wife Barbara (Felicity
Kendal), willing but not too meek, snub-nosed and tomboyish but

still a sexual fantasy for wistful males such as Neil's father in *The Young Ones*, he quits his job. The Goods opt for a life outside the rat race, raising pigs and chickens, using animal faeces as an energy source. This horrifies their conservative neighbours, Jerry and Margo Leadbetter. Jerry works at the same company as Tom did, while Margo, his snooty wife, maintains the upper-middle-class appearances of their domestic life. Both couples are unencumbered by children.

It would have been a mistake for Esmonde and Larbey to have made Tom and Barbara hippies. It's key that they are a very English couple, in accent, breeding and their Famous Five-type have-a-go enthusiasm. They are not countercultural but aspirational, pursuing a suburban dream of their own, albeit an unorthodox one, striking a chord with millions of bored householders, lacking only the will, or a Briers or a Kendal at their side, to pursue the sanitised version of domestic self-sufficiency portrayed here. As the series progresses, however, their alternative lifestyle becomes secondary to their relationship with Jerry and Margo. Not only are they entwined in mutual sexual attraction (male attraction, at least – Jerry for Barbara, Tom, after a couple of glasses of homemade wine, for Margo), but they are closely matched class-wise as well as domestically, despite their diverging lifestyles. The final episode of the series sees them bonded against a common scourge: after a party, the four return to the Goods' house, only to find that it has been broken into and vandalised. This episode was shot in 1977; around the same time, a public information campaign doing the rounds depicted a group of well-spoken neighbours in a respectable-looking neighbourhood clearing up the debris from a spree of vandalism the previous night. Apparently, these hoodlums had arrived from some other neighbourhood and spent an hour trashing the front gardens and garage doors, uninterrupted by the residents ('I watched the whole thing,' grumbles one) and without police intervention ('What's the point?'). The way these characters talked, it was as if this was a regular occurrence. 'There's nothing you can do!' despairs one, only for the voiceover to differ and supply a phone line for suburbanites victim to serial outrages like this.

I puzzled over this film, as I lived in such an area and recollect such mass hoodlum attacks occurring precisely zero times, and, knowing how handy some of my adult neighbours were, they would do more than glower from behind net curtains if they espied any rampaging hooligans. It felt more like a metaphorical fear, of breakdown and decline, a vague, spurious air of moral panic, bolstered by the arrival of punk rock, misinterpreted as a mass outburst of juvenile delinquency. 'The sort of people who do this are the sort who call the police "pigs",' declares Margo, and for once this isn't Margo out on a snobbish limb; we are invited to nod along. As it was, it was a 'Margo' type, in the form of Mrs Thatcher, who would take firm change of the nation in 1979, to banish the various wreckers of civilisation and begin the real work of respectably tearing down, bit by bit, the taken-for-granted fixtures and fabric of the post-war British state.

RACE TO THE BOTTOM – *LOVE THY NEIGHBOUR, MIND YOUR LANGUAGE, IT AIN'T HALF HOT, MUM*

Comedies like *The Good Life* shied away from matters of race; ITV's *Love Thy Neighbour* (1972–6), somewhat foolhardily, did not. Written by Vince Powell and Harry Driver, two white men, it starred Jack Smethurst as working-class racist Eddie Booth, horrified by the arrival of neighbours Bill and Barbie (Rudolph Walker and Nina Baden-Semper). The impact of Barbie was softened, even for Eddie, in that she is an impressive bit of 'crumpet', and she and Eddie's wife Joan (Kate Williams) get along famously. Eddie and Bill, however, are at perpetual loggerheads, principally because Eddie, far from protesting he hasn't a racist bone in his body, makes no bones about showering Bill with white supremacist contempt at every opportunity.

It was an advance, of sorts, on *Till Death Us Do Part*. In *Love Thy Neighbour*, Bill and Barbie were at least bona fide West Indians in talking, starring roles. As for Eddie Booth, a small, portly man whose sins are compounded by his trade unionism, he commands little of the inadvertent charisma of a Garnett.

In a 1976 interview in *Look-In* magazine, which unfortunately praises the programme for 'bringing light relief to one of the darker problems in society today', Jack Smethurst claimed *Love Thy Neighbour* had helped defuse racial tensions, but that's debatable, to say the least. Eddie repeatedly uses the phrase 'nig-nog' to Bill, rather than 'nigger', as if 'nig-nog' is a more pre-watershed friendly, golliwog-cuddly form of racist terminology; 'sambo' also, every use of which saw a spike in the laugh track. This was small consolation to some people of colour, however, such as writer Neil Kulkarni, an Asian boy in the mid-seventies who, from watching *Love Thy Neighbour*, knew to brace himself for the names he was going to have hurled at him the next day in the playground. (Asian people were treated atrociously in the series.) What's more, since for the series to function Eddie and Bill had to spend a great deal of time in each other's company, at work, in the pub, on the doorstep, Bill had to let many of the epithets gobbed at him by Eddie pass, such as the time when they travel together to a TUC conference and Eddie calls Bill a 'Black spoilsport' for refusing to have any truck with his attempted peccadilloes on the road.

Love Thy Neighbour propounds various fictions. The show implies that far from being institutional and widespread, seventies racism is contained solely in isolated personages like Eddie, the only racist in the show's village, to paraphrase *Little Britain*. All the other characters, including pub companions like Jacko and Eddie's wife, treat Bill and Barbie with colour-blind respect. The series is also guilty of equating racism with silly, male fractiousness. (They are at political loggerheads also, Eddie and Bill, since Bill is a Tory.) Bill is a 'real' West Indian, but his constant references to his own blackness and

'Black Power' are the projections of white scriptwriters. Nothing about the way he talks feels real at all. He's a blowhard, at times as much so as Eddie. The nearest they actually come to blows is a backyard boxing bout, dancing aggressively around each other but clearly with no intention of throwing a punch. At times, what with the eye-rolling of the wives at the combativeness of their husbands, and the anti-trade unionism slipped into the series, there are echoes of *Carry On at Your Convenience*; the series suggests that most seventies politics, be it racial or economic, was a blustery slanging match, a 'both sides' affair which only required some female common sense to set right, though chance would be a fine thing. In the *Look-In* article, Nina Baden-Semper remarks, 'I think the series shows that any kind of human problems can be balanced with good humour on both sides of the fence. I just wish people would shut up, stop arguing and get on with living.'

The scriptwriters, too, felt that there was an equivalence between 'nig-nog' and Bill's occasional retort 'white honky', as if the word 'honky' were of equal violence and severity to white people as 'nig-nog' was to Black people.

However, if the show was sympathetic, in its way, to Black British people, Asian people fared much less well. Take a scene in which an unconvincing shopkeeper wearing a turban who bobs his head as he graciously utters to his customers such seventies-TV Indian dialogue as 'Long life and happiness to you and yours' is confronted by Eddie, not realising he is the new shop owner and accused of thieving. 'I caught you with your black paw in the till, you pilfering Paki.' The shopkeeper, as if racially incapable of anger, continues to beam broadly. But anger there was and would be.

Vince Powell went on to create *Mind Your Language*, which premiered in 1977 on ITV. It starred Jeremy Brown teaching English as a foreign language at an adult education school. Students are from Spain, Greece, Italy, Germany, as well as India, all struggling with the mother tongue. In their foreign obtuseness, they are constantly getting it wrong. The verbal kinship of 'massage'/'message' makes for a typically amusing slip-up. When asked to form a sentence including the word 'catalyst', the Spanish student stands up and discusses how Spain boasts a great many Roman Cat'olics among its population. This sparks off a furious argument with the hot-headed Italian, who insists his country is the most Catholic. There's a Sikh character who constantly uses the phrase 'a thousand apologies'; in all the years I have known my Sikh relatives, whenever they felt the need to issue an apology to me, they managed fine with just the one. As for the constantly bowing Japanese student, it feels as if only budgetary restrictions prevented the production team from sounding a gong every time he appears in shot.

Coming from a nation of monoglots like the English, it is a bit rich to mock those who at least have a working grasp of a second language; what's further implied in *Mind Your Language* is that despite their adult status, the classmates, in their arrested state of linguistic development, are more like schoolchildren. They are certainly treated as such by the haughty head of department, Miss Courtney, who adds to the general *Please Sir!* air of the show, whose classroom of adults were at least meant to be fifth-formers.

In a 1979 documentary, the brilliant academic Stuart Hall shows two clips of comedies which reveal less-than-latent attitudes towards race revealed in British sitcoms. One is from *Mind Your Language*, and it's both deplorable and unfunny. He also shows a clip from *It Ain't Half Hot, Mum*, which was also pretty deplorable, but to me, at least, rather funnier, benefiting as it did from the pedigree of its scriptwriters, its well-sketched cast of characters and its keen eye for British hierarchical structures. *It Ain't Half Hot, Mum*, about a Royal Artillery concert party based in Deolali, India, was written by Jimmy Perry and David Croft, and demonstrated many of the strengths of their most famous creation, *Dad's Army*, and, in Windsor Davies's Sergeant Major Williams, a character who doubled me up more often than any of the characters from Walmington-on-Sea. 'You may think it's a good thing that the British are able to laugh at their own past,' said Hall, 'but the British Empire was no joke for those on the receiving end.'

And it is problematic, especially the early series featuring Michael Bates in blackface. Though his family was originally from Cheshire, Bates was born in Jhansi, Uttar Pradesh, India, and cited his Indian origins as giving him the right to play an Indian character, the obsequious pro-Empire bearer Rangi Ram. He does a fine job in his intonations. But would a white South African feel that he had the right to black up and play a Black South African because they were from the same nation?

Dino Shafeek made quite a living playing Indian characters of pronounced Indian-ness in a range of films and shows, from *Carry On Emmannuelle* to *Minder*, as well as *Mind Your Language*. In *It Ain't Half Hot, Mum*, he plays the chai wallah Muhammad, who, despite his Indian accent exciting titters from the studio audience every time he opens his mouth, has at least a certain wry dignity about him.

The bulk of the show concerns the sergeant major's relationship with his concert party charges, a motley platoon, from the diminutive, pith-helmeted Gunner Sugden to university-educated 'Mr La-De-Da Gunner Graham'. He is determined to make men of them, mould them with his own two fists. The funniest scenes are on parade, as he excoriates them with both rough sides of his tongue, relishing his own inventive stream of unanswerable sadism as he mimics Gunner Graham's effeminacy or stares murderous daggers at drag queen Gunner 'Gloria' Beaumont. The word 'poofs' is fired with machine-gun relentlessness.

Williams is racist, bristling when forced to apologise to a local Indian official, whom he clearly regards as a sub-species, or when vowing vengeance on the Japanese for getting their 'little yellow hands on our empire'. But he's complicated; for a while, he is in a relationship with a local woman, and he does find himself sharing his thoughts and emotions with characters like Rangi in particular. The conclusion of the series is sentimental but pleasing. The outwardly genial and kindly Captain Ashwood and Lieutenant-Colonel Reynolds want nothing to do with the concert party or the sergeant major when they are finally demobbed, being anxious to return to the old class order, with themselves remote at the top. However, a camaraderie has developed between the sergeant major and the concert party, despite all. 'I'll never forget you,' he declares. As for Muhammad, as they depart for England by boat he calls after them sorrowfully, declaring he will miss their 'jolly japes'.

It is years since these series were broadcast on mainstream TV. In their time, there were certainly people who considered them demeaning. And yet, many people from ethnic minority backgrounds loved these series. In his memoir *Broken Greek*, the music journalist Pete Paphides relates how his father used to laugh like a drain at the Greek character in *Mind Your Language*. My former Indian in-laws, meanwhile, were not just fans of *It Ain't Half Hot, Mum*, particularly the deceptively wise punkah wallah, played by Babar Bhatti, and his long Urdu monologues, culminating in pithy English summaries. As my ex-brother-in-law Gurbir Thethy explains, they could identify with any non-white representations on TV, not just Indian characters. 'One of their favourite programmes was *Love Thy Neighbour*, especially because the Black neighbour would get one over the white guy as often as vice versa,' he says. 'They especially enjoyed *It Ain't Half Hot, Mum*, for obvious reasons. They were just so pleased to see a version of themselves on the TV. It was proper appointment TV. Then when *Mind Your Language* came along, they couldn't believe they were seeing an actual Indian be-turbanned character, as opposed to Michael Bates blacked up in *It Ain't Half Hot, Mum*.'

BENNY HILL

Such sentiments are widespread. There's a pitiful Benny Hill sketch featuring a Mr Chow Mein, rehearsing for a job as a ventriloquist, despite hilariously getting his 'l's and 'r's mixed up, the single Chinese contribution to seventies British comedy. Below the line of the YouTube clip of this sketch is the following comment: 'My late Nana from Hong Kong absolutely loved this, couldn't stop laughing – yet today the offended-on-other-people's-behalf-brigade would be all over it. If a Cantonese granny didn't have a problem why should anyone else?'

No doubt the Cantonese granny did laugh at Benny Hill, as hard as Pete Paphides's father laughed at *Mind Your Language*. But this is the laughter of scarce recognition, rather than the acuity and wit of these series; it is the joy and relief of coming across people of your own colour or nationality represented on TV. It doesn't vindicate these shows or shut down criticism of their crude stereotyping, which had its own adverse side effects. The Cantonese granny deserved better than Benny Hill. Gurbir's parents deserved much, much better than *Love Thy Neighbour*. They deserved less patronising or stereotypical attitudes inadvertently revealed by white scriptwriters and production teams, and more consultation. It would be a long time coming.

That said, it was perhaps better for these shows to have appeared than never to have been commissioned at all, and for TV comedy simply to have consisted of entirely white characters and extras, with offence to minorities tastefully avoided by omitting to represent them altogether. Shows like *It Ain't Half Hot, Mum* are best regarded as imperfect, and somewhat slippery, stepping stones, commissioned in the belief, as expressed by the ITV executive Humphrey Barclay, that 'seeing different races on screen would familiarise and naturalise them to a white majority viewing public'. Well, no and yes.

I once found myself in the lobby of New York's Gramercy Park Hotel, there to interview a rock band. There was a big screen in the hotel bar broadcasting Benny Hill made up as Molly Weir, the Scottish actor widely known for her adverts for the detergent Flash. The sketch should have made no sense to anyone who didn't grow up with these adverts in the UK in the 1960s and 1970s. However, an elderly American couple sitting at the bar were watching the sketch, laughing merrily, if not comprehendingly. This was Benny Hill, America's favourite English funny man, doing funny stuff.

Although he was as British as brown sauce, Hill had an international reach akin to that of Mr Bean. He'd broken America not least for the quirky reason that the length of his one-hour shows lent them well to American TV's advert-heavy format. And so he would acquire some improbable transatlantic fans, from Snoop Dogg to English expat Charlie Chaplin, who kept a library of his shows.

Ben Elton was forced to clarify a supposed remark he made in Q magazine that Benny Hill's comedy acted as an incitement to violence against women, which he said had been wrenched out of context. Hill is often considered to epitomise the sexism of seventies TV, with women's roles reduced to scuttling about in states of undress. (This might well have been an unnerved response to the burgeoning 'women's lib' movement, which confronted assumptions about womanhood that had been uninterrogated since time immemorial.) Conversely, there are claims that Hill was an underrated comedian, a worthy addition to a great tradition going back to Chaplin himself.

Well, here's some Benny Hill. A sketch featuring Benny as a signwriter commissioned by a white-coated therapist, played by his bald-headed little sidekick, to put up a plaque outside his office. Benny paints the word 'THERAPIST' over two lines so that it reads 'THE RAPIST'. A shocked gaggle of 'dolly birds' flocks to the scene to give the poor fellow a scolding.

Looking back, with appalling exceptions such as this, it's hard to feel either outrage or admiration at his work. There was, in deference to the American audience, of whose existence he was aware, a lot of parody of American shows like *Charlie's Angels*, involving much cross-dressing. As with *Python*, male cross-dressing wasn't just an easy means to raise a laugh but also a way of bypassing the involvement of actual, multidimensional female protagonists. There is also a lot of fast-cranked mime, almost silent comedy, which might have piqued Chaplin's interest, as well as securing Hill broadcasters in more than ninety countries. The shows are sexist, but Hill's hapless, leering male characters never get anywhere close to having it off with the notional representations of womanhood who flit, suspendered, in and out of his ken. One sketch features him approaching a young woman and lifting her bodily from the ground, receiving a volley of head slaps for his pains. The reveal is that he's been reading a book entitled *How to Pick Up Women*. In Benny Hill-land, the chance of getting your leg over is as remote as winning the football pools.

Much of the problem is Hill himself. With comedians like Tommy Cooper, Les Dawson and Frankie Howerd, there are worlds to be found in their dolorous gamut of expressions. With Hill, despite the vast range of characters he played, his default reaction is an eyebrow-raised 'Oo-er'. Hill seems to have been a harmless but strange man, frugal despite his vast wealth, bundles of which he preferred to carry about in carrier bags, never marrying, having been rebuffed twice. He lived in rented lodgings, and was reluctant to travel to America and do the chat-show circuit, despite having big fans there like Johnny Carson. The rise of alternative comedy and the attendant backlash against him troubled this eccentric, innocent soul, who never regarded comedy as tribal, ideological or as a carrier of attitude. He didn't have it about him to enjoy a postmodern career boost, the way Frankie Howerd and Bob Monkhouse did. His show was cancelled in 1989 because ITV saw that it was running out of steam, and its star, now in his mid-sixties, looked tired. Three years later, he died.

THE LIVER BIRDS, BUTTERFLIES, MARTI CAINE – THE BIRTH OF WOMEN

As the sixties faded into the seventies, TV found itself reckoning with the tentative liberation of women, as independent agents no longer necessarily tied down or defined by household chores, marriage or motherhood, freer to negotiate their own destiny. In sitcom, series such as *My Wife Next Door* (1972), starring John Alderton and Hannah Gordon as neighbouring divorcees, and *And Mother Makes Three* (1971–3), starring Wendy Craig, reflected the break-up of nuclear family norms. These persisted in Sitcomland, however; *Bless This House* (1971–6), starring Sid James, was quintessential in an increasingly inessential genre. James was the nominal head of a household featuring Diana Coupland as his slightly ditzy wife and two irritating grown-up kids, drama-school representations of the with-it generation. Realistic plotlines included their house being taken over by a stranger claiming squatter's rights, a common occurrence in the febrile imagination of seventies suburban Britain.

Liverpudlian Carla Lane was initially a scriptwriter for *Bless This House*. In the eighties, a decade in which her ill-fated home city was fetishised in TV culture, she enjoyed huge ratings for her sitcom *Bread* (1986–91), but was also reviled by some for stereotyping Scousers. A high-profile vegetarian, she fell for a Chris Morris spoof in the 'Animals' episode of *Brass Eye*, with Morris putting it to her that dangerous bulldogs had their tails wound up to tweak their nervous systems so that 'it goes like a bloody rocket'. Poor Lane sank further into the mire when she opined that prison was too good for these tail-tweakers because 'prison's like bed-and-breakfast these days'.

The Liver Birds (1969–79) was a corollary to *The Likely Lads*, as subliminally reflected in its title. Nerys Hughes starred as Sandra, a young woman of squeamishly delicate sensibilities, flat-sharing with Polly James's earthier Beryl, Terry to Sandra's Bob. Except this was more than mere replication. Even if the scripts of *The Liver Birds* were in no hurry to deliver on the jokes, no hurry at all at times, the well-drawn characters, bearing the unprotected brunt of women's liberation in a precarious coexistence, carried it through several series. Here, at least, was female-scripted female experience, albeit within the slightly mannered bounds of sitcom-ese.

Butterflies (1978–83) and *Solo* (1981–2) were more advanced and mature explorations of the choices facing women in the late seventies, their desires and the possibility of acting on them. In the former, Wendy Craig plays Ria, whose comfortable middle-class existence in Cheltenham, married to dentist husband Ben (Geoffrey Palmer) and with two almost grown-up boys, is far from idyllic. Ben is almost wholly absorbed by his work and his hobby (lepidopterology, the study of butterflies) and oblivious to the needs of Ria, whom he forbids from working. By contrast, he bickers with his two lads for their work-shy, hair-down, carefree attitude to life.

Brian Cooke and Johnnie Mortimer, creators of ITV's *Man About the House* (1973–6), probably weren't impelled by sociological zeal when they conceived this sitcom about a young man, Robin, who becomes flatmates with Chrissy and Jo (Paula Wilcox and Sally Thomsett). The series did, however, point to a gradual parity between the genders and their domestic roles. Robin is horny enough, particularly lustful towards Chrissy (Wilcox). But the show's creators were wise enough not to allow him to have it off, get his leg over, his end away or enjoy any how's your father with his flatmates. He is emasculated, and the show's title charged with irony; the women tell their landlord George that Robin is gay so that he can live in the flat. They are attracted to him primarily because he is a dab hand at cooking, whereas it's all they can do between them to burn a piece of toast. As for landlord and landlady George (Brian Murphy) and Mildred (Yootha Joyce), theirs is a sexless, childless marriage, the pitiful cardigan of a man George incapable of fulfilling Mildred's desires. Their three lodgers take up the rooms their children might have had, these strange, freer-living, frillier, longer-haired children of the Aquarian 1970s.

Paula Wilcox would go on to star in ITV's *Miss Jones and Son*
(1977), as a woman who has a child out of wedlock and must struggle
with the practicalities of a reduced income and the judgemental attitude of her parents and society as a whole. The most helpful person
in her life is her neighbour, Geoffrey, who, in his well-meaning but
shuffling, gauche manner, comes across like a younger George Roper.
For all its worthy intentions, it is stilted by the tropes and cadences of
mainstream sitcom, which it fails to exceed, as well as the perspective
of its writers. Richard Waring, creator of *Miss Jones and Son*, had
first enjoyed success with 1963's *Marriage Lines* (Richard Briers and
Prunella Scales) and also created . . . *And Mother Makes Three*. 1977
was the year of punk, with its concomitant explosion of hidebound
social attitudes. Miss Jones is not quite such a revolutionary. She is
not with her boyfriend because she is 'a bit old-fashioned about living
together'. Meanwhile, taken back to her parents' place after the boy's
birth, she worries about him being in her old room, 'surrounded by
dolls and dresses – I don't want him to grow up peculiar'.

In her excellent 1990 memoir *A Coward's Chronicles*, written when
she knew she had terminal cancer, Marti Caine recalls the atmosphere
in the green room at the theatre where she was performing when the
news of her diagnosis had broken, and her dumbstruck fellow cast
members and crew were taking it in. Caine broke the awkward atmosphere by telling the story of 'the guy next door' who was given only
three days to live. He told his wife, who said that over those three days
he could have whatever he fancied for his tea. The first night, he asked
for a nice bit of steak, which she duly rushed out and bought him. The
second night, he requested fresh salmon, which, once again, she went
out and cooked for him. On the third night, feeling a little guilty at
repeatedly sending his wife out shopping, he said, 'I notice you have a
nice bit of boiled ham in the fridge. I'll have that with a few tomatoes.'

His wife said: 'You can sod off! That's for the funeral tea tomorrow.'

The truism that comedy is a coping strategy for pain and adversity was rarely truer than in the case of Lynne Shepherd, aka Marti

Caine. Born in Sheffield in 1945, she recalled her early years with fondness. However, her father died young, and her mother turned to pills to assuage her grief and loneliness. Meanwhile, her grandfather, 'Pop', the patriarch who had cowed both son and daughter-in-law, abused her sexually. In *A Coward's Chronicle*, there is a publicity shot, hideous in retrospect, published in the *Sheffield Star and Telegraph*, of Caine in a swimsuit, with 'Pop' standing behind a tree leering approvingly at her.

Married with a young family and at her wits' end as to how to meet the costs for her mother's funeral, Caine turned to showbiz, relying on the wit she had sharpened since childhood as a tool against bullies. It stood her in good stead. She recalls an early gig at a notoriously hostile working men's club in Sunderland, the walls of the venue plastered with mashed potatoes following a rowdy get-together of the rugby supporters' club. Initially trembling and 'belching' with fear, she took advantage of the momentary stunned silence at her appearance in a bright pink mini-dress, an inadvertent glam parody. 'Gerremoff!' shouted a heckler. 'If it's as big as your mouth, you're on,' Caine came right back. She realised in that moment the power she wielded as a comedian – far from being under siege, she felt she had the crowd dangling on the edge of her string.

Having put in the years in the most exacting of environments, the working men's club circuit, Caine's skill and timing were diamond sharp, as sharp as a Bernard Manning, a genuine compliment. It was a sharpness born out of necessity. Unlike her male contemporaries, Caine had to deal with being what was considered in the 1970s a rarity: a female comedian. Critics, struggling for comparison, had to reach back to Hylda Baker, to whom she struck a stark contrast. Unlike Baker, Caine had sex appeal in her armoury, as emphasised in her press shots. Moreover, a good part of her act fell back on her capability as a middle-of-the-road crooner. She was no Mrs Mopp-style caricature of lumpen, working-class coarseness. Hers was a balancing act between sequin-thin showbiz glam and the earthy, rueful wit that twitched and lurked and subverted just beneath. She was soft focus but hard as nails, with irony in her soul. And, novel as a comedian like her was to 1970s audiences, she won them over, seeing off Lenny Henry and Victoria Wood to win 1975's *New Faces*.

She was not exactly left-field – she naively played Sun City in 1983, at the height of the anti-apartheid campaign, which would hardly have endeared her to the alternative comedy generation. She did, however, later apologise for this, declaring that if she had been aware of the situation on the ground in South Africa, outside the Sun City bubble, she would never have agreed to perform there.

Despite her great TV success, hosting her own BBC shows and starring alongside Philip Madoc in the sitcom *Hilary* (1984–6), not a lot survives of Caine's comedy work on YouTube. It's possible that some of the material was distinctly creaky even in its own day – I recall a sketch in which she played 'Jane Blonde', a female 007 type. However, the little that does exist sparkles like crushed gems. In 1976, prior to interviewing the Nolans, she riffs with a certain arch elegance on the advantages of having an older lover. 'Reeking of Old Spice, dentures clicking in anticipation . . . I bet teenage lovers never leave their socks on.'

I like to imagine, had she lived, Caine finding a starring role in *Coronation Street*, a show she loved, alongside the likes of Lynne Perrie (Ivy Tilsley), a friend whom Caine describes as 'the best comedian of her day', sparring and trading witticisms with Julie Goodyear (Bet Lynch), Jean Alexander (Hilda Ogden), Elizabeth Dawn (Vera Duckworth), Mavis, Rita, maybe even Sarah Lancashire as Raquel, a worthy addition to that ensemble. As it was, she remained a star, a natural star, until her death in 1995, aged just fifty.

A TOUCH OF CLASS

The traditional relationship between comedy and the upper classes wasn't one of envy, or disdain, or anger at their disproportionate, unearned wealth – hence a long-standing British tradition of monstering trade unionists as a threat not merely to the country's GNP figures but to comedy itself: a grim litany of 'brothers', beginning with Peter Sellers's Soviet Union-loving Fred Kite, whose aim it was to cut the nation down to Ronnie Corbett size, reduce us all to joyless, overalled proletarians who had cowed management beyond all reason. Uppity militants became a comedy staple, in series such as Lance Percival's *Up the Workers* (1973–6), or Miriam Karlin's shop steward Paddy Fleming in *The Rag Trade* (1961–3, 1977–8), with typically weak textile workshop manager Peter Jones at the perpetual mercy of her catchphrase 'Everybody out!' There was also the episode of *Sykes*, 'Job', aired in 1972, in which Eric repeats the Britcom trope of the worker who raises the ire of his union rep by working too fast, with Jimmy Edwards playing the role of the factory manager easily dominated by the stern, accented shop steward, helpless as Heath.

There was a drip-feed of this, not least from Britain's favourite 1970s impressionist, Mike Yarwood. Amid his roster were impersonations of trade union leaders, the likes of Jack Jones, dour, regional sorts whom in one sketch he had reading in gloomy tones children's stories 'by the Brothers Grim'. That these were recognisable to mass audiences reflects the high profile of trade unions. However, it also reflects the invidiousness of their task of protecting workers' rights, being routinely portrayed as sour killjoys who thrived on industrial strife.

Such was the conservative leaning of British comedy – that the urge for betterment with which, say, Harold Steptoe is consumed must never be consummated. That wouldn't be funny. In the 1974 Christmas episode of *Steptoe and Son*, Harold unearths a bit of memorabilia containing his school motto: 'Know thy place and be grateful.' He trembles with rage. It's not just the British class system that has kept him in his place but the diktats of British comedy. In sitcom in particular, things must be reset to the status quo; everyone must return to their place. Comedy and high ideals are a mismatch; there is no laughter in paradise. It's a stretch to argue that the anti-union streak that runs through British comedy was wholly responsible for the rise of Margaret Thatcher, who rose to power as much on a promise to curb the supposedly excessive power of trade unions as anything else. Tabloids such as the *Sun*, *Mail* and *Express* supplied a relentless feed of 'Red' bêtes noires, menaces bent on turning the lights out in Britain at the drop of a motion. But like the ITMA gang back in World War II, comedy did its bit.

By the 1970s, the word 'satire' belonged squarely in the sixties, a decade that felt like a long time ago. These were politically moderate times. The Wilson–Heath–Wilson sequence of governments between 1964 and 1976 gave the misleading impression that politics was a perma-see-saw between Labour and Conservative, with the same two men at the helm, pursuing pragmatic policies on a day-by-day, crisis-by-crisis basis in the face of slow decline. TV political comedy fell to the impressionist Mike Yarwood, who had ample opportunity to hone his takes on the thoroughly imitable Wilson and Heath (though as the broadcaster Stuart Maconie delicately observed, there was always an essential 'Yarwoodness' about his impersonations). Wilson puffing away on a pipe, prating about the pound in your pocket; Heath's shoulders shaking as he laughed at his own jokes.

Carry On at Your Convenience (1971), meanwhile, was a straight-up exercise in union-bashing. Kenneth Cope co-stars as Vic Spanner, a union rep and cheap knock-off of Peter Sellers's Fred Kite in *I'm All Right, Jack*, right down to his manner of speaking as if reading out the minutes from a branch meeting. Kenneth Williams plays W. C. Boggs, owner of the ceramics factory, but such is the slant of the film that he is relatively sympathetic, especially when he gets well into the spirit of things on a work outing and recites a ribald limerick. And there's Sid James, chuckling again, the foreman whose common-sensical attitude naturally sees him side with management, knowing his place. As this made-up story puts it, the activities of the unions are deplorable and most of the other workers, with the exception of dimwit Bernard Bresslaw, just want to do an 'honest day's work' rather than fuss about their rights. Finally, the strike-breaking cavalry arrives in the form of a regiment of women, led by Spanner's mother: 'Shift your arse out of the way and let these good people do their work.' Whereupon she takes her son over her knee and gives him a spanking. (Interestingly, the film did not fare well at the box office, the didactic, anti-union tone of the dialogue perhaps being off-putting to cinemagoers used to unbridled mirth from the series.)

Williams would have sympathised with Spanner's mother. He became more right-wing with age, developing a sympathy for the political wing that would have the least truck with gay rights, for example. He appeared on *Parkinson* and, ruining the fun as he was often wont to do, delivered a dyspeptic anti-union tirade in front of his embarrassed-looking fellow guest Maggie Smith. Williams, Sims, Windsor, James, Hawtrey, Butterworth made the best of often tired material and intermittently brightened our lives with their seaside familiarity, representing a bawdy levity we recognised in ourselves, a consolation for our ongoing British predicament. And yet, looking at the tawdry, never-changing rates he and his fellow *Carry On* actors were paid throughout the series, despite its enormous success, the thought occurs: Kenneth, you guys really should have unionised.

FAWLTY TOWERS

Unions were the bane of John Cleese's Basil Fawlty, a scourge of the era of 'bloody Wilson!' in which *Fawlty Towers* (1975–9) was broadcast. But this antipathy was a reflection on Fawlty, this tall, small man with a grudge against modernity.

In 'The Wedding Party' episode, Basil, on realising that the young couple on the other side of the hotel desk are unmarried, refuses to allow them to book a double room. 'It's against the law,' he tells them. What law? they ask. 'The law of England,' snaps back Basil.

Basil Fawlty is a character who abides by all the unwritten laws of England, concerning propriety, respectability, tone, though his contempt for his fellow countrymen, except for his social betters, leads him to commit acts of staggering rudeness. If, as I for one believe and a TV industry poll conducted in 2000 agreed, *Fawlty Towers* is the greatest ever English sitcom, it's because, prior to Alan Partridge, he was the most exhaustive comedic human exposé of the English psyche – its irascibility, repression, superiority/inferiority complex, anger, frustration, hauteur and, above and beneath it all, anxiety and embarrassment.

Basil feels like a creature from the 1950s stranded in a modern, too-permissive England in which riff-raff appear to have the upper hand. He would have felt happiest in the England of the 1950s, just demobbed from the Korean War, pre-Suez, pre- the Common Market and the Beatles and sexual intercourse, when the restoration of Winston Churchill to Downing Street seemed to nip the onset of socialism in the bud and class distinction was still observed.

Basil Fawlty was inspired by Donald Sinclair, a Torquay hotelier. Staying at the hotel with his fellow Pythons, Cleese noted that Sinclair received every request, however routine, with undisguised exasperation. The guests, Sinclair felt, obtusely regarded his establishment as some sort of hotel, and himself as some kind of manager. Cleese recalled asking Sinclair to order him a taxi, and the hotelier retorting, 'Oh, I suppose so!' – as if Cleese had asked if he could borrow his car.

Basil's first few exchanges in 'A Touch of Class', the debut episode of *Fawlty Towers*, are pure Sinclair, as he casually sprays venom at everyone from striking dustmen to the guests who fall short of the 'tone' he wishes the hotel to maintain. When a new guest arrives, he can say nothing to dampen Basil's irritation. 'Have you BOOKED?' Basil spits. 'Well, no – are you full?' 'Full?' replies Basil to this idiotic question. 'Full? Of COURSE we're not full.' It's the moment the guest reveals himself to be one Lord Melbury that Basil transforms from Sinclair impersonator to Fawlty, paradigm of the English condition, instantly reduced to a puddle of fawning. 'You never get it right, do you?' observes his wife, Sybil (Prunella Scales), in 'The Psychiatrist'. 'You're either crawling over them licking their boots or spitting poison at them like some Benzedrine puff adder.'

Cleese was perfect for the role of Fawlty. It's strange to think that others, including Denholm Elliott, were considered for the role. In his *Python* and pre-*Python* days, it always fell to him to play the pin-striped establishment figures, as their self-confidence was ingrained in him, in the way that it was not in a Palin or a Jones. Yet he also understood the concurrent anxiety of the well-to-do. As he told *Der Spiegel* in 2015, 'safety and respectability was everything. People were terrified of being caught doing anything that wasn't respectable.'

Al Murray once accused one of his audience of being 'too tall', and so is Fawlty. Cleese is the perfect height to convey the too-tallness of this actually rather small man, destined to be laid low by his own pretentious folly. It enables him to peer down with contempt at the majority of his guests in all their pudgy, suburban mediocrity, or occasionally outright uncouthness. 'Have we got enough bananas in this week, dear?' he remarks obliquely, as his eyes fall scornfully on Nicky Henson's open-shirted, medallion-wearing Mr Johnson. However, when confronted with doctors, leading Rotarians or peers of the realm, he is forced to stoop to adopt the correctly obsequious posture.

He couldn't have been played by a portly actor; as the farce in each episode builds, for which he is inadvertently responsible or over-anxiously takes responsibility, he spends an inordinate amount of time running, scuttling, barrelling, limbs flailing frantically, up and down the needless staircase on the hotel's first floor or out of the hotel door to stop a laundry van, one of whose baskets may contain a dead man. Furthermore, when he finally loses it completely, his elongation is ideally suited to doubling up, crumpling in a heap, crouching into a bouncing foetal ball or breaking into a goose-step, barking Teutonically.

Because *Fawlty Towers* just pre-dates the election of Margaret Thatcher, she features fleetingly: in 'The Psychiatrist', Mr Johnson, to Basil's quiet fury, jokes that the smallest book in the world is the wit and wisdom of Margaret Thatcher. It's 1979, but Basil's complaints are still against Wilsonian 'socialism', a layabout's paradise. 'What's happening to this country, it's bloody Wilson!' he shrieks, at the culmination of a disastrous fire drill. Basil embodies an English time bomb of self-pitying resentment, petty frustration and pent-up fury that would propel Mrs Thatcher to power at the same time as *Fawlty Towers* closed its doors for the last time.

Fawlty Towers' mounting chaos and manic loss of self-control could only be achieved by tight, meticulous writing and intensive revision on the part of scriptwriters Cleese and his wife Connie Booth. Her contribution was indispensable. Having married in 1968, she and Cleese had written together prior to *Fawlty Towers* – on *Romance with a Double Bass*, a forty-minute movie adaptation of a Chekhov story – and even attempted a TV thriller, though this project was abandoned early on.

Although the work he and Chapman produced together for *Python* was indisputably brilliant, Cleese ultimately found the partnership frustrating as he had a very meticulous and rigorous way of applying himself to writing, whereas Chapman worked more fitfully and was apt to be lost to the pub if his nostrils twitched at the aroma of a hostelry. Despite the fact that Cleese and Booth's marriage was in trouble in the mid-seventies, they actually found amicable respite co-writing together, and Booth was a blessed contrast to Chapman.

Cleese praised Booth as a fount of funny ideas – only Michael Palin, he said, was her equal in this respect in his experience – as well as being good on character. More acute was his observation that 'I take a script along obvious lines, moving towards farce, whereas Connie stops me doing the obvious.' This enabled Cleese and Booth to straddle the difference between mere sketch-writing, taking ideas on a brief journey to their logically absurd conclusion, and the more rounded art of sitcom-writing.

There was a further advantage to working with Booth as opposed to Chapman. Although Chapman and Cleese were maddeningly different in their approach to writing, they were very similar in terms of class and patrician perspective. Booth brought with her a very different background and experience, having worked, for example, extensively as a waitress while trying to get her acting career started in New York, as well as coming from a family who were more openly combative than Cleese's own, buttoned-up parents, as well as, of course, having the female experience of life.

There is a reason why Cleese never again matched the quality of *Fawlty Towers*, and that reason is largely Connie Booth. In innumerable ways, her contributions enrich the show, make it hum with humanity, so that it is not merely a rickety set of one-dimensional, human-shaped props for the ridiculous Fawlty to flail and bluster at. She helps create the obstacles, the complications that heighten the comic stress and thereby raise the quality of the series. Never the obvious.

Graham McCann, in his excellent study of the series, notes that the scripts generally ran to around 135 pages, twice the length of the average seventies sitcom. Cleese was much taken with classic farceurs like the turn-of-the-century playwright Georges Feydeau, but also contemporaries such as Alan Ayckbourn, at the height of his fame in the mid-seventies thanks to TV adaptations of works like *The Norman Conquests*. Ayckbourn's characters, though well observed and finely drawn, often felt secondary to the magnificently elaborate and symmetrical comedic structures he built to house them in.

Not that this was always a guarantee of comedic sturdiness. 'The Builders', the second episode in series one of *Fawlty Towers*, is its least impressive edifice. Sybil is an enigmatic character. It's unclear what she ever could have seen in her husband, with whom she is at perpetual odds. Her only stated reason for their staying together is that they have already done so for a long time. And while she is clearly far more capable than Basil of addressing guests with the proper measure of politesse, and takes charge when necessary, she also spends a lot of time on the phone gossiping, planning leisure activities, going conveniently absent for key stretches of the shows. All to the good. Any kind of *Good Life*-style uxorial affection would be the death of *Fawlty Towers*, while Sybil's indolence, into which the show wisely doesn't go too deeply, allows Basil the time and legroom to sow self-defeating mayhem.

In 'The Builders', however, Sybil is more the traditional battle-axe, wielding a golf brolly like a mace. Add in the abuse by one of the labourers of the hapless Spanish waiter Manuel as a 'Dago twit' and the Irish builders, headed up by O'Reilly, a stock Irishman played by David Kelly, who attempts to make up in charm for what he lacks in competence and whose shoddy workmanship must be rescued by the stolid, English Mr Stubbs, and it's all a bit bog-seventies. Still, there are peaks of excellence, as Basil threatens to blow all his blood vessels at once as he loses control. He sarcastically spanks his own backside, slaps his own head, screams with impotent petulance, strangles a garden gnome.

Critics weren't immediately taken with *Fawlty Towers*. They might have echoed the misgivings of Ian Main, the BBC script editor who cited, among other things, the weak pun of its title. Episode three, 'The Wedding Party', however, is a full demonstration of the show's powers. There's so much to commend, not least Manuel's revels on his birthday night and the subsequent hangover which sees him fall asleep in a laundry basket. Sexual envy, resentment, prudishness and faint longing are an undercurrent throughout. Sybil, enjoying a drink with a bawdy male friend, is illustrating one of life's great sadnesses – that the people with the most annoying laughs are also the most easily amused. 'Like machine-gunning a seal,' he hisses at the major, who introduces Basil to Mrs Peignoir, an elegant Frenchwoman and antiques dealer whose roguish flirtatiousness both flatters and disconcerts Basil.

Sex is in the air this warm, sultry evening, and Basil, who's having none of it in more ways than one, takes it out on his guests. A young, frisky couple, anxious to check in to their room, ask for a double bed. When Basil realises they are unmarried, he acts to stem this tide of sexual licentiousness currently overwhelming Torquay and denies their request on legal grounds. Whereupon the bloke settles for two single rooms, 'if that's all right with the police', before Sybil overrules Basil.

Basil is still fuming at this humiliation when the young man arrives back at the desk, realising he has no batteries for his electric shaver. Basil thinks he wants them for some sort of sex device. 'I know what people like you get up to and I think it's dis*gusting*.'

What do you mean? says the guest. I was only asking if you had a couple of batteries for my shaver.

'That's what I was referring to,' Basil musters, slowly quailing inside. 'It is, of course, dis*gusting* that you haven't shaved, but understandable, sometimes I forget to shave too and that's also dis*gusting* . . .'

As he unleashes a silent scream, we realise that mortification is one of Basil's strongest emotions. As further wedding party guests arrive, a series of embraces between father and daughter and family friend Polly (Connie Booth), which he accidentally witnesses, impels him to delay the arrival in the room of the mother, as he takes on board the potential embarrassment of the situation. Why should Basil, normally so carelessly brusque with his guests, care if one of them is exposed as a philanderer? You suspect his inspiration, Sinclair, would have pulled up a chair and enjoyed the ensuing kerfuffle. Instead, Basil frantically diverts the mother into an unused room. He follows that up by eavesdropping in the corridor, imagining an orgy to be in process. He decides to confront the entire wedding party and throw them out. Only when Sybil explains the actual relationship of the wedding party to Polly does Basil once again crumble inwardly. 'What have I done?'

However, admission of error is unthinkable, the loss of face intoler-able. 'Is that what made Britain great?' he yells, when Sybil suggests he apologise, before doubling up like a Python Gumby: 'I'm seew sorry, I've made a mistake!' The lengths to which some Englishmen will go to avoid to owning up to a mistake are considerable, and Basil goes to every last one of them as he reinstates the wedding party ('My wife has made a terrible mistake').

'The Hotel Inspectors' follows, in which Basil and Sybil are tipped off that they may come under scrutiny from roving officials in Torquay. For Basil, this means the enormous wrench of treating the guests with due deference. In fairness, he is tried to his limits by Mr Hutchinson, played by Bernard Cribbins, whose extended, punctilious demands for service are supremely calibrated to wind Basil up. It is the bane of Basil's life, and an affront to the status for which he pines, that he can maintain his lordly Towers only by performing menial chores for assorted 'proles', especially a high-maintenance one like Hutchinson. Initially, Basil treats him with unconcealed asperity ('Why don't you talk properly?'), only to collapse into servile solicitude when he comes to believe Hutchinson is the hotel inspector, only to rise again with wrathful, unwarranted vengeance on him when he turns out to be a spoon salesman.

Fawlty Towers was developing a momentum and raising high expectations in its audience, triggered by the sedate, chamber strains of the Dennis Wilson theme tune. It was a gleeful certainty that by the end of each episode, things would have descended into a full-on, orchestral cacophony of atonal mayhem. So it was with 'Gourmet Night', in which, in his attempts to cleanse his establishment of the lower orders, Basil sets up a dining event, to whose advert he has appended the words 'no riff-raff'. Only four people turn up, the Twitchens and Colonel Hall and his wife. So over-excited and awestruck is Basil that he forgets his own name, let alone that of one of the guests, but this is a tiny precursor of the cataclysmic events to follow, precipitated by Kurt, his drunken chef.

Cleese's physical comedy is a joy. Screaming the word 'duck!' at Polly, as he returns to the dining area, flapping his arms and quacking loudly, he morphs instantly into the suave gait of a maître d' the moment he is in the sightline of the guests. But the centrepiece is his assault on his malfunctioning little red Austin 1100 at a kerbside.

Basil is the victim of his own cheapness, but the car seems to symbolise clapped-out Britain. The year 1975 was when British Leyland (who manufactured the occasionally temperamental Austin 1100) collapsed and had to be partly nationalised. It had fallen foul of all of the ills of the seventies – inflation, the three-day week, the oil crisis – as well as poor or misplaced innovation. British Leyland's failure greatly exercised car-obsessed Britain. It spoke of wider failings and the ongoing mediocritisation of a once proud nation. The futile thrashing Basil administers to the vehicle with a tree branch is an act of primal, political rage, to which the audience's response is part sympathy, part serves you right. Mainly, though, it's all about the pleasure of watching the veneer of Basil's propriety peel away to reveal a yelling, frustrated maniac.

Finally, 'The Germans', two episodes soldered into one. The first part features a head injury to Basil, following his rage at his guests' failure to distinguish the semitone of difference between a fire and a burglar alarm, the fall of a moose's head and an actual fire in which he nearly burns Manuel alive. The major is on particularly fine form, especially when he is convinced that Manuel's booming voice from behind the hotel desk is the moose's head atop it talking to him.

The major was played by Ballard Berkeley, an actor with an intriguing history – a sometime flatmate of Cary Grant, he was a special constable during World War II. When the Café de Paris took a direct hit, Berkeley arrived at the underground ballroom to find bandleader Ken 'Snakehips' Johnson, a leading figure in Black British music in the 1930s, decapitated and rows of formally dressed audience members sitting at their tables, looking unscathed but actually quite dead. Following the war, he made a career out of playing aristocratic types but never any quite so addled as the major. A permanent resident, he gets a modicum of deference from Fawlty, whose rudeness to him is only ever under his breath ('drunken old sod'). He is, like Basil's Empire coin collection, something of class to have about the place, even if his currency is obsolete. The major is a fellow whose marbles have long since returned to Greece of their own volition. His role, as with Manuel, is to let Basil down in his hours of need, by failing utterly, despite his game efforts, to grasp the point.

In 'The Germans', however, he delivers the series' most infamous line, recalling taking an old girlfriend to a cricket match to see India, whom she regards as 'niggers'. He upbraids her, indignantly. 'No, the West Indians are niggers. These people are wogs!' Technically, it's the perfect major joke; as with his rise to the defence of the hotel in the face of an American guest's insults – 'No, I won't have that! There's a place in Eastbourne . . .' – you think he's going to show some old-school uprightness, only for him, as ever, to let you down. But it's Cleese and Booth who let the viewer down, in this instance, though sadly the joke would have raised a great laugh in 1975, as would Basil taking a hop back when he is confronted with a Black doctor at the hospital. *Fawlty Towers* may be the apex of British comedy but it did not always rise above the social attitudes of its day, when blackness was considered 'other', comical, peripheral on national TV. The joke is a jarring, needless, one-off reveal of an un-endearing racism on the otherwise endearing major's part, and suggests an indifference to the hurt it causes on the part of the creators. It should have been cut. If you wouldn't do it now, you shouldn't have done it then.

As for the Germans, even Basil would not have acted as he did were it not for his head injury. Some viewers are uncomfortable that the shrieking audience laughter at Basil goose-stepping about the lobby is the suppressed guffawing of British Germanophobia. However, the German guests themselves are refreshingly unstereotypical and their dignity marks a contrast with the Nazi cartoon figures still stomping around Basil's arrested psyche in lieu of actual 1970s West Germans. (According to a German-born friend of mine, *Fawlty Towers* has a strong cult following in his native land, particularly this episode;

indeed, they complain only that the episode isn't tough enough on the Germans themselves.)

Four years passed between series one and two of *Fawlty Towers*. The breakdown of Cleese and Booth's marriage was a factor, though not only were they determined to continue working together, their resolution to outdo the first series prompted an even more thorough scripting process.

The BBC bridged the gap by repeating the original series three times. The *Fawlty Towers* team received raises, though not over-generous ones. John Cleese was paid £9,000 (about £43,000 in today's money) and Andrew Sachs (Manuel) £350 for their work on a series that would garner viewing figures of eleven million per week.

The opening episode of the second series, 'Communication Problems', was broadcast in February 1979. Other than the makeover of the lobby in more subdued colours and the introduction of Brian Hall as chef Terry, there isn't much evidence of the passing of time. I couldn't help noting in the following episode, 'The Psychiatrist', that Basil's grey suit with tapered trousers, supposed to denote ultra-squareness, actually made him look ultra-hip, as if he'd come back from watching Joy Division at the Futurama, compared with young Mr Johnson's hairy-chested medallion-man look, considered risible in the post-punk era.

Thatcherism hasn't yet happened. In advance of her in 'Communication Problems' is Joan Sanderson's hectoring, misery-making Mrs Richards. She has a hearing aid which, in her financial meanness, she refuses to turn on, forcing Basil to bellow exasperatedly. One sympathises with him in his clashes with this gorgon in tweeds. When she complains about the view from her room, Basil asks what she expected to see. 'Sydney Opera House? The Hanging Gardens of Babylon? Herds of wildebeest sweeping majestically . . . ?'

Basil may be a reactionary, but his rants are the stuff of comedy modernism, masterclasses in scathing, erudite sarcasm, in sync with the acidic disdain punk rock unleashed on a moribund Britain. It's strangely unsurprising that John Cleese and Johnny Rotten draw on similar wells of scorn, despite Basil and Rotten belonging to opposite ends of the social spectrum. (Ironically, both would come out in favour of Brexit, as if they felt that Britain in 2016 needed the same jolt out of its complacency as in the 1970s.)

Often, Cleese's sarcasm grenades come in volleys of three. To the spoiled boy in 'Gourmet Night' who complains his chips are the 'wrong shape', Basil asks him which shape he would prefer – 'Mickey Mouse shape? Amphibious landing craft shape? Poke in the eye shape?' Or, to the guest who asks for breakfast in bed: 'Rosewood, mahogany, teak? Sorry, I was wondering what you'd like your breakfast tray made out of.'

This is the acerbic voice of advanced late-twentieth-century comedy, one adopted by Blackadder, another man at odds with his times, brought face to face with the myriad imbecilities of Olde England. Often, you feel it's not Basil talking but Cleese. 'Look, it's not a proposition from Wittgenstein,' he says to Manuel, as if Basil were as acquainted with the *Tractatus* as he is Peter Benchley's *Jaws*.

Communication problems are a theme dear to Cleese – he talked about 'communication difficulties' being one of the reasons for his schism with the rest of the Python members. But in the case of his dealings with Manuel, there's a simple, farcical delight in watching Basil's blood pleasure rise, and his lanky body contort, as he is unable to elicit basic comprehension in times of urgent need.

'The Psychiatrist' takes advantage of its unusually long permitted running time of thirty-six minutes. As with 'The Wedding Party', it's largely about sex, and the starved Basil's deeply inhibited, repressive prurience. This unmatched, immaculate piece of comedic design, in which doors are opened and shut at all the perfectly wrong moments, all stems from Basil's determination to catch out his nemesis, the uncouth and, to his eyes, simian Mr Johnson, bringing a woman back to his room. Basil is undone at every turn, including a scene when, up a ladder looking to peer into Johnson's room, he ends up looking into that of the psychiatrist; another where he accidentally molests a young Australian guest, convincing Sybil he is having an affair; and eventually, in what he hoped would be a Poirot-type moment of truth, finding himself saying hello to Mr Johnson's mother.

Basil is triggered when he discovers Dr Abbott is a psychiatrist. Although he is dismissive of psychiatry as a 'load of tommy rot', he obviously fears these doctors will subject his mind to an X-ray examination, revealing all kinds of sordidness lurking in the still, slimy waters of his subconscious. He misunderstands when Dr Abbott asks him how often he and Sybil take holidays – 'How often do you manage it?' – assuming that, sex being the topic on his brain, it is on theirs too. 'My wife didn't see how you could manage it at all,' remarks Abbott. To which Basil blunders, 'About three times a week, actually. That's normal, isn't it?'

The 'Waldorf Salad' episode addresses another topic close to Cleese: the transatlantic divide. It's late evening, and enter Bruce Boa's Mr Hamilton, an American, and his (English) wife, with whom Basil is quite charmed – less so when Mr Hamilton appears, ranting about the failings of England, from its narrow roads to its 'Mickey Mouse' currency. Hamilton explodes when he learns that the restaurant has closed for the evening and bribes Basil to reopen it. Following an argument with Terry the chef, whom he dismisses for the night, Basil surreptitiously takes over in the restaurant, playing out the roles of both himself and the chef for the benefit of his guests. Confusion arises when they order a screwdriver (a vodka and orange) and a Waldorf salad, of which Basil has never heard. Mr Hamilton, who possesses not an atom of English shyness when it comes to complaining about poor service, advises Fawlty to lay it on the line to his chef, to 'bust his ass'. Basil retreats to the kitchen for a showdown with the imaginary chef, then returns, assuring Mr Hamilton he's just 'smashed his backside' for him.

The charade collapses, and Mr Hamilton leads a revolt of the

English guests, who finally speak up, despite Basil's Churchillian speech in which he is about to outline certain English values of far, far greater importance than money. 'I'm not happy,' objects one guest. Basil erupts. 'This is . . . typical – absolutely typical – of the kind of *arse* I have to put up with from you people.' (The defiance of 'arse' is pleasing – so superior to 'ass', one thing we Brits do well.) 'You ponce in here expecting to be waited on hand and foot, when I'm trying to run a hotel . . .' As for complaints, well, he says, this is the sort of restiveness which reminds him of 'how Nazi Germany started', a foreign mess which, to Basil's mind and that of many others, it once again fell to the English to sort out. With a dismissive "*Raus!*" he expels his guests and then himself, leaving the hotel for good, it seems, striding out bold as Brexit to take back control for a few yards, before the reality of the cold English rain forces him back indoors.

'The Kipper and the Corpse' is based on an anecdote Cleese heard from a hotelier of the difficulties staff face when trying to remove guests who have died during the night. Such a fate has befallen Mr Leeman, whose demise Basil fails to notice while serving him breakfast in bed, too preoccupied with railing against socialism. Only when Polly spots that the guest has joined the choir invisible does Basil break into a panic, suspecting he might have been done in by an out-of-date kipper.

Basil and Manuel's efforts to remove Mr Leeman's body are thwarted by the damnable insistence of hotel guests on coming and going from their rooms and by Miss Tibbs, who tries to help them out, only to fly into hysterics when she realises they are carrying a corpse. Polly overdoes her efforts to calm her down, knocking her out cold; now her body must be discreetly stowed away somewhere.

Long-term residents Miss Tibbs and Miss Gatsby are, like the major, a living, breathing part of the fixtures and fittings; it's a mystery akin to the endurance of the Boris Johnson Appreciation Society why they retain a soft spot for Basil, living off every drop of the superficial unctuousness he bestows on them, regardless of his many rudenesses

– shooing them out of the gourmet night to make do, like the rest of the riff-raff, with a trough of baked beans 'garnished with a couple of dead dogs', or, as here, bundling one of them into a wardrobe. Yet they continue to regard him as the epitome of charm.

There would be a two-week wait for the series' fifth episode, 'The Anniversary', due to a BBC strike. A further bout of industrial action meant that 'Basil the Rat', the last ever episode of *Fawlty Towers*, wasn't broadcast until 25 October 1979.

Although there's gold in both these episodes, 'The Anniversary' in particular feels like the first episode in an ill-advised third series. Having forgotten his and Sybil's wedding anniversary the year before, Basil is planning a surprise party for their fifteenth. However, his pretence of having forgotten yet again backfires – Sybil storms out, just as some of their close friends are arriving for the do. A terrified Basil persuades Polly to impersonate a bedridden Sybil, but the game is truly up when Sybil returns. The funniest sequence is when, rather than try to save the marriage, Basil waives it, and her, rather than face the excruciation of being found out in his charade.

There is an intriguing exchange between Polly and Basil in which she pours out years of grievances – and now he expects her to impersonate his wife. It's a moment that feels like it might be channelling some of the energy of Cleese and Booth's disintegrated marriage and its presumably attendant rows. However, it also raises the question of why Polly, level-headed, a college graduate, chose to stay on for so long, providing the one plank of sanity across the gaping Fawlty hellhole. There have been various, strenuous efforts to explain this, but most likely is that we are simply required to suspend disbelief.

Polly is more of an ally to Basil in his myriad predicaments than his wife, and more than once helps bail him out of his deceptions. Polly's is a generous, necessary role. Though she gets the odd bit of vengeful fun – spicing up the sausages of a pampered pooch who bit her, for example – she doesn't get the bigger laughs. She has to do the menial but vital work of seeing to it that, for twenty-five or so minutes at least, a *Fawlty Towers* episode doesn't collapse like the unsupported wall in 'The Builders'. As with *Monty Python*, sanity is a vital component in *Fawlty Towers*, sanity and humanity. In some ways, the comedy is a plea for it, rather than some wilfully zany rejection of it. Connie Booth, both as writer and as Polly, supplies both, ensures that the series is grounded, never spirals off into wanton, Milligan-esque frenzy.

Manuel is the most loveable character in *Fawlty Towers*, though has also been considered problematic in later times, as his imbecility is equated with his foreign-ness ('He's from Barcelona,' Sybil will often explain to guests perplexed by his incompetence). He wasn't a novel creation – *Bless This House* had already featured a 'zany' Spanish waiter, played by Ronnie Brody, in 1973. Cleese insisted that Manuel was not a xenophobic stereotype but designed to compound and intensify Basil's frustrations. This may be so, but quite a few members of the British audience watching in the 1970s would have been taking their first, tentative European holidays and encountered Spanish waiters whose limited command of English was proof of the meanness of their intelligence; maybe they laughed a little too heartily at every '*Qué?*'

Manuel is barely treated as human by Basil, more like a monkey on a rope. Manuel lopes about with a simian gait, like a Barbary ape lured off a rock and stuffed into a white jacket. He is subject to constant corporal punishment – cuffed, slapped, splatted across the forehead with a spoon, poked in the eye, assaulted with a saucepan. It is all terribly cruel, but then, some of the most satisfying moments in comedy, from Laurel and Hardy to Baldrick to *Bottom*, involve severe blows taken to the head. All we need is assurance of the imperviousness of the recipients. Furthermore, albeit unintentionally, he visits far more pain on Basil than he receives in return – when he tells Sybil that Mr Fawlty 'looking in window to see girl' (Mr Nicholson's girlfriend, not the Australian girl) and she 'goes crazy', for example, or in 'Communication Problems', when he triumphantly clears his throat and declares, 'I know no-thing,' ruining Basil's scheming.

However, Manuel's devotion to Basil is unwavering. He regards him as his benefactor and, when Basil eventually opens the door to the blazing kitchen in which he's locked him in 'The Germans', his lifesaver. Basil spares none of his feelings, and yet those feelings for Mr Fawlty are so strong that he will scuttle instantly to his side at the snap of his fingers. When choosing a name for his beloved rat, Manuel naturally opts for Basil.

Manuel could never be presented as a comic creation in our own time, when Europeans are accepted by most Britons as sentient members of the human race – and nor ought he to have been in 1975. Andrew Sachs, who played him, was German-born and had come to England as a child, knowing but a single sentence of English. In time, he acquired the language with the accent-less fluency of a native-born speaker – as so many did. Over the course of four years, by contrast, Manuel's English barely improves. Were it to do so, that would arguably make him redundant as a comic character, but it does confirm the notion that foreigners are inherently imbecilic, that to be 'from Barcelona' is an unfortunate condition. Sachs was once asked in an interview if he had ever met a waiter like Manuel and had to confess that, despite repeated trips to Spain, he had not. Of course he hadn't. Manuel reflects no reality; he is a comic creation, co-conceived by Cleese, who, despite presenting Fawlty as a relic of British exceptionalism, shows how he was occasionally guilty of the trait himself.

That said, while the major's errant lines are easy to excise, for those who have grown up with *Fawlty Towers* since childhood, Manuel is more difficult to do away with (not least because of his own child-likeness). He is responsible for so much of the comedy, not just the communication difficulties he presents at vital stages in the episodes but also the violence – which was an issue that concerned interviewers of Sachs at the time far more than any stereotyping. Manuel is, for those of my own generation, hard to forsake but may leave present and future generations coming to the show for the first time colder. Modern writers worth their salt, when creating a sidekick, would have thought harder, done better.

Although there have been developments in British comedy since the seventies, *Fawlty Towers*, despite its rickety sets, stands firm as Britain's finest piece of sitcom architecture. Subsequently, the closest Cleese came to emulating the manic, raging, forlorn character of Basil was in the Michael Frayn-scripted movie *Clockwise* (1986), the story of a punctilious headmaster whose journey to a conference is beset by a series of calamities. Containing the immortal line, 'I can take the despair. It's the hope I can't stand,' it's as near as we will ever get to a *Fawlty Towers* movie.

Cleese would achieve further cinematic fame with *A Fish Called Wanda* (1988), but became an increasingly remote figure with the passing of time, one whose judgement did not improve with age. With *Fawlty Towers*, it feels like he is not just critiquing a certain kind of Englishness but also reflecting a process of 'un-Englishing' himself, loosening certain of the inhibitions of being English. Basil is afraid of psychiatry. Cleese himself, however, overcame his own 'very British' misgivings and embraced psychiatry and the mental unbuttoning it involved, joining a psychotherapy group led by one Robin Skynner, albeit at the over-analytical expense of his comedy. Basil was stuck in a single, abject, sexless relationship, whereas Cleese enjoyed a varied if turbulent love life with multiple wives. He not only took an American wife but also embraced California's sun-kissed antidote to the small, narrow tepidity of his homeland. (Although these feelings must have been mitigated when he learned that an American studio was planning their own version of *Fawlty Towers* – with Basil written out.) Basil was uncomfortable around Germans and apt to commit the odd gaffe when addressing them. Cleese, however, was a Germanophile. Speaking to *Der Spiegel* in 2015, he said, 'When I later learned German, I came to prefer your culture to the French culture. I found that Immanuel Kant is the most important philosopher I ever read. Your music is the finest in the world, you have wonderful painters . . . My main regret in life is that German is not my first language.'

And yet, speaking to the *Daily Telegraph* in 2011, he expressed wistfulness for the passing of the English middle-class culture which had nurtured him. 'There were disadvantages to the old culture, it was a bit stuffy and it was more sexist and more racist. But it was an educated and middle-class culture. Now it's a yob culture . . . London is no longer an English city, which is why I love Bath,' he said. It was as if he hadn't quite managed to excise a small chunk of his original breeding, which had became stuck in his system, ultimately proving infectious. Finally, from the vantage point of the Caribbean, he came round to Basil's way of thinking on Europe, urging Britons to vote Leave.

MONTY PYTHON – THE MOVIE YEARS

John Cleese's Python writing partner Graham Chapman was similarly able to command an authentically patrician air – when playing the colonel, for example, who walks into sketches to object to the silly turn they have taken. 'I do my best to keep things moving along . . . Now, let's have a good, clean, healthy outdoor sketch.' Originally, there was a notion of pitting the Cambridge men, Cleese and Chapman (as well as Idle) against the Oxonians Jones and Palin, but the dynamic most common in Python is of the taller Cambridge men, born to command, towering over the physically shorter Jones and Palin, often hunched in postures of social inferiority when across the desk from their betters, mumbling in a variety of haplessly provincial voices.

The experience of making a film based on the best of the *Python* sketches, *And Now for Something Completely Different* (1971), persuaded the group that they could be more ambitious in their forays into cinema. Hence *Monty Python and the Holy Grail* (1975). This retelling of the Arthurian saga benefited from the shrewd decision to cast Graham Chapman in the 'straight' role of King Arthur.

Chapman as Arthur is as much a figure of sympathy as of fun. One shares his exasperation at the persistence of the Black Knight, still goading him to fight on even after Arthur has lopped off all his limbs ('All right – we'll call it a draw'). One certainly feels for him in his encounter with Cleese's French soldier, jeering at him from atop a castle as he announces his mandate to seek the grail ('We've already got one . . . it's verra nice . . . your mother was a hamster and your father smelt of elderberries!'). His follow-up, like some present-day phone customer failing to get satisfaction from a call centre, is as English as Arthur himself: 'Is there anyone else up there we can talk to?' One understands the distraction he's driven to by Palin's anarcho-syndicalist Dennis, when he explains how he ascended the throne courtesy of the Lady of the Lake. 'Supreme executive power derives from a mandate from the masses, not some farcical aquatic ceremony!' While Arthur does, strictly speaking, reveal the 'violence inherent in the system' by slapping Dennis around the head, he's just trying to be king, out of solemn duty rather than lust for power, and he's faced with idiots at every turn.

There is one absurdist running joke in the film: that, due to budgetary constraints, Arthur and his knights must ride around on non-existent horses, prancing along to the clop of coconut shells. Interestingly, the budget for the film was raised thanks to UK prog-rockers of the day, including Led Zeppelin, Pink Floyd, Genesis and Jethro Tull, all fans of the show, chipping in. It might be a stretch to describe *Python* as 'prog com', but the medieval world conjured by co-director Terry Gilliam chimed in with the bucolic, mystical preoccupations to which prog was grandly prone.

Key to *Grail*, however, was the gruelling realism of its location settings. *Python* the series dealt in minimal props and stock outfits, low budgetary fare. For *Grail*, with co-director Terry Jones on hand as historical consultant, they concocted an authentic period environment of mud, mess, mist and steaming filth, in which peasants scrabbled desperately for sustenance or through which wooden carts bearing plague victims wended – in which the only way, indeed, that you could tell Arthur was king was because he was the only one who didn't have shit all over him.

Grail was a success, the birth of *Python's* second life in cinema. It was mandatory at this time for half-hour comedies to make the transition from small to large screen, with somewhat variable results. *Steptoe and Son* had transferred very well, its first outing in particular. However, film versions of *On the Buses*, *Bless This House* and *Man About the House* live on only as shuddering artefacts of seventies kitsch. *Monty Python and the Holy Grail*, however, was of a different order, different even from TV *Python* insofar as it created a world unto itself, visually immersive and thought through. In its misty atmospheres, rural squalor and bloody violence, it strangely prefigures John Boorman's altogether more earnest *Excalibur* (1981).

For years hence, to catch screenings of the *Grail* (these were the days before video), or to buy and memorise the LP recording of its best sketches, was to mark you out as a young person of quality, distinction and esoteric taste, above the vapid pap doled out to the mindless masses. *Python* films engendered the same superiority complex as that of Genesis fans. Only Peter Cook and Dudley Moore's Derek and Clive recordings were considered more 'underground' than *Python*. But the adulation, however snobbish, was deserved.

Following the release of the movie in 1975, the Python's began to think about the follow-up. The genesis, as it were, for the movie that would eventually be released in 1979 was a title idea suggested by Eric Idle: *Jesus Christ: Lust for Glory*. However, after considering the idea of a piss-take of the Messiah, they concluded that his core message really didn't warrant mockery; it was, indeed, intrinsic in their own basic ethical decency. The real fun to be had was what happened when he tried to disseminate his message: how it was taken up, fatally misinterpreted, fought over. A foretelling of the sort of fractiousness that can arise when Christ's message is received from afar occurs in the Sermon on the Mount scene, in which the real Jesus briefly appears, before the camera pans right back to those gathered almost out of earshot from Christ. 'Speak up a bit!' shouts one. They then ponder over the meaning over the words 'Blessed are the cheesemakers', before shushing one another and a fight breaking out.

The lead role went to Chapman once more, given his vague resemblance to a might-be Messiah. In *Grail*, Chapman had functioned as a beacon of bemused sanity as Arthur. In *Brian*, he would be the mouthpiece for the scream for sanity and common sense that resounds throughout *Python*. He is swept up in events beyond his control, buffeted between madness, mayhem and even a UFO. He's cast into the maelstrom of current affairs when he develops a hatred for the Romans, on discovering that his father was a Roman centurion who raped his mother. He joins the People's Front of Judea, where he develops an infatuation with Judith, a young revolutionary, and becomes involved in a plot to kidnap Pontius Pilate. He's arrested but flees his captors, evading them by posing as a preacher, mouthing platitudes he vaguely recalls from those bits of Jesus' sermon that filtered through to him. Suddenly, Brian is greeted as a Messiah, hailed through a mixture of mishap and hysteria, in which shoes and gourds become tokens of sacred significance.

Brian flees his disciples ('Fuck off!' 'How shall we fuck off, oh Lord?'), only to open his window and find them gathered below in their multitudes. The following exchange, a forlorn voice of modern, secular reason in the face of religious mania, is purest *Python*: 'You don't have to follow anyone! You are all individuals!' 'Yes! We are all individuals!' 'You are all different!' 'Yes! We are all different!' (Solitary voice: 'I'm not.')

The surrealism of TV *Python* is mostly abandoned with *Brian*: the repeated or overlapping sketches, the random man in a bow tie dancing to East European guitar music, the TV announcers sitting at desks in the middle of fields. Brian is couched in an epic, well-realised period setting, with a romantic subplot, a moral, a narrative through which are threaded a series of brilliantly enduring characters and sketches. Palin's at his best: as a fully fit beggar, cured of his leprosy by Christ and now struggling to make a living; as a prisoner chained up in a dungeon, whose fate doesn't dispel his disdain for namby-pamby approaches to crime ('Nail them up! Nail some sense into them!'); and as a weak-'r'd Pontius Pilate, aristocratically oblivious to his speech impediment, not least when it comes to his best friend 'Biggus Dickus'. ('He wanks as high as any in Wome.')

Cleese is dominant: as the centurion who, like a sadistic classics schoolmaster, makes Brian rewrite his graffiti in correct Latin a hundred times across the city walls; and as Reg, leader of the People's Front of Judea. One could argue that imperialism has not entirely been a source of civilising benefit to occupied countries, as is implied in the 'What have the Romans ever done for us?' sketch, but given that at this point Cleese was probably the funniest man in the world, he more than just about gets away with it. Elsewhere, the satire at the expense of the far left is more acute: the factionalist animus of the People's Front of Judea against the Judean People's Front, the resort to drafting resolutions as opposed to taking effective action, and the exasperation with the common people ('What Jesus fails to appreciate is it's the meek who are the problem') all ring sadly true.

Monty Python's Life of Brian is possibly the funniest British film ever made, but the circumstances surrounding its making and reception were more dramatic. EMI had picked it up; however, having just dropped the Sex Pistols, following their foul-mouthed tirade on the Bill Grundy show, they would drop *Life of Brian* when the script hit the desk of chief executive Bernard Delfont in 1978 ('I'm not having people saying I'm making fun of fucking Jesus Christ!').

Idle went in search of alternative funding. Once again, rock came to the rescue, in the form of George Harrison, who had assisted in the creation of Idle's Beatles spoof *All You Need Is Cash* (1978), a mockumentary about the Rutles. Harrison remortgaged his house and office premises to raise the cash.

The film did generate controversy, with those who had not seen it raising the angriest objections. Cleese and Palin were invited onto a late-night chat show, hosted by Tim Rice, pitted against Malcolm Muggeridge and Mervyn Stockwood, Bishop of Southwark. Anyone expecting a flippant face-off between Eminent Piety and Juvenile Insolence would have been disappointed. Cleese and Palin won the debate by virtue of taking it seriously. Theirs were the voices of reasonableness, sobriety, anti-extremism. Muggeridge and Stockwood, meanwhile, came across as off-hand, condescending, dismissive, ill prepared for in-depth debate and, in gesture and manner, a bit rich. In their complacent, waffling grandeur, they represented the sort of supposed authority figures, winging it in a certain tone of voice, that *Python* had always sought to lay low. Muggeridge vaguely and grandly attempted to dismiss the film on comedic merit, opining that it was 'a squalid little number', 'tenth rate', barely worthy of an undergraduate revue, but this was wholly unconvincing to anyone with any actual sympathy with, and exposure to, modern comedy. He excoriated them for depicting Jesus as a 'derisory and absurd figure', which Cleese denied – they had been at pains to do nothing of the kind. Muggeridge also made an observation that has been repeated many times subsequently by Christians when under the satirical cosh: that if they had made this film about Muhammad, 'the anti-racialists would have risen up in their might', as if anti-racists were a fringe militant group. 'Four hundred years ago we'd have been burnt for this film,' says Cleese. 'Now I'm suggesting we've made an advance.'

Stockwood, meanwhile, rambled spuriously about the supposed triumph of Christianity over Maoism in China, as if *Life of Brian* had been an attempt to destroy Christianity, with Cleese looking on at him with ill-disguised exasperation, like Basil Fawlty having to listen to an interminably fatuous monologue from the major. Palin was seething at the end of the interview, when Stockwood slipped in a low blow – 'You'll get your thirty pieces of silver' – just as the lights were dimming and the Pythons had no chance to answer back. Afterwards, Stockwood genially approached him – 'Thought that went rather well' – before taking a glass of whisky. The lack of seriousness of the man astonished Palin.

That *Life of Brian* was not blasphemous should have been obvious to anyone prepared to give it a fair viewing, to say nothing of whether 'blasphemy', certainly as understood by a figure like the conservative activist Mary Whitehouse, should be regarded as an ethical or artistic failing. The advance Cleese suggests is palpable in this debate. His and Palin's secular decency clearly holds far more sway with the TV audience than the gaseous piety and irrelevancies of Stockwood and Muggeridge, delivered as if from a pulpit to a bored, half-full church. Surely their day was all but done. Sadly, however, it was the party favoured by Whitehouse who won out in the UK that year, and liberalism which would find itself on the defensive.

Coming out as it did in 1979, *Life of Brian* prefigures the lurch into religious irrationalism that would unsteady the world from that year onwards, from the Islamic takeover of Iran to the 'Moral Majority' of Christian fundamentalists who would hold unwelcome political sway in America. The political critique of *Brian*, mostly directed against revolutionary leftists, remains very funny but is of diminished relevance compared with the rise of Thatcherism and Reaganomics, which would disfigure the 1980s. Only with Mr Creosote, Terry Jones's obscenely bloated, exploding diner in the 1983 film *The Meaning of Life*, did *Python* really get to grips with the phenomenon of individualistic greed.

Today, you might lodge a few small objections to *Brian* – for example, about the moment when Brian asks his mother (Terry Jones) if she'd been raped ('Yeah . . . at first . . .'), or Eric Idle as a gaoler's assistant using a stammer for laughs, the odd 'Ooh-ducky' voice, which was still considered fair comic game in 1979. Larger objections might have been levelled if the film had featured more of

Idle's Otto, a Germanic-looking figure obsessed with Jewish racial purity, who wears an insignia on his helmet resembling a Star of David twisted into a swastika. Fortunately, Otto was mostly consigned to the cutting-room floor.

The spirit of *Python*'s logical absurdism was carried on right through the remainder of the century and beyond – by Mitchell and Webb, Armstrong and Miller, in *Smack the Pony* and others. The Pythons themselves had fine later careers: Idle's Rutles mockumentary, a cut-off from his *Rutland Weekend Television* series (1975–6); Palin and Jones with *Ripping Yarns* (1976–9); Cleese with *Fawlty Towers*. Gilliam's visual sense, meanwhile, blossomed into a body of work as a Hollywood film director of eccentric, glorious renown. With age, and showing their age, the Pythons gathered together for reunions, retrospectives and reminiscences, becoming increasingly cranky, in some cases, at 'political correctness'. They were wrong. But their work was done.

CARROTT AND CONNOLLY – FUNNY AS FOLK

Much of the comedy in this chapter was of the suburbs, the shires, the robust North, designed primarily to placate and entertain the *Mirror-* and *Mail*-reading middle-aged. Comedy was a long way from becoming the new rock and roll, which impinged rarely, and then cringe-makingly, on its storylines.

Antithetical to this was Billy Connolly. Originally with the Glaswegian folk rock group the Humblebums, he emerged from a similar comedy/folk background as Jasper Carrott: both had hits in the mid-seventies, Connolly with a parody of Tammy Wynette's 'D.I.V.O.R.C.E.', Carrott with 'Funky Moped'. I probably never laughed harder in my life than when our music teacher, Mr Phillips, trundled in the school gramophone player and played the B-side to 'Funky Moped', a parody of *The Magic Roundabout*, with suggestive 'boings' from Zebedee, featuring Dylan telling Dougal to piss off, and Dougal doing so, all over Florence. Carrott went on to be the sort of comedian who was always a Corporal Jones-style step behind the times, even down to naming his TV show *Carrott's Lib*, long after the last drop of mirth had been wrung from parodying the term 'Women's Lib' – but for that belly laugh, I am indebted.

Billy Connolly, meanwhile, is comedy's equivalent to a seventies guitar hero, a fretboard warrior, trailing his long locks behind him as the gales of his virtuosity blow back in his face. Despite his many TV and film appearances, he was never one of those comedians who regarded stand-up as a mere springboard into sitcom, or even straight drama. The stage was his element, the place he truly belonged, striding up and down, gesticulating, riffing, exclaiming, tearing down the house with the raucous power of his lungs; he had the sort of physically imposing presence that would make hecklers think twice. He accrued a lifelong wealth of material in his days as a boilermaker in the Glasgow shipyards and as a drinker: the mawkish Scotsman in his routine bawling songs to the bonnie country he loves, 'Even though I'm farr away!', to which his son replies, 'But father – you're in the living room!'; the two Scotsmen in Rome – 'Fantastic, I wonder who papered that ceiling' – trudging through the ponderous dirge that is the English national anthem and proposing that it be replaced with the theme music for *The Archers*; or his country-and-western parody 'My Granny Is a Cripple in Nashville', with its mounting, blackly comedic pile of tragedies. Mere description of his routines does him less justice than most – like Tommy Cooper, he was the sort of comedian whose very presence onstage summoned guffaws out of thin air. Unlike many, he survived the interrogation of alternative comedy no problem. From the seventies but not of the seventies. Indeed, in a programme broadcast during that decade, Connolly opined:

The British people are not overtly racist, but given the opportunity they switch on to racism very quickly. You know, they listen to so many broadcasts on the radio about how desperate the situation is with Pakistanis and West Indians flooding into the country – a total lie – and then mohair-suited comedians pouring out racism to the extent that Black comedians are doing it, which I find desperately dangerous. I feel dirty. Comedians play a very important role in society; you should see things that the average guy in the street can't see and point out the absurdity in something that's just accepted.

BLACK AND WHITE COMEDY

ITV fared better on racial matters with *Rising Damp* (1974–8), created by Eric Chappell. It was another departure from the nuclear family structure, set in a shabby Victorian townhouse converted into bedsits that was, home to the jetsam of an increasingly unravelled Britain. Rupert Rigsby, played by Leonard Rossiter, is the embodiment of British male post-war disappointment and decrepitude. Rigsby imagines that it is the younger generation who represent the country's decline, rather than his own delusions, diminished powers and obsolete worldview. The elegant Frances de la Tour, who plays Miss Jones (what was it with Miss Joneses in the seventies?), is the not-quite-mother of the house, the object of Rigsby's politely unrequited affections.

Rossiter is a twitching mass of magnificence as Rigsby, a towering rendition of a stooped, small man. Chappell is a fine scriptwriter, but Rossiter makes a veritable skeleton dance of his dialogue, his every utterance addled and itching with nerves and a seething, anxious interior life, flinching, darting, pecking aggressively, riding invisible punches.

One thing that commends *Rising Damp* is the inclusion of Don Warrington as Philip. This was certainly not the first time a Black man had been given a role in a UK sitcom. However, whereas in previous sitcoms that tried to address race Black people were assigned peripheral, non-speaking roles or were played up for their exotic-ness, Philip is an unflappable young man who is more than a match for

Rigsby's constant stream of racist assumptions and insinuations, born as much out of jealousy for the fact that Miss Jones has the hots for him as his skin colour.

'You couldn't wear black, you'd disappear,' jeers Rigsby to Philip at one point, during a sartorial discussion. 'A few beads and a shrunken head.'

'I think one shrunken head's enough, Rigsby,' retorts Philip. Granted, the seventies audience's laughter at Rigsby's jibes suggests some of them may be guffawing along with the racism under the cover of laughing at it, but at least Philip gets an effective final word.

Rising Damp is exceptional in the 1970s – a good ITV sitcom. Why the station, with its various regional services, was unable to produce little but low-grade brown sauce in terms of comedy is hard to fathom, but it remains true that the funniest ITV show of this era was *Coronation Street*, guided as it was by the queer eye, the shrewd sense of character and language of its founder, Tony Warren.

In 1976, *The Fosters* arrived onscreen, a UK adaptation of an American sitcom of the same name, acquired by Michael Grade. It represented the first British sitcom with an all-Black cast, the original series having been written by African American writers, though in the UK it was developed by writer Jon Watkins, a white man. It lasted only a season and suffered for trying to find a place for its characters within the non-threatening rhythms and language of conventional sitcom. The controller of London Weekend Television, Cyril Bennett, felt obliged to issue a pusillanimous assurance that the show would contain 'no racial overtones', which left it with little room for manoeuvre.

The most positive contribution of the series was its opening credits, a weekly montage of Black British life in 1976, in all of its street bustle and joy, integrated with young whites and South Asians, adding to the gaiety and flavour of the British nation and weaving into its fabric at all levels – before referring to the actual setting of the show, a cramped and socially isolated flat in a tower block. It was also a showcase for Norman Beaton, a Guyanan actor who spent his career playing genial, patriarchal types aged circa sixty, as in the more successful *Desmond's* (1989–94) on Channel 4, before dying, sadly, aged sixty. It was an introduction for the teenage Lenny Henry too, who featured prominently in the credits, having already made his name a year earlier on *New Faces*. For Henry, the show was a learning experience in the practicalities of television – where to stand, where not to stand, as well as general mentoring that would set him in good stead for the future.

Mixed Blessings (1978–80), meanwhile, addressed the 'problematic' issue of racially mixed marriage, with mixed results. The series was created by Sidney Green, who had previously co-scripted *The Strange World of Gurney Slade* (1960), starring Anthony Newley. *Mixed Blessings* tells the ongoing story of Thomas Simpson (Christopher Blake), who marries a Black woman, Susan Lambert (Muriel Odunton). For all the show's sympathy towards its lead couple and the grief they must take from their respective parents, there's an ingrained, unconscious bias in the script, in which Susan's blackness is more a subject for comment, even comedy, than Thomas's whiteness; he is, after all, the member of the 'default' host race. Still, *Mixed Blessings* represents an advance on *Love Thy Neighbour* and its blizzard of racial epithets.

Lenny Henry's stint with *The Fosters* was a stepping stone in what is the most remarkable career of any Black British comedian. Henry is not just a hugely talented but also a hugely beloved figure in British life, let alone British comedy.

Growing up in Dudley, Henry didn't particularly identify with Black actors on TV, cast in peripheral roles. He wanted to emulate the stars, principally white, 'cool-talking, martini-drinking, gun-toting' heroes. Later, he was inspired by Mike Yarwood. His formidable Jamaican-born mother, of whom he lived in fear, urged her kids to 'h'integrate', an injunction Henry followed. He couldn't have remained oblivious to race and to racism had he tried. At school, in the late 1960s and early 1970s, he was called all the names the kids might well have picked up from other race-based TV shows or simply from home. He soon learned to use his wits as a weapon. He was not naturally given to surliness or militancy – in later life he would chide himself for not having taken a tougher stand against racism. 'If you're practically the only Black kid in school, you get this desperate urge to mix, to please everybody, be everybody's mate,' he told me.

Henry was, however, profoundly influenced by the handful of Black British comedians who attained national familiarity (alongside the likes of Bernard Manning) on *The Comedians* – Sammy Thomas, Jos White and Charlie Williams. He noted how they would have to get in first with mandatory, self-deprecating jokes about their blackness; Jos White's catchphrase was 'I'm browned off.' Once that was done with, however, White delivered jokes in the seasoned working men's club idiom, expertly timed. Fella goes to the barber's with his son, asks how much is a haircut? Four and six, says the barber. How much is a shave? A shilling, says the barber. All right, shave his head, says the fella. In terms of accent, delivery, subject matter, body language, there was nothing exotic or 'other' about White. His success was deserved but depended on his 'h'integration'.

Charlie Williams, too (to Billy Connolly's despair), felt obliged to preface his act with references to his blackness, the proof required by white audiences that he could laugh at himself, being of a funny tinge. Once allowed simply to be funny, however, he had a wonderful style, telling jokes rendered in the most Barnsley of Barnsley accents, laughing infectiously at his own jokes, his thorough enjoyment at being onstage filling the room with the helium of joy. He 'h'integrated' a touch too much, unfortunately, spraying racial epithets with the same gusto as the next (white) comedian, playing in Rhodesia during the Ian Smith era, defending the golliwog logo and urging immigrants to conform to the extent he had. His career declined, though it seems cruelly ironic that he as a Black comedian should have been punished in the name of anti-racism in comedy.

Henry made his debut in his mid-teens on *New Faces* in 1975. His reveal to the world was a Frank Spencer impersonation, shot from the back in Spencer's recognisable mac and beret, only for him to swivel round to reveal – that's right, he was Black! Although he also did a mean Stevie Wonder, the disconnect of a young Black man doing flawless impersonations of white TV personalities such as David Bellamy, Tommy Cooper and Ken Dodd would prove ingratiating and a boost to Henry's career. It also slyly implied: we know all about you people, to the last detail. What do you know about us?

Less fortunate was his contractual obligation to perform with *The Black and White Minstrel Show*, a mystifying staple of 1970s British television, drawing as it did on the Great American Songbook. Enduring this show as a child, I was galled by its gruelling quaintness – the racism didn't even occur to me, any more than it did with the Black character on the front of the *Sparky* comic; it didn't occur to me that these caricatures could possibly refer to human beings of any kind. Efforts had been made to pull the show but were rebutted in 1967 by a senior BBC figure, Oliver Whitely, who wrote: 'The best advice that could be given to coloured people by their friends would be: "on this issue, we can see your point, but in your own best interests, for Heaven's sake shut up."'

Henry recalls in the first part of his autobiography the quiet shame of his family at his participation in the show. He writes movingly also of his fellowship with the troupe, the dancers and 'minstrels' themselves, who were, in their own way, indentured. Despite the show's popularity, when they tried to ask for a raise, they were told by their manager, also Henry's own, that since no one would recognise them beneath their black make-up, they were effectively showbiz nobodies.

Henry's journey was one from centre- to left-field; but he learned key lessons from watching and working with the likes of Don Maclean and Cannon and Ball, who might sound like bywords for big-bow-tied seventies naffness but from whose technical excellence he was shrewd enough to learn. Henry was in showbiz, in big-time telly, on *Tiswas* and *Three of a Kind*; he might have seemed a world away from the angrier, conscious manifestations of Black British culture in those angry times, from Stuart Hall to Linton Kwesi Johnson, whether flinging flans and emitting elongated 'ooookkkkkaaaaaayyyy's on Saturday mornings or participating in funny but orthodox sketches with Tracey Ullman and David Copperfield, parodying primary-school nativity productions, for example, in the evening. Henry was, however, an unmistakable product of Black Britain, conscious and observant of his origins. Having met Dawn French, he became aware of the burgeoning alternative comedy scene and, ever the alert student of his discipline, understood that comedians like Alexei Sayle represented a radical shift from the traditional stock of lazy stereotypes to a new comedy which, however seemingly deranged, drew on life as lived, in its everyday banality, absurdity.

With the assistance of co-writer Kim Fuller, Henry created characters drawn from his own heritage: from Theophilus P. Wildebeeste, a lewd parody of alpha soul males like Teddy Pendergrass, to ducker and diver Delbert Wilkins and Grandpa Deakus, caricatures but accurately and affectionately drawn, as far a cry from the blackfaced minstrels he had performed alongside just ten years earlier as could be imagined. He also had licence to lampoon the increasing number of Black eighties superstars, from Sade to Run-DMC, Prince to Michael Jackson. He also lent credibility to Comic Relief in its early fundraising efforts from 1987 onwards, which no number of red noses could entirely subdue.

In 1989, he was certainly deemed more than sufficiently credible to be interviewed for *Melody Maker*, which was how I met him. He was initially more concerned with sizeism than racism:

I'm fed up of these articles that kick off with these descriptions of my 'considerable bulk'. I did this recent one and it went on about 'his considerable bulk. His enormous frame. He bit into an apple . . . God, he was huge!' . . . Never mind the interview, let's do a bloody weight assassination!

I very much liked him; he was forthright and funny, not at all truculent, but with an undoubted edge. I suggested to him maybe he came across as nice, obliging, the sort of person of whom people felt entitled to make excessive demands as well as excessive criticisms.

Yeah, people think I'm a bit of a pushover but I do get upset. I did one interview in the music press where this guy wrote this long preamble basically saying that he had this Black mate who didn't like me – complete and utter bollocks it was! And basically it was because he didn't have the courage in the interview to say that I wasn't Black enough for him.

The interview was around the release of a video of his stand-up, *Lenny – Live and Unleashed*. It was, I was able to say, his funniest work to date. But there was a seriousness about Henry at this time too. 'I'm really beginning to feel that I wanna say stuff, I don't need a character to talk about racism, or sexism – I wanna say it myself.' His 'Fred Dread' character, a take on Linton Kwesi Johnson, delivers a rap in this routine which isn't parody but sorely meant. 'On television when I did Fred Dread it usually ended up saying [gurgling laugh] "I didn't mean it really." But for the film we thought, sod it, let's go for it.'

In more recent times, Henry has become active in seeking greater representation for people of colour on TV, especially as writers and producers, something he also touched on in our interviews. He, more than most, understands the importance of that from personal experience. A guilty conscience, some might say, given his early work, and to a degree they'd be right. There's a tendency, especially among the famous, to adopt a defensive, double-down,

I-was-never-wrong stance. Not Henry: he is self-critical to a fault. He has always been serious, and even when the material wasn't up to snuff, always innately funny.

ALTERNATIVE – THE MOMENT THAT CHANGED EVERYTHING

As well as the coinage of the word 'sexism', the late seventies saw an increase in anti-racism and anti-homophobia, and alternative comedy was a part of that thrust, coming in the wake of the post-punk movement and its attendant social consciousness. However, alternative's beginnings weren't hugely, overtly political. Rather, it was a wayward gathering of energies, preceded by a seventies comedy folk scene that included Jasper Carrott and Billy Connolly, as well as the continued traditions of the Satire Boom of the sixties, culminating in the Secret Policeman's Balls of the late seventies, at which Rowan Atkinson made his first appearance.

The wrecking-ball attitude of early alternative comedy was personified by Malcolm Hardee, who, although he rarely appeared on TV, is considered a legend among his comedy peers. He would later be described by Rob Newman as a 'living legend, a millennial Falstaff', while Stewart Lee wrote that in any decent country he would be regarded as a national institution.

Hardee's contribution is hard to quantify because his influence was more as an example and enabler of others. Or, as Arthur Smith put it, 'Everything about Malcolm was original except his stand-up routine.' He embodied the anarchic quantum energy necessary to wrench British comedy out of its rut. Described as an 'English comedian, author, comedy club proprietor, compère, agent, manager and amateur sensationalist', Hardee was a man whose very life, in all its hilarious chaos, was his art, as revealed in his autobiography, *I Stole Freddie Mercury's Birthday Cake*. A South London boy who spent some of his early years in an orphanage and borstal, he entered showbiz to channel his propensity towards mischief, which had seen him spend a further stint in prison. He joined a surreal sketch troupe, the Greatest Show on Legs, became a regular at Soho's Comedy Store, cradle of alternative comedy, and eventually opened the Tunnel Club, at which, as compère, he would, in his own, uniquely tough way ('This next act's probably a bit shit'), nurture future talents including Harry Hill, Paul Merton, Vic Reeves and Jo Brand, who earned their spurs during the 1980s facing down hecklers. In 2005, Hardee drowned, swimming from the floating pub he owned at Greenland Dock back to his houseboat. But his work had long been done.

Soho's Comedy Store was the initial crucible of alternative, launching the careers of the likes of Keith Allen, Tony Allen and Andy De La Tour. Coincidentally, it opened in May 1979, the month Margaret Thatcher was elected prime minister, and throughout the decade that followed it represented a cultural point of opposition to her administration and its attempts to roll back the frontiers of the welfare state. The Store's first MC, Alexei Sayle, was indisputably of the left, though he specialised in absurdist juxtapositions of political earnestness and 'low' culture. In their own way, however, the alternative comedians were also looking to roll back the frontiers of seventies Britain. Their ambition was to create new and enterprising options other than the closed shop of old-school entertainers with their ostensibly working-class appeal but backward, reactionary outlook.

Alternative comedy's revolt manifested in absurdism, surrealism, scatology and slapstick. It was also, as Frank Skinner has pointed out, more observational, autobiographical, bristling with attitude and opinion, putting out onstage what the old, bow-tied school of comedians kept strictly offstage or behind a wall of jokes about Englishmen, Irishmen and Scotsmen. Alternative comedy broke down that wall. It was about confrontation – with audiences, with what comedy was supposed to be about. It was heavy rather than light entertainment, often only just staying the right side of what John O'Farrell characterised as a 'new puritanism'.

There were direct links between the rise of the new comedy and the rise of punk – itself a reaction against the state of seventies, Labour-dominated Britain, despite eventually becoming a rallying point for anti-Thatcherism. Alternative comedians would support alternative bands: Ted Chippington supported the Fall; Peter Richardson opened for Dexy's Midnight Runners. Meanwhile, John Cooper Clarke was the first of a new wave of 'punk poets', spitting out gobbets and couplets of acerbic disaffection into the microphone that were a million miles from the whimsy of Pam Ayres. Their ranting ranks included Seething Wells, Benjamin Zephaniah, Joolz, Craig Charles and Porky the Poet (aka Phill Jupitus). Theirs were often Northern tales of the reality of life in Thatcher's weather-beaten Britain, railing against macho bigotry (Wells's take on the reality of 'Tetley Bittermen') or English hypocrisy (Clarke's 'You'll Never See a Nipple in the *Daily Express*'). None of this had been touched on in the seventies working men's club variety show *The Wheeltappers and Shunters Social Club*.

Many of these comedians and ranters would ultimately become footnotes, overtaken within a couple of years by the new vanguard of alternative comedians about to hit the nation's TV screens. Channel 4, inaugurated in 1982, and initially brave, was one outlet. It immediately commissioned *The Comic Strip Presents . . .*, scripted by Peter Richardson and derived from a troupe which itself was an offshoot of the Comedy Store, featuring in its cast Dawn French and Jennifer Saunders, Rik Mayall, Ade Edmondson, Nigel Planer and Keith Allen. Many of these films, generally scripted by Richardson and Pete Richens, were limb-from-limb satires on the sort of entertainment that had been taken for granted for decades. 'A Fistful of Travellers' Cheques' sent up the macho, taciturn spaghetti Westerns; 'The Bullshitters' similarly took apart *The Professionals*; while 'The Strike' and 'GLC' would parody Hollywood clichés in their treatments of the miners' strike and 'Red' Ken Livingstone's stewardship of London's Greater London Council respectively. *The*

Comic Strip's knowing take on mass entertainment as well as its handling of the hot political issues of the day was an advance even on Peter Cook and Monty Python, and remains unmatched in its acuity. Comedy was about to make a huge advance.

THE 1980S

THATCHER, THE RESISTANCE AND ACKNOWLEDGEMENT

Much as the most significant music of the 1980s was, albeit indirectly, determined by punk, so the bulk of the best comedy of the decade was determined by the alternative impetus. There was consternation on the part of long-established comedians that the assumptions underlying their work were obsolete and they needed to be done away with. Much as Billy Bragg was the go-to representative for those grabbing for an exemplar of the politicisation of pop music, so Ben Elton was invariably cited for having politicised comedy practically single-handedly (others, such as the Marks Steel and Thomas or Jeremy Hardy, were less frequently mentioned).

However, the effect of Elton and his generation on British comedy, far from reducing it to tub-thumping polemicism, was more raucous, shamelessly puerile, self-deprecating and brilliantly self-conscious in the way it interrogated comic conventions.

That said, much as Pink Floyd didn't fade away just because Johnny Rotten wished it so, neither did the old guard, or the old ways. Margaret Thatcher was, after all, PM throughout the entire decade, and though she was an Aunt Sally to be militated against, the old-style variety and sitcom shows that persisted in the eighties reflected the abiding conservatism of the country.

THE YOUNG ONES, BLACKADDER – THE MORALITY OF SCATOLOGY

'Rik Mayall is putrid – absolutely vile. He thinks nose-picking is funny and farting and all that. He is the arsehole of British comedy.' – Spike Milligan

In the 1980s, it's striking that the most leading-edge, intelligent comedy – from *The Young Ones* and *Viz* through to *Blackadder* – was also the most scatological. In 1986, I interviewed Ade Edmondson, aka the psychotic punk–metal hybrid Vyvyan in *The Young Ones*. In person, he is the opposite: quiet, dry, reflective. He'd just published a Christmas-stocking filler, *How to Be a Complete Bastard*, an extension of the Vyvyan character, full of nob, pants, belching and poo jokes. I asked him how long he thought he could carry on in this vein. 'Until the word "bottom" ceases entirely to be humorous, I suppose,' he replied, urbanely. That day has come and gone. But in 1986, it was still as long awaited as a Labour government.

Viz was founded in 1979, in Newcastle, by Chris Donald and his brother Simon, their drawing career having started in school. 'We used to pass around these books, with these cartoons of really fat people we'd drawn, being sliced up by bacon slicers or put through pencil sharpeners and coming out the other end in spirals,' Chris Donald told me in 1987, when I interviewed him in the magazine's modest offices in Newcastle. At that point they were selling 63,000 copies per issue. The next time I interviewed Donald, two years later, that figure had risen to a million.

One inspiration for *Viz* was Rik Mayall and Ade Edmondson, who toured Newcastle around the time of *Viz*'s inception. 'I didn't know people could be so relentlessly, pants-pissingly funny,' said Donald. *The Young Ones* (1982–4) was the comic wing of the counterculture of the late seventies and early eighties.

The Young Ones blew open a generation gap, the biggest since *Python*. 'My parents would never watch *The Young Ones* – comedy was a big unifier in the household, but now it was a dividing line,' recalls broadcaster Al Needham. Lise Mayer, one of the show's co-creators, spoke of how they interspersed the show with one-frame random images. 'It was fun to mess with people in new ways,' she said of these entirely meaningless shots, which those struggling to keep pace with the show's anarchic tangents assumed they were meant to decipher also. The most perturbing random touch was a recurring image of a 'fifth housemate', slumped, ignored, in the Young Ones' house, fringe obscuring their face. He or she can be seen as early as the opening episode, as eerie as the girl in *The Ring* who crawls out of the TV screen at the end of the movie.

Much as punk represented an explosion of the turgidity and bland gloss of 1970s rock and pop, so *The Young Ones* shattered the glazing of TV comedy. Its two series see them constantly tear through walls – fourth walls or actual, filthy walls. Explosions are rampant and often apocalyptic, such as the plane crash that wipes them out at the end of the first episode, or the double-decker bus they take over a cliff edge in the final episode.

The Young Ones was born out of individual cabaret/comic turns, including Rik Mayall's prickly and self-important anarchist, 'people's poet' Rick. Meanwhile, he was working with Ade Edmondson as the Dangerous Brothers, street entertainers driven to psychotic extremes by famished desperation. Edmondson was generally the victim of slapstick violence in the Dangerous Brothers; as Vyvyan Basterd, he would be its perpetrator, Meanwhile, Nigel Planer had created Neil, a morose, pacifist Peace Studies student. The show yoked all of these characters into a student house, with *Comic Strip* compère Alexei Sayle as the landlord and his various relatives. Mike, the fourth member of the house, was played by *Comic Strip* outsider Christopher Ryan.

Mike isn't as funny as the other three; his 'And I'm not talking about . . .' to-camera catchphrase barely stood the test of its own time. And yet he's important, the unnerving father figure of the house, domineering, despite his lack of inches. Despite having no dog in the tribal fracas waged by the other three (Neil, hippiedom; Rick, agit-punk; Vyvyan, punk/metal), he is the coolest housemate, unflappable, above the slapstick fray inflicted and endured by his housemates. When Vyvyan claims to have struck oil in the cellar, the hierarchy of the house is quickly established. Mike is El Presidente,

Vyvyan his violent henchman, while Neil and Rick are forced to prostrate themselves on the floor as Vyvyan assails Rick's testicles with a baseball bat ('Ha! Missed both my legs!'). It was appropriate that Ryan played one of the Driscoll brothers in *Only Fools and Horses*, a role to which he brought the same insouciant menace.

One of the great ironies about *The Young Ones* is its mockery of the counterculture from which it springs, simply because they knew it so well. Had *The Young Ones* been an American creation, it might have revolved around a bunch of cool, left-field college kids, record-store prowlers and hip underachievers surrounded by Reaganite fools, meatheads, airheads and uptight conservatives. That sort of self-congratulation did not sit well with Mayall, Mayer and Elton, who saw themselves in an English tradition of self-deprecation, in which to be very funny was to be very uncool. And so, Neil's peace, love and vegetable rights ethos does not bring him to a state of nirvana but reduces him to the house slave, a life full of hassle, bummers and downers. Vyvyan's hardcore punk take has made him, with apologies to the Sex Pistols, a moron, a potential H-bomb. As for the *NME*-reading, Echo and the Bunnymen correspondent Rick, he is a monstrously conceited offshoot of the undercurrent of self-righteousness that began to flow and spout when punk, politics, PC and anti-Thatcherism emerged. He wears his various lapel badges, from CND to *Blue Peter*, with ostentatious smugness: the original virtue signaller but full of vice. He screams the word 'fascist' multiple times but is, as Mayall observed, full of fascistic tendencies himself. His espousal of Cliff Richard signifies the impotence of pop/rock as a revolutionary force. He dreams of being the 'people's poet', uniting the tribes of early-eighties music – punks, rastas, skins – but his self-important, attention-seeking efforts to galvanise the masses barely reach across the kitchen table, let alone the streets, shot down with a 'Shut up, Rick' from Vyvyan or Mike. He makes punk's antipathy towards hippiedom ('Bored! I might as well be listening to Genesis!') a personal matter between him and Neil, the only housemate he can get away with bullying.

Rick is a cowardly, spotty, neurotic, virginal, insecure nerd, a personification of all the foibles of right-on-ness. However, Mayall invests him with such raucous, pop-eyed, gurning, scathing energy that he is the largest, loudest and most vivid character in the house, if not, as he believes, the 'best person' in the house.

The old-guard comedians would have been incapable of this level of satire because they didn't have either the close-up knowledge or wherewithal to deal with all this spiky eighties stuff. Comedians like Ted Rogers or Jim Bowen were only just getting over Mick Jagger. Had they attempted to laugh at it, the results would have been embarrassing. Ben Elton, however, despite being saddled with the invidious reputation of being Mr 1980s Right-On PC, was in a much better position to mock – despite being a comedian prone to sermonising and occasional excruciating moments, such as when hosting a concert to celebrate Nelson Mandela's release and declaring, 'The show must go on – as indeed does the struggle.' And yet he, in the opening *Young Ones* episode, nailed the frantically with-it condescension of early youth TV, with its clichés such as presenters doing links from the scaffolding, 'Because that's what this programme is about – shock!'

The Young Ones celebrated and unleashed the punkish energy of its time not by making heroes of its characters but in other ways. Bands were featured, including Madness, Motörhead, Dexy's Midnight Runners and Amazulu. This expediently increased their budget since it allowed them to be filed under 'variety'. The show's slapstick was in parallel with the raucous, manic puerility of punk. For Ade Edmondson, it was going back to basics. 'We're aiming for pure comedy, like Tommy Cooper. Just trying to make people laugh their bollocks off, that's all,' he told me.

The Young Ones is propelled by cartoonishly implausible comedy – Vyvyan survives decapitation when he pokes his head out of the window of a moving train. None of it is very socialist. The Futurist poet Marinetti once said that art should be about 'violence, cruelty and injustice'. It can feel like *The Young Ones* and, indeed, comedy successors like *Blackadder* and *Bottom* professed the same 'values'.

The corollary to that, however, is its radical restructuring of comic form, much as punk eventually restructured rock form. Walls are walked through, floors fallen through, other dimensions entered as the shows peel off into sketches involving ghosts and talking hamsters. All channels are open.

In an interview with an Australian journalist, Rik Mayall observed that his was the first generation of comedians to have grown up in the age of television. *Monty Python* had begun to parody TV tropes, but generally, the generation of comics who entertained us in the 1970s had not had their sensibilities formed by prolonged exposure to television, an infant medium in the 1940s and 1950s. Morecambe and Wise, Les Dawson, Tommy Cooper, far from young ones in their TV prime, were the children of wartime, music halls, variety, *Singin' in the Rain*, of stage curtains and stock characters.

The housemates spend a sizeable chunk of time crowded round the TV set, viewing its transmissions with no great avidity but beset with sheer boredom, a particular early-eighties kind of boredom which was of a stretching, sublime, staring-at-walls quality extinct in the twenty-first century. One watched television not because it was good but because it was on.

TV is referenced throughout the series: *Grange Hill, University Challenge*, a snatch of sitcom in which a man finds himself trousers down and astride his dog just as the vicar is visiting for tea. It's a step beyond the sort of gameshow/political mickey-takes of which the Pythons were fond. Python themselves get the treatment in a brief sketch in which Alexei Sayle funny-walks into a shop and asks the assistant (Mayall), 'Do you sell cheese?' 'No,' replies Mayall. 'Well, that's this sketch knackered, isn't it?' says Sayle, and funny-walks off.

The Good Life is featured when Neil's parents, blazered and twinset suburbanites, visit. Its theme and opening credits strike up, only for

Vyvyan to burst through them like paper, gobbing invective and delivering the closest the series gets to a direct rant, not against the mediocrity but the cosiness the series represents, the amiable docility it engenders and the cosseting fiction that 'everyone in England is a loveable English eccentric'. It's what *The Young Ones* has bloody, bloody, bloody well come to drive out.

Ah, the scatology; 'bottom', 'pants', 'fart', 'bogey', the deliberately quaint but raucous rudeness which wafted like wet raspberries through every episode, loud and furious yet limp and unthreatening, like Rick's threat to give Vyvyan a 'ruddy good punch on the bottom' for his ungallant remarks about Felicity Kendal. This puerility that so appalled Spike Milligan was a reminder that the show's makers were not long out of short trousers themselves. At the time, it was facetiously cathartic: a regression to the happiest days of our lives, practically wetting ourselves as schoolkids at the word 'bum'. The directness was the point. 'For years in comedy you had what was known as the double entendre,' Ade Edmondson told me. 'And now, what seems funny is the single entendre.'

In other words, all this was a plea for honesty and directness in a coyly censorious and duplicitous media age. During a Dangerous Brothers sketch, an angry Jennifer Saunders asks the boys, 'What's the rudest word you can say on television?' Meanwhile, in a *Grange Hill* sketch in which Ben Elton's schoolboy collides with teacher 'Mr Liberal', Elton says, 'C'mon sir – we're the only schoolkids in Britain who don't say f—' (scene cuts away).

Being so puerile, Rick and Vyvyan are also undersexed and beyond gauche in their dealings with women, with Saunders once again playing the appalled victim of their clumsy attentions. At a house party, Vyvyan demonstrates his prowess by dropping down to the floor and thrusting repeatedly ('Want to see how many press-ups I can do?'), while Rick curiously pulls a tampon from her handbag, the first time he has ever seen one. The casual sexism of predecessors such as *The Likely Lads* and *On the Buses*, in which the lead characters were presumed to be confident cocksmen, casually working their way through a series of available 'dolly birds', was thus debunked.

Even when they go to the pub, these anarchic, wall-crashing, countercultural tearaways reveal themselves as innocents. They go to the pub, but that's because that's what you're supposed to do, isn't it? But once in there, they're like virgins to the experience. Even this congenial and not-hard-to-navigate aspect of adulthood is beyond them.

The Young Ones was succeeded by *Filthy Rich & Catflap* (1987), written by Ben Elton, and later *Bottom* (1991–5), in which Mayall and Edmondson, now the Older Ones, socially marginalised and incapable of little beyond inflicting extreme violence on each other, took their partnership to bleak, Beckettian extremes – waiting on a park bench without even the hope that a Godot might turn up. It was an opportune time for *The Young Ones* to quit. By 1984, the counterculture driven by punk was beginning to peter out, tired and suffering the attritional effects of the now-dominant Thatcherism that was coming to determine the character of the decade, in pop as well as politics.

In *The Young Ones* episode 'Bambi', the four housemates, representing Scumbag College, were pitted against the (posh) Footlights College, whose team comprise Ben Elton and three relative unknowns – Stephen Fry, Hugh Laurie and Emma Thompson, representing Oxbridge but also real-life products themselves of the Footlights. Along with Oxonians Rowan Atkinson and Richard Curtis, Fry and Laurie would be mainstays of *Blackadder*, which, following the Manchester/Liverpool post-punk hiatus represented by Mayall, Elton and Sayle, suggested a shift away from anti-establishment, spiky surrealism – though certainly not a cosy restoration of the comedy norm. And with plenty of bottoms still in store.

The Black Adder (1983) was co-conceived and written by Richard Curtis and Rowan Atkinson, who had come to prominence at 1979's Secret Policeman's Ball, thanks to two sketches in particular: one in which Atkinson deployed his oddly precise diction in reading out a school register of increasingly absurd and misshapen surnames; then, in a sketch led by Peter Cook as leader of a doomsday cult, he plays a hooded disciple, who asks with strange, hollowed vowels, 'Will the wind be so mighty as to lay low the mountains of the earth?' The Department of Silly Voices had a new minister. Meanwhile, his 'rubber face', the odd, twitching relationship between his nostrils, lips, jowls and eyes, was an instrument that enabled him to play a host of unmanly males, such as the mime artist Alternative Car Park on *Not the Nine O'Clock News*.

By 1983, it was appropriate that he have his own comedy vehicle. Curtis felt that when it came to contemporary sitcoms, *Fawlty Towers* had scorched the earth; anything set in modern Britain would have to bear comparison with Cleese and Booth's masterpiece. So they decided on a medieval setting, with Atkinson playing Edmund, the self-styled Black Adder, in a historically counterfactual series set in the late fifteenth century. In this alternative medieval Britain, Richard III is a kindly monarch who wins the Battle of Bosworth Field but is then accidentally slain by Edmund, who cuts off his head when he fails to recognise him as he takes his horse in a mix-up. Richard III's nephew, Richard, Duke of York (Brian Blessed), takes over in his stead as the fictional Richard IV.

Edmund is a pitiful contrast to his booming father the Duke of York; the entire series seems designed less as a meditation on 1480s mores, more a vehicle for Atkinson the physical comedian, a weedy, snivelling mass of slithery intonations and nerdy, knock-kneed body language. Edmund is forever trying to impress his father, who favours his older brother Harry and has problems even remembering Edmund's name. Though he is appointed Archbishop of Canterbury, only his friend Lord Percy (Tim McInnerny) is a more pathetic creature than Edmund; even Edmund's servant, Tony Robinson's Baldrick, is more intelligent than him. Though it had its moments, *The Black Adder* was a cluttered, broad, messy battlefield of a show, uncertain of its purpose.

However, the Black Adder did return, as Blackadder, in 1985, the beneficiary of two masterstrokes which would establish the sitcom's success. The first was to bring on Ben Elton as co-writer – he brought focus, structure and a twenty-something sensibility which he had developed as scriptwriter and co-creator of *The Young Ones*. Elton's introduction also saw a greater emphasis on the scrofulous despotism, ignorance, hypocrisy and moral squalor which were endemic in British history. In an era in which the Conservatives were urging us to hark back to the supposedly superior values of bygone eras, the Victorian for one, this was salutary. In his stand-up, for which he first achieved national recognition in 1985 as host of *Saturday Live* (which also featured Rik Mayall and Ade Edmondson as the Dangerous Brothers, along with Stephen Fry, Hugh Laurie and Harry Enfield), Elton would rail against the cruelties of Thatcherism with an indignation that some felt bordered on the hectoring and didactic. *Blackadder* was a means whereby he could channel this indignation into a hilariously physical as well as verbal comedy of turnips and codpieces, well-wrought similes and daftly contrived farce, whose ostensible juvenilia was put to the higher purpose of exposing and ridiculing the very worst, and still not entirely extinct, aspects of our British heritage.

The second series also saw Blackadder man up, ditching the mass of geeky physical tropes with which Atkinson had made his name. This incarnation sees Edmund as a courtier in the Elizabethan age treading a fine line between favoured status and decapitation, often seeking to out-grovel fellow courtier Lord Melchett (Stephen Fry). However, Atkinson does not play Edmund as an oily, twitchy creature of ambition and fire but as a more rugged, impressively callous cynic. He regards the idiocies of late-sixteenth-century England with contempt and despair, the perspective of a twentieth-century man caught up in the era. Not that he's troubled by any liberal conscience or compassion, as seen in the casual cruelty he heaps on a now much dimmer-witted Baldrick, whom he treats as a human footstool, as well as his tirelessly fatuous, dead-from-the-ruff-up 'friend' Lord Percy.

Rik Mayall sensationally upstages Edmund in the manhood stakes as Lord Flashheart, in a pants-swelling, thigh-slapping, cock-thrusting display of screaming bravado: 'Hello, Melchett. Still worshipping God? Last I heard, he was worshipping *me!*' As oversexed as Rick was undersexed, Flashheart showed that Mayall, like Atkinson, could play the alpha male when required.

However, there's no dominating Miranda Richardson as 'Queenie' Elizabeth, a squeaky cross between Violet Elizabeth Bott and Stalin, still attended to by her 'Nursey' (Patsy Byrne), who has never shed the habit of addressing 'Queenie' as if she is five years old. Queenie, though given to adult crushes, is a woman-child, preserved as such in supreme privilege, finding joy in silly court games and present-giving, whose every whim must be indulged on pain of having one's head casually chopped off.

Edmund must placate the poker-wielding, baby-eating Bishop of Bath and Wells, flit deftly between a drinking contest involving fake plastic breasts and dinner with his ultra-puritanical uncle and aunt, and deal with Captain Rum, played by Tom Baker as the saltiest of seadogs, despite his total incompetence as a sailor. Throughout, Blackadder maintains a balance between kissing up and kicking down. However, he kisses up with only partially disguised scorn and kicks down (to Baldrick) with a familiar ease rather than ill temper. Baldrick, meanwhile, is so fully accepting of the social order that he barely seems to notice the pain inflicted on him by Blackadder. Hence the moment in *Blackadder the Third* (1987) when Blackadder tells Baldrick, 'Life isn't fair. If it were, things like this wouldn't happen,' before clouting him by way of demonstration. *Blackadder the Third* sees Edmund's social status decline further; over the centuries he has been reduced from prince to courtier to butler to Prince George (Hugh Laurie). He has retained his acid sarcasm, however, of which the obliviously dunderheaded George is a frequent target, as well as a viperish eye for the main chance. He's less dashing than his Elizabethan predecessor – more Colin Jeavons than Colin Firth. The relationship is Jeeves and Wooster *in extremis*. George is genial but cluckingly imbecilic, working his jaw constantly as he lets out a stream of self-absorbed jabber, and utterly dependent on Edmund, incapable as he is of negotiating his way into a pair of trousers.

Curtis had feared emulating *Fawlty Towers*, but by the time of *Blackadder the Third*, they were channelling Basil's sardonic verbal savagery, paying homage with Fawlty-esque, three-pronged jibes. For example, Blackadder, when the young prime minister declares he is putting up his own brother as an MP: 'Pitt the toddler? Pitt the embryo? Pitt the glint in the milkman's eye?'

There was a Shakespearean quality to Blackadder's language, rich in simile, invective and mocking bombast. No longer afforded the expensive location shots of the first series, but working within the budgetary confinement of a few small sets, the real extravagance was in the dialogue, which aptly conveys the debauchery, squalor, decadence and inelegant incapability of the Georgian era. Random examples:

Fat Tory landowners who get made MPs when they reach a certain weight.

As useful as a catflap in an elephant house.

You talk like a plate of beans negotiating their way out of a cow's digestive system.

I am therefore leaving immediately for Nepal, where I intend to live as a goat.

Sometimes I feel like a pelican – whichever way I turn I've got an enormous bill in front of me.

Amid all this, however, is the rankness of bracingly lowbrow humour involving naughty bits: Baldrick's uncle who played 'second codpiece' in the theatre ('Did he have a large part?'); constant references to trousers, buttocks, testicles, nipples; the fart joke when George creaks the floorboards trying to stand in the manner of the theatrical hero; a French revolutionary who complains about being 'hung like a baby carrot'; and puns about briefs. Mere *Carry On* carrying on into the eighties, some might say, but there is no bawdiness about *Blackadder*. There's a reductive egalitarianism about this humour, as if to say: be we prince regent or serf, we are all pissers, farters, bearers of nipples, our pants filled with private parts and rear ends which shit also.

As in *Blackadder II*, Edmund is a character with the cadences and sophistication of a twentieth-century man. He is surrounded by deliberately broad, stock types of the age: ghastly, red-faced sadists; grand thespians; Robbie Coltrane playing Dr Johnson with three drug-addled, declaiming aesthetes, Shelley, Byron and Keats, in tow, gruff Yorkshire industrialists; and French fops. He taunts them with a dry, malicious wit that is way above their heads and centuries ahead of its time – repeating the word 'Macbeth' in front of the actors, forcing them into a painful, nose-tweaking ritual to expel the bad luck it brings, or unnerving Johnson by complimenting him on completing his dictionary with an array of made-up words, including 'contrafibularities'.

He is happy with the class set-up: 'Toffs at the top, plebs at the bottom and me in the middle making a fat pile of cash out of both of them.' He also makes a side living selling George's socks, for which Parliament had awarded him a £59,000 grant.

And yet *Blackadder the Third* is implicitly, unmistakably about the absurdity, the iniquity of social injustice – think of Sir Talbot Buxomly, who uses his servants to eat off ('Why should I waste money when I have men standing idle?'), or, as Edmund himself puts it, when explaining to George the rise of revolutionaries in England and their demands: 'peace, freedom and a few less fat bastards eating all the pie'. Only in the final series would the writers reveal the show's latent moral seriousness.

By the time of *Blackadder Goes Forth* (1989), Edmund has been reduced to captain. It had been just six years since *The Black Adder* debuted, but with each series Blackadder seemed to have aged several years. He feels middle-aged here, a career soldier who imagined he would never face any more dangerous foe than squads of pygmies armed with sharpened pieces of fruit. Now he's in the frontline trenches in 1917, bogged down in a squalid, muddy, futile madness that matches anything Bosworth had to offer but with twentieth-century machinery thrown in, too.

Blackadder Mark 4 seems tired, as if from the wearying trials of his ancestors. Private Baldrick is so dim he barely has the cognitive ability to move, but Blackadder can no longer be bothered to inflict on him the physical abuse of previous series. Hugh Laurie's George, meanwhile, is a lieutenant, as chinless, gurgling and idiotic as Prince George but reduced from monarch to mere well-connected public schoolboy. Enthused by the juvenile, sanguine, patriotic fervour which saw him and his chums leapfrog all the way to the enlistment office in 1914, he has no idea that the caper he has signed up for might involve mortal danger. When crawling on their bellies through no man's land, George asks Blackadder what they should do if they hit a landmine. The normal procedure, Blackadder advises him, is to 'jump 200 feet into the air – and scatter yourself over a wide area'.

Right behind them – thirty-five miles behind them – are Tim McInnerny as Captain Darling and Stephen Fry as General Melchett, reprising some of the braying, barking spirit of Wellington in *Blackadder the Third*. Thanks to the precise intonation and timing of Atkinson and Fry, in particular, whenever Darling is addressed by his surname it raises a laugh. It's the mark of a show which makes a genuine virtue of broadness. Darling, a pen-pusher and a pusher of other men into danger zones, rightly suspects Blackadder is engaged in a series of elaborate ruses to avoid orders to clamber over the top and be riddled with bullets. This makes Darling's lip curl, though when he himself is sent to the front he's hardly over-keen on the prospect. General Melchett, meanwhile, though hale, genial, a sport – he broke wind for his college – grandly assumes his men will feel the same enthusiasm for their sacrifice of advancing a few feet into no man's land as he does.

Dad's Army is referenced. In the opening episode, 'Captain Cook', Jones's 'Permission to speak, sir' is invoked by Blackadder, a permission he denies George when taking credit for one of his paintings to General Melchett, in the hope it will see him transferred to Paris. Then, in 'Corporal Punishment', there are echoes of the episode in which Mainwaring finds himself in the dock, with his nemesis Captain Square sitting as judge. Here, Blackadder is court-martialled and facing execution for eating Melchett's beloved carrier pigeon Speckled Jim, and, due to a Baldrick cock-up, finds himself represented by George, the world's worst barrister. In case this wasn't clear enough, two of the members of the firing squad are named Jones and Frazer.

Blackadder Goes Forth, however, is as dissimilar to *Dad's Army* as World War II was to World War I. There is no nobility, only futility, while zeal for the war, as displayed by George, is a sign of stupidity, not decency. Even Baldrick, for so long an unquestioning bondsman, is stirred by the dissenting voices of the Russian Revolution. And whereas death is kept safely at bay in *Dad's Army*, in *Blackadder* death is at hand and imminent. Each of the previous three series ended in death, and so does *Blackadder Goes Forth*, but on this occasion there's an unprecedented shift to the sombre – a comedic ceasefire, just as George, Baldrick, Blackadder and Darling await the blast of the whistle which will send them over the top to their slaughter, the battlefield then morphing into a field of poppies. It works devastatingly well because it is true to the show's underlying morality. *Blackadder* had always been the least earnest of critiques of the sort of societies that pre-dated the liberal and civil one many of us are able to take for granted today – feudal, rancid, cruel, ignorant, repressive. But in 1989, there were still living survivors of the Great War, and the nod to the Cenotaph made by the series was a masterstroke, as appropriate as *Dad's Army*'s final toast to the Home Guard.

That said, *Blackadder Goes Forth* was up to this point as pungent with puerile humour as its predecessors: 'pumped thoroughly in the debriefing room', 'pull strings and fiddle with knobs', 'belts off, trousers down, isn't life a scream', 'a good line in rough shag', 'I've got to admire your balls', 'tackle out', 'right up your alley', 'horrendous uprisings from the bottom', 'the pants haven't been built that'll take the job on'. This even excites comment from Baron von Richthofen, eager to learn from his British captors about 'your jokes about the breaking of the wind. You find the toilet so amusing . . . For you, it is the basis of an entire culture.'

Although sitcom would change in the 1990s, the *Blackadder* series still stands up today. It is verbally dextrous and, despite the vulgarity, a genuine, knowing advance on the standard-issue reactionary comedy of the decades preceding it. However, there are also the first seeds of what will later become annoyingly whimsical. There is a certain port-swilling relish about Fry's use of rude vocabulary, as in his own small contribution to *Blackadder* – 'You twist and turn like a twisty-turny thing.' It's an ominous harbinger of how comedy would play out in less talented hands and mouths in everyday discourse, often from loud, well-spoken sorts, oblivious to how absolutely irritating everyone else finds them – in more recent times, the sort of people who would use compound insults like 'cockwomble' and 'spunk-trumpet'. Earlier came 'The Stonk', the single released by Hale and Pace for Comic Relief in 1991, featuring Jonathan Ross and others making that groin-thrusting movement popularised by Rik Mayall in *Blackadder*, and you realised that something in comedy had died and was starting to smell unfunny.

TO THE MANOR BORN, THE HITCHHIKER'S GUIDE TO THE GALAXY – THE EIGHVENTIES

In the 1985 TV version of ingenious farceur Alan Ayckbourn's play *Absurd Person Singular*, we see three couples across three successive Christmas Eves. The husbands are a banker, an architect and an ambitious but socially inept young contractor, Sidney (played by Nicky Henson, ten years earlier the medallion man in *Fawlty Towers'* 'The Psychiatrist'). In act one, he is eager to please the architect and banker, but they regard this upstart with superior class and professional disdain. By act three, their fortunes have declined and they find themselves in the ignominious position of looking for favours from Sidney, whose dominance is finally confirmed as he plays ringmaster over them in a humiliating party game.

Absurd Person Singular was written in 1972, but by 1985 the play felt politically prophetic. Thatcherism had prevailed. The little men like the estate agent in *Abigail's Party* (1977) hadn't fatally succumbed to their own stress. The little men had won. The Brittas Empire was theirs. Timothy West's coarse, callous 1930s arms dealer in the sitcom *Brass* (1983–4, 1990), Bradley Hardacre, sadistically ruled the roost, his pleasure in laying men off quasi-sexual. The wankers had won. Jim Davidson, on mainstream TV, crowing, after the Falklands campaign, 'We're not doing so bad – just won a war.' The wankers had won. The incursions of alternative comedy, *The Young Ones*, Alexei Sayle, *The Comic Strip* were cathartic, brash, put the opposition to shame, but theirs were the sardonic, baleful cries of the losers. In the battle between alternative and the cynical but highly effective Conservative mantra 'there is no alternative', the latter had won. The Tories would enjoy landslide domination throughout the decade, with old assumptions buried deep below the landscape they had created, a landscape to which British comedy had to reconcile itself. And the comedy that won in the primetime popularity stakes was more likely to be *Daily Mail* suburban-based than deconstructive.

In what my friends Al Needham and Taylor Parkes describe as the 'Eighventies', that period in which the seventies had expired but the eighties were yet to assume their shape, the dominant sitcom in BBC1-land was *To the Manor Born* (1979–81), created by Peter Spence and starring Penelope Keith. On the face of it, she was another Thatcher proxy, whose hectoring femaleness made her an Aunt Sally, but also someone who commanded fear, a faint shame even, deep down in the bosoms of her snickering critics.

Despite her brusqueness and obsolete values, however, Audrey fforbes-Hamilton isn't exactly a Thatcherite. Granted, she loathes the Labour Party, whose occasional periods of government she compares to 'wars, plagues, floods and famines'. However, when visiting a railway station, she is appalled to learn from the man behind the counter that a line is being shut down for unprofitability. 'It's not meant to be profitable, it's meant to be a service,' she retorts. Coming from old money, she disdains Richard DeVere, Czech by descent but fully anglicised, a nouveau-riche arriviste who made his pile in supermarkets. Fforbes-Hamilton is reduced to selling him the manor and moving into the lodge when she learns of the very careless husbandry of her deceased spouse. She scorns DeVere as a mere 'grocer'. Hardly Thatcherite.

You could describe Peter Bowles's DeVere as an extremely well-laundered Robert Maxwell: genial, informal, unbothered by the ancient protocols and 'duties' required of the lord of the manor. He represents a mockery of Audrey's snooty, fastidious uptightness and naive adherence to feudalist ways. Urbane and comfortable in his own skin, with no snobbery but no coarse hint of accent either, he's certainly no Sidney, twitching with the resentful, small-minded rapaciousness of the nouveau Thatcherites.

The supporting cast of *To the Manor Born* in the fictional Grantleigh are reassuring in their knobbly eccentricity, such as the Miles Malleson-esque Ned, or well-bred amiability, such as Audrey's old school chum Marjory (Angela Thorne). Grantleigh anticipates

Dibley, of which Dawn French would become vicar: a major-esque, harmless, picturesque England, Midsomer *sans* murders.

At the series' end in 1981, 17.8 million people watched Richard and Audrey marry at last, Audrey having been restored to the manor. It was a synthesis of old and new England, far from the madding ravages of eighties Britain; like Charles and Diana's wedding, that moving merger between ordinary posh and mega-posh, or even Ken and Deirdre Barlow in *Coronation Street*, weddings were the great healer for torn eighties Britain, however forced or temporary. Audrey and Richard, however, would celebrate their silver wedding anniversary in 2007. That, as Oscar Wilde might say, is fiction.

Also of the eighventies was Douglas Adams's *The Hitchhiker's Guide to the Galaxy*, a 1978 radio series, adapted for TV in 1981. It belongs to a culture subsequently dubbed 'hauntological': with its retro-futurist analogue synthesiser soundtrack, it triggers the same associations as *Blake's 7*, mid-morning BBC Schools TV programmes and paternalistic public information films, the era so observantly lampooned in Peter Serafinowicz and Robert Popper's *Look Around You* (2002–5). It was an era in which the future loomed uncertainly, possibly one in which space travel would take a further leap and bound, in which robots might feature in our lives, whether as domestic labour-savers or humanity's nemesis. The dark rafters of space still hung high in the collective imagination.

The Hitchhiker's Guide, however, which wears its philosophical wit lightly, punctures many of the delusions of sci-fi, certainly the idea that extensive exploration of life, the universe and everything would solve very much. The meaning of life? Forty-two. Ask a silly question . . . It tells the story of Arthur Dent, who with his Doctor Who-like helpmate Ford Prefect manages to escape an earth scheduled for obliteration by an alien species, the Vogons, to make way for an inter-galactic highway, much as Arthur's own house has been scheduled for bulldozing. There is no escaping the petty ordinariness and banal self-centredness of humanity, one which prevails throughout galaxies, across species. Most of the series' humour arises from this bathos. No one talks in lofty, deep-throated, alien-like terms but in the small, informal idioms of everyday English. Even the dolphins, who turn out to have been far wiser than humans, have a matey tone about them, as their last message to humanity reveals: 'Cheerio, and thanks for all the fish.'

Hitchhiker's, with inventively wry gloom, deflates the notion that there is anything bigger and better out there, reduces the unknown cosmos to the scale of England, in all its middle-management medi-ocrity. It cleared the space for *Red Dwarf* (1988–), whose title speaks to the indomitable smallness of the human condition, even when unbound from earth. *Red Dwarf* was anomalous, really. The eighties, the no-more-Apollo, no-more-James-Burke, no-more-documentaries-about-the-microchip-revolution decade, were the beginning of the post-space age. In the seventies, speculation was that we would have landed on Mars by now. However, as the space shuttle *Challenger* dis-aster of 1986 tragically illustrated, we were barely capable of exceeding the bounds of our own atmosphere without burning up. The dreams of the 1960s and even the 1970s had been supplanted by the brutally imposed 'realities' of the 1980s.

DUCKING AND DIVING –
MINDER, ONLY FOOLS AND HORSES

From Dent across the universe to Daley. *Minder* (1979–94) was more comedy-drama than comedy, but few remember it for its not-very-authentic depiction of London's underworld, as conveyed by a jobbing and dependable cast of character actors and veterans including Brian Glover, Pete Postlethwaite, Lionel Jeffries, Max Wall, Suzi Quatro, Roy Kinnear, Brian Blessed and Rula Lenska. Dennis Waterman starred as Terry McCann, an ex-boxer in the employ of shady 'import/export' entrepreneur Arthur Daley (George Cole). Luckily for Arthur, for a hard case, Terry's a soft touch, although he has his limits. What's more, Terry's moral compass functions far better than Arthur's, so deficient it's as if it were one he sold to himself. So, when Arthur has Terry mind his second-hand car dealership, a teenager comes in, considering buying one of Arthur's dodgy vehicles. Learning that it would be his first car, Terry dissuades him from buying any vehicle from Arthur, knowing the state it's probably in. Your first car should be special, he tells the bemused lad, packing him off to some more reputable dealership.

At the beginning of the series, there is a bit of menace about Arthur, but this eventually dissipates. What's funny is the oleaginous cheek of his sales patter, the dodgy schmatter and malfunctioning gadgetry down at his lock-up. His victims are merely the VAT man, the taxman and geezers like Dave, landlord at the Winchester, sweet-talked into buying crap off him when he ought to know better. Arthur's charm is mysterious; Terry himself, when asked why he doesn't up and leave him, says he can't, after all Arthur's done for him; when pressed on precisely what that is, he's stumped. It's not even like they're blood, the sort that binds Steptoe to his unscrupulous, exploitative father. Arthur is a con man who has conned all around him into remaining in his circle of influence, including, apparently, 'er indoors, a formidable woman who nonetheless allows Arthur licence to roam. Perhaps his greatest con is against himself, into thinking he is a fellow of status and propriety, entitled to the respect due an entrepreneur. His wounded indignation when challenged by Terry, or his police nemesis Inspector Chisholm, is more than performative.

The success of *Minder* was, believed John Sullivan, the reason he was commissioned to write *Only Fools and Horses* (1981–2003), following the success of the amiable *Citizen Smith* (1977–80). It began two years after *Minder* and did seem a bit conspicuously imitative at the time – a London-based trader in dubious goods relying on his wit and charm. David Jason as Derek 'Del Boy' Trotter continued in the tradition of *Citizen Smith*'s Wolfie, with his indomitable optimism. Whereas Wolfie believed that this time next year, he would be at the forefront of a socialist revolution, Del Boy believed that this time next year, he'd be a millionaire.

Early episodes are blighted by references to the 'Paki shop', jarring even for 1981. Someone presumably had a word because these dried up and *OFAH* evolved, as the eighties wore on, into the last sitcom that was both critically acclaimed and mainstream, hugely popular. This was in part due to Sullivan's way with comic set pieces and sight gags – the scene in which the Granddad sends a chandelier crashing to the floor of a great hall as Del and Rodney are waiting to catch the one adjacent to it, for example. Or there's the surreally dim-witted Trigger, he who claims to have saved the council money by owning the same broom for twenty years, albeit with multiple different brushes and handles, and who constantly refers to Rodney by the name of 'Dave'. When sent by the landlord of the Nag's Head to ask Rodney what Del will be naming his baby so that they can go halves in a Guess the Baby competition, Trigger returns with the information that if it's a boy, 'they're going to call him Rodney, after Dave'.

Although its cast of regulars gives the series a joyful, familial feel, the relationship between the morose Rodney and older brother Derek is central. Come the late eighties, Del Boy eagerly embraces the yuppy era. He wears the tag with pride. When he meets two actual young yuppies and refers to them thus, they bridle. 'We're not yuppies,' says one of them. 'Oh yes, you are,' Del assures them, without sarcasm. He starts drinking cocktails with plastic umbrellas and carrying a Filofax simply because these are the things that maketh the yuppy. When their Uncle Albert goes missing and they find themselves down at the docks, Rodney embarks on an extended, long-faced lament at how the area is becoming besieged by property developers, and Del replies, 'Yeah – great, isn't it?'

But Del Boy is more than an enthusiastic creature of the Thatcher era. He adopts the yuppy tropes because he is quite hilariously lacking in taste. And his enthusiasm for Docklands development isn't born out of cynicism or greed but wide-eyed optimism. Del Boy is a creature of the sixties, a more sanguine era in which the future seemed sunlit and it was possible for a young man like Del to dream. Rodney, by contrast, has come of age in the early 1980s, a precarious era in which there is far less reason for hope. Sadly, his attempts to better himself, very often with a view to impress women, do bear out Del's frequent description of him as a 'plonker'.

As for Del Boy, no amount of adversity can subdue his brazen optimism or brass neck. The series persisted until 1996, when Sullivan decided that the Trotters should stroll off into the sunset with Del Boy's dream of becoming a millionaire granted, thanks to an extremely valuable antique timepiece unearthed in the lock-up. But Del becomes bored. For him, the essence of life is going down the market to sweet-talk punters into buying tat, or trying to offload Romanian wine or malfunctioning remote controls to some mug. It's all about the game. Win it, and it's over. Which is why, in a short-lived return to our screens, they had Del lose the entire fortune on some reckless investment, returning to his old flat in Nelson Mandela House, the home he loves best.

As *Minder* and *Only Fools and Horses* were in full flight, the *NME* ran a think-piece lambasting a culture that made heroes of duckers and divers like Daley and Del Boy, entrepreneurs who made a dubious living by disregarding the rules and regulations supposed to keep capitalism in check. What did it say about us that we put such characters on a pedestal, made heroes of them, with their shameless pursuit of spondulicks and nice little earners? Yet I was one of many anti-Thatcherites who felt no contradiction between my hatred of the Tories and love of Arthur Daley and Del Boy. Maybe it was that their low-level shenanigans took place in the shadows of far worse and more unpleasant villains, be it the Driscoll brothers in *Only Fools and Horses* or the various underworld characters to whom Terry was compelled to dish out right-handers in *Minder*. Or that they were never party political (when Arthur stands for political office it's as an independent). There was, by contrast with the thuggish, humourless

Tories, little damage done by the scamps Del Boy and Daley, and to laugh at their efforts to flog their dubious wares was certainly not to admire them, or to yearn for laxer trade regulations, or to seek to emulate their lifestyles. Also, in an era of wrong things, even if, like Sergeant Bilko, they didn't always do so with a smile, they did the right thing. They weren't entirely unscrupulous. They were heroes, if sometimes reluctant ones, whose values and sense of class, such as they were, had been forged in earlier times.

EVER DECREASING CIRCLES AND THE SHADOW OF SEVENTIES SITCOM

Following the success of *The Good Life*, Richard Briers initially faltered. But then came *Ever Decreasing Circles* (1984–9), written by *The Good Life*'s John Esmonde and Bob Larbey. Among the strangest successes in British TV history, largely due to Briers's recognisability, it saw him play a character who was the very opposite of Tom Good.

In 1984, Martin Bryce would have been considered a broody eccentric. Watching it today, it's clear that he is on some sort of spectrum. Living in a suburb in East Surrey, he has a fixed, appointed role as local 'organiser' of local sports clubs and is rigidly set in established routines, the sort against which Tom Good rebels. His life is disrupted by the arrival of neighbour Paul Ryman (Peter Egan), a genial fellow, ex-Army and Cambridge blue, effortlessly good at everything, so much so that you wonder what he is doing running a local hair salon. Paul endures Martin's constant, resentful grumbling at him, his ill-concealed jealousy, with endless good humour. Martin is lucky to have him as a neighbour – lucky, too, to be married to Ann, whose romantic attraction to him is mystifying; there is far more chemistry between her and Paul, but it's as if they have tacitly agreed not to have an affair for the sake of the man-child Martin. They are not quite plausible, and not particularly funny in their own right. Their function is to act as buffers of companionship to Martin, in all his haplessness, to allow us to laugh at him rather than pity him.

Martin does have some good qualities: he rescues a child from drowning, for example, but in so doing reveals aspects of his own arrested development, being unable, emotionally, to take in what he's done. 'My underpants are wet through!' he complains, and when he eventually takes on board his heroism, he makes a thorough bore of himself by swanking relentlessly about it, bringing a scolding from his wife. A plaque is erected in his honour on a park bench; we see him sitting at it, fussily polishing it. Nothing is ever quite right. In the last series, when he and Ann move house following the arrival of a baby, Martin's last act is to move a telephone receiver that is out of position. A perpetual mass of nervous, sometimes aggressive anxiety, Martin can never relax, the way Tom was wont to, over a glass of home-brewed wine, reflecting smilingly on his blessings and, literally, domestic Felicity.

Martin represents a heart of darkness towards which the suburban sitcom has, in those decreasing circles, swirled. It is not cosy. It is existentially fraught. Martin is a visibly faded presence at its centre. Ricky Gervais cited *Ever Decreasing Circles* as a major influence. But one shouldn't over-egg Martin's symbolism as eighties man. Like Frank Spencer, or even Hancock, he is a lonely, anomalous figure. What is happening in the eighties is happening to other people, not him.

SUE TOWNSEND, VICTORIA WOOD, JO BRAND

Still, sitcom bumbled on in the eighties, from the foreigners-are-funny capers of *'Allo 'Allo!* (1982–92), or *Oh! What a Funny Resistance*, to Carla Lane's *Bread*, a cheerful take on the economic ravages which besieged Liverpool, to Laurence Marks and Maurice Gran's *Birds of a Feather* (1989–98, 2014–20), whose lead characters, played by Pauline Quirke and Linda Robson, were named Sharon and Tracey, but which didn't always live up to the high comedic promise of that nomenclature. Some of the acutest social commentary of the disintegrating eighties came in Sue Townsend's Adrian Mole diaries, later adapted for television, commencing with 1982's *The Diary of Adrian Mole, Aged 13¾*. Occupying a mid-point between *The Diary of a Nobody* and *The Inbetweeners*, the *Diary* is a study in painful adolescence, with Mole not just chronicling his own anxieties about his acne and penis development but also shedding light on his dog-rough family circumstances, his school bullying at the hands of Barry Kent and coping with the style revolution brought by punk rock, which has arrived late in his home county of Leicestershire. The *Mole* chronicles are no light entertainment taking place in well-tended suburbia. Unlike, say, William Brown, Adrian Mole is the victim, rather than the perpetrator, of the action, which involves feral dogs, fist-fights, domestic estrangement. He is certainly one of the losers, in a decade in which the cosy ties of yore are pitilessly fraying and there is less and less of such a thing as 'society' as we knew it.

Fortunately, there's a resilient obtuseness about Adrian, a dogged, idealistic earnestness: just think of his desire to help out the 'poor and the ignorant', despite themselves, and his conclusion that in order to associate with society's most disadvantaged, his best friend should ideally be an old African woman. Upon reading George Orwell's *Animal Farm*, he resolves to become a vet. He also resolves to stop eating pork, wanting nothing more to do with pigs after their disgusting behaviour in the book. However, like Orwell, he had to fight back nausea at the actual working classes, particularly his revolting pensioner friend Bert Baxter, while he is capable of snobbishness and a feeling that he naturally belongs on a higher social plane, hence his infatuation with the awful Pandora.

The success of Sue Townsend was a heartening reminder of the advance women were making in the eighties, not just as performers, often decorative and under-used, but among the vanguard of writers and observers. Victoria Wood was another. She reminds me of Kate Bush, who thrived in the post-punk 1980s, although really she was of hippy-ish origins, mentored by David Gilmour of Pink Floyd rather than inspired by Johnny Rotten. Wood came to prominence in the post-alternative comedy environment but was forged in pre-alternative times. On *Victoria Wood as Seen on TV* (1985–7), she recalls, improbably, Ken Dodd in her body language, the way she scans the audience and the velocity of her performance. Her garish colour schemes, as if she has thrown together every bad sartorial mid-eighties idea for her outfit, are also reminiscent of Doddy's own joyfully colour-clashing garb.

Some are sceptical of Wood's radical credentials; in her cultural study *Steal as Much as You Can*, Nathalie Olah suggests that Wood 'played within the rules of the British establishment, carefully crafting their brand of comedy so as not to offend the sensibilities of the upper classes too aggressively'. Maybe; there is a cosiness, a warm familiarity that exudes from Wood's parodies of soap opera, shopping malls, daytime TV. It's deceptive, however, this odour of Shake n' Vac, and it can come back to bite, especially when Wood is in lacerating, satirical mode. She writes with a literary elan about a world she understands more than the vast majority of her male contemporaries would deign to. Wood understands the comedic weight of the words 'Regency stripe' when describing a pair of curtains and where that stripe registers on the Pretension-ometer. With the exception of a few dependable male regulars, she wrote for women, top-drawer actors like Celia Imrie, who in Wood's *All Day Breakfast* (1992) perfectly spoofs the strident but coy advertising of the day with Sonara: The Slimline Towel with Built-In Redial, in which the power-dressing executive constantly on the go on her mobile ('Hello, bank manager?') needs a towel which will readily absorb the menstruation-denoting blue liquid she pours all over it. There was Susie Blake, as well, the newscaster whose rictus smile belied a snobbish froideur. 'Apologies to our viewers in the North. It must be awful for you.'

Julie Walters had a particularly strong relationship with Wood. *Acorn Antiques* was one example, a parody of the low-budget production values of shows like *Crossroads*, in which she tutored her film crew in the visual vocabulary of getting everything just wrong – cutting to actors frozen in position prior to action, for example. You'd have to have been common enough to have watched *Crossroads* to get this, of course. Walters bustles around as Mrs Overall, constantly serving up beverages to Celia Imrie's proprietor 'Miss Babs', their relationship a keen parody not of real-life mistress–servant relationships but the cosier TV version, the way the British liked to think the classes related with one another: hierarchical but caring, up to a point.

dinnerladies, broadcast between 1998 and 2000, was for many Wood's supreme achievement, elevating female experience with its rich gamut of characters and pedigree actors, the menfolk playing a conspicuously subordinate role. Only Wood could have created this world. Indeed, she was sole scriptwriter, dispensing with a script editor. One masterstroke was to bring in Thelma Barlow, aka Mavis Riley in *Coronation Street*, who deserved a vehicle for her abundant comic talents and the chance to play an alternative character. Her panic when she accidentally ingests a dose of Viagra is pure Wood-ese, the language of all her characters, but here particularly rife with prim hysteria and, in this instance, a revulsion with the male condition: 'What will happen when it gets down there and finds there's nothing to pump up? . . . What else will I get? Nose hair? Weeing at random, missing the bowl altogether?' Anita, played by Shobna Gulati, was a fine and thoughtful creation also, sweet if not bright, poignant in her desire to have a family and kids.

dinnerladies featured a raft of guest stars drawn from both soap and mainstream sitcom, including Eric Sykes, Janette Krankie, Lynda Baron, Jack Smethurst and Kate Robbins. However, *dinnerladies'* broadcast on BBC2 could not but feel avant-garde, despite its household faces.

As TV became more risk-averse, Wood found herself in the ignominious, undeserved position of having to deal with young, 'creative' junior TV executives explaining to her the nature of comedy. There's no doubt she was an influence, but it's enough to say that had there been no Victoria Wood then there would have been no Victoria Wood. She was a pioneer, a master of observing everywoman mores and concerns, but in many ways a one-off whose moment should never have passed.

I first encountered Jo Brand at a comedy fundraiser I was reviewing for *Melody Maker* in the late 1980s. Compèred by Arthur Smith, it was a surprisingly testy affair at times, with Ben Elton heckled for not having written a new set of material for the occasion and Jeremy Hardy, among the most impeccably left-wing comedians, loudly upbraided for a supposedly egregious non-PC remark, an accusation that clearly left him hurt. I was most impressed on the evening by Brand, in her guise as the Sea Monster. In terms of her garb and haircut she seemed to be playing up to the stereotypical ardent *City Limits*-style feminist of the age, but she wasn't man-hating and certainly not humourless. Her jokes, delivered in a deliberately mechanical, two-note sing-song, matter-of-fact tone, were at the expense of her own appearance – 'I was always asked to play Bethlehem in the school nativity play' – though without either guilt or shame. She made herself out to be among the most fantastically obese, ugly women ever to have lived – and what of it? I was reminded a little of Cyrano de Bergerac, when a foolhardy soldier mocks the size of his nose, only for him to come back during the subsequent sword fight with a series of quips of his own, far superior to any his foolish abuser could ever conceive, before finishing him off. No insult delivered by some braying, drunken heckler could shock her or come remotely close to matching her own wit.

Born in 1957 and brought up in London, Brand hardly had an impoverished upbringing but had, by the time she ventured into the world of stand-up, developed a carapace of resilience which was more than just a defence mechanism. As a child she experienced violence at the hands of her depressive father; as a young woman unwelcome sexual advances, including from a man who flagged down her car, only for him to thrust his penis through her wound-down window. As a psychiatric nurse she experienced the base, humiliating bodily mess of humanity on a daily basis, and some of its most broken characters. As a fledgling comedian she found herself abused by hecklers, one of the most vicious of whom turned out to be a member of the club's security. You could say she had experienced life as a series of unsafe spaces. But she weathered it all.

Jo Brand's qualities are deceptive. In her memoir, *Look Back in Hunger*, she recalls being invited to present prizes at her old school. The headmistress introduced her thus: 'There are girls who are hugely academically gifted who apply themselves to their work and there are others who mostly fly by the seat of their pants. Please welcome Jo Brand!' However, though she is clearly no stranger to the pleasures of not being arsed, Brand was actually diligent in her school lessons and competitive in sports. While she may do a sterling impression of a very lazy person, her career, since she debuted on *Friday Night Live* (previously *Saturday Live*) in 1988, has been pretty tireless. She has been much in demand on a range of shows, including *The Brain Drain*, *QI*, *Would I Lie to You?*, *Have I Got News for You* and *Taskmaster*. She has never pretended to have any great skill as a character actor. She is, generally, herself.

JULIAN CLARY AND THE SINGLE ENTENDRE

Antithetical to *Round the Horne*'s Julian and Sandy were Rob and Michael, the gay couple who appeared in *Agony* (1979–81), starring Maureen Lipman as a put-upon agony aunt. The series, co-written by Anna Raeburn, was praised for its depiction of cisgendered gay men as regular, settled, well adjusted, rather than mincing, screaming 'poofters'. Although records show no evidence of anyone laughing themselves to death, à la *The Goodies*, at *Agony*, the understated depiction of Rob and Michael made for courageously enlightened, progressive television.

Come the eighties, and Julian Clary would synthesise these approaches, retaining the progressiveness of Rob and Michael along- side the rampant queeniness of Julian and Sandy. Initially going under the name of the Joan Collins Fan Club, decked out in the loudly effete, Hi-NRG bondage garb of the eighties, Clary's act was festooned with puns that hurt so good ('That fair put the willies up me'), but there was none of the denial of his sexuality which, perforce, John Inman and Larry Grayson had had to maintain. It didn't turn out that he was married all along. He spoke of special- ising in the 'single entendre' in his act, most famously at an awards ceremony, when he casually announced that he had just been fisting then-chancellor of the exchequer Norman Lamont backstage – a cue for a joke about red boxes. As a boy, he told me in 1990, brought up in a Benedictine Catholic school, where the wearing, say, of gold eye shadow was forbidden, he developed 'a more discreet code, a certain language and demeanour – wearing odd socks, walking with a certain gait, which infuriated [the monks], but they couldn't get you for it'. In adulthood, however, Clary decided: enough with the coding. 'Noël Coward was a confirmed bachelor for forty years. This is 1990, for heaven's sake. I can't be bothered with all of that.'

Clary had a soft-spoken manner: his rapport with the public on his game-show vehicle *Sticky Moments with Julian Clary* (1989–90) was reminiscent of the gracious condescension of Dame Edna Everage. When I interviewed him, he was thoughtful, reflective, conscious of his act and its implications, ambivalent about though not dismissive of the commercial end of the TV pool in which he quickly found himself. He was aware of his history and of the history of waspishness, which was his stock-in-trade. 'With all these drag acts in the music hall in the 1920s, they were very sharp-tongued in putting down hecklers because if the audience didn't like them, they didn't get paid. So these hecklers were, in effect, jeopardising their wages.'

YES MINISTER, THE NEW STATESMAN, SPITTING IMAGE – THE EIGHTIES THAT DIDN'T HAPPEN, THE EIGHTIES THAT DID

Margaret Thatcher would not have been sympathetic to Julian Clary. She was an unabashed homophobe who actively introduced legislation (Section 28) against the 'promotion of homosexuality'. Her antipathy to the anti-apartheid movement, as well as her destructive, far-right policies, excited an active response among younger 1980s comedians. And yet, in the finest political comedy of the 1980s, it's as if she had never happened.

Created by Antony Jay and Jonathan Lynn, *Yes Minister/Prime Minister* (1980–8) stars Paul Eddington as Jim Hacker, former editor of the magazine *Reform* turned politician, with Nigel Hawthorne as Sir Humphrey Appleby, his private secretary, later permanent secretary. Hacker's political party is unspecified; he exists in that non-ideological zone where Labour right and Tory left overlap.

Jim Hacker is full of grand, unorthodox schemes – one involves scrapping Trident and bringing back national service. It is Sir Humphrey's task to see to it that these schemes are either kicked into the long grass or quietly strangled at birth. Sometimes it is enough for him to congratulate Hacker for being 'courageous' and watch the blood drain from Hacker's face.

It's tempting to view Hacker and Sir Humphrey as a latter-day Jeeves and Wooster. However, while Hacker may start out each episode as a wide-eyed neophyte with no grasp of the cynicism and nuance of Whitehall politics, he's a quick learner, capable of evolving rapidly into a seasoned political player, peering over the rims of his glasses, taking great pleasure in turning the tables on Sir Humphrey.

Meanwhile, Sir Humphrey is not as omniscient as he might believe. He is perturbable and can be outflanked. Take the episode 'One of Us' (1986), in which it is revealed that, based on his complacent assumptions about fellow Varsity men, he failed to spot that the former head of MI5 was a Russian spy. In notes discovered after the spy's death, he is described as 'that prize goof Appleby'.

If anyone approaches the Olympian stature of Jeeves in *Yes Minister/Prime Minister*, it is Sir Arnold Robinson (John Nettleton), a retired cabinet secretary whose counsel Sir Humphrey often seeks. Sir Arnold is a figure of immense pinstriped dignity, a fount of political knowledge and the most cunning of manipulators, understanding the vanity of MPs and scornful of any independent initiatives they take. He regards MPs the way Jeeves regards Wooster: as mentally negligible, malleable.

Yes Minister/Prime Minister was, for a mainstream BBC comedy, an urbane, erudite achievement, a series in which the viewer is assumed to know who Bartók is, for example. It was highly verbal, not least in Sir Humphrey's circumlocutory, over-elaborate explanations designed to fog Hacker. It's replete with aphorisms ('lulled into a true sense of security', 'you can't check on everything – you never know what you might find') and euphemisms (to fiddle the figures becomes to 'periodically restructure the basis from which statistics are derived'), as well as double-edged blandishments: Hacker is offered a post because, feels the cabinet secretary, he enjoys the advantage of an 'open and uncluttered mind'.

How wounding, however, was the satire? So wounding, apparently, that Margaret Thatcher declared it her favourite TV programme. She was prime minister for the duration of *Yes Minister/Prime Minister*'s existence. But then, for all its insider wisdom about the machinations of Parliament and the civil service, the show was far truer about the fudge and stalemate of British politics in the 1970s, essentially a centre-right continuum from Heath through to Callaghan. Thatcherism saw the country yanked to the right and old permanences and assumptions upended. *Yes Minister/Prime Minister* was an anachronism in its own time, with its pretence that sensible men in suits were curbing the reckless ideological ambitions of politicians. This is most exposed when the show must refer occasionally to the reality of the Falklands conflict. In the shaded, grey universe of this show, such a campaign would have been averted long in advance by discreet manoeuvring to preserve an uneasy peace.

The New Statesman (1987–94) overlapped briefly with *Yes, Prime Minister*. It was a wholly different animal, however. Rik Mayall had asked Laurence Marks and Maurice Gran to write a sitcom in which he would star as Alan Beresford B'Stard MP, the size of whose majority was in inverse proportion, his wife reminds us repeatedly, to the size of his penis.

There is no coyness about B'Stard's politics. He is a Conservative who shares his middle name with Norman Tebbit, blue in tooth and claw. It's said that B'Stard was based on Alan Clark MP, the philandering bounder who once turned up to the Commons drunk after a convivial wine-tasting event. However, Clark was a more complex character than B'Stard, who is without nuance or scruples. We see in the opening episode how he attains power by arranging a car crash in which his SDP and Labour rivals perish, though so dithery are these two candidates that they would probably have collided with each other regardless.

This was 1987, Margaret Thatcher had just won a third consecutive election and the country had never been bluer. Hence B'Stard, a wealthy man who extorts, insults, runs over peacocks, abuses waiters or kicks away the crutch of a Falklands survivor just for the sadistic hell of it. He treats his assistant Piers Fletcher-Dervish as Flashman might a younger schoolboy, subjecting him to physical punishment for any mistake or slip of the tongue. He feigns the unctuous public facade all MPs are supposed to maintain but can never be bothered to do so for long. 'I don't need money but I do love blackmail,' he says, in a scene which concludes with him uttering a very sarcastic 'Yes, prime minister' to camera.

A scene with Nicholas Parsons in a deranged quiz show called *What's the Question* captures the giddiness of the late eighties, the delirium of Leslie Crowther hosting *The Price Is Right*, the country's collective eyes revolving with pound signs, having taken leave of its centrism. B'Stard can ride out every crisis because everyone else is as contemptible as him in their own way, whether conniving or simply weak. The opposition are impotent huffers and puffers who still haven't quite come to terms with what's hit them.

The New Statesman has little of *Yes Minister*'s wit. 'God, you're ugly.' 'Shut up!' 'You know how nobody likes you and you haven't got any friends?' The satire is ITV broad, the peccadilloes low-grade. But this is how debased Britain had become. Satirical salvoes like 'greed is good' and 'loadsamoney' were grist for the slicked-up boys in braces flaunting their wads of notes, an era in which socialism was as defunct as your grandad's old trousers. This was the level of comedic commentary Britain deserved, certainly the clowns, crooks, grotesques and ogres running the country now that the 'wets' had been displaced: the crude and futilely flung revenge of the losers.

The New Statesman crackled principally because of Mayall's performance. No one played unmitigated, loud characters with such flamboyance and fine detail as he. B'Stard's speeches are about the 'dilution of our national spirit' and nonsense about French bank robbers swarming through the Channel Tunnel. Mayall preens, snorts, throws back his head, leers, glowers, eyes dancing with barely concealed, devious ill intent. In one prophetic speech he excoriates the European Union. Why should we Brits kowtow 'to the continent that produced Hitler, Napoleon, the Mafia and . . . the Smurfs'? Almost thirty years later, the country, or at least its decisive elderly section, took B'Stard at his word. Sadly, even

Mayall himself in 2014 dressed as Hitler in a campaign against Britain joining the euro. 'I'm an independent sort of person,' he explained. 'If we join the euro, then the people in Brussels will take even more decisions on our behalf.'

The rise of Margaret Thatcher had been too much for Mike Yarwood. He made a few game attempts to impersonate her, but floundered painfully. Yarwood himself was a victim of Thatcherism; his impressions, his unabrasive style, were irrelevant to the more polarised eighties. Yarwood suffered a personal toll as his career went into a tailspin.

In his stead arose ITV's *Spitting Image*, first broadcast in 1984 and eventually commanding audiences of fifteen million. Its stars were the latex caricature puppets of Peter Fluck and Roger Law, which they had hitherto created for photo shoots in *Private Eye*. Law had history in the world of satire: back in the early 1960s, he had worked at Peter Cook's Establishment club as an in-house illustrator and unofficial bouncer, leading the charge in fist-fights against the local gangsters.

Spitting Image was only fitfully brilliant but consistently, pitilessly crude and derisive about not only politicians but also the celebrities and sports stars of its media age, who seemed to put themselves about more garishly than their predecessors. It provided early voiceover work for Steve Coogan and Harry Enfield, but also for one Steve Nallon, a fellow pupil of mine at St Michael's College in Leeds. Nallon's impression of Margaret Thatcher was among the show's best features. Cleverly modulated and more keenly observant than the general, standard-issue Maggie impersonations of the time, it caught the full range of her heavily coached voice, from unctuous insincerity to the fingernails-on-blackboards abrasiveness she adopted when lambasting the reluctant wets in her cabinet. One of *Spitting Image*'s finest sketches has her assembled in a restaurant with her fellow ministers. She gives her order to the waiter. 'And the vegetables?' 'They'll have the same as me.'

Spitting Image was spectacularly insolent. One sketch involved Cliff Richard's long-disused semen, elderly and hobbling around on walkers inside his sac. In a sketch based on *The Price Is Right*, a show that captured some of the acquisitive hysteria that gripped Britain once Thatcherism really began to kick in, Leon Brittan can be seen charging about screaming 'Come on down!', revelling in the great sell-off of state assets. Everything was cranked up beyond ten. Parliament was depicted as akin to a borstal canteen, tabloid journalists as pigs, home secretary Kenneth Baker as a slug, Roy Hattersley spittle-spraying and jowly. When they could not find an aspect of a politician they could adequately caricature, they simply made something up, investing MP David Mellor with terrible BO, for example.

The royal family were lampooned as aristocratic grotesques whose continued existence added inadvertently to the gaiety rather than prestige of the nation. One sketch saw them in rock garb, throwing heroic, strenuous poses as they shredded with guitars, à la the group Queen. The Queen Mother was portrayed as a tipsy, earthy, Beryl Reid type, though this might have been over-affectionate towards a woman onto whom the general public tended to project virtues and homely characteristics she did not, in fact, possess. Another sketch, meanwhile, shows Prince Andrew fretting that his wife is taking advantage of her royal status for mercenary ends, which, given his own future dealings, feels retrospectively flattering.

In their expectorating raucousness, the *Spitting Image* royal sketches contrast in their inelegance with a parody of the deferential tones of BBC-speak on royal occasions, delivered by David Frost on *That Was the Week That Was* back in the sixties, on the imaginary occasion of the sinking of the royal barge. 'The sleek, royal blue hull of the barge is sliding gracefully, almost regally, beneath the waters of the Pool of London . . . And now the Queen, smiling radiantly, is swimming for her life. Her Majesty is wearing a silk ensemble in canary yellow.' Ironically, the writer of this sketch, Ian Lang, went on to become a Conservative MP, a vegetable, under Mrs Thatcher.

Spitting Image wasn't always sure-footed. The huge lips they imposed on Tina Turner and Frank Bruno would be a matter of concern today, and the less remembered about their Björk puppet, the better. Even when they were funny, they occasionally got things wrong. They had a monotonous Steve Davis trying to figure out a 'devil may care' nickname for himself, like fellow snooker player Alex 'Hurricane' Higgins. He comes up with 'Interesting'. Davis himself loved the sketch and even titled his company Interesting Productions. The irony was, Davis genuinely was among the most interesting individuals snooker ever produced, not least for his obsessive love of avant-garde and prog rock. What's more, *Spitting Image*'s latex caricatures were a liability inasmuch as they lacked responsive facial mobility, for which the great deal of rocking and wobbling they did on screen wasn't really a compensation.

Despite the drubbing delivered to the other political parties, there was a clear anti-Tory bent to *Spitting Image*. Thatcher was a primetime Aunt Sally figure, a right-wing grotesque whose sense of compassion was as convincing as Cruella de Vil cooing at a puppy. The UK laughed and voted overwhelmingly for her in 1987, the same as they had in 1983 and 1979. When she stood down, she was replaced by John Major, whom *Spitting Image* depicted as a sorry, grey-faced born loser, pushing peas around a plate at his dreary dinner table; once more, millions laughed, and in 1992, they voted him into office for another five years. 'At first we were stupid enough to think we were going to make a difference with our humour,' Law once observed, 'but I don't think, in retrospect, that it did make a difference.'

That *Spitting Image*'s primary target, the Tories, flourished in parallel with the show was indicative of the uneasy symbiotic relationship between satire and the establishment, much as the celebrities it mocked thrived rather than withered as a result of being lampooned on the show. It was as if the Tories were sealed in the inevitable firmament, the natural order of things, by being such regular objects of satire, rather than in danger of being dragged down. *Spitting Image* was no more able to depose the Tories than it was the monarchy. Ardent fans of Thatcher and Major did not revise their opinions, chastened by exposure to the show. They merely dismissed it as juvenile – cruel, even. Conversely, *Spitting Image*, in common with satire at large, had no effective way of conveying the tragedy of Tory rule – the attritional ravaging of working-class communities, the consequences of long-term unemployment, the rise in homelessness, the imbalance between rich and poor, capital and labour, the sadistic, pseudo-moralistic assault on gay people, minorities, immigrants, single mothers, which were so brutal as to become ingrained, even after the political pendulum swung back to the 'left', under Labour. Such serious excoriation wasn't in their remit; lampooning Tory MP David Mellor for his imaginary bad breath was.

Back in 1982, in a similar spirit to *The New Statesman*, ITV had commissioned the series *Whoops Apocalypse*, written by Andrew Marshall and David Renwick, which reflected a widespread anxiety about imminent nuclear war in the Thatcher/Reagan years. For much of the eighties, this cloud of fear was so pervasive that it seemed fatuously optimistic to think that there would actually be such a thing as the nineties. But there was: a nineties few, if anyone, anticipated.

UNTROUBLED TIMES
THE 1990S

The nineties were unexpectedly glad times. Wim Wenders's *Wings of Desire*, released in 1987 and set in a Berlin divided by a wall, was based on the supposition that the wall was as fixed a future prospect as the Chinese one. In early 1989, the Soviet Union still existed, East Germany remained a dictatorship, Margaret Thatcher was still in office, Nelson Mandela in jail, Mike Tyson world heavyweight champion. By 1991, all had seen their fortunes reversed. That Tyson suffered his first shock defeat the night before Mandela was released from jail only exacerbated the sense that the world was shifting on its axis, revolving towards the light.

For those of the comedic left-field, there was the shock of the demands of wearily chanted slogans and faded T-shirts at last being met. What now? Conversely, there was a feeling, relished by some, that with the demise of the Soviet Union, the 'left' had lost its superpower representative and that liberal democracy now had the road ahead to itself – free play for the West. Francis Fukuyama published *The End of History*, in which he argued that the age of political extremism, from Nazism to Stalinism, had given way in the post-Cold War era to the 'final development' worldwide of liberal democracy. While most if not all on the left greeted the fall of the Berlin Wall with delight, there was a seed of doubt, borne out by the post-Soviet development of Russia, that the West, for which read capitalism, neoliberalism and foreign interventionism, as well as democracy, might not be the shadowless prospect some anticipated.

For now, however, there was euphoria, relief from the angst and declinism of the past two decades, which would eventually make itself felt in the world of comedy as it conflated with other worlds, like rock and roll, and became the object of mass celebration as well as mere laughter.

David Baddiel was among the first to experience the epiphany that would set him on his own particular road. He was among a number of comedians who felt clamped by the imperatives of eighties alternative comedy, whose circuit took in countless benefits and causes, whose gravity could not but add a pervasive worthiness against which the natural comic instinct baulked. In his book *Sunshine on Putty: The Golden Age of British Comedy from Vic Reeves to* The Office, Ben Thompson recounts Baddiel talking about going to a screening of *Henry: Portrait of a Serial Killer* (1986), and a woman at the Q&A session afterwards complaining, like *Kind Hearts and Coronets'* Edith D'Ascyone objecting to the amount of drinking that went on at the village public house, about the amount of violence in the film. Upon which another audience member retorted, 'Fuck's sake, what did you expect? It's not called *Henry the Elephant*, is it?' In this riposte, Baddiel found a release. 'I think it was at that point that the eighties fell away for me, or at least that seriousness . . . I was never going to be that intense again.'

Slowly, like the anxiety about nuclear war that had haunted imaginations throughout the eighties, culminating in *Threads* (1984), the eighties of *City Limits*, Red Wedge and Joy Division, the 'seriousness' to which Baddiel alluded did give way to a slow-dawning relief, to a hedonistic euphoria, one reflected in the launch of *Loaded* magazine in 1994, which sought to re-establish a laddish, strictly up-tempo sense of fun, of football, lager and 'birds' (albeit strictly inverted-comma'd) and short skirts in lieu of eighties dungarees. It was as if a Soviet-style Ministry of Taste in these matters had suddenly been disbanded. *Men Behaving Badly* (1992–8), a sitcom starring Martin Clunes and Neil Morrissey in which men behaved badly, swiftly followed.

As did *The Fast Show* (1994–7). Anxious to get past alternative eighties connotations, *The Fast Show* vowed that it would avoid overtly political content. (That said, they did feature a memorable character, a Conservative MP, Sir Geoffrey Norman, who met every accusation with a flat denial, including, when pulled over by the police and asked if he was the driver of the vehicle, 'No.' Boris Johnson must have been taking tips frontline: on a walkabout once he told a member of the public there were 'no cameras here', staring into a TV camera as he did so.) There were other indicators. Jack Dee, for example, whose exceptionally jaundiced stand-up act poured scorn on the everyday rather than politicians. When I interviewed him, we discussed our mutual love of Sam Kinison, a renegade American comedian who flew in the face of every decent liberal tenet, doing a pro-drink-and-drive bit and lambasting starving Ethiopians for not living 'where the food is at'. 'We've got deserts in America, we don't fucking live in them!' We marvelled at how and why he was able to make such appalling sentiments work as comedy.

And yet, the nineties represented a golden age for comedy not because it threw off the shackles of political correctness but because it took PC on board. The seventies were not back, any more than they were in music, despite the Stone Roses ushering in a brief return to flares circa 1990. No more would Englishmen, Irishmen and Pakistanis walk into bars. Ultimately, the 1990s would see 'political correctness', the fashionable, pejorative term of the decade, triumph and be much the better for it.

FRY AND LAURIE, ALEXEI SAYLE, FRENCH AND SAUNDERS – INFECTING THE MAINSTREAM

Stephen Fry and Hugh Laurie had become household names in the 1980s via *Blackadder*. Their sketch show, *A Bit of Fry and Laurie*, however, wasn't broadcast until 1989. Given that the duo, unlike Ben Elton, were willing to do TV adverts and given their provenance as Cambridge Footlights graduates, one might have expected from them something polished but whimsical, amusing but middle-of-the-road, the sort of comedy that wears a long scarf around its neck. Smug, perhaps. However, amid its slapstick, erudite, postmodern, fourth-wall-breaking stuff and daringly obscure parodies (of a BBC Shakespeare workshop, for example), *A Bit of Fry and Laurie* had teeth, bared and angry, especially when it came to Rupert Murdoch. In one sketch, a parody of *It's a Wonderful Life*, Fry's angel shows Laurie's Murdoch the world as it would have been had he never been born: a much better place.

Alexei Sayle, too, had to wait a long time for his own TV vehicle. The host of the Comedy Store finally got to star in and co-write *Alexei Sayle's Stuff* in 1988. Defying baggier late-eighties fashion, he stuck defiantly to his tight suit, white socks and pork-pie hats, wandering up and down the streets and humdrum byways delivering his routines like some eccentric travelling preacher. Despite adhering to leftist politics, he treated his upbringing – his parents were both members of the Communist Party of Great Britain – much as Les Dawson might, as a source of surreal, self-deprecating humour. He said that his bed was 'three inches from the ceiling because underneath it were 20,000 unsold copies of the *Morning Star*'. His comedy veered between headbutting bluntness and sketch material not a million miles away from *Python*. He never shied from impoliteness towards showbiz contemporaries whose existence offended him in any way. He positioned himself, in one monologue, as antithetical to Clive James. 'I prick pretension whereas Clive James is a pretentious prick.' But he wasn't vain – bouncing onstage as 'Steamboat Fatty', for example, only to be greeted by the dancing kiddie Mouseketeers with a 'Who is this fat bastard?'

When he was political, he was, at times, uncannily prescient. From a sketch about residents being killed by elephants falling through their lofts, he proceeded to a TV debate in which a Tory minister is challenged about 'notorious new tower blocks in Newham constructed not from high-tensile concrete but with coconut meringue'. The minister's response: 'Yes – basically the thing is this. I want to go home now to my mummy.' The Grenfell tragedy, and the pitiful political response it engendered, was three decades away.

French and Saunders, too. They'd previously appeared in *The Young Ones*, *Girls on Top* (alongside Tracey Ullman and Ruby Wax, an unsuccessful, too on-the-nose attempt to do a female *Young Ones*) and numerous episodes of *The Comic Strip*. The wheels of TV commissioning grind exceedingly slowly, and it was only in 1987 that their sketch show debuted. The alternative had become mainstream, but it had taken a while.

Like Victoria Wood, French and Saunders lampooned areas of TV-land where male comedians failed to venture: daytime TV, kids' TV and fly-on-the-wall docs in which they played, among other roles, hotel cleaners and animal welfare officers. Whereas Wood opted for inventive, baroque dialogue, however, French and Saunders preferred a more naturalistic approach, lots of mumbling and overlapping, an advanced chemistry developed through their long working relationship.

One of their best sketches was about a scatterbrained, ageing sixties child (Saunders) whose rather more straight and responsible daughter tells her to turn down the rave music she's wigging out to as she's trying to finish her homework. This inspired inversion formed the basis of Saunders's *Absolutely Fabulous* (1992–2012), which became a phenomenon like no other TV show, its very indulgence and indiscipline part of its appeal; its excess was its essence. Saunders played Edina Monsoon, who had somehow managed to form a successful PR firm, while Joanna Lumley was thankfully persuaded to play her best friend, the monstrous Patsy, a scowling goddess of toxicity who held fast to a sinecure at a fashion magazine. Julia Sawalha played the sensible daughter, Saffron.

Patsy and Edina are children of London's swinging sixties and have never stopped swinging, leading financially secure lives of daily debauchery, beginning around early lunchtime. Hardly blissful lives, however, as both are consumed with insatiable frustration,

resentment, even, while their inability to hold their champers leads
to many a slapstick pratfall as they decant themselves in and out of
taxis throughout the series. Watching other people have a good time
is no formula for comic success, and it's crucial that the pair extract
so much grief from their riotous living. And yet, at the same time,
there is a certain vicarious, Bollinger joy about their unrepentant,
ongoing drive to preserve their mode of living; not so much *24 Hour
Party People* as *24 Year Party People*.

Absolutely Fabulous mirrors a society fresh out of recession,
about to embark on a hedonistic spree. But Edina also personifies
the underlying sense of ennui engendered by Western prosperity.
Whereas her daughter Saffron is a pillar of sensible stability, Edina
is a perpetual, twitching mess of fickle dissatisfaction, pursuing then
discarding New Age fads, lacking the concentration or stamina to
see them through, or changing decor purely for the sake of change,
as bored as an adolescent surrounded by everything money can buy.
There is no evolution in *Absolutely Fabulous*, no Palace of Wisdom at
the end of their road to excess. Each week Patsy and Edina fall drunk
into the same ditch, climb out, pass out, resume at midday.

Still, few fans of *Absolutely Fabulous* shared Saffron's puritanical
disdain for the frolics of Patsy and Edina. It became somehow a part
of the world, a favourite of the people it sought to lampoon. That it
was abbreviated to *Ab Fab* was telling, since Edina felt in part like
an indictment of the sort of people who come up with abbreviations
like *Ab Fab*. There was something carefree about its very structure,
while the supporting cast seemed at times to be simply chums along
for the party, the wine freely dispensed in the home or in the office.
One episode features guest appearances by Saunders's husband Ade
Edmondson, Meera Syal, Jo Brand and Helen Lederer, as well as Jane
Horrocks, making it feel like *Last of the Summer Wine* in reverse. Still,
to complain about this is like taking a spade to a Harrods soufflé.

Moreover, this same episode features a wonderful plotline, in
which Edina is anxious that an old friend of hers, an erstwhile

arch-minimalist played by Miranda Richardson, is coming to visit with her husband (the magnificent Patrick Barlow). We see Patsy and Edina visiting them, years earlier, at their gleaming white apartment, unencumbered by regular furnishings, unsure where even to put the bottle of wine they have brought, which quite capsizes the feng shui of the room. Edina tries a bit of last-minute decluttering of her kitchen, but she needn't worry. When Richardson and Barlow arrive, it is with their baby and the bags and bags of paraphernalia that come with newborn infants.

June Whitfield was the ideal candidate to play Edina's mother in *Absolutely Fabulous* – playing a cunning variation on the 'June Whitfield' type, as straight as a knitted cardigan but with an impending battiness which belied her disingenuous put-downs of her ludicrous daughter. She was not just the best but probably the only actor for the part.

Whitfield was such a steadfast, immensely capable, in-demand presence in British comedy for over half a century that it was easy to take her for granted. Interviewed in 2013 as recipient of the Aardman Slapstick Comedy Legend Award, she related with a gentle roll of the eyes how Roy Hudd had described her as 'the comic's tart', having worked alongside everyone from Arthur Askey to Julian Clary, Wilfred Pickles to Jennifer Saunders. Starting in 1953, she played Eth in Frank Muir and Denis Norden's *Take It from Here*, her repressed 'hot-blooded' sexuality expressed in tones that fluttered around in the upper register; she was still active in 2016.

Despite her versatility, from playing a 'tart' in *Steptoe and Son*, with her temporary clutches on old man Albert, to a prim, sexless wife in *Carry On Abroad*, her essential, unassuming warmth shone through to a degree that made her feel like family to generations of TV viewers, a much-treasured symbol of continuity. She was, in the course of her long and busy career, daughter, lover, sister, wife, aunt, mother, grandmother, Everyenglishwoman, as summer-like as the month of June itself. Unpretentious to a fault, she recalled a guest appearance in the episode of *Friends* set in London, in which she was bewildered by the principal cast members of the sitcom each having their own dressing room, outside each of which stood a minder. 'Who did they think was going to attack them, the other members of the cast?'

It might have been protested on her behalf that she deserved a vehicle of her own, rather than playing foil at various times to the more wayward, less reliable likes of Tony Hancock, who leant on her impeccable professionalism, but she demurred. She didn't want to be the one who had to take the flak if the series were a flop.

Despite her unfailing modesty in the face of the awards with which she was showered, June Whitfield's career endured because she knew what she was about, knew what comedy was about and retained a sly wit that did not wither with age, as evidenced when she reprised her role as Mother in *Absolutely Fabulous: The Movie* (2016).

Absolutely Fabulous was not so much a sitcom as one year-long sketch, but as well as being extremely clever, it's emblematic of times we'll probably never get to live through again. Following the series' success, Dawn French sent her partner in comedy, Jennifer Saunders, flowers, with a note reading, 'Congratulations, you cunt.'

Jo Brand, meanwhile, consolidated her popularity in the 1990s with the Channel 4 series *Jo Brand Through the Cakehole* (1993–6). There, she demonstrated a full awareness of her actual splendour, hair gothically teased up with jars of gravity-defying gel, descending a staircase flanked by two fat male go-go dancers in cages, one wearing pink Spandex leggings. As well as her customary self-deprecation, she lampooned New Labour, whose impending abandonment of its traditional values she noted, and the creeping outsourcing of the NHS and new bureaucratic initiatives with brainstormed titles such as 'Centres of Excellence'. She would go on to create her own take on the NHS with *Getting On* (2009–12), co-created with Joanna Scanlan and Vicki Pepperdine, who co-starred as health workers on a geriatric ward.

'I became a nurse – thanks, Hattie Jacques,' Brand once remarked in a routine, but both the almost documentary-like realism and the advanced sensibilities of *Getting On* are a far cry from the quaint frolics of *Carry On Nurse*. Since Brand's Kim Wilde often cannot speak her mind, the camera dwells studiously on her countenance: those large, expressive, withering, empathetic eyes, that face a creased trove of life lived.

BADDIEL, NEWMAN, FOOTBALL, ROCK AND ROLL, OLD AND NEW

One of the great truisms of the 1990s was that comedy was the new rock and roll. This was epitomised by David Baddiel and Rob Newman playing the Wembley Arena to a previously unheard-of audience of 12,500 people in 1993. Cambridge graduates, they had teamed up with Steve Punt and Hugh Dennis for *The Mary Whitehouse Experience* (1989–92), swiftly transitioning from radio to TV. The series wasn't always as splendid as its title. The mixture of themed monologues and mini-sketches felt Footlights-ish, unable to shed a precocious air of chortling self-satisfaction. A sketch about striking teachers saw them asking for a 12 per cent rise. 'How do we get it?' they chanted. A teacher reverses the placard and shows the mathematical workings. There were instances, too, of Baddiel's relief from the need to be intense, as in a sketch which waxed amused on the topic of tramps. 'How does one become a tramp? They're always saying, "Oh, I had a bit of bad luck." But if I have a bit of bad luck, like I go to the newsagent's and it's closed, I don't go straight over to the bin and think, "I wonder if there's some food in there?" And not go home for twenty-seven years.' Newman chimed in with an impersonation of a tramp busking badly, which the duo compared to Bob Dylan.

All this was several shades of dire, but not all of it was that bad. And when Baddiel and Newman got their own series, they carried over one of their earliest efforts and by common consent their funniest work: 'History Today', in which they played a pair of very elderly academics whose TV discussions invariably descended into puerile playground insults. It's the sort of comedy that thrives on the audience knowing what's coming. So, a discussion on Romanticism and the industrial age would trigger a reference by Newman to a harrowing memoir titled *My Life as a Prostitute*, 'by your mum'. Whereupon Baddiel would retort: 'See a pond or a lake or a large puddle? That's your bed, that is. You're on the cover of *Bedwetter's Monthly*.' Timeless juvenilia, but enough to propel them to the sort of mass onstage adulation normally enjoyed by a Prince?

Certainly, Baddiel and Newman associated themselves with contemporary pop and rock in their use of house music for intros, or, in the case of their Wembley appearance, clanging, generic indie rock. They would reference the Cure, the Charlatans, Ride – big fish in the music press but esoteric to mainstream audiences. They also benefited from a shift in popular culture away from the tribal and fragmentary towards a desire for sixties-style mass gatherings, collective euphoria. This might first have been reignited by the spectacle of Live Aid, then rave culture and the pacific pop state engendered by ecstasy. It was as if comedy demanded a similar structural response, to adapt itself to the mass delirium of 'Things Can Only Get Better' times. And so, much as the Beatles were not the most important thing about their Hollywood Bowl performance, their playing drowned out as if it were negligible, so it was to a degree with Baddiel and Newman at Wembley, playing material with which the audience were as familiar as Take That fans were with their heroes' tunes, the laughter of surprise replaced by the sort of cheer that greets a greatest hit.

Baddiel and Newman would have been uncomfortable with this, deep down. But they were distracted by a growing personal animosity. They split up and went off in opposite directions. Newman would repudiate his earlier work. 'It's easy to make cold, sardonic and sneery comedy – lord knows I've fallen into the trap of doing that in the past. I've tried not to in the last decade or so,' he later said. His solo career felt like a penance, saw him tackle the same sort of radical subject matter as Mark Thomas, taking on Peak Oil, the American military-industrial complex and berating the Perrier Comic Awards since Perrier was owned by Nestlé. Baddiel, by contrast, teamed up with Frank Skinner, a partner with whom he was far more clearly at ease, for *Fantasy Football League*, broadcast on BBC2 between 1994 and 1996. *FFL* took an irony-laden look at the world of football, its missed sitters, dodgy haircuts and pre-war footage. They made dire missteps – a blackface incident discussed elsewhere in this book and another item which saw them accused, on air, by Sylvia Kristel of racism; as a star of the seventies *Emmanuelle* film series, Kristel was clearly invited on in the postmodern, laddish, wah-hey spirit of the time, but her guest appearance backfired. Generally, however, the duo established an easygoing comic ambience akin to that of a bachelor's untidy apartment, the set based on the flat the pair shared in real life; it was comedy you could flop down into of a Friday night, but put together with deceptive skill. Far lazier, more tedious footballing bantz would follow in their wake.

In my book *1996 and the End of History*, I suggested that the year represented a subconscious, collective yearning to replicate 1966, politically, musically, in football terms, with Labour leader-in-waiting Tony Blair as Harold Wilson, Oasis as the Beatles, and the England national team at the Euro '96 tournament as the 1966 World Cup winners. At the zenith of the comedy/rock and roll moment, Baddiel and Skinner teamed up with Ian Broudie of the Lightning Seeds and recorded the single 'Three Lions', a song that reflected, humourlessly and with wounded passion, on 'thirty years of hurt', marked by successive England failures at international tournaments, usually at the hands of the Germans. For those uninterested in football, the song might have felt obscene in its patriotism and sense of entitle-ment; for those who, like myself, had endured those England failures on a biannual basis since 1970, the song invoked memory pangs of intense frustration, which didn't necessarily imply a reactionary lament for the UK's decline as a world force. What's more, it was an anthem for an English flag that, given the general wave of enthusiasm for Euro '96, felt temporarily detoxified, inclusive.

The 1996 tournament saw England reach the semi-finals. They were level, in extra time; a 'golden goal' would book their place in the final. However, Paul Gascoigne, a yard or so short of pace, perhaps explained by his riotous living off the pitch, failed to connect with a cross that would have seen him tap into an open goal. England's opponents, Germany, won on penalties. Furthermore, to scotch the idea that they were a nation lacking humour, the German fans sang 'Three Lions' as the national team paraded the trophy back home, and the song reached number 49 in the German charts. A moment, for good or ill, had passed, like the ball to Gascoigne, gone astray. Lives went on. David Baddiel and Rob Newman eventually made up and became friends again.

THE TRIUMPH OF POLITICAL CORRECTNESS

There was, however, a counter-narrative to the notion of the nineties as the decade in which comedy loosened its eighties-imposed corset of political correctness, learned to laugh again, to booze, shag, talk about 'birds', lighten up on racism, give the heavy political stuff a miss. Comedy in the 1990s may not have been overtly political, was no longer alternative, with denizens of the old left-field having become mainstream household names. But it was more 'correct', in multiple, tiny ways, in its observations, its finely wrought details, its representations. Pre-eighties, pre-PC comedy was characterised by its laziness in its stereotypes, its unexplored assumptions about people of colour, women, 'gays', workers, foreigners; there was an incuriosity on the part of scriptwriters, producers and executives to explore in greater depths the lives of Britons, how they talked, behaved and felt, what idiosyncratic characters they harboured in their ranks. Characters were stock, from sharp-tongued charladies to doddery old men, to pious vicars (a stereotype later comprehensively turned inside out by *Rev* [2010–14], starring Tom Hollander), mincing, woofter-ish nancy boys, henpecking, sexless wives, busty barmaids, Jack the lads, foreigners and people of colour whose every utterance affirmed and emphasised their foreignness and racial orientation, whether Irishman, Scotsman or Pakistani. And Germans who, like Dennis Waterman's Teutonic character in *Man About the House*, were still wistful about losing the war.

There was no undoing the impact of alternative comedy, no way of rolling back to the saucy seventies. Comedians, writers, producers would have to think harder, display greater sensitivity. Far from being inhibiting, doing away with a whole array of stock characters resulted in an efflorescence of comedy which introduced fresh angles, more nuanced characters, greater diversity, better ideas, keener observation, turning over rocks that had sat unexplored for too long and letting ideas teem out from underneath. This was manifested in the brilliant *Smack the Pony* (1999–2003), among many others.

Harry Enfield was a Dick Emery for the 1990s, his use of repeated catchphrases being distinctly Emery-esque. But whereas Emery's characters came from staid, predictable stock, Enfield's creations were far better thought out and crafted, grotesque and exaggerated but hooked to recognisable aspects of real life. Kevin the teenager captured adolescence moroseness in a way never attempted before; 'You don't want to do it like that' encapsulated in a single phrase a certain kind of older English male who had managed to go about his meddling business unobserved for decades. And while Enfield may have affected to scorn political correctness, he had in his armoury such characters as Tory Boy, a zitty, blustery, repugnant little adolescent fogey based on a bad memory of young William Hague, and Mr Cholmondley-Warner (played by Jon Glover; Enfield played his colleague Grayson), a black and white throwback to a more stilted, paternalistic age, who hosted public-information films, prefaced by tootling brass and the exhortation to 'Look, listen and take heed', including perhaps the most magnificently funny riposte to archaic sexist assumptions: 'Women. Know Your Limits.' Political correctness worked. Harry Enfield was proof.

Paul Whitehouse, who made his name alongside Enfield, was one of the co-stars of *The Fast Show*, co-inaugurated by Charlie Higson. Initially, the show was indeed fast: snippet-like sketches of strange characters wandering on screen to utter their inscrutable yet irresistible catchphrases. 'You ain't seen me, right?' 'This week, I shall be mostly . . .' 'Brilliant . . .' With successive series, however, the characters were given more room to go through their inevitable motions. 'Coughing' Bob Fleming, the rustic TV presenter whose initial tickle in the throat generally descended into a hawking catastrophe; Mark Williams's competitive dad, who heckles his own son during a school Shakespeare performance; Arabella Weir's character, who makes a practical suggestion among a group of men, which is ignored, only for one of the men to make the same suggestion, which is agreed on unanimously. The letter was pleasingly feminist, but *The Fast Show* was never angrily polemical. John Thomson's jazz-club host, an oblique piss-take of *The Old Grey Whistle Test*'s 'Whispering' Bob Harris; Ted and Ralph, with its strange, unrequited infatuation between young master and older servant; or crusty Rowley Birkin, his every utterance a swill of incoherence, were but further examples of how the diktat of PC to avoid stereotyping back in the eighties led eventually to a collective release of the comic imagination come the nineties. Even when they 'did' foreigners – as in the 'Channel 9' sketch, where the weather, as read by Caroline Aherne, is always '*scorchio*' – it wasn't in some obvious 'Els Bells' *Carry On Abroad* style. The seed of Channel 9, the recognition factor, was common to anyone who took a holiday in Southern Europe at that time, idly switched on the TV set and looked on uncomprehendingly.

The fruits of the alternative comedy explosion were a long time growing, in some cases almost twenty years. It took a good while for a younger generation, with very different sensibilities, to assume their place in the new hegemony. But assume it they did. Trad hetero sitcom was displaced by *Terry and Julian* (1992) and *Gimme Gimme Gimme* (1999–2001). *Father Ted* (1995–8), being an Irish production, is technically outside the remit of this book but deserves mega-honorary mention not just for the way it reset the lexicon of the broad, laugh-tracked sitcom but also for the panache and confidence with which it presented as one of its main characters a very thick Irishman without falling foul of the accusation of dealing in anti-Irish stereotyping. *Rab C. Nesbitt*, played by Gregor Fisher, created by Scottish writer Ian Pattison, managed to take over its sixty-five episodes from 1988 the cliché of the 'see you, Jimmy' drunken Scot and build on it an immense, complex, Falstaffian creation, surrounded by a cast of characters who were born out of recognition, rather than distant assumptions about the sort of folk who dwelt in places like Govan. *Rab C. Nesbitt* was never less than erudite; at one point, Rab's wife Mary quotes Samuel Beckett in her exasperation: 'I can't go on. I'll go on.'

Or there was *Spaced* (1999–2001), created by and starring Simon Pegg and Jessica Stevenson. *Spaced* feels like a sitcom largely rooted in nineties experience, one of soft drugs, cheapish lodgings, raves and frequent trips to Blockbuster video, in which fantasy and the mundane, worn cushions of everyday, domestic reality merge. Or *The League of Gentlemen*, which premiered in 1999, which was in gestation through the nineties – the comedy troupe comprising Mark Gatiss, Steve Pemberton, Reece Shearsmith and Jeremy Dyson that was formed in 1995. It found itself hitting the headlines during the blackface furore of 2020, but it by no means deserves cancellation, such is the lurid richness and diversity of the dark flowers in its particular back garden. Set in the fictional town of Royston Vasey, named after Roy 'Chubby' Brown, a misshapen, offensive creature of comic bastardy who nonetheless had the wit to agree to appear in the show, *The League of Gentlemen* seemed to trade on soft Southern ideas about the grimness and hideous surreality of life in the North, of the morally deformed characters festering and lurking among the cobbles, ginnels, ghostly mill towns and forbidding corner shops, too insignificant to be bulldozed. This was a far cry from the authentic representation of *The Royle Family* (1998–2000); it was a feat of comic evocation, dreamlike, transcending the very idea of what comedy was, insinuating itself into other parts of the body and mind than just the funny bone. It was no surprise that the tentacles of their sensibility would reach over into more dramatic terrain. Mark Gatiss would be responsible for reboots of *Sherlock* (2010–17), *Doctor Who* (2005–) and *Dracula* (2020). As for Steve Pemberton and Reece Shearsmith, they went on to make the macabre, supernaturalist comedy-not-comedy *Inside No. 9* (2014–), though ironically, it's in this series that they created one of the most touching tributes to the spirit of bad comedy long banished from the screens: the episode 'Bernie Clifton's Dressing Room' (2018), in which they played a Little and Large-type act, Cheese and Crackers, reunited thirty years after falling out.

FROM *ON THE HOUR* TO ALAN PARTRIDGE

There is no one in modern British comedy, not even Stewart Lee, who is as deadly serious about his work as Chris Morris. Like Lee, he eschews comedy panel shows, chuckling along with his peers and making sidelong observations about current affairs or observational jokes. You would never see him interviewed on a chat show, dropping the mask of the Jeremy Paxman-type news presenter of *Brass Eye* or *The Day Today*, the hostile interrogator, and showing the world the reflective, nice, liberal bloke he is when the cameras stop rolling.

This isn't because he's a surly bastard; by every account, he's a charming and decent man. It's because he has always regarded comedy as more than just a way of raising a few cheery laughs to make us feel better and more relaxed about ourselves and the world. He seeks through his comedy to raise taboos and anxieties, explore the out of bounds at dead of night. He's unafraid of invoking death, cancer, paedophilia, psychological cruelty. He was dubbed a satirist, but his satire isn't so much about lampooning current affairs as the norms, tropes and clichés of the media environment, the way in which news is presented to give a spurious, arbitrary and undeserved sense of authority.

Moreover, he acquired, through his background in radio, a sense of how to make the best and most inventive use of the tools of the trade. Much as producers like Conny Plank and Brian Eno learned how to use the studio as a musical instrument, Chris Morris has done the same for comedy. His technical intricacy is a significant part of his genius. He has the dexterity of a hip-hop producer or a Dadaist. There is work of his which, wilfully, transcends comedy and the limits imposed by the need to maintain light-heartedness. Some of it is equivalent to that barely translatable German concept known as *Hörspiel,* a sort of radio theatre which draws on all of the medium's strengths to create hyperreal effects. As the radio historian Tim Crook said of *Hörspiel,* 'It is auditory in the physical dimension but equally powerful as a visual force in the psychological dimension.' Take the 'Temporary Open Space' monologues first broadcast on Morris's GLR show in 1993. Read by one Robert Katz, these monologues strike a desolate, gagless note, using sound and text to create a character and a situation skirting the borders of comedy, but which recall also, in their psychogeographic distress, *Robinson in Space* (1997), a cinematic meditation on the 'problem of England', with an unseen narrator.

In 1993, Peter Cook entered the Radio 3 studios in the guise of Arthur Streeb-Greebling for a series entitled *Why Bother?* Although Cook took the sole writing credit for the series, which consisted of five ten-minute programmes, his interlocutor was no mere straight man, but perhaps the one man on earth who could push Cook deepest into the forest of his comic imagination. Morris's take wasn't simply to lob gentle balls to Cook for him to run with, but to throw up startling propositions, such as that, in a forthcoming lecture, Streeb-Greebling was set to reveal 'the fossilised remains of the infant Christ'. Cook picks this up at once; the remains were the relics of several failed attempts to launch the Messiah on earth. 'A remarkable discovery in the Promised Land – by some accident, this tiny little form had been preserved perfectly – I brought it home and had it examined in my institute.' There is a feeling in *Why Bother?* that a baton is being passed from one great, soon to be late, comic to another.

Chris Morris was born in 1962 in Colchester. His father was a GP, and his was a prosperous, upper-middle-class privately educated, upbringing in an old Victorian farmhouse. It was a privileged life, but by his own account a dull one, in which he found worlds of solace in the radio, not least the Goons. He graduated from Bristol University, gaining a degree in zoology – appropriately, since there's something zoological about Morris's fascination with the human animal, as if he's the dispassionate member of some higher species, observing us. After graduating, he went on to play bass in a number of groups: another significant string in his bow, as some of his most acute parodies are musical – Pulp, the Pixies – while with *Jam* (2000) he tried to find a way of merging the usually antithetical sensibilities of comedy and music.

He moved into radio, first at BBC Radio Cambridgeshire, where he discovered the technical wherewithal to splice together spoof items during studio downtime. He gravitated to GLR and was a regular on mainstream radio in 1994. Three years earlier, however, he had joined the team of *On the Hour*, a Radio 4 parody of a current affairs show. Here he would work with Steve Coogan, Rebecca Front, Stewart Lee – and also Armando Iannucci, who was in charge of the show. Iannucci can be credited with the concept that would also inform *The Day Today*; as he put it, 'Suppose you produced a news programme which was absolutely authentic but gibberish.' This was something Morris was already doing on his GLR show, delivering fabricated, absurd news stories delivered in the brusque, polished tones of a BBC newsreader to make them ring true.

Messing with the content, messing with your head, skewing norms. *On the Hour* was adapted for television as *The Day Today* in 1994, and the team took full advantage of the new medium to parody the over-excited, self-important tone and graphics with which shows like *Newsnight* used to convince their viewers that they were being mainlined the truth, stamped with the BBC guarantee of veracity. *The Day Today* is regarded as satire, but as a rule it didn't deal in topical issues, jovial wisecracks at John Major's dullness or the peccadilloes of lecherous backbench MPs. There were exceptions: the absurd insistence that Sinn Féin's Gerry Adams's words in interviews must be spoken by an actor is referenced in an item in which the party's deputy is forced to inhale helium 'to detract seriousness from his statements'. However, it was, in general, a satire not of content but of form.

Content-wise, the gibberish headlines made for a joyful use of language and surreal juxtaposition, a rampant march of balderdash to the boinging rhythm of TV headlines. 'Portillo's teeth removed to boost pound'; 'Where now for man raised by puffins?'; 'Headmaster suspended for using big-faced child as satellite dish'; 'Bryan Ferry bathmat poisonous, say lab'; and 'Branson's clockwork dog crosses Atlantic floor'. All of this was embellished by the sort of propagandising drivel of which TV news agencies are so fond: 'Bagpiping fact into news'.

Chris Morris's news anchor parodies Jeremy Paxman, though with a few Michael Buerk-type tics thrown into the mix also. He has the air of a man who takes no nonsense, while broadcasting nothing but nonsense. 'As City markets crashed and flew off, the government tried to stabilise the economy with an emergency currency based on the Queen's eggs, several thousand of which were removed from her ovaries in 1953 and held in reserve.' He postures as a champion of truth, but he's no radical. As much as anything, he's in it for the bullying, particularly at the expense of Patrick Marber's Peter O'Hanraha-hanrahan. It's his cruel pleasure.

The show certainly stands up comedically today, while its satire, if anything, saw TV news strangely spurred into becoming more like *The Day Today*, then chastened into becoming less so, especially as satellite rivals such as Sky upped the competitive stakes. Today, however, the faux-attack dogs like Paxman and John Humphrys are no longer on the airwaves. A contemporary satire of the BBC would take it to task for its docility, its attempt to maintain balance in a world rendered lopsided by the likes of Johnson and Trump. But that's for another generation of comedians to deal with.

The year 1997 saw the launch of Morris's next project, *Brass Eye*; perfectly titled, it calls to mind programmes like *Brass Tacks*, but after a second's contemplation you realise it's a description of a useless, sightless organ. As with *The Day Today*, the credits parody the ludicrous, sledgehammer tactics that graphic designers of current affairs use to bludgeon us with the idea that TV news comes with the stamp of bona fide credibility.

Morris reprises his Paxman-esque interviewer, but this time there are underlying themes to the show: credulity, sensationalism, moral panic. He also reprises his radio prankster, certainly a man of brass balls, the sort required to exclaim 'Christ's fat cock!' when interviewing Cliff Richard, for example. Also, in the 'Drugs' episode, he shows some courage when posing as an undercover reporter pestering a dealer in an alleyway with requests for a string of non-existent stimulants such as 'yellow bentines'. What's impressive isn't just the way Morris puts himself out there in what could be a potentially hazardous situation, but also how, while doing so, he unspools a wonderful line in dialogue that lies somewhere between Edward Lear and James Joyce's *Finnegans Wake*: a prose poetry constructed from phantom fears and misapprehensions about drug use. It's the dealer you feel sorry for in this item – he's a working bloke who just wants a quiet life – rather than feeling afraid for Morris. And, if there's just a suspicion that Morris is making comedy out of desperate lives, that's compensated for back in the studio, where he turns to camera after a satisfying hit, nailing hypocrisy at the heart of the drugs debate in the media, particularly when some of the hysteria is generated by users themselves. He can handle his hit, he says, but 'what about people less stable, less middle-class, less educated than me – builders and Blacks, for example?'

The most spectacular coup in this series was Morris's success in persuading high-profile and breathtakingly gullible celebrities and politicians to read out arrant nonsense to camera – not just utter nonsense, but with non-too-subtly coded messages baked into it saying, 'This is utter nonsense.' Bruno Brookes, Bernard Manning, Noel Edmonds, Rolf Harris and Jimmy Greaves were among those warning of the danger of a new drug that hit had the street known as cake. 'It's a made-up drug,' they were told, whatever that meant, but still they didn't twig that it was a made-up drug. The most satisfying victim was Noel Edmonds, who had made a career out of prattling half-arsed non-jokes on TV and radio, fully confident that he possessed a sense of humour, as well as a pedigree as a patronising prankster of the public. But it was with a straight face that he addressed to camera the effects of cake on a part of the brain known as Shatner's bassoon.

Four years later, a special on paedophilia saw yet more celebrities duped: Dr Fox informing us that paedophiles had more in common genetically with crabs than humans, and Gary Lineker urging us to support a charity called Nonce Sense. 'Paedogeddon!' was broadcast in the midst of a national moral fever following the murder of Sarah Payne, when mobs took it upon themselves to attack the premises of paediatricians since they were obviously in on it too. The hypocritical indignation it engendered in the tabloids was predictable, as were the political opportunists, like Home Office minister Beverley Hughes, who condemned the show while confessing they'd not watched it.

Still, Morris did operate close to the line. *The Day Today* featured a brief shot of Joy Division's Ian Curtis's rotted corpse swinging from a noose. Morris would, rightly, apologise for that, having realised Curtis's daughter had watched it. Morris is conscious of boundaries. He knows there is a line. He treads around it, for sure, but he's not in comedy for the cheap sake of offence or revelling pointlessly in political incorrectness. He's audacious but with a far stronger and more active ethical sense than his more commercial comic peers, who steer clear of the areas he explores, mainly out of career self-interest and a need to ingratiate.

The year 2000 saw Morris bring *Jam* to Channel 4, an adaptation of his radio series *Blue Jam* (1997–9). Hitherto, his TV comedy had been conventionally lit. With *Jam*, Morris was set on creating a dark ambience, an atmosphere not normally considered conducive to harvesting chuckles, an audiovisually warped experience that, indeed, was in keeping with the Warp aesthetic of Aphex Twin and filmmaker Chris Cunningham. *Jam* was a blues for the unnerving sense of foreboding that lurked beneath the tranquil surfaces of the pre-millennial 1990s, an electric, washed-out blue, featuring perverse shifts in colour, tone and pitch which suggested that we were entering psychological zones, stumbling on taboos, horrors, which most of us would prefer not to dwell upon.

The opening sketch set the tone. A husband and wife sit down at the table with a best friend, played by Kevin Eldon; the visual atmosphere is sallow and woozy; the soundtrack is 'Pendulum Man', by Bark Psychosis, one of the unfunniest pieces of music ever recorded. They explain the favour they would like him to do for the sake of their son Ryan. It's of an appallingly sexual nature. The mother goes further, explains how she is sleeping with her son disguised as younger women to encourage him not to take the deviant path of homosexuality. This isn't the comedy of double takes, wrinkled noses, glances to camera or raised eyebrows; Eldon's face is a picture of coagulating horror. It's very funny indeed, but not so much side-splitting, more like your sides are bleeding pus.

Jam, in the elements it melds so grotesquely, is as near as British comedy has got to a *Gesamtkunstwerk*, a total work of art involving mixed media. The music used included Brian Eno, the Propellerheads, DJ Shadow, Low and David Sylvian. It lasted a single series. *Brass Eye* had been hampered by attempts at intervention by Michael Grade, hence Morris putting up the bridge-burning subliminal message 'Grade is a cunt' at the end of series one. He would still work in TV, however, co-writing *Nathan Barley* with Charlie Brooker in 2005 – a prophecy of a Shoreditch to come, in all its hipsterish, decontextualised, steampunked semiotic whimsy, all those cereal cafes and penny farthings. *Nathan Barley* nailed it before it even happened.

But TV and radio miss Chris Morris. Channel 4 has never been as transgressive and brave since *Jam* and *Brass Eye*. Nor radio. Nor any other comedian. We miss his solemn, morally driven, uncompromising artistic ambition, his aversion to low-hanging opportunities for laughs, which makes Morris so lethally serious, so very funny.

Alongside Morris and Armando Iannucci, Steve Coogan initially made his name with first *On the Hour* and then *The Day Today*. Alan Partridge was created in 1991, originally as a sports presenter. Coogan had down pat the flat, glib vowels of the modern walking-and-talking-to-camera broadcaster, from Fred Dinenage to Alan Parry – assured and assuring, matching the 'sports casual' appearance of his pullovers. However, he is almost surreally inept. 'Goal!' he cries, over footage of a ball hitting the back of the net. 'And again!' he declares, as the scorer immediately whacks the ball back over the line in celebration.

In these early series, Partridge was a sidekick, blushing under the sneering glower of Chris Morris's Paxman-esque host. However, with *Knowing Me, Knowing You* (1994), Coogan and co-writers Armando Iannucci and Patrick Marber decided to give Alan Partridge his own chat show, and in so doing lent him a seething, interior life of prejudices, pathologies, deep-seated insecurities and right-wing resentments constantly poking through the blandly accomplished but brittle surfaces of his safe-pair-of-hands presentational style: a lexicon of Little Englander preoccupations, ranging from an encyclopedic obsession with traffic-flow systems to homophobia. He represented the reactionary smallness of an Englishman who would have felt more in his element in an earlier era. He twitched with respectable rage, teeth constantly bared in a snarl of resentment that the world has fallen from a state of Dave Lee Travis grace, and him with it.

And then, eighteen years after *Fawlty Towers* and, coincidentally, after eighteen years of Tory rule, came *I'm Alan Partridge* (1997), another comedy series based in a hotel featuring a more modern archetype of Englishness: Alan Partridge. However, there are significant differences between Partridge and Fawlty, in the characters, the sitcoms they inhabited and the Englands they came from.

His very nomenclature represents one advance on *Fawlty Towers*, the most feeble aspect of which is Basil's surname. It's as if the creators of Coogan's character had elected to call him Alan Pratt. As for the series *I'm Alan Partridge*, it was aptly named; it's his desperate mantra. If he didn't keep chanting it, he might evaporate into non-broadcasting oblivion. He is in the potential throes of such a crisis now; his last series of *Knowing Me, Knowing You* saw him accidentally discharge a firearm into a guest, which he tries to pass off as a mishap comparable to the excreting elephant on *Blue Peter*. He's reduced to presenting a radio show in Norwich at 4.35 in the morning, the sort of slot where the hits of the seventies and eighties go to die. Desperate to get back on TV so that he can exist again, he lunches with head of BBC Television Tony Hayers, which ends in Hayers refusing to commission Partridge for another TV series, turning down his pitches for new shows ('Youth hostelling with Chris Eubank? Monkey tennis?'). Partridge, his always paper-thin filters burned out, pursues him around the restaurant with a lump of cheese.

Unable to buy the house he hoped to purchase, Partridge is caught in a quandary in the form of the Linton Travel Tavern, a roadside hotel, until such time as one of the ideas he records in memos to his assistant/slave Lynn hits the jackpot. He's a long-term resident at the hotel, the sort of transient, beige, green and formica place no ordinary resident would think of spending more time in than they would a lavatory. There is no proud Fawlty-like proprietor at the Tavern, and while general odd-job man Michael seems happy enough with his lot, when not experiencing episodic flashbacks to his army days in the car park, the manager, Susan, with her perma-smile fixed like a name badge, the constantly corpsing receptionist Sophie (Sally Phillips) and her lover Ben, always just on the right side of sardonic, have no investment in the place beyond the wage it pays.

Partridge, however, takes a strange joy in the ennui the hotel externalises, whether dismantling a Corby trouser press, perusing the porn channels, trying to game the buffet system with his big plate or taking the time to critique the size of the complimentary soap bars. The place has its attractions, among them the pretty Susan, whose glue-on politeness he takes as a cue to be overbearingly flirtatious, while he enjoys a friendship of sorts with Michael – an underling, naturally, but someone he holds in a little bit of awe on account of his army background, someone who has lived out his own grenade-flinging combat fantasies.

Fawlty Towers was much less interested than *I'm Alan Partridge* in the minutiae and mundanity of hotel life; the hotel was there as a point of congregation where classes and types could present themselves for Fawlty's disdain or fawning, depending on his social opinion of them, or issues such as psychology, Germanophobia or the Anglo-American divide could be explored via arriving guests. For Alan, however, it is a representation of an abiding, persistent, deadening British mediocrity, for which he is one of the nation's voiceover men. It's part of a hinterland of windscreen wiper fluid, astroturfing, fungal foot powder, water breaks, photocopier toner, Sue Cook, Castrol GTX jackets, China Crisis, Roger Moore, Jet from *Gladiators*, fitted kitchen suppliers, supplementary auxiliary speakers from Currys, tungsten tip screws, plywood – bland stuff, a cumulative indictment of an England's drearing in 1997, still familiar decades on.

Another dissimilarity between Alan Partridge and Basil Fawlty is that while both have excruciatingly poor social skills, unlike the frequently mortified Fawlty, Partridge is barely capable of embarrassment. Yes, when Lynn or Sophie take a peek in the contents of his top drawer he'll shut it with spectacular alacrity, but he'll quickly get over it. Whereas most of us will recall unbidden moments of our past in which we made fools of ourselves or terrible faux pas and endure a deep, frigid shudder of the bowels, Alan, whose entire history comprises such moments, is free of retrospective agonies. When a sex game with an employee involving chocolate goes wrong, there's no 'Quick! In the wardrobe!' moment when there's a knock at the hotel-room door. He answers it, in a bath robe liberally smeared in brown and a 'What of it?' expression. Basil's class consciousness has invested in him a deep sense of social shame; Alan has none.

Unlike Fawlty, who does without friends, Alan does have an urge for matey male companionship in particular ('Dan! Dan! Dan! Dan! Dan! Dan! Dan!'). He's fascinated by the condition of being a man, not quite feeling one himself. He tries to have a drink with the producers of the waterways ad he is doing, and within three-quarters of an hour is rendered insensible. The trouble is, he has absolutely no idea how to talk to people, only to talk at them, always broadcasting, and, like a broadcaster, unable to allow dead air. He is fluent in effluent.

If Basil Fawlty was a creature who would have been in his element in the 1950s, Alan's spiritual kinship is with the 1970s, the decade in which Fawlty is exiled. His crowning moment as a rock fan, he reveals, was seeing the Electric Light Orchestra at the Birmingham NEC in 1976. He is pals with Bill Oddie, star of strictly seventies comedy *The Goodies*. When lifting his spirits he sings 'Jet' by Wings. His argot is just a touch out of date for the 1990s – 'Up yours!', 'Sunshine', 'You big spastic!'

I'm Alan Partridge, like *Fawlty Towers*, is full of huge moments, etched permanently on the collective memory: the car scrawled with 'COCK PISS PARTRIDGE', his suggestions to Graham Linehan and Arthur Matthews for a slogan to modernise the appeal of Ireland ('Dere's more to Oireland dan Diss'), being incapacitated by a dead cow, the entanglement with Lynn in the telephone lead, forcing the hand of a dead man to 'sign' a new contract for him, the ill-fated attempt to nab a motorway cone, and his on-air encounter with Chris Morris's farmer, in which he endures a verbal beating that puts him back in the humble place he endured on *The Day Today*.

However, as with all Partridge productions, it is the cumulative detail that makes these episodes perennially watchable. Even in silent mode, just watching Alan's eyes dart, his jowls freeze, the various tics and signs of a furtive yet ill-concealed interior life is as constant a joy as, say, watching Basil Fawlty in the slow throes of realising that he has hold of completely the wrong end of the stick.

Also, the writing. Not just the dead-on acuity ('cracking owl sanctuary'). It's an unfiltered stream of wildly inappropriate nonsense in the tones and cadences of everyday voiceover telly speak, but it yields infinite variations: 'an infected spinal column in a bap'; as the ill-chosen narrator for a new-age cassette: 'Please relax, I can't emphasise that enough'; during sex: 'That's first class.' Not relishing the prospects for leisure boating in Norfolk in the age of global warming, Partridge alludes reassuringly to the 'pot-smoking, whore-ridden waterways of Amsterdam' in the Hamilton's Water Break video. It's an unrelenting stream of thoughts conceived in the mouth. Even when he has run out of words, sitting in a car with Lynn, his jaw continues to rotate, his lips move – 'talk-ing'.

Lynn is superbly played by Felicity Montagu. Part Manuel in her willingness to be at Alan's beck and call at the snap of his fingers, part Polly in her protectiveness of Alan and willingness to help haul him out of scrapes, no part Sybil at all, Lynn endures low wages, total inconsiderateness and brusqueness from her employer because she loves him, brooding with jealousy when he takes an interest in other women. However, it's a far more complex love than the mere amorous, unrequited longing of Ruth Madoc's Gladys for Simon Cadell's Jeffrey in *Hi-de-Hi!* It's maternal, servile, platonic, sibling-like. She gets to occupy the void left in Alan's life that comes from his fundamental difficulty in respecting women or forming relationships with them. Her life, her terrible life with Alan, is the only one she wants – 'intimate but affection-free', as scriptwriters the Gibbons brothers put it. Put upon she may be, but she is strangely proud and strong-willed, with an acerbic, judgemental eye for the foibles of others. She is not among the ranks of the blessed meek.

Montagu is responsible for a number of distinctive comedy creations: as Bridget Jones's horrible colleague Perpetua, or the vicar's wife with the substantial, heaving bosom in Julia Davis's *Nighty Night* (2004–5). However, Lynn outdoes them in both depth and longevity. In a 2019 interview with Alice Jones in the *i* newspaper, Montagu describes how she 'lives' her characters, building up for them rich backstories in her head, forming such a strong association with them that when Lynn's mother was killed off at the beginning of the second series of *I'm Alan Partridge*, she felt genuine grief. In the same interview, disappointingly, Montagu is disparaging of the #MeToo culture in somewhat histrionic terms – 'It's so PC out there at the moment, it's like the Ku Klux Klan.' And yet a character like Lynn's is precisely the product of a more carefully thought-through approach in lieu of the lazier, stock approaches and attitudes PC came to drive out.

To magic up genuine laughs from Alan and Lynn's relationship does everyone involved credit, though it is interesting that for the *This Time with Alan Partridge* series twenty-two years later, the writers felt obliged to give her a little more agency, a shadowy touch of the Lady Macbeths, her devotion to Alan hardened into a lifelong compulsion. 'Lynn would lay down her life for Alan,' Coogan once said. 'She's like a lioness. She is a loyal servant to her master but Lynn is a bit more manipulative of Alan than he realises.'

And yet, at the very end of *I'm Alan Partridge*, there is a moment of joy of sorts between them, as they tidy up following a disastrous party involving a racist guest, a drunken Michael and Susan finally blowing her top and serving Alan notice to quit the hotel. With everyone gone, Lynn has Alan to herself; they tidy up together to the chimes of the theme to *Black Beauty*. England, old England rolls strangely on.

There were further iterations of Partridge – a second series in 2002, with Alan living in a caravan following a breakdown, which felt a little broad at the time because it retained a laugh track, considered passé by many after *The Office*. Removed from that context, it has many good moments, however ('Stop getting Bond wrong!'). The character then fell into abeyance as Coogan began to pursue other projects, including a career in cinema. Following a BBC mocku-mentary, *Anglian Lives* (2003), recounting the life of Partridge, Alan disappeared for several years. You sensed Coogan's interest diminish-ing in the character with every 'A-ha!' hollered at him every time he ventured out into the high street.

Alan Partridge was revived when brothers Rob and Neil Gibbons sent the production company Baby Cow scripts reimagining the character still hanging on to his broadcasting career at North Norfolk Digital Radio. The results were broadcast on YouTube in 2010, then on Sky as *Mid Morning Matters with Alan Partridge*, and are among his best work. This is a modified Alan – no longer a 'homosceptic' after a positive encounter with Dale Winton, he is experiencing stirrings of 'woke'-ness, though mainly to preserve what hope he has of a future in the media. The Gibbons Partridge has moved with the times but remains his essential self, with added wrinkles, a constant drivel of asides which betray a character still hostage to all his old issues. Sidekick Simon (Tim Key) is his studio dogsbody, an unpaid intern lacking Alan's misplaced self-assurance, whom Alan dominates and intimidates, while regarding him as a great mate. *Scissored Isle* followed in 2016, showing Alan extending into other areas, including that of confrontational investigative reporter. It was never that Alan had any interest in or aptitude for this sort of work; empty and imitative, he simply considered this was the sort of work a wide-ranging broadcaster should be doing.

This had been preceded by a book, then a film, in which Alan was cast in an almost heroic mould, forced to act as a negotiator in a hostage situation, allowing some of his *Bravo Two Zero* fantasies to be fulfilled. And then, in 2019, Alan returned to mainstream TV, on the *One Show*-esque *This Time with Alan Partridge*. Much as the second series of *I'm Alan Partridge* fazed some viewers due to its laugh track, *This Time* initially felt odd for its lack of any studio audience, let alone studio laughter. However, despite the relative lack of big comedy bombshells of old, its mix of location items and Alan's blundering attempts at chemistry with co-host Jennie Gresham (Susannah Fielding) won over most sceptics. Again, Alan professes to have evolved in his sexual politics, beginning one episode riding into the studio in an open-top car accompanied by some 'dolly birds'. However, this is quickly revealed to be part of a theatre piece in protest at sexism, with one of the 'birds' revealed to be a 'shaved boy' named Peter.

Despite Alan's feminism, however, as co-host with Jennie he's constantly verbally manspreading, cutting across her, blurting thoughts which would be better left locked deep in his head than aired on TV. Her face is a picture every time he utters a gaffe, gulping as if swallowing a grenade, constantly forced to rearrange her expression to maintain BBC light entertainment equilibrium.

The longevity of Alan Partridge is extraordinary. Contrast that with Basil Fawlty, who would, if still alive, be in his late eighties. He all but disappeared, revived just twice after 1979, both cornily – in 2006, Cleese for a song titled 'Don't Mention the World Cup', to coincide with the tournament taking place in Germany, and in 2016, in a Specsavers advert, reprising the bit in the 'Gourmet Night' episode when he gives his car a damned good thrashing. As for Partridge, we shall grimly enjoy what he makes of England now that his Brexit dreams have come true.

THE ROYLE FAMILY, REALISM AND THE DECLINE OF THE LAUGH TRACK

When viewing the playback of the pilot of *The Royle Family*, Manchester comedian Caroline Aherne, who created the show along with Craig Cash and Henry Normal, was so horrified that she offered to pay to have it binned. Thankfully, the prospective bill for doing so was so hefty that she demurred. The show took one or two terrible shellackings on its first broadcast, notably from the *Guardian* writer Charlotte Raven. Her takedown was gleefully reprinted in full in a paperback edition of the show's scripts. Despite Aherne's lack of faith in the first episode, she and Cash had the vision, tenacity and courage to fight against the BBC when they tried to insist that the show had a laugh track, which would have been ruinous.

The Royle Family represents authoritatively the people it depicts. This is enhanced by the use of 16 mm film and a single camera rather than the artifice of studio lights and multiple angles. The characters aren't creatively exaggerated, or saddled with dramatic licence. They aren't idealised, nor are they patronised. The sense of authenticity is most evident in the accents, deeply ingrained as they are: the way docile Dave practically drools his dialogue, or how Denise's utterances, which can barely be bothered to crawl out of her mouth at times, are tinged with nicotine, or the rasp of Jim's every exclamation, rich with a lifetime's bad living.

The Royle Family is of a piece with the untroubled nineties. It's a comedy about a low-income household, dependent on benefits but with no Ken Loach-style tears of rage or despair at their poverty or lack of opportunity. Their means and their pleasures are modest, but they exude a cosiness that can be bought for the price of a pack of teabags, a telly and an old sofa. There's something universal about the company they keep one another in the warm blaze of the cathode rays. There's a scene in *The Crown* featuring the Queen, Princess Margaret and the Queen Mother crowded on a sofa, gazing with square eyes at their rented TV set, which reverberates with irony to fans of *The Royle Family* but does illustrate the commonality of British life they represent.

The Royle Family was a show in which nothing happened, more than twice, in every episode. Plenty was said, little was done; no one got into a tricky situation; no stranger or unexpected event occurred which threatened to upend their lives. The only dramatic rumblings are of digestive systems. It's significant that its actors were drawn from the world of soap – Sue Johnston and Ricky Tomlinson had been husband and wife in *Brookside*, while Geoffrey Hughes (Twiggy) played Eddie Yates in *Coronation Street*. *The Royle Family* was for those who liked the quieter, less melodramatic passages of *Coronation Street*, the soap as opposed to the opera – those moments when you found yourself on your settee staring fondly at ordinary folk in inconsequential mode. Why not make a series that was composed almost entirely of such moments? Ambient comedy?

Craig Cash and Caroline Aherne would go on to narrate *Gogglebox* (2013–), a show about ordinary people watching TV, but at least in *Gogglebox* the couples, friends and families featured did actually engage with and discuss the shows. In *The Royle Family*, the TV is a constant but background drone, occasionally audible during a conversation, the family staring at it, watching and not watching, as if it were an open fire, functioning essentially to provide half-light and warmth. Arguments erupt, they bicker, but these pungent moments dissolve quickly into the air, like one of Jim's farts.

The theme tune, Oasis's suitably mundane 'Half the World Away', could be young Antony's (Ralf Little) internal monologue, with its vaguely restless lyrics. He is the one who does eventually get out and get on, first with the rock group he's managing, even taking them to London, to the derision of Jim, who has never been to London, then acquiring a girlfriend from a 'higher' social stratum and getting himself a job that involves a suit. Again, however, he doesn't speechify dissatisfiedly about wanting to get on, the way Bob Ferris in *The Likely Lads* might. He merely gravitates, over time. In the meantime, he is as happy as any family member to settle into the plumped-up torpor of his own chair, adjacent to the rest of the family. This is a family absolutely at ease with one another in the upholstered nest of their own company.

Cash was the son of a joiner who grew up in Stockport; Aherne was brought up in Manchester. They were of Northern working-class stock, which was less of a rarity in the comedy world back in the 1990s. Not that *The Royle Family* is exactly a proud representation of salt-of-the-earth Mancunians. There is a division of labour within the family, with put-upon Sue Johnston as Barbara Royle and dogsbody son Antony reluctantly doing most of it. Aherne's Denise is idle in the extreme, something father Jim has the gall to observe, sitting in his own throne of indolence, only discomfited when his underpants creep up his arse crack, the result of shifting his buttocks when het up. ('These underpants cost a quid and I've got 70p of them up me arse.') Much of the little that happens pertains to Jim's backside, his flatulence, his bowel movements. Lesser scriptwriters might have gone for a storyline in which Jim tries to turn over a new leaf, with hilarious consequences, or in which Denise tries to give up smoking, only to drive everyone up the wall with her withdrawal symptoms. Granted, there is the episode in series two in which Barbara reaches the end of her tether and walks out, but of course she returns, and after some desultory patching up involving Jim agreeing to make a cup of tea, everything returns to normal, the old fault lines; something ventured, nothing gained. Back to the settee.

The determination to dispense with a laugh track as well as a studio audience was vital too, inasmuch as the scriptwriters didn't have to conform to the artifice, the spiked dialogue of tradcom, in which a gag or half-gag has to be uttered by one of the cast every ten seconds, in violation of the actual, natural rhythms of domestic conversation. This is very noticeable when you see the *Royle Family* Comic Relief specials, which take place before a live studio audience. It's a grisly glimpse at what might have been if the BBC had had its way.

Daringly, *The Royle Family* shows the characters cracking their own jokes and laughing heartily at them, Jim in particular. But these aren't really the jokes, funny as they can be; they're observational moments. They're in the script because that's the sort of joke a bloke like Jim would make and the sort his family would laugh at. Much of our own laughter derives from banal, Beckettian passages of silence and repetition. Barbara to neighbour Joe, who has badly injured his fingers in a cheese-grating accident, and whom she feels could do with a biscuit: 'Do you want a Club for later? Antony, go and get Joe a Club for later.'

Norma/Nana, played by the superb Liz Smith, previously best known for Peter Tinniswood's *I Didn't Know You Cared* (1975–9), is an exquisitely observed type of old lady, not necessarily Northern in origin – she reminds me of one of my own grandmothers, London-born. From her piety and strange non sequiturs ('I don't like to root, not on the wedding day') and her immense nosiness, culminating in the woman-crush she develops on Valerie, mother of Antony's girlfriend, to her bristling, prim airs to her naughty indulgences and the way she insists on relating none-too-scintillating anecdotes to each family member in turn, she is very possibly the finest and truest old lady in British sitcom.

It's one of the show's great achievements that Jim doesn't come across as an offensively negative caricature. He is, after all, bone idle, useless at grafting – as seen when he and Twiggy attempt to strip wallpaper – and a burden to his wife. However, he earns his place on the throne as king of the Royles through the Falstaffian energy he devotes to everything but getting off his arse. He warms the room, and for all his petty, temporary rages he exudes a funda-mental joy that comes especially to the fore when it's time to get the banjo out for a sing-song. Much is said in *The Royle Family* but much is unsaid – all of which makes it excusable when the pregnant Denise's waters break in the bathroom, and Jim's emotions gush out too, in a lengthy declaration of all the love between father and daughter that runs like an underground river throughout the series. This is the difference between *The Royle Family* and, say, Mike Leigh's *Abigail's Party*, which itself makes hay of the gruelling banality of British small talk. In *Abigail's Party*, we are meant to feel contempt for most of its characters; it's the function of one woman in the play, the tall, posh lady, simply to regard them with silent horror. With *The Royle Family*, there is mutual love, and love on the part of the viewers. Small wonder that, once the three series had ended, they would go on to become BBC TV's go-to Christmas family, for a series of one-off specials. They are not emblems of working-class virtue or a haw-haw-ing satire on working-class vice. They say but don't say, 'Here we are, this is who we are. And we shall not be moved.'

FROM REALISM TO SURREALISM

Much of the post-*Python* sketch comedy would tend towards the troupe's 'straighter' aspects, using absurdism in a cleverly logical manner to make a rational point, such as Mitchell and Webb's takedowns of conspiracy theorists and homeopaths. Surrealism, or more accurately Dadaism, in all its wilfully anti-programmatic randomness, as evidenced in Milligan's *Q* and early *Python*, its juxtaposition of seemingly unrelated elements to produce bizarre compounds, blossomed again with the emergence of Vic Reeves and Bob Mortimer. Reeves, aka Jim Moir, had been become acquainted with the Dada movement at art college and would later present a BBC4 show on the topic. This was evident in sketches like the 'Living Carpets', whose headwear recalls the masks the Dadaists wore in their wilfully provocative theatre presentations.

Dada shared with the Futurists a love of outrage, while it was also influenced by Cubism. Dada was born in 1916 out of rage with the obscene mass slaughter of World War I. Its artistic response was similar to that of Milligan to the senselessness and tragedy he witnessed while on service in World War II. The Dadaists themselves took refuge in neutral Zurich, where they inaugurated themselves at a cafe nightclub, the Cabaret Voltaire. Embracing primitivism, performance, sculpture, stream of consciousness, poetry produced by cut-up techniques, cinema and photomontage, Dada was a fertile expression of a nihilistic age, tearing up the world and its contents with disgusted gusto and hurling the pieces back in its face. Although they were mischief-makers, the Dadaists were, according to those who witnessed their meetings, not over-endowed with what we British would classify as a sense of humour.

With *Vic Reeves Big Night Out* (1990–1), Reeves concocted an elaborate nonsense, couched in the mediocre razzle-dazzle and pizzazz of the low-budget light entertainment fare on which he as a lad would have been forced to subsist. He redefined 'variety' to mean any old junk thrown together, from foodstuffs to the stuff of broom cupboards, a randomness that exceeded the merely wacky, that was completely unmoored from the usual confines of performance comedy. A song celebrating smells: 'I love the smell of manure . . . I love the smell of Frank Muir'; the helmeted Man with the Stick, who carried objects on the end of his stick; Bob Mortimer inserting a pen attached to a pipe into an onion – all this was sheer Dada, redolent of Max Ernst's *Celebes* or the rubber gloves that were a recurring motif in de Chirico's landscapes.

There was one vital difference, however, with Reeves and Mortimer, not just from Dada but also from Milligan and *Python*: there was no rage about Vic and Bob. There was none of Milligan's atheistic disgust with humankind, or *Python*'s underlying, humanistic despair. Vic and Bob represented pure, weightless fun, uninhibited by missionary purpose but generally untainted by any of the unreconstructed dodginess which age has revealed in Python and Milligan in patches. With Python, it was essential that they never so much as smirked at their own material. With Vic and Bob, the opposite is true. Theirs is the comedy of smiles; it's essential that they be grinning the whole time, exuding levity, joy, absolute free play.

Vic and Bob chimed in nicely with the 1990s, which was, for British and Americans at least, the most euphoric and light-hearted decade since records began, a time in which for all its tribulations, existential dread had, temporarily at least, been lifted with the end of the Cold War. Comedy blossomed after the trials and concerns that had given rise to the 'alternative' scene, but Vic Reeves and Bob Mortimer were no restoration of the 'pre-PC' days. There was no relapse into lazy habits; rather, they gave vent to limitless imagination. All of this was evident on *Shooting Stars* (1993–2011), in which they sashayed round the over-lit vacuous chasm of modern celebrity culture, their hapless celeb guests putty in their hands, put through the mill of ridiculous quiz rounds such as the 'true or false' game ('True or false – mice change their appearance on Saturdays so that they can watch *Grandstand* without being bothered by cats'), try to recognise popular songs rendered by Reeves in the 'club style', have Reeves rub his thighs at them if they were considered sexy, an act so obviously off-kilter as to evade charges of sexism.

In terms of durability, it might be that future or even present younger generations may be puzzled by some of their humour and its references to Frank Muir, or Vic Feather, or *Grandstand*. As it is, they are loved in a way few others of their generation are, especially Bob Mortimer. His appearances on *Would I Lie to You?* are masterpieces of invention/anecdotage in which he has variously claimed to perform his own dental surgery, be a qualified dog masseur and to break eggs into his bath, a tip he learned from fellow Middlesbrough man Chris Rea. What is remarkable is how many of these tales turn out to be true; there is about Mortimer a supremely calibrated comic mind, combined with a guilelessness, an absence of cynicism. And as he tells his tales, he laughs – the laughter of a deep, uncomplaining peace with this world.

GOODNESS GRACIOUS ME AND THE STALLED RISE OF ASIAN COMEDY

Lack of Asian representation in cultural and sporting fields was once often met with the reply, 'But they don't come forward.' But who would wish to 'come forward' into such casually discriminatory worlds? However, the mid-nineties at last scotched the idea that it was the fate of British Asians to be passive, peripheral players in their own society.

Goodness Gracious Me (1996–2001) was long overdue. Its best-known sketch is 'Going for an English', in which a group of Asians go to an 'English' restaurant, treat the waiter with boorish contempt, order the 'blandest item on the menu' and generally reverse the treatment meted out by curry-and-lager-chugging lads on Saturday nights immemorial. This was a step up from a Rowan Atkinson monologue, the previous comedic word on the subject, in which he brownfaced as an elegant and sympathetically pained Indian waiter politely laughing along to diners' jokes: 'Yes, indeed, I will "popadom" on the table.' It was only unfortunate that the biggest laughs Atkinson got were when he broke off to bark at his staff in Atkinsonian Indian-ese.

Having married into a Sikh family in the 1980s, I had some insight into lifestyles of which I might otherwise have known little. Particularly funny for me was Meera Syal as a sultry, would-be man-eater, confident she could entrap any male with the 'timeless dance of seduction', before demonstrating the awkward, not terribly seductive hops and hand movements of the bhangra dance. Also, the Indian mother who deplores anyone spending any money on practically anything when she could run it up herself simply using a 'small aubergine'. Or the proud father who insisted on the Indian origin of all things ('Superman? Indian. Where else can a man run faster than the train?'). All this was not just funny but authentic, as was the smattering of non-English dropped into the dialogue, particularly 'chuddies' (underpants). Happily, the show didn't suffer mere niche appeal; it was as well that it was mainstream-broad in places. It was widely popular and made stars of Syal and Sanjeev Bhaskar in particular, though respect is due to co-stars Kulvinder Ghir and Nina Wadia, as well as my friend Sharat Sardana, who died aged forty in 2009 and who, with his co-writer Richard Pinto, was responsible for much of the show's most memorable material, including the 'Going for an English' sketch.

Sadly, once *Goodness Gracious Me* finished its run, commissioning editors seemed to decide that Asians had had their show and therefore had no further need to complain of under-representation. It's only relatively recently, with shows such as the brilliant, audaciously disconcerting *Man Like Mobeen* (2017), that the stories of British people of colour, told by British people of colour, have reappeared on our screens.

SATIRE IN THE UNTROUBLED NINETIES

How fared satire in this untroubled decade? *Spitting Image* took its last bow in 1996, as viewing figures declined. The 1990s was an altogether different decade from the 1980s, less tribal, building towards a crest of euphoria that would see Tony Blair elected as Labour leader a year after the show finished. As much as anything else, politics would become blander post-Blair; younger, smarter, more plausible estate-agent types would gradually emerge in lieu of the ageing, caricaturable gargoyles of a previous generation.

That said, in the 1990s, *Have I Got News for You*, hosted by Angus Deayton and featuring as team captains *Private Eye* editor Ian Hislop and comedian Paul Merton, was often uneasy viewing, with a confrontational edge that distinguished it from later, rival shows like *Mock the Week*, in which comedians delivered satirical set pieces which could seem smug. The 1990s was its heyday; despite the derisory contempt it exuded, particularly from Hislop, it had something about it of the lairy glee of the decade as a whole, for the West a peaceful and prosperous time relatively speaking, lapping about in the End of History hiatus.

Random nineties moments: the US president promising to 'sort out' the Ulster problem, someone telling us how to run the country causing great upset, said Hislop, 'because that's the Germans' job'. Doubtless that jibe about the EU felt harmless enough in 1992, when our membership of that body was safe as houses. Tory sleaze was the political order of the day in the 1990s; an accumulation of it would bring them down the way Profumo helped do for them in the early 1960s. Minister Alan Clark, for example, hit the headlines for bedding both the wife and the daughter of a judge, James Harkness. *HIGNFY* highlighted a quote from the daughter, regarding her liaison with the senior Tory: 'All I got were a few minutes of sex. I remember feeling dirty. He made me feel like a dog. There was no tenderness, no love. He came round the next night and I slept with him again.'

HIGNFY in the 1990s was at once cosy and edgy, giving house room not just to Boris Johnson but also to other characters who would gravitate from the eccentric to the dangerously unhinged. Sportscaster turned conspiracy theorist David Icke is invited on the show. 'We need a miracle, David,' says Merton, as they fall behind to Hislop's team. Happy days. 1995, and there's a fresh-faced Alex Salmond, who later went on trial for sexual misconduct charges, only to be acquitted. But then there was Paula Yates, who, in one of the show's least cosy moments, tries to give a joshing Ian Hislop the evil eye; he had recently made certain remarks about her breast enlargement surgery. 'Don't even look at me, you sperm of the devil.' 'Even your insults emanate from the genitals!' retorts

Hislop, the audience on his side. Yates died in 2000 of a heroin overdose.

1996, and there's Charles Kennedy, a convivial man whose self-deprecating geniality makes his party, the Liberal Democrats, come to seem a more left-of-centre option than the authoritarian New Labour. Following a battle against alcoholism, he died, too soon, in 2015. Martin Clunes and Neil Morrissey appear, amiable paragons of the decade's laddism. Peter Stringfellow is invited on and teased for his sixteen-year-old girlfriends. Piers Morgan unwisely attempts to follow in Paula Yates's footsteps by trying to pick a fight with Hislop. Having asked why people find it funny when Eddie Izzard uses the word 'jam' but not him, Hislop points out to Morgan that 'people like' Izzard. 'Don't try the popularity line with me, Hislop. Do you like him? Does anyone like him?' Morgan asks the audience. In their response, they indicate that they do like Ian Hislop – rather a lot, in fact. But what might seem to be a humiliating setback somehow only abets Morgan's eventual ascent to transatlantic stardom. He thrives somehow on ignominy.

The photo round shows an old, black and white image of a cavalry man splayed across the rear end of a horse. Suggestions are invited for captions. A returned Paul Merton offers, 'Don't take a photo of me now, I'm fucking a horse.' He may have felt the show was 'in a rut' but it was absolutely made for him, and he it; it's the element that's perfect for his quickfire, reactive humour, even if there are stretches where he seems bored and detached from proceedings and indifferent to its political component.

1997: Labour win by a landslide, and Hislop gloats openly in front of disgraced Tory MP Neil Hamilton and his wife Christine. 'The most brilliant evening of television I have ever seen in my whole life,' says Hislop of the BBC's election coverage. 'Did you stay up for Portillo?' he asks, of the MP renowned as a Brussels-baiting 'bastard' who lost his seat but successfully recast himself in the guise of a thoughtful and amiable broadcaster.

By 1996, *Have I Got News for You* had already been broadcast for six years. Hislop, Merton and host Angus Deayton were the show's perfect triumvirate. Despite the thousand cuts it administered in its heyday, and despite the edge it retained over other satirical UK shows, there remains an uneasy sense that institutions like *HIGNFY* are not really determined to tear the country a radical new arsehole but rather to feast, week in, year out, decade in, decade out, on a reliable flow of folly, humbug, hypocrisy, over-promoted buffoons and out-and-out silliness. In the economically cosy and pacific nineties, especially in the pre-social-media age, the clamour for serious social change was barely audible. In our own, disaffected era, it is much more so. Still, however, it is the same set of faces in *HIGNFY*'s chairs, men settling into middle age and not exhibiting any great, fundamental desire to upset the applecart, merely to highlight the odd bad bit of fruit. When radical change actually does rear its imperfect head, it, too, must be mocked as mercilessly as the rottenness it seeks to supplant, for satire must have no favourites; this is what it does and this is why its ability as an agent of change is so limited.

Indeed, too good governance carries with it perils of its own for the satirists. In the sixties, there was genuine fear at *Private Eye* that Harold Wilson's incoming Labour government would be so worthy as to deprive them of the rotten targets they had feasted on in the Satire Boom, the Macmillan/Douglas-Home years. This was followed by genuine relief when they realised the Labour government was quite capable of yielding a plentiful supply of venality and incompetence of its own, even inebriation in the form of perpetually 'tired and emotional' foreign secretary George Brown.

The 'nineties' were in decline by 1998, as the political, cultural and sporting euphoria of the middle of the decade began to dissipate, supplanted by what musician Tricky described as 'pre-millennial tension'. This culminated in the Y2K bug scare, but the glitch was successfully anticipated; planes did not come crashing down from the sky when 2000 arrived. New Year's Eve brought no sense of imminent catastrophe – the skies remained blue and the comedy drifted steadily in the right direction, out of its Dark Ages, into an emergent new light.

CRUELTY AND KINDNESS
THE NOUGHTIES

Catastrophe did strike very early in the twenty-first century, but British civilisation did not fall – rather, it fell prey to a vague sense of existential boredom and a political mood of disillusion born of increasingly grudging support for a Labour Party that failed to live up to the delirious sense of optimism of election night in 1997. The turn of the millennium lacked the moral impetus and sense of hope and impending elation of the turn of the previous decade, with walls collapsing, Mandela freed. The sour fruits of this tendency were varied in quality; however, following on from *The Royle Family*, there were also immense feats of naturalism in the field of sitcom, nuanced, wise, hilarious, affectionate comedies which seemed to consign the sitcom laugh track, and all the artifice it engendered, to permanent obsolescence.

In two fell strokes, 9/11 shattered the placid complacency of the End of History. It brought the illusion of eternal global peace to a violent, sickening halt. In the coming days, there was talk of a jihad-related World War III, a perma-winter of fear. The world was perceived to have been transformed into a dreadful, darker place. Our lives and carefree behaviours would be altered beyond recognition.

On 10 September 2001, the schedules had included *Never Mind the Buzzcocks*, a repeat of *Birds of a Feather* and *'Orrible*, a debuting sitcom written by and starring Johnny Vaughan as a chirpy, ducking-and-diving West London cab driver. Much as some said there could be no poetry after Auschwitz, could there be comedy after 9/11? Could we ever again chuckle as Mark Lamarr presided over a panel trying to pick out the former Paper Lace bassist from a line-up? Or smile with cosy familiarity at Sharon and Tracey's 'chance'd be a fine thing'-style dialogue? Would we ever even come to appreciate, undistracted, *'Orrible* – the *Minder* of the twenty-first century, potentially?

However, much as Tony Blair was re-elected twice more, the nineties spirit persisted. The hole blown in the fabric of Western culture by 9/11 was stitched up rapidly. The Iraq War happened but not to 'us'. Light entertainment resumed its trajectory with *Pop Idol*, the death knell for pop music as it was known in the twentieth century. As for *'Orrible*, it was cancelled after one series. Vaughan put the problem in a nutshell in 2004: it was 'shit'.

Since the 1920s, decades had tripped easily off the tongue and assumed their successive identities as instant signifiers sprang to mind. The twenties, thirties, forties, fifties, sixties, seventies, eighties, nineties, the . . . noughties? The decade feels nondescript, not so much because nothing happened but because cultural activity was so diffuse, so diverse, that it left a hollowness at its centre, a lack of high-quality common denominators. The only sure means of recognising the passage of noughties time was by the size of the mobile phones.

In rock, the corollary to the manufactured, point-missing pop generated by *Pop Idol* was 'landfill indie', a series of determinedly orthodox, retrograde guitar bands, the equivalent of trad-jazzers in the 1960s. *Two Pints of Lager and a Packet of Crisps* (2001–11) could be described as landfill comedy. It reflected the desultory mood of the time. Much of it featured characters sitting, talking, getting slowly drunk, as if waiting for something to happen; when it did, it was often more soap-operatic than comic (shootings, relationship break-ups). Created by Susan Nickson and set in Runcorn, it starred, among others, Ralf Little and Sheridan Smith, both of whom had appeared in *The Royle Family*, which invited adverse comparisons.

In some respects, *Two Pints* was leading edge, with its serio-comic tone, as well as interactive elements, such as the end of series eight, when the audience were asked to vote on a plot outcome. It also incorporated blooper and outtake episodes into the main body of the series, as well as DVD extra-style interviews involving cast members and crew, lending the show a further 'reality' dimension. It also took scatology to impressive new levels, such as the episode in which Gaz wanks himself thin.

That apart, its gags, pace and dialogue felt like a throwback to the seventies – surprisingly, given the youth of its creator, born in 1982. 'You'd make a good student . . . being such a great big tart!' could have been delivered in *The Liver Birds*. Or Jonny telling his mate, 'I'll hurt you – I know feng shui.' Such were the fields of corn through which viewers were invited to run on a weekly basis. But run with it they did. The series lasted between 2001 and 2011. It felt impossible to watch BBC3 for an hour without colliding with an episode of *Two Pints of Lager and a Packet of Crisps*. It represented continuity, companionship, fictional flatmates for many in uneventful but vaguely fraught times.

However, the noughties also saw a slew of comedy through which ran a conspicuous streak of cruelty.

Take Sacha Baron Cohen. *Da Ali G Show*, first broadcast in 2000, was an instant sensation. Although he was a resident of Staines, Ali G was decked out in the paraphernalia of what might pass for a young male Brit with a distant, immersive obsession with US hip-hop culture. He passed, too, in his role as spoof interviewer, for the sort of vacuous would-be hipster who might front a flashy, fast-cut Yoof TV show, certainly in the eyes of interviewees/victims like Rhodes Boyson, Paul Daniels, Mohamed Al-Fayed and astronaut Buzz Aldrin. You could see his interviewees regarding Ali G with a mixture of bemusement and strained politeness at his idiotic line of questioning, their elderly opinion of youth culture low enough to think Ali G might be a plausible representation of it. If slighted, Ali G would ask of his victims, 'Is it because I is Black?' Here was where Cohen showed his genius in evading, by the tiniest of margins, political incorrectness. In his goggles and garish trackies and the hue of his skin, he might just about pass for Black and, as he calculated, none of his guests ever dared challenge him on his racial orientation.

Still, when Ali G interviewed perfectly nice members of the public, including a pleasant woman attempting to teach him Welsh ('Now the people at this university might all sound like divs but that is because they are speaking the language of Wales'), you felt a pang for some of his victims. This was more pronounced with Baron Cohen's character Borat, as evidenced in his movie *Borat: Cultural Learnings of America for Make Benefit Glorious Nation of Kazakhstan* (2006). Again, Borat courts offence but evades the accusation of xenophobic mockery of the nation of Kazakhstan by adopting a make-up which no Kazakh would recognise as resembling, let alone caricaturing, themselves, making umbrage harder to take. Instead, he trades on Western ignorance of what a Kazakh would look like, while his broken, heavily accented English allows him to get away with terrible comments, including appallingly anti-Semitic ones, for which, again, Baron Cohen gets a pass, being himself Jewish.

Borat's encounters were increasingly with regular people – the elderly, sometimes. More than once, interviewing older men who stated that they were retired, he replied in his 'Kazakh' accent, 'You are a ree-tard?' and, well, I wouldn't be happy if that had been my dad. Sometimes, the niceness of his American hosts/victims seemed not to warrant his duping of them. Baron Cohen as Borat always exposed himself, in terms of attire and situations mere mortals would find too mortifying to endure on screen – sporting a mankini, or wrestling furiously with his obese, naked sidekick. I laughed; often, however, I felt like I was revisiting the laughter of the schoolyard, in which 'divs' and 'ree-tards' featured prominently. Victoria Wood did not laugh; she couldn't abide his treatment of his victims.

Jesse Armstrong and Sam Bain's *Peep Show* (2003–15) starred David Mitchell as Mark Corrigan, a loan manager who shares a Croydon flat with his old but antithetical university friend, dim-witted musician and slacker Jeremy (Robert Webb). *Peep Show*

is an odd-couple comedy but much more. Its use of inner monologues and cameras attached to the protagonists' heads, to give the
viewer the feeling of being inside theirs, was ground-breaking. Still
more so was that here was a comedy in which pretty much everyone
was unsympathetic: the awful Geoff, Mark's romantic rival; Sophie
(Olivia Colman), initially the fragrant object of Mark's desire, who
becomes more awful as she deteriorates into a bad drug habit; her
awful family; the awful Johnson, a slick alpha male with a transatlantic accent which makes 'Kettering' come out as 'Keddering';
the awful Toni, the awful Australian girl on whom Mark develops
a crush; the awful shit who hosts a party at the house he inherited
from his parents ('Money's like an energy – it flows towards me');
the awfully naive, awfully posh Big Suze; the irresistibly awful Super
Hans (Matt King), drug-addled and yet as self-assured as Mark is
full of doubt, even when it comes to the naming of the pub Jeremy
has somehow come into and he plans to co-run: Free the Paedos.

   Peep Show conveys a Croydon-centred dystopia that's arrived
ahead of schedule, a world in which the oxygen of decency and
consideration has been sucked out. Adrian Mole-like, Mark disdains
the new world he has grown up into, taking refuge in grammatical
corrections, military history and a centre-right emphasis on personal
responsibility. His stuffiness is risible, however, rather than admirable, offset by his desperate sexual longing to have just the odd splash
of the action that flows to Jeremy constantly. But it's a cruel world
Armstrong and Bain created, with no comforting moments of hope
or redemption. Cruel is funnier.

   Damon Beesley and Iain Morris's *The Inbetweeners* ran initially
between 2008 and 2010. It exists in the same universe as *Peep Show*
but at secondary-school stage. Again, there are elements of Adrian
Mole, particularly in Simon Bird's character and narrator Will, the
too-straight victim of a world that rains scorn on him ('Briefcase
wanker!' a pupil spits at him on his first day at Rudge Park
Comprehensive, a puppy-eat-puppy environment). Will's mother is

mumsy but more of a hindrance than a help in protecting him from the cruel world. Greg Davies's schoolteacher is like a bullying Rick from *The Young Ones* grown up into stocky, cynical adulthood: the anti-Mr Chips. Mark, the school bully, operates with the free hand bullies customarily have.

The Inbetweeners does contain one or two likeable characters, like Charlotte, who pays kindly attention to Will and his group, but mostly they are left to fend for themselves, pooling the meagre resources of their characters. There's Simon, seemingly tender and romantic, yet the slightest wrong word from his family can send him into a massive strop, flying to the garden shed roof to sulk, to their amusement. Neil is the happiest of the group, maintained so by his cheery gormlessness. He doesn't ask much. Sitting down to do a piss rather than standing up he regards as an occasional 'special treat'. Then there is Jay, the Spoofer McGraw of the foursome, peddling a perpetual pack of lies about his sexual experiences, a transparent cloak for his sexual inadequacies. In fact, the nearest he gets to a sexual liaison with a woman is when, working a shift in an old people's home, he riffles through some drawers in search of stimulus for his masturbation and comes across a photo of a young woman, only to be interrupted, mid-wank, when he realises he is in the bedroom of said young woman, now an old woman, gratified to have been the source of Jay's photographic pleasure.

The scriptwriters of *The Inbetweeners* took immense pleasure in heaping up the worst imaginable humiliations any school lad could endure without combusting through blushing. There was occasionally the hint of a bit of learning at the end of each episode, but what had really happened was that our hapless young heroes had been hauled over the coals of teen embarrassment for maximum fun, unadulterated by pity.

Cruelty of another sort abounded in Julia Davis's *Nighty Night* (2004–5). No one has delved further into the darkness of gross, excruciating depravity and horrific moral dereliction for our amusement and delectation than Davis. *Nighty Night* stars Davis as Jill Tyrell, owner of a beauty salon, who, openly consumed with self-pity when she learns her husband Terry (Kevin Eldon) has cancer, makes a play for another man, Don (Angus Deayton), inveigling herself into the sympathies of his wheelchair-bound wife Cathy (Rebecca Front) as she seeks to bed Don, even flirting with their young son to advance her cause. Inconveniently, Terry responds well to treatment, prompting Jill to install him in a hospice and tell her friends Terry has died. Furthermore, she maintains a relationship with Glenn (Mark Gatiss), who has come into money. *Nighty Night* is pure comedy uncut by sentiment. Davis's performance is a toxic confection of discreet manipulation on the one hand, open, animal lust to achieve her ends on the other, her eyes constantly scanning and working over her victims even in her most unctuous exchanges. As fatale a femme as ever stalked a screen.

The noughties were different times. The difference could be marked in the Frankie Boyle who in the next decade was a purveyor of left-of-centre political decency, on Twitter or on his own TV show *New World Order* (2017–), on which he made sure to have predominantly female guests, and the Frankie Boyle censured in 2009 by the BBC Trust for describing swimmer Rebecca Adlington as 'someone who's looking at herself in the back of a spoon'. It's the difference between the Russell Brand who more recently, albeit clumsily, attempted to set himself up as a well-meaning, wide-eyed idealist and beacon for youth disaffected by the political status quo, and the Brand who in 2008 made prank calls on his Radio 2 show with Jonathan Ross to the elderly Andrew 'Manuel' Sachs, leaving a series of snickeringly unpleasant comments on his answerphone, including observations about his granddaughter.

THE RETURN OF BLACKFACE

Despite a progressive sense that the alternative ethos had purged British comedy of the sins of the sixties and seventies, leaving a scene more reflective of, and truthful about, lives as they were actually lived, the noughties saw . . . a return to blackface, as if censure of the Two Ronnies and their Indian waiter sketch (and other such transgressions) had never happened. There were multiple examples. Mainstream ones included Ant and Dec in *Saturday Night Takeaway*, blacking up as Jamaican women Patty and Bernice in a 2003 sketch, and, bizarrely, Charlotte Church as 'Charlie Chapel'. But the phenomenon spread further left-field. Vic Reeves and Bob Mortimer blacked up as Otis Redding and Marvin Gaye; Leigh Francis as Craig David in *Bo! Selecta*. The Papa Lazarou character in *The League of Gentlemen*, meanwhile, a kidnapper dredged from the darkest fathoms of that collective's imagination, resembled infamous old photographs of Louis Armstrong blacked up at the Mardi Gras carnival. Noel Fielding blacked up as the 'Spirit of Jazz', Howlin' Jinny Jefferson, in *The Mighty Boosh*. There had been recent precedents – particularly shameful was David Baddiel on *Fantasy Football*. Baddiel blacked up as Jason Lee, with a false pineapple on his head to boot. This was part of a campaign of 'banter' at the Nottingham Forest striker's expense. Lee made it known that he was upset by the portrayal. Harry Enfield, meanwhile, at the height of Black Lives Matter, went on radio to defend his having blacked up as Nelson Mandela. He justified it as being 'so wrong it was right' and made a distinction between his own blackface and that of 1930s characters.

Enfield was always a contrarian, despite rising to fame in the eighties alongside Ben Elton, as if he felt he had something to live down being thus associated with alternative comedy. However, his non-apology was telling. Of course his blackface wasn't malignant, old-school racism. It was suspended by a healthy pair of postmodern inverted commas. Baddiel, Reeves, Mortimer could indulge their licence as comics to blackface because, as ought to be self-evident – c'mon, this is us! – they were highly intelligent comedians with advanced modern sensibilities and a sense of irony that precluded any possibility that they were racist. Why, they were so anti-racist they could get away with 'racism', so smartly laundered were their credentials. And, in their time, mostly post the 1990s, pre-Twitter and the era of viral indignation, they did indeed get away with black-face, with relatively little demur.

Others, however, apologised profusely. Ant and Dec and Leigh Francis (aka Keith Lemon) were among those to offer contrition for their past blackface errors; Craig David said that he considered *Bo! Selecta* to have affected not only his career but also his mental health. Matt Lucas and David Walliams of *Little Britain* also expressed their regrets; Walliams used blackface to play the character Desiree DeVere, Lucas to play Pastor Jesse King. 'We want to make it clear that it was wrong and we are very sorry,' Lucas tweeted. In 2017, interviewed by *The Big Issue*, he added, 'I wouldn't make that show now . . . We made a more cruel comedy than I'd do now. Society has moved on a lot since then and my own views have evolved.'

Though not as good as the similarly character-based *The Catherine Tate Show* (2004–9), *Little Britain* (2000–7) was a smart, often funny series and highly regarded by most critics in its time. The sleazy Tory MP played by Walliams forced serially to come to the gate of his country house with his family in tow to explain away his latest 'acci-dental' peccadillo and the tiny Dennis-Waterman-in-*Minder* and his meetings with his agent were highlights, while Vicky Pollard was a virtuoso creation, her blurted torrents of self-justification defying comprehension.

And yet there was a reactionary undertow to their work, conscious or otherwise. 'We're ladies, don't you know' (they're not really ladies, you know) sits poorly in the context of trans rights. 'The Only Gay in the Village', meanwhile, feels like another dig at a supposedly persecuted minority ('Don't know what the fuss is, everyone's into gay rights nowadays, get past it'), while Lou and Andy, carer and cared for, show what idiots nanny liberals are: these so-called disabled are taking us for a ride. Even Vicky Pollard stands accused as an example of 'chav'-baiting. As for the 'Thai bride' Ting Tong, what on earth were they thinking there, drunk on their own success, pushing the envelope in completely the wrong direction?

The noughties also saw the proliferation of panel shows like *Mock the Week* (there is a certain noughties cruelty in that 'mock'). Despite the fact that the generic comedians who populated shows like *Live at the Apollo* were all too eager to ingratiate, a generation of anti-Jack Dees bounding onstage in perpetual warm-up mode, staring wide-eyed, open-mouthed from posters as they pointed at copies of their own DVDs, never, ever putting each other down, you sensed a keen ambition among these hopefuls – not to cultivate a slow-cooked persona but rather to get their crack in, in the thirty or so seconds of vital TV exposure available to them on whatever TV vehicle/charabanc they were rocking up in.

Jimmy Carr epitomised the new breed. He may have looked like a former ventriloquist's dummy, but as with any such 'dummy', his appearance belied a ruthlessly succinct wit that sailed close to, or even right into, the winds of offence. Sample jokes:

> Dwarves are often overlooked. Tell you what I know about dwarves – very little. I can say that, they look up to me.

> I asked my Welsh friend how many sexual partners he's had. He fell asleep counting.

Ricky Gervais, too, took an odd turn in the noughties after finding success with *The Office* (2001–3). The post-*Office* Gervais, however, struck me as a character who saw fame as a licence to behave with a certain kind of boorish, self-satisfied arrogance.

Thin-skinned, also: after some mildly disparaging criticism from Ian Hislop, he took to ending his show by calling him an 'ugly little pug-faced cunt'. When called out for use of the word 'Mong', he retorted, like some out-of-work seventies comedian, by referring to the 'humourless PC brigade'.

However, what grated more was his own overbearing presence in, for example, the podcasts he did with Karl Pilkington. For many, Pilkington's bizarre take on the world was reason enough to chuckle. But if he was a funny enough character in his own right, why did he need Gervais and Stephen Merchant riding shotgun with him, constantly making with the 'How mad is that?' commentary and manic guffaws? Moreover, it felt like schoolboy baiting, as if Pilkington were some shambling creature with a rope round his neck, a freak-show exhibit.

That guffaw of Gervais's, 'AHAHAHAHAHAHA', resounded unpleasantly through his post-*Office* career, not least in *Life's Too Short* (2011–13), which, in a very knowing, postmodern, ironic way you'd have to be triply sophisticated to understand, you understand, was a series revolving around jokes at the expense of a dwarf.

In a piece in *Tribune* in June 2020, Jason Okundaye recounted the wider culture of cruelty in noughties light entertainment. There was *The Weakest Link*, in which Anne Robinson recast herself as a twenty-first-century Cruella, ritually humiliating her contestants.

> In one of her 'spiky' exchanges, Robinson notes that her contestant is a single mother to three boys, before subsequently asking 'how many ASBOs?', 'are you on benefits?' after forcing the contestant to reveal details of her broken-down marriages. It beggars belief how conduct like this was treated as a palatable feature of daytime television less than two decades ago.

Okundaye berates a series of noughties shows, all of which had a punch-down, bread-and-circuses, Darwinian quality to them: *The X*

Factor, *Big Brother*, *Supernanny*, *Wife Swap*, *The Jeremy Kyle Show*, *Fat Families* and *There's Something About Miriam*. *The Jeremy Kyle Show* was particularly obnoxious in that it larded into the mix a nauseating dose of moralising to its parading of 'chavs'. Okundaye saw these shows as of a piece with the desire of the Labour party of Blair/Brown to appease right-wing media observers in particular, with their determination to get tough on the lower orders, scroungers, benefit fraudsters, young criminals – no socialist mollycoddling for them! Although New Labour performed some good deeds, far from dismantling the structures established by Thatcherism, or trying to scotch traditional prejudice against immigrants, union activism, the unemployed or single mothers, they too frequently pandered to it – in Blair's case, with a glint of demonic fervour.

Okundaye's argument has merit; the rise of reality TV coincided with a grim 'realism' of the sort Mark Fisher alludes to in the title of his book *Capitalist Realism (Is There No Alternative?)*, published in 2009. Reality TV bred contempt rather than compassion, and may have helped condition Britons for the very real cruelty of the austerity years, in which the already impoverished and disadvantaged were made to pay for the banking crisis of 2008; there was, after all, no alternative. That insidious, deliberately discouraging, almost Dalek-like mantra still held British voters – Conservative, Lib Dem and many Labour – in its thrall.

But how does that account for the penchant for cruelty across the board, from *Jeremy Kyle* to *The Thick of It*? It was, perhaps, the air of lassitude that permeated the long nineties. Not even 9/11 was able ultimately to dispel a grey air of uneventfulness, of a collective shuffle rather than any great leap forward into the future. The moment of giddy idealism, of imminent sunlit uplands encapsulated in New Labour's theme 'Things Can Only Get Better', gave way to a dull, cosy, cynicism, a weary contempt for politicians but also for idealism. Things couldn't get much better than this, it seemed. The comedy of cruelty – of people bored of the futile fight against inequality, bored of political correctness – thrived in such a vacuum. Gordon Brown's tired countenance, a contrast to the beam and gleam of Tony Blair, epitomised a political movement that was sclerotic, pragmatic and had long since departed from any sense of hope or guiding principle, had run its course. The alternative posed as the decade drew to a tired close? David Cameron. Presenting himself with estate-agent, pinstripe-thin plausibility, he stated that he wished to become prime minister because, with supreme, Etonian self-confidence, he 'thought I would be good at it'. His pitch, the gall of it given what he would visit on Britain, was one of 'compassionate Conservatism'. Dave, in tandem with the equally fresh-faced and plausible Liberal Democrat leader Nick Clegg, was an antidote to the exhaustion of Brown's fatally compromised Labour, promising an end to the belligerence of Brown, Alastair Campbell and his fictional counterpart, *The Thick of It*'s Malcolm Tucker. It was a confidence trick, and a jaded electorate, many of whom had forgotten what left and right were, went for it.

RORY BREMNER, *THE THICK OF IT* – SATIRE IN THE NOUGHTIES

Come the new millennium, come Rory Bremner. He started showbiz life as a prodigious impressionist on shows like *Rory Bremner – Who Else?* (1993–8) who could be relied on to deliver a spot-on Murray Walker but who evolved, with the assistance of sixties *That Was the Week That Was* veterans John Bird and John Fortune, into the most acute observer of the deceptively slick politics of the Labour years, during which time trouble was brewing beneath the glossy surface. His 2001 election special (now under the name *Bremner, Bird and Fortune*) was a delight. Labour put in an uninspired performance; however, they were up against a Conservative Party bereft of ideas and relevance, led by William Hague, the very imitable William Hague, as Bremner found to his joy.

In an age in which politicians were becoming that much harder to tell apart, ideologically and in terms of recognition factor, Bremner did an exceptionally able job. Few impressionists would have dared to do a Peter Mandelson as Bremner does him, following the minister's hard-won victory in Hartlepool, when he delivered a somewhat extended speech by way of tribute to himself. Bremner has Mandelson intoning, in those rather mean tones of his, the lyrics to Gloria Gaynor's 'I Will Survive'. He also does a fine Paddy Ashdown, former warrior leader of the Liberal Democrats, staring out at the world through narrowed eyes in a thoroughly self-vindicating manner.

His Tony Blair, however, was his centrepiece, filmed, for much of this episode, on his battle bus, accompanied by his press secretary and sole confidant Alastair Campbell, offering constant over-the-shoulder advice ('You can say what you like about the future . . . just don't talk about the past'). He gets Blair's perma-mode perfectly: a shifty mass of compromise and self-justification, blinking as he thinks the unthinkable behind a rictus smile. We see his Blair interviewed by Peter Snow, brimming with vacuous, end-of-history hubris, wondering aloud if elections should be done away with altogether: 'Why not replace the ballot paper with a consumer survey?'

The pinnacle of the show is when Bremner's Blair and Campbell (Andrew Dunn) arrive at a Labour rally in advance of the actual Blair and members of his cabinet, warning that 'anyone who comes after me is an impostor'. Bremner-as-Blair then joins the cheering crowd as the real Labour politicians arrive, attracting the attention of Gordon Brown by trilling the word 'Gordon!' in faultless Tony tones. Brown looks round and, realising who it is, reacts with a rare expression of absolute joy.

In 2020, it emerged that Rory Bremner may have helped avert a Tory revolt back in 1993 after he prank-called a Eurosceptic MP, Sir Richard Body, one of a band of querulous right-wing MPs, pretending to be prime minister John Major. With no other intention than testing the quality of his impression, Bremner-as-Major successfully pleaded with Body to back him, thereby swinging vital support for Major at a critical juncture in the Maastricht talks. This might have been British satire's most decisive moment, such as it was, accidental as it was, helping keep the country in the EU for another twenty-three years.

Armando Iannucci created *The Thick of It* (2005–12) having argued the case for *Yes Minister* as the best ever British sitcom. He admitted also the influence of *The Larry Sanders Show* (1992–8), a brilliant, naturalistic exposé of the fraught goings-on behind the curtains of a late-night US TV chat show. In *The Thick of It*, the hand-held camera is forever on the move, scurrying in fretful pursuit of stressed staff around the offices of party HQ.

Although Iannucci initially declined to say so, the party in *The Thick of It* is Labour. As with *Yes Minister*, however, political belief barely seems to exist or matter. The party's offices are staffed by ministers and special advisers who, with the exception of the precocious if invertebrate Ollie Reeder (Chris Addison), are pudgy mediocrities who have risen like bits of plywood atop the choppy waters of government. Their day's business is to advance or protect their own careers, landing others in the shit if necessary, or inadvertently starting and trying to put out fires. Their proximity to the levers of state lends them a cocksureness in between crises, and they address each other with competitive playground taunts conspicuously lacking in affection. These are fleeting moments, however, as it only takes head of communications Malcolm Tucker (Peter Capaldi) to stride into the room to reduce them to quailing mush.

The Thick of It resumes a theme from *Yes, Prime Minister*: that government is really run by unelected figures who operate behind the scenes. In *Yes, Prime Minister*'s day, Sir Humphrey's discreet and tactful job was to curb the initiatives of ministers. In *The Thick of It*, Tucker, widely supposed to be based on Labour's head of communications Alastair Campbell, is openly aggressive about his intentions and certainly not inclined to waste politeness on anyone so lowly as a minister.

One imagines a youthful Tucker, his socialist fury stoked by the oratory of union chiefs like Jimmy Reid. One has to. The show is deliberately sketchy about his backstory, lest it soften or humanise him. He has certainly retained the fire in his belly, but it has managed to burn away most of his scruples, leaving only an essential structure of resentment of the chinless political classes and a vengeful desire to win at all costs. With the exception of a fellow Scot, press officer Jamie McDonald (Paul Higgins), he has no friends in his workplace and harbours deep contempt for his colleagues, whom he sees as soft, stuttering flab where once there was steel and muscle in the party.

For Tucker, the sacking of a minister is not the hardest part of the job but the part he most relishes. This is established when he calls in secretary of state Cliff Lawton (Tim Bentinck). It begins as a cordial exchange, with lots of naturalistic conversational overlap. But then it takes a downward turn as Tucker makes it clear to Lawton that, given the adverse press he has been suffering, he must resign. It's nothing personal: 'No one who matters thinks any the less of you over this . . . so far,' says Tucker, menacingly. Lawton tries to draw himself up to his full ministerial height, but Tucker joyfully cuts him down. 'Get used to Cliff,' he snarls.

Tucker's contempt isn't based on ideology; if he were an old Labour firebrand, he would hardly be in the position he is in. If the party has lost something of its founding vision, then so has he. His energies are sublimated in alpha-macho excoriation of his colleagues as he bends and lashes them to his will, tearing them down verbally and threatening imaginary/imaginative physical punishments if they don't. He's at once a reproach of how soft Labour has become and the embodiment of how centralised and ruthlessly authoritarian it now is at top level: no longer a broad church but an instrument of will, the will simply to prevail.

Tucker's swearing is, in the best sense, gratuitous. Which is why Iannucci called for the services of Ian Martin, a 'swearologist', to work up Tucker's rants to a whipped cream of vituperation. To Ben Swain MP: 'Your hands were all over place, you were like a sweaty octopus trying to unhook a bra.' To Nicola Murray MP: 'You're not a grandee, you're a fucking bland-ee. No one knew what the fuck you stood for, political fucking mist, no substance, no weight. You have all the charm of a rotting teddy bear by a graveside.'

Despite its ostensible naturalism, *The Thick of It*'s scripts are a fabrication of supremely honed witticisms which no human could hope to maintain. It is an exercise in language as much as an analysis of noughties government. They're useless and hopeless in various ways, and that's that. Politics is a series of cock-ups.

Not that these weaklings aren't played with great strength. Addison's Ollie is constantly punished for his youthful self-satisfaction as Tucker commandeers him, and even his sex life, for his schemes. Terri Carr (Joanna Scanlan), the director of communications, retains a stoical resilience in the face of universal contempt, holding fast to her small dream of one day owning a tea shop. Rebecca Front, as Nicola Murray MP, carries herself with the same invidious, haunted haplessness Theresa May later had as PM, enduring gales of harassment from Tucker. It's one of the show's delicate features that its women face the same abuse as the men without it feeling sexist or problematic.

Labour is supplanted by the Tories towards the end of *The Thick of It*. The essential stand-off is between Roger Allam's Peter Mannion, secretary of state for social affairs, and Stewart Pearson (Vincent Franklin), spin doctor. Mannion is of the Hush Puppy, easy-going wing of the Conservatives, with no ideological axe to grind but resistant to change, especially the new-fangled nonsense spouted by fangler-in-chief and 'tranceiver' Pearson. When he is ousted, however, Pearson's worm turns spectacularly:

I've spent ten years detoxifying this party. It's been a bit like renovating an old, old house, yeah? You can take out a sexist beam here, a callous window there, replace the odd homophobic roof tile. But after a while you realise that this renovation is doomed. Because the foundations are built on what I can only describe as a solid bed of cunts.

It's a glimpse into the future. *The Thick of It* was brilliant but its relevance has been swept away by the political tide. Labour saw a resurgence of its left wing, which came close to power in 2017, only to be put down in 2019. Brexit happened. The Peter Mannions were sacked from the party; the soft centre has collapsed. In Malcolm Tucker-land, ministers were extremely vulnerable to the sack, with the government willing to throw to the wolves any minister who tarnished their image. In Boris-Johnson-and-Dominic-Cummings-land, no one resigned; Cummings brazened out accusations that he had broken the government's own guidelines on travel restrictions at the height of the Covid pandemic. The Tories discovered that the pressure Tucker felt he had to bow to didn't exist for them. If you were shameless enough, you could do as you pleased. A new show was thus created, broadcast daily: The Shitshow.

LOCAL COMEDY, LOCAL PEOPLE –
PHOENIX NIGHTS, GAVIN AND STACEY

And yet, amid the desultory mood of cynicism and low-level sadism that pervaded noughties comedy, a much richer and more authentic sense of regional locality and character could be cultivated, away from the generic Southern pubs and suburbs – comedies that showed Britain was not so little after all, but ran wide and deep.

Peter Kay's *Phoenix Nights* (2001–2) was one example. Kay was notorious for his elephantine memory of the disregarded trifles and Angel Delights of decades past, waxing reminiscent and vividly about the seventies and eighties, when he was an infant. But *Phoenix Nights*, co-created with Neil Fitzmaurice and fellow Boltonian Dave Spikey, is garish, hilariously grim in its depiction of a place you know, grew up in, love, got out of the moment you could.

Set in Bolton's Phoenix Club, it stars Kay as truculent wheelchair user Brian Potter and focuses on his efforts to outdo rival club the Banana Grove by laying on ever more lavish events and turns. These include inept psychic Clinton Baptiste, who, after a portentous introduction shrouded in lights and dry ice, announces himself with a reedy 'Y'all right?', before coming to grief as, alighting on a particularly burly fellow, he says, 'I'm getting the word "nonce".' Elsewhere, Potter converts a male toilet into a children's adventure playground, and a bouncy castle turns out to be a giant cock and balls. If all this seems crude and far-fetched, that's counterbalanced by the *vérité* of the production. The Phoenix Club, whose glitterball and tinsel only exacerbate the drabness of the establishment, is the sort of place where the overripe pop-cultural produce of yesteryear comes to rot: the mullets, the underwhelming, over-familiar, fizzless pop music, the shiny jackets – futile, misplaced protests against the dourness of a Lancashire town. Indeed, the visual ambience of *Phoenix Nights*, realised in brilliant, knowing detail by its creators, generates laughter in its own right, while avoiding caricature or condescension.

Like *Phoenix Nights*, *Gavin and Stacey* (2007–10) afforded a deep-dyed sense of the accent, feel and metre of provincial life, twinning Essex with Barry in South Wales. The titular couple, played by Mathew Horne and Joanna Page, are ostensibly the subject of the show, straight characters around whose relationship much funnier characters orbit. It was created by Ruth Jones and James Corden, who play Nessa and Smithy, whose relationship, following an initial one-night stand, is wary, intermittent, unresolved. It does, however, result in Nessa becoming pregnant.

The cast of family and friends includes Julia Davis as Dawn, whose flaming, apocalyptic rows with her husband, Pete Sutcliffe, followed by equally swift reconciliations, erupt throughout the series. Larry Lamb and Alison Steadman play Gavin's parents, the

Shipmans, while Rob Brydon plays Bryn West (note the recurring theme), Stacey's uncle, ever present and willing to help, but who lives under the constant shadow of a past incident with his nephew Jason, awkward but never divulged.

Dominant, however, is the unsmiling Nessa, sometime bouncer, one-time paramour of John Prescott, more of a man than all the men put together, more of a woman than the women also, whose various, not always scrupulous, money-making initiatives she approaches with the same matter-of-factness and absence of shame or anxiety.

The series revolves around various events that bring the families and all who sail with them together; as with *The Royle Family*, it combines high comedy with the spectacle of characters we have come to love having a good time, which should not work as well as it does in this exceptional series.

Barry deserves a casting credit in *Gavin and Stacey*. It is true to the place, which is depicted lovingly in the wider-screen format that by now was opening up visual opportunities on what was no longer the small screen of TV. Barry-towners felt represented; and even if you didn't come from there, you could identify, vicariously, with that feeling of representation of a region, and the characters, terraces, mundane beauty, minor madness and eccentrics that abide in such areas.

THE OFFICE – A NEW NATURALISM

When Ricky Gervais made his mark with *The Office*, someone who knew him in his previous life as a concert promoter and would-be pop star told me: 'It's like the quiet kid you sat next to in school, and haven't thought about for years, suddenly painting *Guernica*.' Gervais had previously been in a couple of groups, including one regrettably named the Passiondales. He then went on to manage Suede, who would achieve the stardom he had vainly aspired to, before putting on gigs in the early Britpop years. There is certainly an overlap between David Brent and Gervais himself. Those who knew him back then do not recall him being the full-blown embarrassment realised in *The Office*, however, but rather as managerial, businesslike in suit and tie, settled into a bureaucratic role, keeping his opinions to himself. Nearing forty, he had the air of a man who had come and gone and accepted as much.

Clearly, however, on the inside ambition was still roiling. He met Stephen Merchant when they worked together on XFM radio, where Gervais began to forge a persona that felt like it belonged on the margins of TV, trying just a bit too hard. Transposing Gervais/Brent into a workplace, however, in the dullest of towns (Slough) and the dullest of industries, stationery production, was a masterstroke, setting Gervais/Brent's ambition, improbable, sad and risible as it might seem in a man of his age and thwarted history, with tremendous self-deprecation at the heart of the show.

When Gervais and Merchant pitched the show, they did not merely send a script but filmed sample scenes with key actors, to convey precisely the feel they had in mind. As with *The Royle Family*, it was vital that there be no laugh track, no studio lighting, but the grain of truth that comes with documentary-style footage, hand-held cameras zooming in slightly invasively at key moments. The conceit is that they are being filmed for a reality doc about office life, with central characters interviewed, in which the views they express are very often at odds with the reality depicted in the footage, or, in David Brent's case, spectacularly contradictory.

First broadcast in 2001, *The Office* brutally realises the world of work as experienced by so many in its many shades of grey as the new century dawned: the carpets, the managerial tiers, the suits, the vertical blinds across the windows. *The Office* was as monochrome a colour TV series as was ever broadcast.

In the second episode, Brent is giving a new worker a tour of the office and stresses that at Wernham Hogg they are fully online, spelling out the words 'world wide web'; it was still a slight novelty.

It altered the dynamic of office life, however, in which workers sat glumly transfixed in their own workspaces, their greying faces fixed on their screens; offices that had once clattered with typewriters or with the more frequent ring of telephones or the bustle of human beings interacting away from their desks now resounded to the low-level thrum of collective yet solitary activity. *The Office* is undercut by a sense of quietly desperate mundanity. People hate their jobs but hate more the prospect of losing them, the threat of which hangs over Wernham Hogg, Slough branch all through series one. It was probably as much its depiction of the present-day reality of the workplace as its comedy which saw *The Office* proliferate in different guises worldwide: Slough as universal condition.

With the exception of the appallingly keen-as-mustard Gareth, these are people, like receptionist Dawn, who just want to get through the day and get back to their creative hobbies, maybe vegetate to *Big Brother* or, like Tim, have a big old wank. The tentative relationship between Tim and Dawn, engaged to the rather surly and probably quite hard Lee, who works in the warehouse, distinguishes *The Office* from other sitcoms. Events are coming to a head. Brent, it turns out, cannot get away with doing virtually no work other than prowling around the office, believing himself to be 'an educator . . . a motivator of people. I excite their imaginations. It's like bloody *Dead Poets Society* out there,' but in reality a man whose intervention in any conversation immediately kills the mood. The blank, gravestone stares of non-amusement which greet practically his every utterance fail to deter Brent, who is too absorbed in his own nervous, gurgling laughter. He's incorrigible, the embodiment of a broader tendency in the modern workplace: a failure among a particular tier to understand that when they seek to boost their workforce's morale, especially through a tenth-hand idea of 'fun', they merely add insult to injury.

Comic Relief represents a particularly exquisite torture in this respect, with its compulsory enthusiasm and red noses. In an episode based around Comic Relief Day, Gervais and Merchant the comedy critics rise to the fore. By this time, Comic Relief was beginning to feel staid, less than radical, a lot less than funny. Brent is all for Comic Relief. It fits right in with his self-image as entertainer and altruist, as well as office manager: 'We are raising money for people starving to death. If I make people laugh along with saving lives, sue me.'

Brent is an indictment, if not of British comedy, of the British attitude to comedy as harboured by some: that it can be dolloped everywhere into every situation like custard, with cheer inevitably following. 'Would you like to be known as a funny man or a great boss? To me, they're not mutually exclusive,' he says in a to-camera interview, as if he is either. Brent believes that simply by reciting old *Monty Python* sketches, he is rendering himself an honorary Python, as opposed to a pest. He regards any opportunity to give a presentation in the workplace as a stand-up routine, including when the Swindon office merges with the Slough office and an informal greeting is laid on. Brent goes to the trouble of putting out chairs, talks to the Swindon manager Neil as if he is his warm-up man, then goes and delivers a fabulously ill-conceived routine, one of the high, excruciating points of the series. He reads out from a card about a tendency to 'pisspronunciate my worms', then, when it falls flat, blames the 'audience' for not recognising it as a *Two Ronnies* joke. The next card from which he reads involves a bit about a former worker called Eric, supposedly prone to the catchphrase 'I don't agree with that in the workplace', first in the style of Columbo and then as Basil Fawlty, complete with goose-stepping and comb under the nose. It occurred to me as I first watched this that I hadn't laughed so much at a sitcom moment, doubled over at the sheer crest of embarrassment attained, since the actual *Fawlty Towers* episode imitated by Brent, 'The Germans', back in 1975.

Brent certainly knows his comedy, much of it old-school. He sees a lineage of genius: 'Milligan, Cleese, Everett, Sessions.' He's on an awkward cusp between the 'traditional' sense of humour and political correctness, which he tries to absorb as he does the memos on health and safety, but tends to come a cropper. He is pious about anti-racism but doesn't understand why a joke about a Black man's cock is offensive and stereotyping. 'It's not an insult, is it? It's a compliment, if anything.' Meanwhile, he can't conceal his real attitude towards the disabled when he bends over to a woman in a wheelchair during a fire drill and, as if addressing a hard-of-hearing 105-year-old, says, 'We're going to get you out of here, all right?'

The Office would set the tone for twenty-first-century entertainment, with its desire for naturalism as opposed to artifice, the CCTV patina of reality in the way we actually interact, unscripted, halting, pauses speaking greater volumes than sentences, which are often broken, overlapping, delayed. Of course, *The Office* was scripted, meticulously realised but not slickly; much of its humour lies in the cracks in the lines, the half-sentences, the thoughts allowed to die away before being abruptly resumed, all of which has to be seen to be appreciated. In the second episode, when, having made a show of throwing his answerphone out of the window, as if its three messages are enough to drive a man to distraction, Brent accidentally drops it in the waste-paper bin. 'It's fine . . . fine, that one – it's – that's okay – it's that – take the – er –,' he blurts, fragments of embarrassment and hasty sweeping-off which look like nothing on paper but speak volumes on screen revealing the ignominious vistas of Brent's character.

In *The Office*, humour and character are revealed not in polished, uninterrupted quips followed by short pauses for audience laughter but in thoughts suppressed or clumsily blurted, a lexicon expressed by a highly nuanced group of actors versed in the way Brits in particular self-consciously interact, in a mass of half-jokes and hesitancies, afraid to admit their true intentions, thoughts and desires, which are revealed only in stolen glances or momentary, frozen expressions of wistful introspection.

The naturalism of *The Office* would become the default setting for twenty-first-century sitcom – *Outnumbered*, *This Country*,

People Just Do Nothing, Detectorists. The laugh track did survive and even thrived, as writers like Graham Linehan successfully created a new grammar based on *Father Ted* in *The IT Crowd* and *Count Arthur Strong*. However, a series like Lee Mack's *Not Going Out* (2006–), more traditional in its approach, felt eerie in its orthodoxy in the post-*Office* world, strangely stilted in a world in which, cumulatively, stilts and artifice had been withdrawn, old prejudices dismantled and people of all sorts, all backgrounds, not just the hapless white male, were revealed for who and what and how they were. It presaged a shift from cruelty in the noughties to kindness in the decade that followed.

CODA

STEWART LEE AND THE COMEDY OF MUSIC, THE MUSIC COMEDY

As someone for whom music and comedy have been twin passions since I was so high, I've always been interested in their interrelationship, or even lack of it. Having begun my writing career as a writer for *Melody Maker*, it's a theme dear to me. I've touched on it at various points – the ruefully familiar soundtracks of Laurel and Hardy, the bracing symphonies of the Ealing comedies, the lugubrious theme tunes of dolorous sitcoms like *Hancock*, to the parallels and interfaces between *Python* and later alternative comedy and countercultural phenomena such as prog rock and punk.

More often than not, however, comedians are inclined not to be particularly intense music fans, and are inclined to chuckle at musical pretensions. But then came Stewart Lee, whose highly developed sensibilities as a music lover were brought to bear on his stage work, bringing the music/comedy relationship to a new level – a performer for whom comedy wasn't merely the new rock and roll but the new avant-garde.

In 2005, Lee wrote a piece for *The Wire*, in which he recounted a gig by the improv guitarist Derek Bailey. He recalled a moment in which the septuagenarian Bailey accidentally bumped into the back wall of the stage, his guitar clanging resonantly as he did so. Apparently pleased by the accident, he deliberately struck the wall with his instrument a second time. 'I laughed, and despite the wealth of different responses Bailey's music had already offered me, I never thought it would provoke laughter,' wrote Lee. He later learned that Bailey had played in the orchestra pit on the road with Morecambe and Wise. For Lee, this figured. 'Banging your guitar into a wall by accident, and then doing it again on purpose in a spirit of clownish curiosity, seems to me like a classic Eric Morecambe move.'

The relationship between humour and music is fraught. Like ice cream and gravy, I used to maintain, they should not mix. They debilitate one another. Humour in music, be it quirkiness, parody or amusing lyrics, punctures and deflates; music at its best is ecstatic, brutally intense, sublime, light of being or weighty with significance, but always, if it is truly to have an impact, humourless.

As for comedy, it was always traditionally felt that music was its enemy: a form of unwanted 'relief'. My earliest disappointment, akin to opening a grandmother's biscuit barrel and finding it full of cotton reels, was when Ken Dodd appeared on TV only to burst into mawkish song. Why wasn't he waving his tickling stick or labouring down the jam butty mines? When Barbara Dickson did a number midway through a *Two Ronnies* show, or Dana appeared to chirrup some ballgowned ballad on *The Tommy Cooper Show*, it seemed to me that I was being forced to serve a penance for laughing too hard at Cooper's spoon, jar, jar, spoon routine.

Music-as-comedy represented for me an unwanted respite, a toning down, a turning down of the heat. The comedy numbers of Victoria Wood, Josie Lawrence, Richard Stilgoe were too light, too enervated, a tickling of the ivory ribs rather than the winding gut-punch of the best humour. Even 'Always Look on the Bright Side of Life', which concluded Python's *Life of Brian*, felt like a dampening concession to the pro-musical brigade. Music and comedy were bad for each other. Why did people insist on conjoining them? As a music lover who felt that music was as serious as your life, and as a comedy lover who wanted comedy to make me laugh so hard I might shit my sphincter, I was convinced that comedy music was an insidious combination beloved by those guilty of that very British trait – a compulsion to tone down, not up.

This was especially true of the post-punk era, when I admired groups like Wire, Suicide, Cabaret Voltaire, Throbbing Gristle and Joy Division, groups who weren't there to entertain, any more than the free-jazz men and women of the 1960s were, but to irradiate audiences, glower at them, decondition them with dub and noise and serrated guitars. These groups engendered a sense that in order for music to be infused with significance and energy, violence had to be done to it, so that it didn't merely become an eternal reiteration of its dead past.

All this was happening at the same time as the alternative comedy scene, which yielded the likes of Malcolm Hardee, Alexei Sayle, Rik Mayall, all of whom were doing violence to comedy, eschewing the balm of Barbara Dickson in these more urgent times. Even *The Young Ones*, however, wasn't the equivalent of the sort of extremists I loved. They had musical interludes, to show they were in tune with the boisterous abrasiveness of early-eighties Britain, but that meant groups like the Damned, Madness, Motörhead, all of whom were tempered by comedy. They could never have had Wire or Suicide on *The Young Ones*.

Come the 1990s, I found comedy hook-ups with music disappointing. Vic Reeves joined forces with the energetically uninspired indie rockers the Wonder Stuff for a one-off single, 'Dizzy'. *The Fast Show* featured Jazz Club ('Nice . . .'), which was funny but depended on its humour for people's bewilderment at progressive music – all that jazzy noodling and pan pipes.

All this is true – except when it isn't. Take, for example, the way Hancock used silence, comedically timed intervals of radio dead air, equivalent to the spaces between the notes in a sparing but highly effective Count Basie piano solo. Attending an Indian classical music concert, meanwhile, I found it was not just breathtaking to witness the feverish spirals of dialogue between sitar and tabla players but also comical, given the way in which they exchanged frantic phrases like a double act, smiling as they did so, eliciting audience laughter.

Or think of John Shuttleworth, brainchild of Graham Fellows, who had a one-off hit in 1978 as 'Jilted John'. Shuttleworth lives in the Sheffield suburb of Walkley and has aspirations as a singer-songwriter, but despite the assistance of his next-door neighbour and excitable 'sole agent' Ken Worthington, makes little headway. When there is even the faintest, phantom prospect of making it down South, he gets cold feet, expressing the fear of becoming 'big-headed', and all comes to grief.

Shuttleworth's songs, rendered in husky, homely tones to the accompaniment of a PSS portable keyboard complete with bossa nova effects, are paeans to the cosy, jejune quietude of Northern life and its creosote aromas: 'Smells Like White Spirit', 'Austin Ambassador Y Reg', 'Dandelion and Burdock', 'Two Margarines', 'In the Garden Centre' and his would-be Eurovision Song Contest entry, 'Pigeons in Flight'. And yet, for all their efforts at comic self-sabotage, there's a strange, genuine beauty to Shuttleworth's songs. Robert Wyatt once described to me during an interview his love of the sweet soar of his Lincolnshire neighbour Fellows's melodies.

Still, I felt, 'serious' music – experimental, electronic, free improv, etc. – was antithetical to comedy – comedy, at least, in the wacky, sidelong, ribald, oops-a-daisy, one-up-the-bottom, eyes-bulging, mouth-open, oo-er, who's-gone-raving-mad-here-missus sense. On the website of the German composer Karlheinz Stockhausen, post-war pioneer of electronic music and *musique concrète*, there is a collection of cartoons at his expense. They include one showing a surgeon explaining to his patient on the operating table, 'No, it's not Stockhausen – we've just dropped a tray of surgical instruments.' The premise of these unamusing cartoons was that avant-garde music – tuneless, atonal, cacophonous – was inherently amusing.

Only in the twenty-first century did I become properly alive to one comedian who gave the lie to these assumptions, one capable of making audiences fall about in Leicester Square but also writing with passion and perspicacity about a whole range of left-field music, from the Fall to Fred Frith, in the *Sunday Times* and *The Wire*.

Stewart Lee emerged in the early 1990s, one of a spate of clever young comics to have emerged in the same tide that brought us *On the Hour* and *The Day Today*, working in a duo with Richard

Herring. He put on shows such as *Lionel Nimrod's Inexplicable World* and directed Johnny Vegas's first DVD. Then, in 2005, he co-created *Jerry Springer: The Opera*, an initially successful venture which might have seen Lee transfer permanently to the West End. However, the production faced protests from Christian groups who deemed the show, sight unseen, blasphemous. They succeeded in suppressing it. Lee was left high, dry and out of pocket by the experience. He reverted to the role of stand-up comedian and became the Stewart Lee which, for all of his previous, diverse endeavours, was the Stewart Lee he was born to be: his own stand-up vehicle. This Stewart Lee could never have done the usual twenty-first-century comic things – appeared on panel shows, fronted his own sitcom or hosted a quiz show. 'Stewart Lee' disdained such things.

'Stewart Lee' as exhibited on the BBC2 series *Stewart Lee's Comedy Vehicle* (2009–16) was no longer a fresh-faced, spiky, ambitious comedy youngster going places. This Stewart Lee was approaching middle age, with kids and financial responsibilities, at odds with twenty-first-century culture, with its Chris Moyles, the rap they have nowadays, the 'fucking *Angry Birds* generation – are you proud of that?' It was also a Stewart Lee who stood at odds with the proliferation of eager young comedians of the *Live at the Apollo* generation, keen to polish their quirky but acceptable, rapid-fire, observational shtick. This Stewart Lee disobeys the Code of the Comedian who, while highly competitive and quietly jealous of any success their contemporaries enjoy, never has a pop at them. He castigates Lee Mack, Michael McIntyre, even Frankie Boyle. Then there's James Corden, who, says Lee, is constantly expressing his admiration for him. 'The feeling isn't mutual.'

Underlying all this, with Lee, is a genuine disdain for a generation of aspirational equivalents to Robbie Williams's 'Let Me Entertain You', whose last wish is to create any sort of discomfiture in their audience. Perhaps Lee's most cutting reference to the twenty-first century's mainstream comedy is not verbal but a bit of physical business, in which he jogs around the mic several times, a keenly observed trope among the McIntyres of this world, the way they enter the stage, signalling upcoming joviality rather than challenge or consternation.

And yet all of this is cleverly framed. The joke is as much on him as it is on his victims, though his victims may smart sufficiently hard not to get that. Take his routine about Graham Norton winning a comedy BAFTA, a broody masterclass of slowly souring grapes. It begins with him reminiscing about the days when he and Norton were in neighbouring morning slots at the Edinburgh Fringe and what a nice fellow he had been, and how ever since, whenever Norton attains another million-pound publishing contract or whatever, he punches the air in happiness for his old mucker. However, he can't let it lie. He does an impersonation of Norton's chat show, feebly inane exchanges about suntans with actors who just have a film out which barely qualify as small talk, let alone comedy. He wonders why James Corden, if he's such a fan of Lee's, didn't rugby-tackle Norton in the aisle after he'd accepted the unjust award.

However, it turns out, under interrogation from the imperious Chris Morris, in one of the interpolations vital to the *Comedy Vehicle* series, that Lee had been mistaken; Norton's award was for comedy and entertainment, not just comedy alone. A sheepish Lee, looking like David Brent taking a rollicking from the new area manager from Swindon, mumbles that if he'd known that, he wouldn't have written the sketch. Maybe he did write the routine in error, the sort of chance mistake that can trigger fine art, or maybe he stepped further back and devised the whole scenario with the error inbuilt. Although he alludes to improv players like Derek Bailey, Lee's comedy is generally scripted, giving the illusion of spontaneity. As he himself put it, his routines are like jazz pieces performed once but then reproduced note for note, night after night. At one point in this routine, Lee says, 'All of this is written . . . what I'm saying right now is written.' It is musical, also, in ways undreamt of in the glib nineties comedy/

new rock and roll formula; the advanced way in which he tinkers with form and content and their interrelationship is surely informed by his advanced appreciation of music in all its modern forms, from Calexico to Steve Beresford.

Lee's routines are full of loops, repetitions, 'callbacks'; he knows and displays the rules in order to break them. Another example is his take on Richard 'the Hamster' Hammond, in which he strikes a more oblique, less obvious chord progression by going for Jeremy Clarkson's sidekick rather than Clarkson himself. After methodically setting up the platform for his loathing, he launches into a blistering, riffing tirade which has all the raging, squally energy of an Albert Ayler saxophone solo as he coruscates the sneery, cackling, mean-spirited, kick-down, half-baked humour of the *Top Gear* ethos. 'Imagine being a gypsy, hahahaha! He's not even got a car – imagine being a lesbian . . . Blah blah, the Welsh – imagine being Welsh and not being English!'

Even when Lee lets rip like this, however, you never feel he's going to pop a blood vessel. His general tone is coolly velvet, occasionally affecting to be searching for the right words and phrases, but that's all part of the artifice, which he declares, over and over, in the Brechtian spirit. 'I want you to laugh in spite of me not because of me,' he tells the audience, a line which on paper reads like a stern aphorism from an East European comedy masterclass, but on stage picks up a belly laugh.

Much of Lee's humour derives from him doing everything that comedians are not supposed to do onstage, like eschewing gags, or telling them simply that he could do gags if he wished to, but chooses not to, tossing aside Lee Mack-type quips about getting semi-hard whenever he sees a pack of Paxo ('Try telling that to the mother-in-law at Christmas! No, that's not quite me, is it?'). Deconstructing rather than putting on an act. Calling his audience 'cunts', frequently turning to the TV camera onstage to berate them to viewers at home.

In this respect, he was influenced by Ted Chippington, an example of the outsider punk spirit on the stand-up circuit. Hecklers are the bane of the life of a low-level stand-up, and much of their skill onstage is in handling and repelling the noise from a crowd determined to get in on, even ruin their act. Occasionally they can put even the biggest names off their stroke. In his fledgling days, a young comedian, later a household name, attempted some stand-up, including a routine in which he announced that he was a schizophrenic. He followed this with a little argument with himself. 'No, you're not. Yes, I am. No, you're not!' Whereupon someone shouted, 'Well, why don't you both fuck off!' Chippington, however, thrived on negativity, invited it, played with it and thereby nullified it. There is audio of him supporting the Liverpool group the Farm in 1985. The jokes are 'terrible', generally prefaced by the studied, lazily repeated phrase 'I was walking down the road the other day'.

Chippington at his peak had a gaunt, penetrating air as he faced down audiences, wilfully provoking a hostile reaction. His best joke saw him walking down the road and asking, 'How far is the railway station?' Fell-a says, 'One mile, roughly speaking,' a line Chippington repeats in a rasping voice. Roughly speaking. 'You didn't find that funny. Well, I did.' Comedy at the end of one of his routines lay in tatters on the stage. Some appreciated him (Phill Jupitus described him as 'this country's Andy Kaufman'); others did not. Following an appearance on *Pebble Mill at One*, triggered by his 1986 cover of the Beatles' 'She Loves You', the presenter told him his was the worst performance he had ever seen on the show. Chippington's response was word perfect: 'Well, I find that quite shocking that you have to say that.'

In the nineties, he gave up comedy and became a lorry driver. 'It got boring when it became popular,' he later told Stewart Lee. 'I couldn't see the point any more – the intention was for everyone to get annoyed.'

There are also echoes of Simon Munnery in Lee's comedy, not least his character Alan Parker: Urban Warrior. When Lee reads out a series of fatuously meatheaded online responses to the killing of

Osama Bin Laden by American forces, he adds, 'Of those four quotes only two of them were made up by me – but such is the depth of your blind anti-American prejudice . . .' He is echoing the misplaced self-righteousness of Alan Parker. 'If we all just peeled off our skins . . . we'd be in agony. That's a small price to pay for world unity.'

Another Munnery creation, his security guard, also specialises in an anti-comedy that knocks spots off the straight version. 'Three security guards go into a pub – nothing happens. That's what we get paid for.'

There are other recognisable influences on Lee. Dave Allen is one, not just in the indulgence he demands with his unhurried, round-the-houses routines but also the intoxicating charm he exudes. Or there is Tommy Cooper, in the way, despite his dolorous air of someone who does not belong under the spotlight, he is in total command when onstage, staring upwards and about, above the heads of the audience, as if inspecting, with total satisfaction, the invisible comedy architecture he has magicked up. As well as understanding the value of a pointless digression, Lee has also mastered the Cooper-esque art of not needing to deliver the punchline to get the laugh; he has guided the audience there already. And so, when he opines that not everyone who voted for Trump was racist, we are already in stitches because we know, via callback to his earlier observation regarding Brexiters, that the next line will be 'some of them were cunts'.

Lee goes to unprecedented lengths in deconstructing, critiquing, framing his work; he's a master builder of the avant-garde school, as well as a master of the time-honoured arts of timing, delivery, weight of emphasis. His audience can take his insults with comfort and joy because they are as fully confident in what Lee is doing as he is. It's a confidence so supreme that he can pull off lines like 'I was using an exaggerated form of rhetoric and implied values to satirise the rhetoric and implied values of *Top Gear* – and it is a shame to have to break character and explain that.' Or, 'If you've not seen me before, I don't think that, I think the opposite of that. I'm going to do it about six times tonight, then about quarter to ten I'll go on about something for too long.'

Daring to go on too long is another example of avant-garde audacity, as is his use of silence. Take his response to a line from Chris Moyles in the second volume of Moyles's autobiography, entitled *The Difficult Second Book*. The half-arsed self-referentiality of this title goads Lee, especially as it's about as far as Moyles's sense of irony and self-awareness go. He reads out one of the first lines. 'When my friends found out that I was writing a book, a few of them asked me what it was about.' Lee mulls this sentence; he wonders at the friends of Moyles, not among the few, who did not ask him what it was about. He falls into a silent mime of incuriosity that begins with slack-jawed indifference, then sees him fiddle idly with his mic stand, before waddling gormlessly across the stage to inspect the curtain. He observes that Moyles intended his volume to be a 'toilet book', to be read while defecating – an ignoble aspiration, contradicted, however, by Davina McCall's back-cover description of the book as 'butt-clenchingly honest'. Slowly and remorselessly, coolly and pedantically, silently inviting the audience to laugh at the punchline before it has been delivered, Lee observes the problem with a toilet book which causes the buttocks to clench.

Lee, however, isn't a mere formalist. He takes on UKIP, Islamophobia, Brexit, as well as the cultural poverty of our times. Voted forty-first best stand-up in one of those TV programmes they have these days, Lee, crucially, refuses to describe himself as, say, a performance artist, insists that a stand-up comedian is what he is, someone with more in common with Michael McIntyre than, say, Bruce McLean. He has pretensions, but no conceit. Stewart Lee is unmatched as a comedian in the twenty-first century.

OUTRODUCTION
KINDNESS AND THE TRIUMPH OF THE WOKE

The Conservatives have been in power since 2010 and, at the time of writing, remain so. They have visited upon us austerity, inequality, Brexit, corruption ('sleaze' is too kind a word), an almost wilful incompetence, lethal xenophobia and migrant-bashing, and a 'culture war', largely provoked by themselves, cynically feeding on their supporters' sense of self-pity – an extended exercise in gaslighting in which perpetrators claim to be victims. Satire has found itself struggling in the face of grotesques like Boris Johnson and Priti Patel – a reboot of *Spitting Image* failed spectacularly because if anything it made the trolls by whom we had the misfortune to be governed seem less awful, less beyond the pale than they actually were.

Despite all that, or perhaps in the face of it, British comedy at its best has become a haven of considerateness, diversity, multiculturalism, richer in its comedic detail and observation and truth to reality than ever before.

Certain notions of what comedy should be, while still prevalent, are increasingly discredited. Take the idea that comedy should be 'edgy', a belief persisted in by, among others, Ricky Gervais. This seemingly sharp, rebel imperative has been exposed, by the stand-up comic James Acaster, as a libertarian pretext for punching down:

Edgy comedians . . . they look like me, race and genderwise . . . no one tells them what they can and can't say . . . they'll come onstage and do ten minutes just making fun of transgender people. And if people on the internet get upset about it, the comedian's like, 'Bad luck! I'm a stand-up comedian. I'm meant to challenge people. What's the matter, guys? Too challenging for you? I'm a stand-up comedian. If you don't like being challenged, don't watch my shows. What's the matter, guys? Too challenging for you? That's my job.' . . . Because you know who's been long overdue a challenge? The trans community.

There was once a pub called the Mucky Pup, my favourite in London. I drank there, did quizzes there, DJ-ed there, danced there, ate vegetarian roasts there. The Mucky Pup is no more; it changed hands. In January 2020, it went under the name the Bill Murray, a comedy club. I was there to see the comedian Bethany Black perform a set to a small but packed house. The melancholy I felt at being on the site of so many memories, now restructured and repurposed beyond recognition, was quickly extinguished by her act. An experienced stand-up, she was engaging, easily confident, her vaguely Northern accent, fast and fluent style and timing triggering associations ranging from Victoria Wood to Ken Dodd and Les Dawson, her tendency to digress reminiscent of Ronnie Corbett. Her set was traditional in other respects: predicaments, tricky situations, the comedy of embarrassment, rude bits, very British fare. And as she casually disclosed, Black is trans, lesbian, autistic, as well as a recovering alcoholic and drug addict. And Goth.

All these multiple streams flowed into the river of her comedy. 'The walk from the car to the venue is the scariest part of my day, this bit's dead easy,' she said. She included a reference to 'slutty mosques', the reason why she involuntarily exclaimed 'Thank fuck for that' to a man who told her he had throat cancer, related the story of a man who refused to wipe his arse because he thought it was 'gay' to do so, a nervous dialogue with her own brain wondering if she was a racist, a routine about finding a pillow in a hotel covered in spunk, and another which culminated in the line 'It's going to look like you're going to be eaten out by Hitler,' the context of which I leave to your imagination.

Discussing responses to her act, she said she was often complimented on being 'politically incorrect'. But she demurred from that.

She disdained, she said, comedians who complained that you 'can't joke about anything any more': what they mean is, 'People have stopped laughing at my boring, tired old fucking stereotypes.' She outlined her own guiding dictum as a stand-up: 'Make sure the jokes you're doing aren't adding to the horrible shittiness of the world . . . People confuse the subject and the object of a joke. Subject can be anything as long as the object of your joke isn't using your power to make someone else feel shittier.' Despite its audacity, its scatology, Black's finely calibrated comedy never failed to abide by that dictum.

More than that, however, Bethany Black made us laugh out loud, caused our jaws to drop into our laps that afternoon, largely because of the combination of her gifts as a comedian and her personal traits, which enabled her to 'see the world in ways which none of you will ever see'.

In 2005, authors Steve Lowe and Alan McArthur published *Is It Just Me or Is Everything Shit? The Encyclopedia of Modern Life*, whose subjects included the politically vacuous Live 8, a grisly spectacle of corporate pop altruism, as well as rapper 50 Cent, Coldplay's Chris Martin, Top Shop supremo Philip Green and the *Daily Mail*. Although theirs was a left-wing perspective, the jaded despair of the title alone suggested an underlying mood of exhausted disaffection with that most nondescript of decades, the noughties.

Over a decade and a half on, one's first gloomy instinct is to call back across the decades: 'Folks, just you wait.' In 2010, Gordon Brown's charms failed to woo an electorate who decided that a change of political curtains was in order. David Cameron, freshly scrubbed and roseate with the glow of a new and ambitious estate agent set himself up in the high street. He was eager to present a detoxified Tory brand, with slogans such as 'Call me Dave' and 'Hug a hoodie', as well as his grand vision of a 'Big Society', in which a notional 'we' were, as the Cameron mantra went, 'all in it together'. A *Guardian* piece by fashion editor Jess Cartner-Morley suggested that Prime Minister Cameron would be restrained by his fragrant wife Samantha from erring into the callous terrain of the old, Thatcherite mode of Toryism.

Hoodies went unhugged, the concept of the 'Big Society' evaporated through insubstantiality, Cameron was called a great many things worse than 'Dave' and the slogan 'we're all in it together' rang bitterly hollow as it soon became clear that society was divided between those in shit creek and those up on the clifftop holding all the paddles. Austerity, an economic policy based on a false notion of the country as a household that had maxed out its credit card, was introduced to make good the financial losses incurred by the global banking crisis of 2008, which saw the banks bailed out and the poor, who had no part in creating the crisis whatsoever, expected to pick up the tab. Sufficient numbers of people, schooled in contempt for feckless, irresponsible 'chavs', as highlighted on *The Jeremy Kyle Show*, were only too happy to see them handed down the punishment they deserved. If Samantha Cameron tried to intervene at all with her husband, it came to naught.

Cameron gave way to Theresa May, who herself was replaced by Boris Johnson, followed by Liz Truss and Rishi Sunak. Politics became more than merely 'shit', dull and uninspiring; it was polarised, deeply divisive. As a bone to his yappy right-wing faction, Cameron had idly agreed to a referendum on Britain's EU membership. 'Brexit' won narrowly in a zero-sum game, thanks to the mendacious efforts of campaigners like Nigel Farage and Boris Johnson. The country was further bisected by the election of Jeremy Corbyn as leader of the Labour Party, which younger voters saw as betokening a much-needed return to a more radical, thoroughgoing version of the party, following the defeat of Ed Miliband, whose campaign had included such dismal attempts to appease floating voters as mugs bearing the words 'Controls on Immigration'. Others saw the appointment of the radical long-time backbencher as an act of wilful suicide, of a party membership taking leave of its senses.

The far left, far right and far centre were at fractious odds, with the proliferation of social media leading to a day-to-day, keyboard-to-keyboard online combat. The UK is divided, culturally, demographically, geographically, ideologically.

It was as if to counter the pain and division, at times seemingly deliberate political callousness and strife, that comedy made its dialectical shift from cruelty to kindness as the noughties gave way to the 2010s. At its best it has become not merely banally escapist but a genuine and humane haven. It is a world away from our broken world, and yet British comedy has never been in a better moral state. It has been strengthened by its inclusivity, its diversity, its (neuro) diversity, all the embedded values of political correctness. It is no longer merely the stories of angry or frustrated white men, though white men are certainly given a more than fair representation in the modern British comic firmament. And it's this concern for inclusion, as embodied in the work of a Bethany Black, that gives rise to the kindness I allude to: a determination never to punch down, a rule to which even Frankie Boyle solemnly abided in 2020, despite his form earlier in his career.

Yes, there remain problems – the sort of blankly, generically ambitious comedians lambasted by Stewart Lee, the domination of satire by chortling Oxbridge types who seem inured to the human misery caused by the politicians whose ribs they dig. There is also the question, as across the board in culture and entertainment, of the avenues sealed off to an increasingly culturally disenfranchised working class, denied the opportunities and entry points they enjoyed forty years ago in more egalitarian times. Such is the fragmentation of modern TV that it is less easy for new comedians, not just because of their multitudes, to became household names à la Del Boy, Tommy, Tony, Harold, Albert, Frank.

Still, comedies like *This Country* (2017–20), *People Just Do Nothing* (2012–18) and *Detectorists* (2014–22), all in their own way derived from *The Office*, strike grace notes of consideration, nuance, a baked-in reflectiveness of the tradition to which they belong and from which they gently depart. Furthermore, as Phil Harrison, author of *The Age of Static: How TV Explains Modern Britain*, points out, characters such as Andy and Lance in *Detectorists* would, just a few years earlier, have most likely been treated as caricatures, losers, English grotesques worthy only of mockery. 'It takes real skill, grace and lightness of touch to imbue such characters with modest but discernible heroism.'

Freed from the hegemony of the laugh track, series like *Detectorists* were able to leaven their comedy with other elements above and beyond the traditional resorts of melodrama or huggy US-style sentimentalism. There's a sort of existential correctness about Andy (Mackenzie Crook, who wrote the series) and Lance (Toby Jones). They are at peace with themselves, a calm which exudes from the flat screen. It was a care that extended beyond the characters, to the audience, as if the actors were conscious of a need not just to raise laughs but also to take on the obligation of maintaining the wellbeing and mental health of those watching. A similar kindness pervades *Mortimer & Whitehouse: Gone Fishing* (2018–), which again represents a shift. It was clearly inspired by Steve Coogan and Rob Brydon's *The Trip* (2010–20), in which the comedians play fictionalised versions of themselves undertaking a restaurant tour of the UK for the *Observer*. The comedy mostly sees them trying to outdo each other's impressions, with Coogan in particular eager to put down his perceived rival Brydon at every opportunity. Theirs is a curious bond of friendship, cemented as much by mutual resentment as admiration.

There is no cruelty in *Gone Fishing*, not even to the fish they catch, which are quickly released back into the water. As well as the ravishing, verdant consolation of the British countryside in which the pair angle, there is a sense of the mutual care between Whitehouse and Mortimer, their non-fictionalised selves, two national treasures treasured indeed as they goad each other affectionately but also share stories of health scares; these are yesterday's young bucks, whom a TV nation has watched grow into middle age.

Toby Jones, Mackenzie Crook, Bob Mortimer, Paul Whitehouse: abiding evidence that despite suspicions to the contrary, white men can be funny. However, the care, the spirit of inclusivity, the advanced sense of political correctness that has pervaded the 2010s and beyond is at last evident in series such as *Stath Lets Flats* (2018–21) or *Man Like Mobeen* (2017–), with its faintly Del Boy-like protagonist (Guz Khan, who co-created the series), who faces up to far trickier and scarier situations than the Trotters ever did. Or *Famalam* (2018–20), the Black British sketch show; or the work of Michaela Coel, whose range, as exhibited in the beyond harrowing *Black Earth Rising* (2018) and *I May Destroy You* (2020), should not distract from her abilities as one of the UK's foremost comedians and actors, as evidenced by *Chewing Gum* (2015–17).

Much as I love these series, I'm going to fall short of looking at them in great detail here because a) many of them are still in the process of taking their historical place, and b) I don't feel it's for me to 'mansplain' them. That's for another book, another author. The same goes for Phoebe Waller-Bridge's much-acclaimed *Fleabag* (2016–19) or the hysterical *Derry Girls* (2018–22), scripted by Lisa Magee and set in Northern Ireland in the 1990s, or the superb Diane Morgan, among others. Just a couple of observations: Waller-Bridge's privileged background has been much remarked upon, but while there's a strong case to be made that writers and performers from poor backgrounds are having an ever harder time making it in arts and entertainment these days, that is a structural problem that should not be blamed on Waller-Bridge personally; her success is thoroughly deserved. She's pushing comedy to the brink, again, with a show that is not mere sentimentality but far more complex, and unexpectedly distressing. All the same, there are would-be Waller-Bridges out there who are denied the opportunities she has enjoyed, solely on the basis of an increasing class divide. In this respect, modern comedy has gone backwards.

Interesting, too, that the series shares a trait with the slightly less critically acclaimed *Miranda* (2009–15), the vehicle for Miranda

Hart. Both make use, ingeniously in *Fleabag*'s case, of the fourth-wall-breaking look to camera, as practised by Stan Laurel and particularly Oliver Hardy in the earliest days of film comedy. It's not just funny but a beautiful act of empathy and of a piece with the tendency towards kindness – kindness not as a trite, greetings-card sentiment but kindness as universal empathy, commonality.

British comedy's current healthy state isn't just down to it firing on all multicultural cylinders. Even the rubbish, such as the dire *Mrs Brown's Boys* (2011–), isn't rubbish because it's a throwback to the darker days of casual racism, sexism, ageism, homophobia, ableism, transphobia, etc. It's pure rubbish, that's all: witless and feebly rude. In a world where it still seems like the bigots, the reactionaries, the unjust, the trolls, the bullies hold cruel sway, in comedy at least they have been vanquished, or banished to the margins at least. Take the reception meted out to Dapper Laughs, the pseudonym of Daniel O'Reilly, whose bantz-addled act was criticised for mocking the homeless and including rape jokes. He was run out of TV-land on a rail, forced to retire the character. There's also Lee Hurst, who reappeared after an initial bout of fame as a right-winger and, in 2020, anti-masker. No Bernard Manning-like status for him. He's a pariah.

The subject of right-wing comedy cropped up in 2020 following a (mistaken) report that new BBC director-general Tim Davie was demanding to see more of it on the Beeb to counter the supposed overall left-/liberal-leaning tendency of its comic contributors. There was one hapless effort, which may or may not have been premeditated, in November 2020, when *Have I Got News for You* featured a comedian who suggested the mass bombing of Jeremy Corbyn supporters at Glastonbury. This prompted a good deal of anger on social media; the retort might be offered, can't you take a joke? Except, in this unfortunate instance, there was no joke to be taken. It's hard to be overtly Conservative and funny, since the party's policies are by nature punch-down, against the poor, those on benefits, immigrants. Granted, Tory sympathisers confect a notion of a liberal elite and the tyranny of 'woke culture', the child of political correctness and health and safety gone mad, but while this might afford the likes of Jeremy Clarkson and others of the ironed-jeans brigade the opportunity for a lazy sideswipe in a *Times* column, it is too lacking in substance to provide the basis for contemporary comedy, with its greater stress on realism, the nuance of lives as recognisably lived. Being a Conservative and also a comedian, as was the case with, say, Morecambe and Wise, is one thing. Making Conservatism the basis of your comedy, especially in its current, toxic condition, is quite another.

Twenty-first-century comedy benefits from coming under the scrutiny of social media. Sites such as Twitter can be sewers, allowing verbal effluent to be displayed in a respectable font in full public view rather than scrawled on a toilet wall or confined to the circulating inner monologues of bigoted nobodies. The creation of vast havens of conspiracy theory and 'alternative facts' on sites like Facebook is another reason to wonder if it might have been better for the health of public discourse had social media never been invented. However, at their best, Twitter and Facebook can offer an effective peer review when obnoxious ideas are aired, holding them to account via peer pressure rather than, as quietly happened in the old days, allowing them to spread their toxicity unchallenged. It's not that you 'can't do/say anything these days', it's just that you had better be prepared to defend what you say if it's objectionable, because you will be called out to justify your terms. That factor has been helpful in improving the care and consideration with which twenty-first-century comedy is created. Which is why Jimmy Carr caught such grief when it emerged in 2022 that on his show *His Dark Material*, he had made a 'joke' about the murder of gypsies being one of the 'positives' of the Holocaust. Twenty years earlier, prior to Twitter, the joke might have passed under the radar. It might have been lapped up by audiences who had regarded comedy as a brief, exhilarating respite from the onerous chore of having to be sensitive to minority groups, perhaps admired by some fellow comedians for its 'audacity'. Anyone who objected might have been regarded as a huffer and puffer. In 2022, it was greeted with a sober, unwavering, collective contempt to which there is no comeback. Different times, indeed.

Social media does, however, also offer a platform for users to vent their low-level grievances. Go on any of the appreciation sites for the likes of *Minder*, *Likely Lads*, *Porridge*, etc., and it's never very long before some disgruntled group member of a certain age bemoans the 'snowflakes' whom they see as responsible for the fact that their favourite series are now banished to the realms of UK Gold. During 2020, on a *Porridge* site, one member claimed that the series was being withdrawn altogether because of the supposedly racist treatment of the Black prisoner, Jim McLaren (Tony Osoba). He offered no evidence that any such decision had been made, nor did the various posters on the thread who grumbled in sympathy ask for any. It was enough for the grudge against modernity and its attendant diversity to be nursed, undisturbed by any further enquiries as to whether it had any basis in truth.

This resentment also reflects a real feeling of having been 'cancelled', a word over-used by the right, whose protests about being denied a platform to air their views are all too often broadcast from very far-reaching platforms indeed, volubly and repeatedly. These are people who feel existentially threatened when they see a Black person in a supermarket advert, or a woman football commentator, or an openly gay character behaving as if their presence on the screen is not some screaming, pantomime outrage.

There was a temporary ban on *Fawlty Towers* following the incident in June 2020 in which a pro-Black Lives Matter group threw a statue of the slave trader Edward Colston into Bristol Harbour. There were fears that an entire pre-'woke' British comedy culture was destined to join the statue in the water and a culture war ensued, in which BLM members quickly protested that they had no interest. They had bigger fish to fry and were wary of efforts by papers like the *Telegraph* to draw them into spurious, diversionary conflicts.

It wasn't for these reasons that *Little Britain* was pulled from Netflix and iPlayer in 2020 for its blackface. *The League of Gentlemen* followed, as did an episode from *Fawlty Towers*, 'The Germans', not because of Basil Fawlty's goose-stepping but because the major refers to 'niggers' and 'wogs' – all of which led to an indignant debate about censorship, and a sense among older white people in particular that they were the victims of this new movement, their treasured heritage being brusquely confiscated.

But here's the thing: the BLM movement, which came into being following the murder of the African American George Floyd in Minneapolis, and in the wake of the toppling of a statue of a slave trader in Bristol, really didn't feel that pulling these programmes was meeting their demands. In fact, they hadn't even made any such demands. As Eleanor Penny tweeted, 'Nowhere in the BLM movements were there massive demands for us to urgently revisit British comedy shows.' Machel St Patrick Hewitt, meanwhile, added, 'No black person went on to the streets to protest because of *Fawlty Towers*. Drop us out of your culture war conversation.'

For platforms like iPlayer or Netflix, removing these shows was an easy, token move, as simple as going down on one knee. A much tougher ask would be to address more systemic issues such as racial imbalances in their own workplaces, or the relative lack of opportunities for those of ethnic or working-class backgrounds. Gagging the major and allowing the opportunity for *Daily Telegraph* columnists to chunter in outrage was, if anything, a worse than useless gesture. However, as Penny added on Twitter, 'We're being baited into a non-event culture battle and the right have leapt on it to moan about free speech because they know they're losing the war.'

However, they are right insofar as there has been a permanent shift away from the comedy of yesteryear. Mother-in-laws, dolly birds, amiable sex pests, comical Asians, nancy boys have all had their day.

They are not merely forbidden; they are bewilderingly unfunny to younger audiences. The privileges of the grumbling white cisgendered male heteronormative hegemony have been rolled back. In our decades of decline, our finest but not so finest hours, comedy has been our supreme consolation prize. Sure, it's been a distraction from the serious business of radicalising and maturing as a nation, imperatives which become more urgent with each passing year, but the excess sublimated energy that traditionally went into British comedy has made for masterpieces of rueful self-reflection, sometimes great art – even better than that, pure laughter. These isles bred giants on whose shoulders subsequent generations of comics stand.

Things have been lost with the new emphasis on naturalism and detailed character observation – a certain silliness, for one thing. Danny Baker bemoaned in 2020 that no comedy will ever put up a scenario in which a character is forced to adopt the disguise of a tree. Moreover, the comedy of manners and embarrassment adds a low-level element of pain, of tension, to contemporary comedy, as opposed to the laugh-track years, in which everyone spoke loudly, unhaltingly, without awkward overlap, and even arch-enemies were wholly at ease in each other's company. That said, there are certain strands of silliness we can manage without; if a comedy based on whoops and daft vocal noises helps make the life of the twelve-year-old with Tourette's a misery in the playground, then perhaps leave that comedy behind in history, eh?

If, despite all, you still think there's a duty for comedy to upset the PC applecart and break modern taboos, then you'd better be good, really good, as in *South Park* good, which is to say, able to navigate through dangerous waters with a seasoned hand and sound moral compass. And since you're almost certainly not that good, then maybe best not bother?

They don't make comedy like they used to, which is at once a good thing, given that back then not everyone got to be in on the laugh, and another reason to seek out and cherish it all the more. As for the best comedy of our own century, well, comedy has never been an agent for radical change and there are no laughs in idealism. The triumph of what is pejoratively referred to as 'wokeness' in British comedy hasn't been that sort of 'triumph'. Rather, it has brought in an unprecedented measure of truth and inclusivity, and a developed, evolved sense of what it is to be us, you, them – all of us. In times when our collective mental health is under great stress, British comedy is en route to becoming, by virtue of not playing it safe, a safe space for all.

SELECT BIBLIOGRAPHY

Barfe, Louis, *Happiness and Tears: The Ken Dodd Story* (HarperCollins)
———, *The Trials and Triumphs of Les Dawson* (Atlantic)
———, *Turned Out Nice Again: The Story of British Light Entertainment* (Atlantic)
Barr, Charles, *Ealing Studios: A Movie Book* (University of California Press)
Beckett, Andy, *Promised You a Miracle: Why 1980–82 Made Modern Britain* (Allen Lane)
———, *When the Lights Went Out: What Really Happened to Britain in the Seventies* (Faber & Faber)
Carpenter, Humphrey, *That Was Satire, That Was: The Satire Boom of the 1960s* (Weidenfeld & Nicolson)
Chaplin, Charles, *My Autobiography* (Penguin Modern Classics)
Corbett, Susannah, *Harry H. Corbett: The Front Legs of the Cow* (History Press)
Davies, Russell (ed.), *The Kenneth Williams Diaries* (HarperCollins)
Dessau, Bruce, *Beyond a Joke: Inside the Dark World of Stand-Up Comedy* (Preface)
Farnes, Norma (ed.), *The Compulsive Spike Milligan* (Fourth Estate)
Fisher, John, *Tommy Cooper: Always Leave Them Laughing* (HarperCollins)
———, *Tony Hancock: The Definitive Biography* (HarperCollins)
Fox, Kate, *Watching the English: The Hidden Rules of English Behaviour* (Hodder & Stoughton)
Hatherley, Owen, *The Chaplin Machine* (Pluto Press)
Henry, Lenny, *Who Am I, Again?* (Faber & Faber)
Lee, Stewart, *How I Escaped My Certain Fate* (Faber & Faber)
Louvish, Simon, *Stan and Ollie* (Faber & Faber)
McCabe, John, and Al Kilgore, *Laurel & Hardy* (Ballantine)
McCann, Graham, *Bounder! The Biography of Terry-Thomas* (Aurum)
———, *Dad's Army: The Story of a Very British Comedy* (Fourth Estate)
———, *Fawlty Towers* (Hodder & Stoughton)
Marnham, Patrick, *The* Private Eye *Story* (Fontana)
Medhurst, Andy, *A National Joke: Popular Comedy and English Cultural Identities* (Routledge)
Morgan, David, and John Oliver, *Monty Python Speaks* (Dey Street Books)

Payne, Robert, *The Great Charlie: A Biography of the Tramp* (Pan)

Purnell, Sonia, *Just Boris: A Tale of Blond Ambition* (Aurum)

Randall, Lucian, *Disgusting Bliss: The Brass Eye of Chris Morris* (Simon & Schuster)

Robinson, David, *Charlie Chaplin: The Art of Comedy* (Thames & Hudson)

Sellers, Robert, *The Secret Life of Ealing Studios: Britain's Favourite Film Studio* (Aurum)

Thompson, Harry, *Peter Cook: A Biography* (Sceptre)

Townsend, Sue, *The Secret Diary of Adrian Mole, Aged 13¾* (Methuen)

Turner, Alwyn W., *A Classless Society: Britain in the 1990s* (Aurum)

———, *Crisis? What Crisis? Britain in the 1970s* (Aurum)

———, *Rejoice! Rejoice! Britain in the 1980s* (Aurum)

Webber, Richard, *Fifty Years of* Hancock's Half Hour (Century)

ACKNOWLEDGEMENTS

My thanks to Alexa von Hirschberg who was hugely instrumental in helping hone and shape *Different Times*, fully understanding what it purported to be and helping me to realise those intentions. Thanks also to Linden Davies and Mo Hafeez in this respect. My thanks also to Hannah Knowles, Mo Hafeez, Ella Griffiths, Rachael Williamson and Melanie Gee who assisted the book through the final furlongs of the editing stage, to Robert Davies and Ian Bahrami for their close copyediting and proofreading, saving me a few blushes with their amendments. Thanks also to Hamza Jahanzeb for assisting with a sensitivity read and to Jonny Pelham for the cover image. Thank you also to my agent Kevin Pocklington and to Lee Brackstone, who first brought me aboard at Faber & Faber and who commissioned this book.

I'm grateful also to my colleagues at the *Chart Music* podcast, Al Needham, Taylor Parkes and Neil Kulkarni who offered suggestions, thoughts and practical assistance, and to Gurbir Thethy for his reflections on how some of the more dubious seventies sitcoms were received by British people of colour such as the Sikh community. Gratitude also to Louis Barfe, whose biographies of among others, Les Dawson and Morecambe and Wise I heartily recommend.

Over the years I've been privileged to interview a number of comedians, invariably kindly and thoughtful about their trade and whose thoughts enrich this text, including Rik Mayall, Bill Pertwee, Ade Edmondson, Eric Idle, Jack Dee, Vic Reeves and Bob Mortimer, *The Royle Family*'s Ralf Little, Julian Clary, Lenny Henry, Stewart Lee. Finally, thanks to my little boy Dara's mum Roshi Nasehi and also my dad for companionship in the onerous task of binging on box sets and black and white British classic movies.

INDEX

Titles of works relate to TV shows unless otherwise indicated.